Effective Leadership in Adventure Programming

— SECOND EDITION —

Simon Priest, PhD

Michael A. Gass, PhD
University of New Hampshire

Human Kinetics

Library of Congress Cataloging-in-Publication Data

Priest, Simon.
 Effective leadership in adventure programming / Simon Priest and Michael A. Gass.-- 2nd ed.
    p. cm.
 Includes bibliographical references and index.
  ISBN 0-7360-5250-X (hardcover : alk. paper)
  1. Recreation leadership. 2. Outdoor recreation--Management. 3. Leisure--Management. 4. Recreational
therapy. I. Gass, Michael A. II. Title.
  GV181.43.P75 2005
  790'.06'9--dc22

                         2005003376   .

ISBN-10: 0-7360-5250-X
ISBN-13: 978-0-7360-5250-4

The Web addresses cited in this text were current as of January 25, 2005, unless otherwise noted.

Acquisitions Editor: Gayle Kassing, PhD; **Developmental Editor:** Melissa Feld; **Assistant Editors:** Michelle Rivera and Kathleen D. Bernard; **Copyeditor:** Jocelyn Engman; **Proofreader:** Erin Cler; **Indexer:** Dan Connolly; **Permission Manager:** Dalene Reeder; **Graphic Designer:** Fred Starbird; **Graphic Artist:** Dawn Sills; **Photo Manager:** Kelly J. Huff; **Cover Designer:** Keith Blomberg; **Photographer (cover):** Art Explosion; **Photographer (interior):** Simon Priest unless otherwise noted here. Photo on page 29 courtesy of North Carolina Outward Bound School; 67 courtesy of Sandra Lynn; 27, 133, 175, 243, 261, 291 courtesy of Taras Ferencevych; 45, 148, 185 courtesy of Browne Center; 84, 117 © Richard Etchberger; 11, 17 © International Stock; 47 © Human Kinetics, Inc.; 113, 249, 264 © ImageState; 145 © Photri/Wallis/Poulet; 199 © Danilo Donadoni /Bruce Coleman Inc.; 236 © Jock Montgomery/Bruce Coleman Inc.; 275, 281 © Keith Gunnar/Bruce Coleman Inc.; 275, 299 © @davidsandersphotos.com; 305 © Sherri Meyers; **Art Manager:** Kelly Hendren; **Illustrator:** Keri Evans; **Printer:** Sheridan Books

Printed in the United States of America   10   9   8   7   6   5   4

Human Kinetics
Web site: www.HumanKinetics.com

United States: Human Kinetics
P.O. Box 5076
Champaign, IL 61825-5076
800-747-4457
e-mail: humank@hkusa.com

Canada: Human Kinetics
475 Devonshire Road, Unit 100
Windsor, ON N8Y 2L5
800-465-7301 (in Canada only)
e-mail: info@hkcanada.com

Europe: Human Kinetics
107 Bradford Road
Stanningley
Leeds LS28 6AT, United Kingdom
+44 (0)113 255 5665
e-mail: hk@hkeurope.com

Australia: Human Kinetics
57A Price Avenue
Lower Mitcham, South Australia 5062
08 8372 0999
e-mail: info@hkaustralia.com

New Zealand: Human Kinetics
Division of Sports Distributors NZ Ltd.
P.O. Box 300 226 Albany
North Shore City, Auckland
0064 9 448 1207
e-mail: info@humankinetics.co.nz

To the gardeners in our lives
for all they sow, nurture, and reap.

Contents

Preface

Outdoor leadership professionals are finding an increasing number and range of exciting opportunities in the field of adventure programming. Quite different from other professional vocations, this field requires you to work in challenging learning environments with a variety of mediums, clients, and professional practices. To demonstrate the range of these opportunities, the following situations portray possible roles you could fill as an outdoor leader.

RECREATION:
THE OUTDOOR INSTRUCTOR

You are teaching a white-water paddling course to a public group, focusing on eddy turns in a series of class II rapids. In preparing for this session, you implement a variety of proactive risk-management measures, including site reconnaissance of the river for any recent changes; use of appropriate risk-management gear, such as personal flotation devices (PFDs) and helmets; and possession and positioning of rescue gear, such as throw bags, Z-pulley rope systems, and rescue boaters. Having previously taught your students appropriate skills through lectures, demonstrations, and actual experience (e.g., practical swim tests, rescue procedures, exit procedures and Eskimo rolls, and paddle strokes in calm water), you are confident that they are ready for the real thing. During the experience, one boater overturns and becomes separated from her boat on a rock in the middle of the river channel. Before you intercede, the class immediately reacts by setting up a Tyrolean system to successfully evacuate the stranded boater to the riverbank as well as a system to retrieve her kayak downstream.

EDUCATION:
THE SCHOOLTEACHER

In working with a high school physical education class, you teach a course in rock climbing using the indoor climbing wall of the gymnasium. The class consists of students with a variety of capa-bilities, and you adapt the curriculum to fit their individual needs. At the same time, you focus on the group dynamics that exist when students place themselves in positions requiring trust and risk taking. While students actually climb, you use appropriate learning progressions and risk management, yet facilitate students' climbing and belaying one another. You coach students to use verbal techniques and considerations, like the full-value contract (a contract emphasizing fully valuing yourself and others), particularly when they are in positions that are especially difficult for them. Several times in this class students become overwhelmed and physically "frozen" with fear. In these situations, you employ a variety of self-efficacy building techniques, such as verbally linking the student to past successes, informing her of the group's support, explaining the options available to her, and helping her focus on difficult areas. After the activity is completed, you reinforce students' learning, debriefing their successes and setbacks through a discussion of feelings, events, and new learning, emphasizing how they might apply their newfound confidence to future school and home situations.

DEVELOPMENT:
THE CORPORATE TRAINER

You are working with managers of a health care company to help them with several troublesome issues. The corporation is experiencing a contradiction between quality and expediency and is looking for your corporate adventure program to provide strategies for how these concepts could work synergistically rather than in opposition. In working with these clients, you design a series of adventure activities related to their identified needs. You focus special attention on the quality of this relationship, creating a metaphorical connection through which the energies, focuses, and outcomes of producing successful methods in adventure experiences successfully resolve the company's specific issues.

Because of its strong relationship to the needs of the company, one of your key activities is the Spider's Web, which involves passing group members through openings in a giant web of rope without letting them touch the strands. You design the initiative for further relevance by presenting it as a task where the employees must demonstrate a model delivery and transfer service by passing employees through a complex network of resources in a caring and efficient manner. The web initiative becomes analogous to the complex interactive system they are working through where each opening becomes a manager's personal area of responsibility to address during the interactive resolution process. Only one person may pass through each delegated area, since to send someone through that opening again would replicate services. You also add a time limit (a common constraint facing this company) of 25 minutes, with a 25% bonus if they complete the task in under 20 minutes and a consequence for every minute it takes over 25 to finish. With this metaphorical framework in place, you begin the activity.

THERAPY: THE FAMILY COUNSELOR

As an adventure professional with a therapeutic training background, you work in a substance-abuse program for youth, focusing on enhancing communication between adolescents with drug addictions and their parents. Your program uses adventure experiences as adjunctive therapy to established treatment plans. Your focus for this session is to redirect interaction between a 14-year-old son and his mother who have become emotionally separated in their single-parent family. Current symptoms of the son's behavior include substance abuse, low self-esteem, and a strong fear that his mother will also abandon him. As you begin, you select the Trust Lean, an activity where one person falls into the supporting arms of another, providing a "mirror image" of what is happening in their relationship and how it influences them. This particular exercise highlights the issues of kids growing up to be adults, figuring out what they are able to accomplish, and testing personal limits. You implement actions as well as verbal techniques that build on these issues, replacing dysfunctional behaviors with relevant functional ones. During the Trust Lean, the mother sees the parallel between her successful interaction with her son and the need for her to have a hands-on relationship with him in order to help him balance his life. Simultaneously, the son recognizes that "staying straight" in the Trust Lean positively affects both his success as well as his relationship with his mother. Following the activity, you facilitate a discussion about the issues of interaction and relationship. Each represents a key feature to solving their various concerns.

PURPOSE OF THE BOOK

These scenarios are actual examples of current applications of adventure programming: recreational, educational, developmental, and therapeutic. While complex, they portray a variety of principles and practices forming the body of outdoor leadership knowledge. In writing this book, we provide guidelines for you as an outdoor leader to enhance your understanding of this rapidly emerging profession. We have organized this book as a course text for preparing undergraduate and graduate students in outdoor leadership, but if you are already working in the field of adventure learning, you can use it as a reference manual. In other words, this book provides a comprehensive source for entry-level outdoor leaders, but advanced practitioners may also find sections that are valuable for their ongoing professional development. In approaching the material, we assume that you are interested in being an outdoor leader and have some personal experience in at least one adventure activity.

HOW THE BOOK IS ARRANGED

The first chapter of this book identifies 12 components that contribute to effective outdoor leadership. Six of these 12 are hard skills that are solid, tangible, measurable, and easier to train or assess and soft skills that are amorphous, intangible, difficult to measure, and tougher to train or assess. We can consider the other 6 components metaskills, higher-order core abilities that integrate other skills in a workable, systematic manner.

Figure 1 portrays the 12 components as building bricks, mortar, and a rock foundation used to construct a wall, analogous to the training you need to become an effective leader. Specifically, we can view the wall of outdoor leadership as being built of soft-skill bricks on top of hard-skill bricks. Metaskills serve as the mortar holding these bricks together to form a solid and cohesive wall. This entire arrangement of outdoor adventure leadership preparation is built on a rock-solid theoretical foundation of philosophy, history, and individual

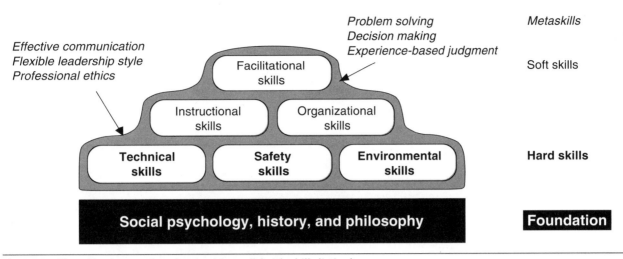

Figure 1   The effective outdoor leadership wall (with skills listing).

and group behaviors. We have written at least one chapter to cover the body of knowledge concerning each of the skills listed here.

The capabilities to perform technical skills in an environmentally sound manner—the hard skills—are common among outdoor leaders. The abilities of leaders to climb, paddle, or peddle; to find their way from origin to destination without getting lost or injured; and to camp along the way without leaving a mess are relatively easy to learn and assess. Since a great many how-to books exist on these hard skills, we devote only three chapters (6-8) to reviewing critical information and refer you to other how-to books in the reference section of each chapter.

Unfortunately, the abilities to instruct, organize, and facilitate participants in adventure experiences—the soft skills—are less common in preparing outdoor leaders. To fill this gap, we devote a number of chapters to these topics. In chapters 9 and 10, we outline how to plan trips and manage risks, reviewing the role of the outdoor leader as an organizer of adventure experiences. Then in chapters 11, 12, and 13 we discuss educational theories and models relevant to teaching in adventure programs and review the role of the outdoor leader as an instructor of adventure experiences.

In chapters 14 through 17, we explain the underlying roles of facilitation and detail techniques for working with groups and individuals in the outdoors, thereby reviewing the role of the outdoor leader as a facilitator of adventure experiences.

Keeping in mind that the hard and soft skills of effective outdoor adventure leadership are interwoven and bound together by metaskills, we devote the next six chapters (18-23) to detailing flexible leadership style, problem-solving and decision-making skills, experience-based judgment, effective communication, and ethical behaviors. We define metaskills as highly specialized skills that when correctly executed permit the most effective expression of all the other skills. Acting like glue, metaskills bind everything together, allowing the hard and soft skills to act synergistically so that your combined competence is greater than the sum of your individual skills. Metaskills allow you to be the most effective you can be. Finally, in chapter 24, we deal with the current trends and issues in the outdoor leadership field. In all, the knowledge in this book will hopefully build you a solid wall of outdoor leadership skills and metaskills. However, as with all construction, the most important feature to a solid wall is constant maintenance once it is built.

Acknowledgments

We would like to thank the following individuals who have raised the standards of our writing by challenging our thinking and coauthoring articles with us. Many of the ideas and concepts found in this book are due to their hard work: Peter Allison, Aram Attarian, Rusty Baillie, Ian Boyle, Camille Bunting, Gaylene Carpenter, Bob Chase, John Corcoran, Jon Dickey, Kathy Doherty, Phyllis Ford, Dan Garvey, Lee Gillis, Laurie Gullion, Don Hammerman, Jude Hirsch, Ken Hult, Jasper Hunt, Christian Itin, Kim Klint, Doreen Leonard, Chris Loynes, Sandra Lynn, Alistair McArthur, Pam McPhee, Peter Martin, John Miles, Jay Miller, Todd Miner, Denise Mitten, Keith Russell, Sabine Schubert, Deb Sugerman, Anna Kay Vorsteg, Jed Williamson, Scott Wurdinger, Rita Yerkes, Carina Ziemek.

Three people deserve special mention: Betty van der Smissen for her critical analysis and suggestions for the risk-management chapter and her outstanding service to the field; Karl Rohnke for unselfishly sharing and having fun doing it; and Craig Dobkin for leading us in play for the most noble of causes—peace, love, and compassion.

Introduction to Effective Outdoor Leadership

Leadership is one of the most observed and least understood phenomena on earth.

—Burns, 1978

Since the beginning of recorded history, scientists known as alchemists have attempted to transmute a variety of common minerals like lead and iron into precious metals such as gold and silver. These alchemists never succeeded, and the secret formula for such transmutation has never been found. Some spent their entire lives searching in vain for a magical element that might make such a change, calling it the "Philosopher's Stone." They believed adding this special stone to a collection of minerals subjected to key processes would result in pure gold! They also believed that the alchemist who found the stone would not only acquire vast riches but also acquire spiritual perfection, everlasting life, and the secrets of the universe.

Preparing effective outdoor leaders for the adventure programming profession can be akin to alchemy. Preparing outdoor leaders is often focused on "transmuting" motivated outdoorsy people into "golden" outdoor leaders. Like the key processes of alchemy, outdoor leadership preparation involves selecting, training, and assessing leadership candidates. However, as with alchemy, outdoor leadership preparation has not always been successful. Something has been missing: either the base elements have been incomplete, combined in the wrong proportions, or the processes have been incorrectly applied. Whatever the case, preparing outdoor leaders has proven far from foolproof. This chapter examines the elements and processes of preparing outdoor leaders and presents an overview of the materials covered in subsequent chapters. To understand the relevance of these elements and processes, let's consider why outdoor leaders are necessary.

NEED FOR EFFECTIVE OUTDOOR LEADERS

More and more people are discovering benefits to participating in outdoor experiences. Leisure service agencies report a growing interest in the participation in risk-related recreational activities. Social services and health agencies note greater use of adventure therapy for clients. Increasing public participation in outdoor pursuits and adventure activities appears to be a trend for the future (Simmons, 2004). People are becoming more interested in and knowledgeable about the outdoors. Educational opportunities devised to enjoy the outdoor experience are plentiful. Today, ultralight equipment and space-age clothing make roughing it considerably more comfortable than it was decades ago. Superhighways lead to the edge of wilderness, providing easy access to pristine areas.

Unfortunately, this growth in outdoor use has brought an increase in participant injuries and environment damage. Careless treatment of inherent natural hazards has often led poorly prepared enthusiasts to injure themselves. In addition, many participants are slowly loving the outdoors to death, ignorantly destroying the very beauty they seek to enjoy. Some people approach the outdoors as a survival challenge in a no-win competition of humans against nature. In beating nature, humans leave the scars of conquest behind: extinct species, trodden vegetation, soil erosion, and litter. In losing to nature, humans also receive a share of injuries, such as negative memories, social embarrassment, physical damage, and occasional fatalities. The time is long overdue to promote a new attitude of humans with nature, where the two coexist in harmony and where neither suffers at the expense of the other.

To achieve a mutually beneficial coexistence, a different approach is necessary. The approach, portrayed through the elements and processes outlined in this text, provides outdoor leaders with the knowledge and processes necessary to enhance safety, increase client satisfaction, and provide greater protection for and client knowledge about conservation necessary to preserve the environment.

EMERGING AND DESIGNATED LEADERS

Before discussing the elements and processes for creating effective outdoor adventure leaders, two processes on how people become leaders need clarification. **Leadership** is a process of influence. In most informal group settings, people who become group leaders influence other members to create, identify, work toward, achieve, and share mutually acceptable goals. Commonly in such situations more than one group member emerges to fulfill different leadership responsibilities.

In outdoor organizations, a sponsoring agency appoints and designates leaders as being in charge of the group. These designated outdoor leaders hold legal and moral responsibilities for teaching and supervising their groups as well as for ensuring safety and protecting the natural environment. Differentiating between these types of leaders is important, because designated leaders can often conflict with emerging ones.

RESEARCH ON OUTDOOR LEADERSHIP

What does it take to be a good outdoor leader? In an attempt to answer this question, several studies have been completed on outdoor leadership competency and curricula. Several researchers have also studied leaders in an attempt to find a consensus on what the qualities of an effective outdoor leader are.

Green (1981) surveyed 61 outdoor leaders in the Pacific Northwest and developed a college course curriculum for land-based outdoor pursuit leaders based on their responses. Among his conclusions, he reported that emergency medical techniques and outdoor living skills are critical to outdoor leaders of land-based outdoor pursuits, and that such knowledge should be obtained before their involvement in an outdoor leadership course. Swiderski (1981) surveyed 148 outdoor leaders in the western United States and found important regional differences on some outdoor leadership competencies related to snow or ice travel and to off-trail navigation. Buell (1981) surveyed 120 supervisors, educators, and leaders of outdoor programs in the United States and Canada over a list of approximately 200 important competencies for outdoor leaders. Priest (1984) similarly surveyed 189 administrators and leaders attending the 11th annual conference of the Association of Experiential Education. Confirming some earlier works, Raiola (1986) developed his own curriculum for an outdoor leadership preparation program. In an international study, Priest (1986) surveyed 169 out of 250 experts from Australia, Canada, Great Britain, New Zealand, and the United States. The top 10 responses from each researcher's list are presented in figure 1.1.

A meta-analysis of these studies (Priest, 1987) suggests that determining the key elements of effective outdoor leadership might be possible. The 12 elements that arose from these studies as critical core competencies are as follows:

technical skills	flexible leadership style
safety skills	experience-based judgment
environmental skills	
organizational skills	problem-solving skills
instructional skills	decision-making skills
facilitation skills	effective communication
professional ethics	

1. **Technical skills** are competencies in the actual adventure activities or outdoor pursuits being led. Two examples are being able to climb at a certain level or standard and being able to paddle a particular grade or class of white water. Outdoor leaders who perform at a higher proficiency than that of the group members seem to have an easier time maintaining control during these activities, enhancing group safety by providing a "cushion of competence."

2. **Safety skills** are those competencies necessary for the enjoyment of the adventure activity in a safe and prudent manner. Safety skills include navigation, survival, weather interpretation, body temperature regulation, first aid, accident response, search and rescue, and water safety.

3. **Environmental skills** are those competencies necessary for preventing damage to the natural surroundings, including practicing and encouraging minimum-impact travel and no-trace camping and modeling behaviors such as carrying out the garbage and not crosscutting switchback trails.

4. **Organizational skills** are those competencies permitting a leader to plan, prepare, execute, and evaluate experiences for the specific needs of particular client groups. For example, outdoor adventure leaders need to manage risks, arrange transportation, coordinate group meals and lodging, schedule activities, select routes, plan contingencies, and secure permits, equipment, and clothing to increase the likelihood of successful experiences.

5. **Instructional skills** are those competencies required for teaching participants technical skills

Green (1981)

Risk-management plans
Small-group dynamics
Liability considerations
Outdoor leadership methods
Judgment
Minimum-impact practices
Decision making
Assessment of group capabilities
Assessment of individual capabilities
Outdoor leadership objectives

Priest (1984)

Ability to anticipate accidents
Wilderness first aid skills
Awareness of group dynamics
Ability to clearly identify problems
Ability to evaluate natural hazards
Ability to foster teamwork
Ability to provide personal growth
Proficiency in land-based activities
Proficiency in water-based activities
Ability to prepare accident responses

Swiderski (1981)

Exercise good judgment
Handle safety problems
Prepare for accidents
Prevent illness and injury
Teach environmental injuries
Follow a wilderness ethic
Model positive attitudes
Demonstrate minimum impact
Recognize own limitations
Recognize problem indicators

Raiola (1986)

Leadership style
Judgment (objective and subjective)
Trip planning and organization
Environmental issues
Risk management
Instructional principles
Navigation
Group dynamics
Nutrition
Field experience

Buell (1981)

Design and use a first aid kit
Have knowledge of group safety
Possess physical fitness
Limit activities to capabilities
Anticipate problems
Provide standard of care
Apply physical and emotional care
Develop safety procedures
Select and implement logistics
Carry out staff preplanning

Priest (1986)

Safety skills
Judgment based on experience
Awareness and empathy
Group management skills
Problem-solving skills
Instructional skills
Technical activity skills
Flexible leadership style
Motivational philosophy
Environmental skills

Figure 1.1 Summary of the top 10 capabilities critical to outdoor leaders based on past outdoor leadership research.

related to the activity, environment, and safety. For example, teaching skiing in a series of progressions, teaching safety by the inquiry or discovery approach, and using effective instructional aids to teach environmental concepts can all be important instructional skills.

6. **Facilitation skills** are those competencies that foster productive group dynamics, enabling clients to complete tasks while developing appropriate interpersonal relationships. For example, outdoor adventure leaders often need to resolve conflicts, communicate effectively, and foster personal trust and group cooperation. They also need to know how to debrief and guide reflection on adventure experiences to generate conditions for optimal learning.

Boardwalks are often established in high use areas to protect fragile environments from negative impact.

7. **Flexible leadership style** means knowing how, why, and when to utilize different leadership styles. For example, under most conditions group decision making is a democratic or shared process. At other times, like during an emergency, leaders need to be autocratic, giving directions and expecting them to be carried out. However, when an experience is progressing well, the leader may abdicate or delegate responsibility to the group. These varying examples highlight the need for outdoor leaders to adapt or flex their leadership style to suit the circumstances (Doran, 2001; Schimelpfenig, 2001).

8. **Experience-based judgment** is a required skill because leaders often confront situations in the outdoors where pertinent information is unknown, missing, or vague. By considering past experiences and using sound judgment, outdoor adventure leaders can substitute predictions for the unknown, missing, or vague information. This type of judgment becomes extremely important when the act of delaying a decision (in the hopes that new information will become available) might result in further problems. Sound judgment comes from surviving past judgment calls (good or bad), analyzing those successes and failures, and applying learning from the analysis to future situations. This generally requires that outdoor leaders gain plenty of intensive and extensive field experience. While experience does not ensure sound judgment, the lack of experience inhibits leaders from soundly predicting what to do when presented with uncertain information.

9. **Problem-solving skills** can be creative or analytical, since a combination of both might work best. Outdoor leaders need to follow analytical processes to recognize problems, define difficulties, anticipate outcomes, identify several possible solutions, select the most probable one, put it into action, and evaluate its effectiveness. They also need to use creative techniques such as brainstorming, extended effort, attribute listing, forced relationships, and deferred prejudice.

10. **Decision-making skills** enable leaders to select the most appropriate option from a collection of possible ones. Outdoor leaders need to be capable of discovering and assessing multiple options as well as capable of selecting the best choice. Some useful methods for decision making include gathering, screening, organizing, prioritizing, and choosing.

11. **Effective communication** is information exchange between two or more people resulting in behavioral change. A message of the information (in the form of ideas, actions, or emotions) is transmitted along an audio, a visual, or a tactile channel. Outdoor leaders need to be able to generate, encode, link, send, transmit, receive, decode, and interpret such messages. They need to use paraphrasing, clarification, and feedback to confirm that the message received was indeed the same message sent.

12. **Professional ethics** refer to the moral standards and value systems that outdoor leaders have and adventure programming demands.

◄ *EFFECTIVE OUTDOOR LEADERS* ►

► Thoroughly understand the 12 elements of effective outdoor leadership and know their personal level of competence in each element.

► Strive to be proficient in all 12 elements and seek to enhance their competence in any weak areas.

For example, challenge by choice (Schoel, Prouty, & Radcliffe, 1988) is an ethic that defines and often guides adventure programming: people have the right to choose their level of participation in activities and not be coerced into performing an action. Similarly, outdoor leaders hold enormous power over clients, and certain ethics guide leaders away from possible abuses of this power (e.g., deception, secrecy, or sexual contact with clients).

CREATING THE APPROPRIATE MIXTURE IN THE RIGHT SETTINGS

Like the alchemists, even if the adventure programming field found the ingredients of good outdoor leadership, they still would face the dilemma of utilizing these elements in the proper mixture as well as under the right conditions to make "golden" outdoor leaders. There currently is no consensus on how best to prepare outdoor leaders, and as a result, several processes exist for producing outdoor leaders. Discussed in greater detail later in this text are three examples of how the field currently creates outdoor leaders:

1. Individual certification (a process guaranteeing that certain minimum standards of competency have been met or exceeded by an outdoor leadership candidate as evaluated by a certifying agency)
2. Program accreditation (a process recognizing that a program or institution has met certain predetermined standards of operation and that the individuals operating under the program's guidelines conduct outdoor experiences appropriately)
3. Outdoor leadership preparation programs (a process where an organization provides one or more training experiences where professionals are trained to be outdoor leaders, often including steps such as screening

and testing, assessment, skill development, leadership field experience under the guidance of a mentor, and required practicum experiences)

Note that within each of these processes is a great deal of variation. This becomes particularly true when considering the wide variety of activities, geographic locations, and populations served by outdoor programs. These processes are not mutually exclusive and some overlapping principles exist.

In short, the process for preparing effective outdoor leaders is far from being an exact science. There is no question that the adventure programming profession needs to train competent outdoor leaders and that this task is becoming increasingly complex. But the magical Philosopher's Stone of outdoor leadership able to provide the remaining answers continues to be a mystery.

The chapters that follow represent the compiled body of knowledge of outdoor leadership and address the 12 elements of outdoor leadership competence. These chapters are intended to aid readers in becoming successful professional outdoor leaders.

SUMMARY

Use of the outdoors for recreation, education, development, and therapy is increasing. Accompanying this increased usage are a greater number of accidents and greater damage to the natural environment, and despite suggestions for a change toward a less competitive and conquering attitude, the problems continue. One solution is to educate users more by preparing outdoor leaders who can supply this education.

Preparing effective outdoor leaders is a lot like the practice of alchemy. Alchemists failed to transmute common minerals like lead and iron into precious metals such as gold and silver, often because they were unable to find the magical agent known as the Philosopher's Stone. Outdoor leadership experts are aware of the elements of effective leadership, but the correct processes for preparing outdoor leaders are still a mystery. The following are elements required for preparing effective outdoor leaders:

technical skills	flexible leadership style
safety skills	experience-based judgment
environmental skills	
organizational skills	problem-solving skills
instructional skills	decision-making skills
facilitation skills	effective communication
	professional ethics

Current examples of processes used to prepare effective outdoor leaders include individual certification, program accreditation, and outdoor leadership preparation programs. But as of yet, the best combination and sequence of these programs remain unknown. The adventure programming profession is still seeking its Philosopher's Stone.

QUESTIONS TO THINK ABOUT

1. Define leadership in your own words.

2. Give three good reasons why outdoor leaders are necessary in adventure programming.

3. Assess yourself on each of the 12 outdoor leadership elements. Write a sentence for each one detailing what you will do to improve your shortcomings for that component.

4. Differentiate between outdoor leadership certification and outdoor leadership preparation.

5. Do you think an elusive Philosopher's Stone exists for the outdoor leadership field? If so, what is it? If not, why doesn't it exist?

REFERENCES

Buell, L.H. (1981). The identification of outdoor adventure leadership competencies for entry-level and experience-level personnel. Unpublished doctoral dissertation, University of Massachusetts.

Burns, J.M. (1978). *Leadership.* New York, NY: Harper and Row.

Doran, M. (2001). A sample course leadership progression. *2001 NOLS Leadership Education Toolbox.* Lander, WY.

Green, P.J. (1981). *The content of a college-level outdoor leadership course for land-based outdoor pursuits in the Pacific Northwest: A Delphi consensus.* Unpublished doctoral dissertation, University of Oregon.

Priest, S. (1984). Effective outdoor leadership: A survey. *Journal of Experiential Education, 7*(3), 34-36.

Priest, S. (1986). *Outdoor leadership in five nations.* Unpublished doctoral dissertation, University of Oregon.

Priest, S. (1987). *Preparing effective outdoor pursuit leaders.* Eugene, OR: Institute of Recreation Research and Service.

Raiola, E.O. (1986). *Outdoor wilderness education: A leadership curriculum.* Unpublished doctoral dissertation, Union Graduate School.

Schimelpfenig, T. (2001). Teaching self-leadership at NOLS. *2001 NOLS Leadership Education Toolbox.* Lander, WY.

Schoel, J., Prouty, D., & Radcliffe, P. (1988). *Islands of healing: A guide to adventure based counseling.* Hamilton, MA: Project Adventure.

Simmons, D. (2004). *American outdoor recreation participation continues six-year ascent.* (Press release: July 28, 2004). Boulder, CO: Outdoor Industry Association. [Available] www.outdoorindustry.org/press.oia.php?news_id=708&sort_year=2004.

Swiderski, M.J. (1981). *Outdoor leadership competencies identified by outdoor leaders in five western regions.* Unpublished doctoral dissertation, University of Oregon.

PART

I

Foundations of Adventure Programming

Philosophy of Adventure Programming

"**W**ould you tell me please which way I ought to go from here?" asked Alice.

"That depends a good deal on where you want to get to," said the Cat.

"I don't much care where," said Alice.

"Then it doesn't matter which way you go," said the Cat.

"—so long as I get somewhere," Alice added as an explanation.

"Oh, you're sure to do that," said the Cat, "if you only walk long enough."

—Carroll, 1916

The act of learning is the result of reflection upon experience.... Having an experience does not [necessarily] result in learning; you have to reflect on it. The purpose of learning is to gain something new and to put that new skill or information to the test of usefulness. In order to learn, one must be willing to risk exposing oneself to new things, [be]

willing to test the validity of old things in relation to the new, and be willing to form new conclusions. I believe that to adventure is to risk exposing oneself to an unknown outcome. Therefore, to learn is to venture into the unknown: to learn is to adventure!

Learning and adventure are both delving into the unknown.... Everyone should have the opportunity to achieve self-fulfillment by engaging in learning that involves stress, striving, self-direction, sacrifice, goal setting, perfecting skills, and working cooperatively with others to achieve goals. That is experiential learning....

The intensity of getting lost in the work of learning contributes in a unique way to the quality of one's life. This occurs during the concentrated activity of perfecting a skill or serving others or protecting oneself from [risk]. This type of experiential learning and its outcomes should be available to each person.

—King, 1988

In the preface, which outlined this book, one of the cornerstones we identified as a critical piece in the wall of outdoor leadership preparation was philosophy. The term *philosophy* is probably distant from the conscious thoughts of clients actively engaged in adventure experiences, or even from the thoughts of leaders immersed in preparing for a trip, busy ensuring that all the equipment, food, and clients are accounted for and nothing has been forgotten.

But as seen in the dialogue between Alice and the Cat, without a strong sense of the philosophical and other theoretical concepts that serve as a foundation for what happens in adventure programming, clients, students, and professionals run the risk of "running around in circles" and not achieving the true potential of adventure experiences.

Philosophy, as used in this book, addresses the concepts of epistemology, how and what we know, and metaphysics, the way the world is, or how we create and view our reality (Crosby, 1981). In the second vignette, Keith King passionately leads readers through his philosophical beliefs on what adventure programming professionals should stress, why following appropriate experiential processes is so important, the direction you should take, and how you should "act" in striving to attain the goals of the adventure experience.

How and what we know about adventure programming allow us as professionals to develop a stronger practice. A "practice" can be defined as a set of rules that provides a professional activity with its structure of *what* should be accomplished as well as *how* it should be accomplished. When we as outdoor leaders fail to have a solid philosophical underpinning on what our clients are doing or how we lead them, we run the risk of acting like Alice. When this occurs, we may lack the proper direction and the ability to match experiences to meet particular client needs, the ability to select one technique over another as more appropriate, and the ability to communicate why one procedure is better than others or even important to use at all (Gass, 1992).

In this chapter, we overview how you can apply the philosophical tenets of adventure programming as a practice through six mediums:

1. Briefly overview philosophical tenets and how past philosophers and educators have presented statements supporting adventure programming.

2. Define various terms used in adventure education to help frame the context, or the way the profession is currently viewed, in the adventure programming field.

3. Outline common products, or outcomes, that generally occur for adventure programming participants, breaking the outcomes down into the two interacting categories of intrapersonal (i.e., individual and emotional) and interpersonal (i.e., group and social) development.

4. Highlight one process for achieving such products or outcomes.

5. Differentiate among adventure programs commonly used in the current field.

6. Summarize the hallmarks of good adventure programming.

PHILOSOPHY: DEFINITIONS

Philosophy comes from the Greek words for "liking" or "seeking wisdom." It considers the underlying principles and the ultimate real truth—versus the ideal truth—of the human condition. As we stated in the preface, philosophy has several aspects that relate to adventure programming. Let's define the following aspects of philosophy: aesthetics, ethics, logic, politics, epistemology, and metaphysics.

Aesthetics is the study of form or artistic beauty, such as the inherent attraction of nature. **Ethics** is the study of conduct or moral living (see chapter 23). **Logic** is the study of thinking or reasoning methods, involving the metaskills of judgment, problem solving, and decision making (see chapters 20, 21, and 22). **Politics** is the study of society or social order theories, such as how people interact in groups (see chapter 5).

Epistemology is concerned with the methods and theories of how we know what we know, in other words, the nature and origin of knowledge. **Metaphysics** is concerned with the methods and theories of the way things are and the systematic investigation of reality. For the remainder of this chapter, we focus on epistemology and metaphysics as they relate to adventure programming and key educational models.

PHILOSOPHICAL MODELS SUPPORTING ADVENTURE PROGRAMMING

Let's look for a moment at five philosophers: Socrates, Plato, Aristotle, William James, and John Dewey. While a detailed discussion of these individuals' work is beyond the scope of this book (see Itin, 1999; Warren, Sakofs, & Hunt, 1995), let's examine how their ideas support adventure programming.

We can trace the foundation of Western thinking and education to the work of the Greek philosophers Socrates, Plato, and Aristotle. Socrates and Plato believed that **virtues,** such as wisdom, bravery, temperance, and justice, were key qualities for young people to acquire in order to assume leadership in an ideal society. They also believed that the best way for young people to obtain such virtues was through direct and purposeful experience and by being involved in situations that impelled them into action (Hunt, 1990). For example, they thought the best way to become wise, brave, temperate, and just was by practicing wise, brave, temperate, and just acts that required people to be virtuous.

While differing in approaches (Plato with rationalism and Aristotle with empiricism), both Plato and Aristotle identified virtues, such as danger, risk, and safety, as important components for human growth. Using the work by Plato and Aristotle, Wurdinger (1995) identified three fundamental ideas that support the basic tenets of adventure programming: direct experience provides one of the best means for learning, building moral character and virtue is highly desirable, and taking risks is critically important to human growth and development.

Building off of his predecessors' works, William James evolved a pragmatic approach to philosophy. **Pragmatism** is the belief that the value of any learning experience is determined by the degree of learning that occurs from the actions and consequences of the experience. As stated by Kraft (1985), "pragmatists do not ignore theorizing or rational inquiry, but rather subject all theory to the crucible of experience to test its 'cash value.' James shared the general American distrust of purely theoretical or intellectual activity and kept asking the question 'What difference does it make?'" (p. 8). The **pragmatic maxim** summarizes the pragmatic approach to philosophy, stating that theories, experiences, and learning only possess value if they are practical, that is, if they help an individual learn and apply new learning to everyday life.

James' book *Talks to Teachers and Students* (1900) discusses 11 aspects of the maxim that examine the utility of experiential education (Donaldson & Vinson, 1979):

1. Clients learn best by their own activity.
2. Client interest is significant to learning.
3. Sensory experience is basic.
4. Effort and vigor make for good education.
5. Education modifies behavior.
6. Good education is holistic.
7. Imitating exemplary behavior is sound learning.
8. Love and understanding are important to learning.
9. Effective learning is interdisciplinary.
10. Respect for individual differences is essential.
11. Sound education is specific.

In the early 20th century, several educational philosophers began to reshape education. Among these innovative educators was John Dewey, the parent of modern experiential education. Dewey (1938) wrote widely on the value of experience in formal education. His ideas were pragmatic and easy to read. He called for education to be real: about life itself, not mere preparation for life. He saw the teacher's role as enabling students to learn about things they were interested in—not directing them to learn from a sterile curriculum. He thought that students should be taught to solve problems in a cooperative manner rather than to memorize facts in a competitive race for the best grades. He believed that a democratic process encouraged free and critical thinking, while the acceptance of authority quenched the fire of questioning. Kraft (1985) paraphrased several aspects of Dewey's work that apply to adventure programming:

> (1) Individuals need to be involved in what is being learned, (2) learning through experiences inside and outside of the classroom, and not just through teachers is vital, (3) learning must be immediately relevant for learners, (4) learners must act and live for the present as well as the future, (5) learning must assist learners in preparing for a changing and evolving world. (p. 8)

When applied to adventure programs, one of Dewey's most critical concepts is the idea of what determines when an experience possesses educational value. Specifically, Dewey based the educational value of any experience on the principles of interaction and continuity. **Interaction** is the ability of an experience to balance the present applications of client learning, such as objective and subjective conditions or external and internal conditions, so that clients are able to extract the true potential from the experience. **Continuity** refers to the ability of the experience to positively contribute to the future learning of the client, that is, how well the client will be able to generalize the experience over time. Dewey viewed experiences not meeting the principles of interaction and continuity as miseducative. We discuss how these two measurements apply to the concepts of facilitation and transfer later in this book (see chapters 14-17).

COGNITIVE, BEHAVIORAL, AND EXPERIENTIAL THEORIES OF LEARNING

Remember, epistemology is the study of the nature of knowledge and the limitations of human understanding (Allison & Pomeroy, 2000). We can group theories of learning into several categories. For the purposes of this book, we examine three categories: behavioral, cognitive, and experiential.

Behavioral theories of learning are founded on an empirical epistemology, which ignores the usefulness of conscious thought and personal experience in favor of external conditioning and control. Behavioral theories are criticized by Torbert (1972), who likens this approach to stimulus and response conditioning in which the "learner is treated as a manipulable black box whose external behavior is to be changed. Phenomena such as 'attitudes,' 'values,' and 'insight,' referring to events within the black box are irrelevant. This total control conforms closely enough to social learning situations in schools (except that schools tend to use their control in inconsistent, ineffective ways)" (p. 39). The obvious drawback to behaviorist approaches is that learners can become dependent on the conditioning environment or external control in the form of an authority figure, such as the teacher, or in the form of the reward and punishment system.

Cognitive theories of learning are based on a rational and ideal epistemology where teaching emphasizes acquiring, analyzing, retaining, and recalling abstract symbols or tidbits of information. Cognitive theories focus on the procedures used to absorb and remember information, like how rote memorization of unrelated facts employs the short-term memory while meaningful learning of concepts that fit into an existing schema (or bank of related knowledge) uses the long-term memory. Hence, if memorized information can be connected in context to existing information, learning will likely be retained for longer periods. For example, you might better study for a test by associating new facts with old memories.

In contrast, **experiential** theories of learning are holistic, incorporating cognition and behavior with conscious perceptions and reflections on experience. Coleman (1979) describes two ways to learn a symbolic language. The first way is experiential and is the "way all children learn a first language: the 'natural' way, by being in the linguistic environment, by trying and failing and finally succeeding, in making oneself understood and understanding others. It is a painful, time-consuming, and emotion-producing experience, but an effective one" (p. 7). The second way is cognitive and is the "typical method of school learning of a second language: [memorizing] the rules of grammar, the meanings of words, not in terms of experience, but in terms of the words of the first language one knows. This process is less painful, less emotion-producing, and less effective" (p. 7). According to Coleman, the difference is that the experiential way "grounds each word, each

phrase in a rich bed of experience. One remembers a word, a phrase, because of the very emotions it provoked when it was not understood by another or when it was understood and evoked a response from the other. One cannot forget it, because its usage is an intrinsic part of the fabric of experience that constitutes one's life" (p. 8).

INFORMATION ASSIMILATION AND EXPERIENTIAL LEARNING

Experiential learning differs from traditional cognitive learning in many ways. Coleman (1979) summarized the major differences between information assimilation, the main avenue by which most traditional cognition is conveyed, and experiential learning by outlining the sequence of each approach (see figure 2.1).

Information assimilation, the main avenue of cognitive learning, begins when the learner receives data in the form of symbols, such as numbers in a book or words in a lecture, about a general principle or particular illustration of the principle. In the second step, the learner assimilates and organizes the information as knowledge, indicating that she has truly learned the information rather than merely memorized it. In the third step, the learner infers a specific application from the general principle, implying cognitive intelligence, which is the

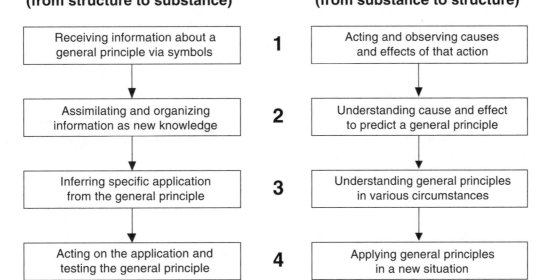

Information assimilation (from structure to substance)		Experiential learning (from substance to structure)
Receiving information about a general principle via symbols	**1**	Acting and observing causes and effects of that action
Assimilating and organizing information as new knowledge	**2**	Understanding cause and effect to predict a general principle
Inferring specific application from the general principle	**3**	Understanding general principles in various circumstances
Acting on the application and testing the general principle	**4**	Applying general principles in a new situation

Figure 2.1 A comparison of information assimilation and experiential learning.

ability to apply learning. The fourth and final step involves actually applying the learning, proving it useful. This sequence progresses from structure to substance.

Experiential learning, however, reverses the four-step sequence of information assimilation, moving from substance to structure. It begins when the learner acts and then observes the causes and effects of the action. Next, the learner derives understanding of the cause and effect from the observations so that he may predict events based on similar circumstances. Then, the learner understands the general principle from which such observations and understandings might arise, forming a working hypothesis. Ultimately, the learner applies the action in a new situation, staying within the limits of the generalized principle, testing the hypothesis. With additional and more varied actions, the learner broadens and deepens this generalization of principles to determine the limitations of the hypothesis.

In comparing the two approaches, Coleman (1979) found information assimilation more time efficient but often less effective in achieving client gains than experiential learning. In other words, the learner can assimilate information quickly and with little effort, yet may retain little. Furthermore, information assimilation depends on a symbolic medium, which can exclude those learners not fluent in the language used. "For children, adolescents or adults who have not mastered the complex systems of symbols used in reading, mathematics and other disciplines, [this] model leads to almost guaranteed failure, as they are unable to translate the learnings into concrete sequences of action" (Kraft, 1990, p. 180). This criticism is echoed by teachers and employers, who frequently state that students know a lot, but have difficulty doing anything with their knowledge. Part of this difficulty is due to institutionalized education's failure to address the last two steps of information assimilation, generalization and application.

In contrast, experiential learning "emphasizes a student's ability to justify or explain a subject rather than to recite an expert's testimony" (Joplin, 1981, p. 20). The emotions associated with experiential learning often aid in learning retention. This approach, however, may be time-consuming and the quality or quantity of learning may vary more widely because each individual may experience different learning from experiential activities. Experiential learning also tends to be more intrinsically motivating, since the action

of learning occurs in the first step, as opposed to information assimilation, in which the action is located in the last step. Initiating learning through action in an attempt to influence or control the environment can provide the impetus to complete the learning process. Schools often try to bypass this motivational shortcoming of information assimilation through extrinsic motivation by mandating attendance, requiring certain courses, and assigning grades. Experiential learning sometimes falls short (as does information assimilation) when addressing the last two steps of the learning process—generalization and application. If learners reflect on the experience, however, they often overcome this shortfall.

Certainly, we do not intend to set up an adversarial relationship between experiential learning and information assimilation; instead, we wish to outline their differences and complementary nature. Kraft (1990) stated that experiential educators who "use 'real life' experiences as their major teaching/learning tool, often ignore or denigrate what laboratory learning theorists have discovered, not recognizing that our carefully [planned experiential] programs make use of the same principles only in a different setting" (p. 176). As an outdoor leader, you stand to benefit from employing both approaches since the strengths of one compensate for the weaknesses of the other. Information assimilation bypasses the need for learners to repeat the centuries of experiential learning that have preceded them. For example, consider whether or not clients need to actually experience frostbite or hypothermia in order to understand them!

For detailed presentations of how many of these and other philosophical tenets have been developed, refer to Crosby (1981), Dewey (1916, 1938), Hunt (1990), Kraft (1985), and Wurdinger (1995).

DEFINING STRUCTURES IN ADVENTURE PROGRAMMING

This section defines many of the key terms used in this book, including the discipline of experiential education, the profession of adventure education, and the field of effective outdoor leadership. As an overview, this glossary helps frame the context of the information that follows in this and subsequent chapters.

We can loosely define **experiential education** as "learning by doing with reflection." This philosophy is based on the belief that people learn best by direct and purposeful contact with their learning experiences. Simply put, the best way to learn about problem solving is not to read about it in a book, but to actively practice solving problems in a hands-on setting. Such learning experiences are realistic: physically active, cognitively meaningful, and affectively engaging. These experiences require learners to accept responsibility for their own actions and to learn from guided reflection on their experiences (Kraft, 1985; Quay, 2003). Indeed, reflection on experience is a precursor to learning, for without reflection, learning loses much of its value.

Outdoor education follows the experiential philosophy of learning by doing. It takes place primarily, but not exclusively, through involvement with the natural environment. In outdoor education, the emphasis for learning is placed on relationships concerning people and natural resources.

Four types of relationships in outdoor education have been identified: interpersonal, intrapersonal, ecosystemic, and ekistic (Priest, 1986). **Interpersonal relationships** refer to how people get along in a group of two or more. Aspects of these relationships include communication, cooperation, trust, conflict resolution, problem solving, and the like. **Intrapersonal relationships** refer to how individuals get along with themselves. Aspects of these relationships include self-concept, confidence, self-efficacy, and so on. **Ecosystemic relationships** refer to the interdependence of living organisms in an ecological system. Aspects of these relationships include basic biological concepts such as the web of life, the food chain, and the energy pyramid. **Ekistic relationships** refer to the key interactions between human society and the natural resources of an environment, or how people influence the quality of the environment (water pollution or strip mining) and how the environment influences the quality of their lives (clean drinking water or beauty).

Historically, two branches of outdoor education have been identified: adventure and environmental. Truly functional outdoor education incorporates all four relationships across both branches.

Adventure education is the branch of outdoor education concerned primarily with interpersonal and intrapersonal relationships. Adventure education uses adventurous activities that provide a group or an individual with compelling tasks to accomplish. These tasks often involve group problem solving (requiring decision

In white-water rafting, working together can be critical for a group's success.

making, judgment, cooperation, communication, and trust) and personal challenge (testing competence against mental, social, or physical risks). To maximize safety, adventure professionals structure risk in a manner that causes participants to perceive it as being enormously high while in actuality it is much lower and more acceptable as a medium for producing functional change and growth. By responding to seemingly insurmountable tasks, participants often learn to overcome self-imposed perceptions of their capabilities to succeed. They turn limitations into abilities, and as a result, they learn a great deal about themselves and how they relate to others.

Environmental education is the branch of outdoor education concerned primarily with ecosystemic and ekistic relationships. While commonly thought of as a separate branch, you can clearly see that neglecting the environmental side of outdoor education threatens the very naturalness and solitude you and your clients seek in the outdoors.

Recreation refers to the activities that take place during an experience known as leisure, which we define shortly. **Outdoor recreation** is simply any activity done outdoors at leisure. Gardening is an outdoor recreational activity, as is racing cars or walking a dog in a park.

Outdoor pursuits are human-powered outdoor recreation. They represent the self-propelled activities performed in outdoor settings. Some common examples include walking, backpacking, rock climbing, mountaineering, skiing, snowshoeing, orienteering, bicycling, spelunking, sailing, kayaking, rafting, and canoeing. They do not include motorized outdoor recreational activities such as snowmobiling, motorcycling, car racing, and power boating, or animal-powered activities such as horseback riding and dog sledding. While these other activities are definitely outdoor recreation, they lack the human-powered, low-impact environmental philosophy that accompanies outdoor pursuits.

For an experience to qualify as **leisure,** it must meet three criteria: it must be a state of mind, it must be entered into voluntarily, and it must be intrinsically motivating of its own merit (Neulinger, 1981). Moreover, in leisure the process is more important than the product. For example, writing for a magazine in order to make money is work, while writing for sheer pleasure is leisure.

Adventure experiences can be leisure experiences. For a leisure experience to qualify as an adventure experience it must meet a fourth criterion: its outcome must be uncertain (Mitchell, 1983).

Uncertainty of outcome can stem from any number of factors. The outcome of an adventure is uncertain when information that is critical to completing a task or solving a problem is missing, vague, or unknown. For example, on an outdoor journey the outcome is uncertain when the necessary skill or confidence may be lacking; when the leadership influence, task definition, or group morale may appear unclear; and when the weather might be somewhat unpredictable. These conditions all lead to uncertainty and therefore risk.

Risk is the potential of losing something of value. The loss may lead to harm that is physical (e.g., broken bones), mental (e.g., psychological fear), social (e.g., peer embarrassment), or financial (e.g., lost equipment). From moment to moment, no one can be fully sure that a loss will actually occur, hence the uncertainty that creates adventure in a leisure experience. Risk is created by the presence of danger.

Danger gives rise to risk, but they are not the same. We may classify dangers as either perils or hazards that may result from both people and their surroundings. **Perils** are the sources or causes of a potential loss. A lightning bolt is one example of a peril that leads to the risk of electrocution. **Hazards** are the conditions or circumstances that influence the likelihood of a loss occurring. An intense thunderstorm is a hazard that includes the peril of lightning bolts.

Human dangers, whether perils or hazards, originate in the leader or participants in a group. Peer pressure, lack of attention, horseplay, and incompetence are all human dangers. These dangers are usually subjective or under the control of the group and its leader. **Environmental dangers,** whether perils or hazards, come from the natural surroundings. Avalanches, white-water rapids, poisonous plants or animals, and temperature extremes are all environmental dangers. These dangers tend to be much more objective than human dangers and are rarely under the control of the group or its leader.

Accidents are unexpected occurrences that result in a loss, such as illness, injury, or fatality. Accidents generally become emergencies when the group or leader is not prepared to respond correctly. The potential for an accident is greatly enhanced when human and environmental dangers occur simultaneously. For example, when kept separate, white-water rapids and horseplay may be fine, but allowing them to occur at the same instance greatly enhances the possibility of an accident. Combining dangers does not mean an accident will always occur, just that one is more likely to occur.

Incidents, or **close calls,** are the unforeseen happenings that do not develop into emergencies. Through effective leadership, some accidents may be prevented or their consequences reduced. We can think of incidents as minor accidents in which the losses are more acceptable, such as minor cuts, scrapes, bruises, and the like. But losses that are acceptable to one person may not be acceptable to another. For example, death may be acceptable to some Himalayan climbers, while a bump on a child's head may not be to the child's mother.

Risk management refers to procedures put in place to reduce the likelihood of an accident or incident. Risk management procedures may be proactive, or primary (completed before an experience); active, or secondary (in effect during the experience to avoid dangers or respond to an accident); or reactive, or tertiary (carried out after the fact). Equipment inspection before embarking on the adventure is a proactive risk management procedure, first aid for and evacuation of an injured victim is an active risk-management procedure, and paperwork done to report close calls or actual injuries is a reactive risk-management procedure.

Challenge is the act of engaging personal competence in risky situations. Risks are present in every adventure experience, creating the uncertainty that makes an experience adventurous. To engage in a challenging adventure experience, adventurers use their competence to risk and resolve the uncertainty of the outcome. If they choose not to use their competence, then the outcome is generally dictated by the random element of chance. Without utilizing some element of competence, adventure experiences are not considered challenging.

Competence is a combination of skill, attitude, knowledge, behavior, confidence, and experience. As with the perception of risk, each adventurer has a perception of personal competence that may or may not be accurate.

We can never know actual values of risk and competence with absolute certainty. At best, we may only estimate them. Professionals develop greater abilities to accurately perceive risk and competence through valid experiences. Effective outdoor leaders with sound judgment and adequate experience generally possess greater abilities to facilitate safer experiences—but not always.

We can use facilitated adventure experiences to enhance learning. By manipulating perceived values of risk and competence while keeping real values at acceptable levels, facilitated adventure experiences are possible. Depending on the objectives and precise control of a facilitated experience, misperceiving novices will slowly recognize relative levels of risk and competence through reflection on the experience. Since the levels of risk and competence are structured by the outdoor adventure leader, the importance of effective leadership becomes both obvious and paramount.

PRODUCT OF ADVENTURE: AFFECTIVE ASPECTS

The product of adventure programs can be cognitive (e.g., fact acquisition), physical (e.g., technical skill development), or affective (i.e., emotional or social development). We can classify affective learning as two interactive products: development of individuals through improved intrapersonal relationships (emotional development), and development of groups through enhanced interpersonal relationships (social development). Secondary aims may relate to the environmental relationships, but the product of most adventure programs is people who understand themselves more fully and relate to others more effectively. The following are some of the many affective outcomes expected from adventure programming:

Intrapersonal: Emotional and Individual

New confidence in oneself

Increased willingness to take risks

Improved self-concept

Enhanced leadership

Increased logical reasoning

Greater reflective thinking

Interpersonal: Social and Group

  Enhanced cooperation

  More effective communication skills

  Greater trust in others

  Increased sharing of decision making

  New ways to resolve conflicts

  Improved problem solving

  Enhanced leadership

Since the major focus of many adventure programs is on individual and group development, we look at the dynamics of individual social psychology and the stages of group development in chapters 4 and 5. These theories are important foundations for any outdoor leader. For now, however, we examine the process of adventure.

PROCESS OF ADVENTURE

While there are many theories on how adventure learning achieves the products we have outlined, probably one of the earliest was the Outward Bound process first described by Walsh and Golins (1976). These authors described adventure education as a process in which the "learner is placed into [a] unique physical environment and into [a] unique social environment, then given a characteristic set of problem-solving tasks [creating a] state of adaptive dissonance to which [the learner] adapts by mastery, which reorganizes the meaning and direction of the learner's experience" (p. 16). In other words, adventure education uses adventurous activities (e.g., outdoor pursuits, ropes courses, initiative games) to provide groups or individuals with challenging problem-solving tasks.

Walsh and Golins (1976) listed seven key elements of an adventure experience: the learner, the prescribed physical environment, the prescribed social environment, the tasks, a state of adaptive dissonance, mastery of learning, and the reorganization of the meaning and direction of learner's experience. Their model incorporates these elements (see chapter 11 for a diagram and more detailed information).

Learner

The learner needs to be motivated and able. In other words, the learner must be open to learning and be capable of physically performing the tasks, of cognitively thinking about and reflecting on the experience, and of dealing with any extreme stress that may arise.

Physically and Socially Unfamiliar Learning Environments

Placing participants into an unfamiliar learning environment can foster a variety of beneficial dynamics. Such environments are valuable because they starkly contrast to the learners' familiar environments, allowing participants to see old behavior patterns in a new light with a richer perspective as well as to notice behavior patterns that they may have overlooked in familiar settings. Unfamiliar physical environments may also allow participants to "try on" new behaviors in an environment that does not encompass some of the limitations or fears of familiar settings. Successful new behaviors may serve as first steps toward integrating behavior changes into more familiar settings.

An unfamiliar yet prescribed social environment can bear greatly on the success of adventure programs. Walsh and Golins (1976) point to the need for creating an "interdependent peer group with anywhere from 7 to 15 individuals who have a common objective" (p. 5). The following are four group dynamics that support adventure programming in a group this size:

1. The group needs to be large enough to produce a wealth of differing behaviors, yet small enough that separate subgroups diversify and form around these behaviors.

2. The group needs to be large enough that conflict results from differing client opinions, yet small enough that the group possesses the ability and resources to resolve any conflicts.

3. The group needs to be large enough to create a collective force through which individuals can and cannot reach certain goals working separately, yet small enough that the group can also support each client's individual goal.

4. The group needs to be large enough that a supportive state of reciprocity occurs, or "an exchange system where by strengths and weaknesses can be traded off within a group" (p. 6), yet small enough that the group members can contribute their

individual strengths, and through such an exchange, utilize the strengths of others.

The unfamiliarity of a learning environment that is full of social and physical risks can also be highly stimulating, enhancing the likelihood that clients will learn. Furthermore, the uniqueness can act as an equalizer, placing learners on par with one another; no one has the outdoor experience to be seen as the expert, so preexisting hierarchies may dissolve or be put aside, allowing people to think for themselves.

Characteristic Problem-Solving Tasks

Tasks in adventure programs should be

- organized—structured to suit the group's skills, needs, and maturity;
- incremental—sequenced with increasing complexity, consequences, and uncertainty;
- concrete—limited by time or space and solved for a real purpose: learners know what they are doing and why they are doing it;
- manageable—solvable with the group's resources and with new learning achieved from previous task completion;
- consequential—structured so that learners get real and naturally derived feedback from the situation, not reward or punishment from you; and
- holistic—structured so that learners need to apply cognitive, affective, and psychomotor/kinesthetic learning processes in a synergistic manner to achieve learning success.

Adventure problems generally present themselves as a challenge and while in some cases initially seem impossible, actually are quite reasonable. Provocative problems can dramatically elicit new learning, and clients are more likely to remember lessons learned for a long time.

Lessons Learned Through Adaptive Dissonance

The lessons learned in adventure experiences arise from a learner's adaptation to a state of dissonance, or the difference between the way the learner perceives their current state of being and the way that learner would like their reality to be (see also chapters 4 and 11). Humans like harmony and generally seek to change a less desirable situation into a more desirable one. By acting to create change and by reflecting on the effectiveness of their actions, participants can learn valuable lessons. In adventure experiences, the lessons are often about individual behavior, group behavior, or the environment.

Mastery of Learning

Success in the adaptive dissonance process is achieved by learners' mastery of the experience. This is generally driven by learners who are motivationally ready, alert in a novel adventurous environment, appropriately supported by group members as well as the leader, and presented with structured problems facilitated for mastery of learning.

Reorganization of the Meaning and Direction of Learners' Experience

The transference of learning from the adventure experience to real life begins with the mastery of new learning, or the sustained successful completion of tasks. When learners master problems through adventure experiences and these associated processes, their lives are often reorganized in meaning and direction in positive ways. The purpose behind achieving this mastery and reorganization is to generalize, or transfer, the successful strategies and associated feelings to other situations. Because transfer is one of the most critical features of adventure programming, we examine this concept in chapter 14.

Leader

Facilitating the Outward Bound process is the leader. As a leader, you direct the learning process by serving learners in a number of roles, some of which may include the following:

- Translator—helping the learner interpret and reflect on the experience
- Initiator—engineering the experiences
- Trainer—teaching skills and conditioning learners for the difficulties ahead
- Maintainer—keeping energy and motivation levels high

Hallmarks of Good Adventure Programming

Successful outdoor adventure programs share the following attributes:

Experiential: Good adventure programming is active rather than passive. It emphasizes hands-on conditions because people learn best by doing and reflecting on their experiences. Activities use perceived risk, yet are relatively safe. The activities are rarely the message or product to be learned; they are more often the medium or process through which learning takes place.

Dramatic: The excitement and emotion of good adventure programming activities focus attention and sharpen minds. Engaging activities demand greater involvement and consciousness. When learners are appropriately engaged, their ability to learn also increases.

Novel: Good adventure programming activities offer a unique context and an uncertainty of outcome. People are placed in situations in which no group member is an expert; therefore, adventures tend to equalize people, breaking down the hierarchical barriers and apprehensions that often exist in organized groups.

Consequential: Errors have potential real ramifications in outdoor adventures, such as getting wet in a canoe or falling from a rope, unlike in a classroom simulation for which points are lost. Furthermore, success and failure are supported by those who really matter: peers and self.

Metaphoric: Adventures are a microcosm of the requirements needed for and changes taking place in the real world. The behaviors demonstrated by individuals and groups during these activities parallel the way they act and what happens to them in daily life. As such, new learning, including skills, coping strategies, and bonding among people, can be analogously applied to future efforts at school, home, work, or play.

Transferable: Testimonials by past participants support the utility of experiential education, and limited research studies substantiate that new learning does indeed show up in daily life. People use adventure experiences to approach their lives from a fresh perspective and with improved effectiveness (Gass, 1985, 1991).

Structured: Tasks are custom-tailored to meet the needs of the client group in good adventure programming. Challenges sequentially increase in complexity and difficulty as people become more competent and need more risk in order to retain a certain level of challenge.

Voluntary: People are not forced to participate in good adventure programming activities. This dynamic gives learners the freedom to learn information and skills that are intrinsically motivating. This independence in the way people learn is often more important than what they learn. It begins with the individual's state of mind and moves toward a leader's confirmation and testimony verifying personal perceptions.

Concrete: In a good adventure program, problems are oriented to tasks with constraints as in the real world. The activities are intriguing, fun, and invigorating, motivating everyone to get involved. The experiences provide opportunities to experiment with new behaviors and skills in a safe environment that supports risk taking.

Holistic: Good adventure programming may incorporate cognitive, affective (social or emotional), and physical and psychomotor learning; may use all the senses; or may accommodate a variety of learning styles.

- Authority—holding influence within the group
- Guardian—being responsible for group safety
- Exemplar—modeling behavior patterns expected of the group

According to Walsh and Golins (1976), the leader "requires the ability to be empathetic, genuine, concrete, and confrontive when necessary. [This means utilizing] reflection, openness, esteem, and acceptance of others, not to be the know-it-all, but the exemplar of spirited, insightful, compassionate leadership" (p. 11-12).

ADVENTURE PROGRAMMING APPLICATIONS

When adventure is deliberately used to achieve the purposes and benefits we have listed, it is called **adventure programming.** As you saw in the preface, we can categorize adventure programming as one or more of four types: recreational, educational, developmental, or therapeutic. A program should be based on the client's needs rather than on the type of client. Corporate clients can engage in more than just developmental adventure programs, for example, sometimes they want a recreational program at a company picnic or conference. And educational programs are not just for school children, for example, therapeutic programs for school children at risk of dropping out are quite common.

Recreation

Recreational adventure programming is aimed at having fun, learning new activities, or becoming reenergized through adventure. Examples include enjoying a canoe outing or learning how to rock climb. Participants in these programs focus on enjoying the adventure. Recreational adventure programming can change the way people feel by reenergizing or revitalizing them. In addition, they may learn a new outdoor skill and then transfer that skill to their own lifelong leisure pursuits.

Education

Educational adventure programming is aimed at understanding concepts, enriching the knowledge of old concepts, or generating an awareness of pre-viously unknown needs through adventure. Examples include teaching the importance of working together as a team or demonstrating the impact of a new way to solve problems. Participants in these programs focus on learning through the adventure. Educational adventure programming can change the way people think by allowing them to see life's issues from a fresh perspective. They gain new attitudes and then transfer these attitudes to their daily life.

Development

Developmental adventure programming is aimed at improving functional behaviors and training people to behave in new and different ways through adventure. Examples include finding positive means to communicate with or trust one another. Participants in these programs want to enhance their interactions in a specific setting, such as school or work. Developmental adventure programming can change the way people behave by showing them successful ways to interact with others. The participants learn new behaviors and then transfer these behaviors to specific real-life settings such as the office or classroom. The efficacy of this program depends on the degree of transfer from the adventure to the participant's reality. In order to accomplish this, adventure experience coordinators often employ strategies such as thoroughly diagnosing a participant's needs, preplanning, action planning, and following up.

Therapy

Therapeutic adventure programming is aimed at changing dysfunctional behavior patterns, using adventure experiences as habilitation and rehabilitation. Examples include dealing with alcohol abuse or overcoming low self-esteem resulting from physical abuse. Participants in these programs generally possess patterns of dysfunction or destructive behavior that may limit or incapacitate their abilities to function in their communities. Therapeutic adventure programming can change people's behavior by showing them the impact of negative behaviors, offering them beneficial alternative behaviors, and augmenting what they may already do well. Clients in therapeutic adventure programs often learn new strategies for coping with personal issues and then transfer these strategies to critical aspects of their daily lives.

◄ *EFFECTIVE OUTDOOR LEADERS* ►

Given these defining terms, products, processes of adventure experiences, and the types of adventure programs, are there philosophical tenets that guide adventure programs? While this philosophy is discussed in several other sources identified earlier, one set of philosophical guidelines for effective outdoor leadership includes (when possible) the following:

► Allow clients to take as much responsibility to solve problems for themselves as possible, unless safety is an issue. The uncertainty of an adventure experience (created by challenging activities in unfamiliar environments with unknown outcomes) is generally aided by not "rescuing" participants from problems.

► Encourage challenge by choice. Forcing people to get involved in an adventure can reduce and even eliminate their perceived freedom of choice. Coercion limits clients from owning their success or failure. Instead they often attribute the outcome to the outdoor leader. Furthermore, injured people may be able to claim negligence against the leader, citing they were made to comply against their will.

► Adapt adventure experiences to suit the varying levels and needs of all members in a group. Leaders should recognize that adventures are a state of mind that often fluctuates according to a participant's perception of situational risks and personal competence. A range of challenges should be made available in the same activity (different watercraft for paddling) or at the same site (various climbs on a cliff) so that participants can select (in consultation with the leader) a level of risk that suits their level of competence.

► Deal in perceived risk with acceptable or recoverable outcomes. Creating conditions that appear risky while minimizing real dangers by using correct safety procedures heightens the perception of challenge. Dealing in real dangers (where a backup system is not possible due to the activity or site) is best reserved for participants who have overcome their misperceptions about risk and are astute in perceiving their own level of competence.

► Empower clients by encouraging them to take active roles in safety and creating challenges that require their competence to counter the risks of the adventure. This approach avoids adventure amusement, where clients have absolutely no responsibility for their own care or actions. They should be put in the primary positions of responsibility and safety whenever possible, with leaders only present to supervise or back up the safety systems.

► Create situations where the consequences (positive or negative) are natural outcomes from the clients' actions (delivered by the environment) rather than artificial ones (from the leader). Learning from mistakes can provide invaluable information. Leaders should avoid rewarding or punishing successes or failures. The negative consequences should be real and natural (e.g., getting wet, walking extra distance when lost, putting tents up in the dark, and going without hot drinks when the stove won't light) as should the positive ones (a beautiful view and sense of accomplishment from reaching the journey's end).

SUMMARY

As we refer to it in this book, "philosophy" addresses the concepts of epistemology, which is the cornerstone of how and what we know, and metaphysics, which is the way the world is, or how a person's reality is created and viewed. Understanding how and what we know about adventure programming allows us as professionals to develop a stronger practice, that is, the set of rules that defines and provides a professional activity with what it should attempt to accomplish as well as how to accomplish it. Without a solid philosophical underpinning, you can lack proper direction, the ability to match experiences to particular client needs, the ability to select one technique over another, the ability to communicate why one procedure is better than others (or even important to use at all!), and so on.

Outdoor education is a discipline within the profession of experiential education. Outdoor education has two branches: environmental and adventure education. Environmental education deals with ecosystemic and ekistic relationships, while the affective aspects of adventure education address intrapersonal and interpersonal relationships.

Outdoor recreation is any activity done outdoors, while outdoor pursuits are those activities that are human-powered rather than motorized or animal-powered. Leisure is an experience in which the process is far more important than the product, which is the opposite of work. Adventure experiences are educational leisure experiences when participation is voluntary, motivation is intrinsic, adventure is perceived as a state of mind, and the outcome is uncertain.

The uncertainty of outcome is possible because of the risks inherent to the activity. Risk, or the potential of losing something valuable, arises from dangers that can be classified as either perils, which are sources of loss, or hazards, which are conditions often increasing the likelihood of loss. Sources of danger occur from the environment or the humans who participate in adventures within that environment. Accidents and incidents occur more often when both the environmental and human dangers combine at the same instant. Safety is the collection of procedures used to reduce dangers and associated injuries.

Challenge results from the interplay of risk and competence. Adventure participants use competence to resolve the uncertainty of an adventure by creating a positive outcome. An adventure that fails to actively engage the participants' competence is merely subject to chance or random event outcomes. Because the participants are not involved, they cannot attribute success or failure to themselves and thus may not gain any empowerment from the adventure.

Facilitated adventure experiences are purposefully structured adventures that aim to empower an individual or group. As an outdoor leader, you are responsible for coordinating these facilitated experiences and for maximizing learning, safety, and environmental protection. You can do this through effective leadership: a process of purposeful action which creates meaningful conditions and may influence outcome.

One model used to describe adventure programming is the Outward Bound process model. In this process, a learner is put in unique environments to solve problems and adapt to the accompanying dissonance by mastering new learning. The seven key elements of this process are the learner, the physical environment, the social environment, the tasks, a state of adaptive dissonance, mastery of learning, and the reorganization of the meaning and direction of the learner's experience. Adventure programming, deliberately used for enhancing relationships, can be recreational, educational, developmental, or therapeutic, depending on the program's purpose. Active experience, drama, novelty, consequences, metaphors, transference, structure, voluntary participation, concrete tasks, and holistic content are all hallmarks of adventure programming.

QUESTIONS TO THINK ABOUT

1. Make a list of the philosophical tenets you believe support adventure programming, guiding how it should be conducted.

2. Draw and label a diagram that shows the relationships between the boldfaced terms defined in this chapter that share connections with one another.

3. Given examples of current adventure programs representing each of the four programming types (here and in the preface), compare and contrast what might occur in each of these adventure programs.

4. Examine the sections "Effective Outdoor Leaders" and "Hallmarks of Good Adventure Programming." Do you agree with all the statements made in these sections? Would you add any conditions or exceptions to make them stronger or more applicable to certain populations? Would you add any other statements?

REFERENCES

Allison, P., & Pomeroy, E. (2000). How shall we "know"? Epistemological concerns in research in experiential education. *Journal of Experiential Education, 23*(2), 91-97.

Carroll, L. (1916). *Alice's adventures in wonderland.* Chicago: Rand McNally.

Coleman, J.S. (1979). Experiential learning and information assimilation: Toward an appropriate mix. *Journal of Experiential Education, 2*(1), 6-9.

Crosby, A. (1981). A critical look: The philosophical foundations of experiential education. *Journal of Experiential Education, 4*(1), 9-16.

Dewey, J. (1916). *Democracy and education.* New York: Free Press.

Dewey, J. (1938). *Experience and education.* New York: Macmillan.

Donaldson, G.W., & Vinson, R. (1979). William James: Philosophical father of experienced-based education. *Journal of Experiential Education, 2*(2), 6-8.

Gass, M.A. (1985). Programming the transfer of learning in adventure education. *Journal of Experiential Education, 8*(3), 18-24.

Gass, M.A. (1991). Enhancing metaphoric transfer in adventure therapy programs. *Journal of Experiential Education, 14*(2), 6-13.

Gass, M.A. (1992). Theory and practice. *Journal of Experiential Education, 15*(2), 6-7.

Hunt, J.S. (1990). Philosophy of adventure education. In J.C. Miles & S. Priest (Eds.), *Adventure education* (pp. 119-128). State College, PA: Venture.

Itin, M.C. (1999). Reasserting the philosophy of experiential education as a vehicle for change in the 21st century. *Journal of Experiential Education, 22*(2), 91-98.

James, W. (1900). *Talks to teachers and students.* New York: Henry Holt & Co.

Joplin, L. (1981). On defining experiential education. *Journal of Experiential Education, 4*(1) 17-20.

King, K. (1988). The role of adventure in the experiential learning process. *Journal of Experiential Education, 11*(2), 4-8.

Kraft, R. (1985). Toward a theory of experiential learning. In R.J. Kraft & M. Sakofs (Eds.), *The theory of experiential education* (pp. 4-35). Boulder, CO: Association for Experiential Education.

Kraft, R.J. (1990). Experiential learning. In J.C. Miles & S. Priest (Eds.), *Adventure education* (pp. 175-183). State College, PA: Venture.

Mitchell, R.G. (1983). *Mountain experience: The psychology and sociology of adventure.* Chicago: University of Chicago Press.

Neulinger, J. (1981). *The psychology of leisure.* Springfield, IL: Charles C Thomas.

Priest, S. (1986). Redefining outdoor education: A matter of many relationships. *Journal of Environmental Education, 17*(3), 13-15.

Torbert, W.R. (1972). *Learning from experience toward consciousness.* New York: Columbia University Press.

Quay, J. (2003). Experience and participation: Relating theories of learning. *Journal of Experiential Education, 26*(2), 105-116.

Walsh, V., & Golins, G. (1976). *The exploration of the Outward Bound process.* Denver: Colorado Outward Bound School.

Warren, K., Sakofs, M., & Hunt, J.S. (1995). *The theory of experiential education.* Dubuque, IA: Association for Experiential Education.

Wurdinger, S. (1995). *Philosophical issues in adventure education.* Dubuque, IA: Kendall/Hunt.

History of Adventure Programming

"World War II was in full skirmish. German U-boats were successfully torpedoing merchant marine and naval vessels crossing the North Atlantic between Britain and North America. Sailors, thrown overboard by the explosive strikes into freezing water, were dying in record numbers. A curious occurrence was noted by observers: the younger sailors were the ones dying, while the older sailors were surviving. An owner of one shipping company remarked, 'I would rather entrust the lowering of a lifeboat in mid-Atlantic to a sail-trained octogenarian than to a young sea technician who is completely trained in the modern way, but has never been sprayed by saltwater' (Miner, 1990, p. 59). Why the difference? What could be changed in the faulty training of strong young sailors to increase their self-reliance and compassionate support of their colleagues?

The use of adventure experiences as a programming tool formally began in the 1940s with attempts to answer these questions. While some authors identify the Egyptians, who explored their world in 2500 B.C., as the first adventurers (Ewert, 1989), many trace the start of adventure programming to the question of the "decline" of youth evidenced by the deaths of young sailors in the 1930s.

In this chapter, we look at the history of outdoor adventure programming. If you are interested in the earlier history of recreation, leisure, and sport as precursors to adventure programming, we encourage you to seek out texts in those fields.

BEGINNINGS

Kurt Hahn can be viewed as the "grandparent" of adventure programming. Hahn was born in 1886 in Germany to Jewish parents, a wealthy industrialist father and an artistic mother. He was influenced early in life by Plato's *Republic* and by an English education at Oxford from 1910 to 1914. After World War I, Prince Max of Baden, Germany's last imperial chancellor, and Karl Reinhard, a German educator, helped Hahn found a coeducational boarding school in 1920 called Salem Schule (translated as *shalom,* or *peace,* school) on Lake Constance. At Salem, the curriculum emphasized personal responsibility, equality, social justice, respect, and service to the community.

Unfortunately, these principles opposed the Nazi movement and so did Hahn. In 1932, he spoke out publicly against Hitler, particularly in response to Hitler's Beuthen telegram, in which Hitler demanded that five storm troopers be released and honored despite their convictions and death sentences for trampling a young Communist to death in front of his mother. With the

rise of the Third Reich, Hahn was persecuted by the Nazis and imprisoned for his statements, beliefs, and religion. He was later released at the request of the British government and exiled from Germany. He went to the United Kingdom and in 1934 opened Gordonstoun School in an abandoned Scottish castle (Richards, 1990).

Gordonstoun operated on the Hahnian principles developed at Salem, but with the start of World War II, it was expropriated by the British armed forces. Hahn moved to Wales where, after joining forces with Lawrence Holt, director of the Blue Funnel shipping line, and Jim Hogan, a British educator, he turned his attention to solving the problem of the dying sailors as well as the needs of other youth. Hahn, Holt, and Hogan believed that younger sailors and other youth needed to be provided with an experience that would turn their attitudes around. Their work came to be known as **Outward Bound,** named after the term given to ships sailing from the safety of harbor into the open seas.

OUTWARD BOUND

Outward Bound began in 1941 at Aberdovey in Wales, not as a center for basic survival training for the military, but as a program for youth, many of whom were destined for armed service. Many of the youth were sponsored by Holt's shipping company; many more were supported by other organizations, such as police and fire departments, local governments, schools, and industry. Outward Bound courses originally lasted one month, because on the last day of the month, company apprentices would have to go home to receive their paychecks! A typical course consisted of orienteering, search-and-rescue training, athletics, small-boat sailing, ocean and mountain expeditions, obstacle-course training, and service to the local communities (Miner, 1990).

How did Outward Bound accomplish its goals in the early days? Let's look at how the program used an obstacle course, a predecessor of the modern ropes or challenge courses of today. Young sailors would swing on old hawser ropes, cross rope bridges between treetops, and climb up and down roped cargo nets or smooth wooden walls. The obstacle course was meant to mimic ships at sea. But not only was this training meant to prepare youth for abandoning ship, it was also devised to increase self-confidence as well as the ability to work well with others. Holt summed up the Hahnian principle of the school best with the comment, "The training at Aberdovey must be less a training for the sea than through the sea, and so benefit all walks of life" (Miner, 1990, p. 59).

After the war, the principles of Outward Bound expanded to address continuing issues of social decline, particularly in youth. The following are six ways in which youth attitudes and abilities were declining that concerned Hahn (Richards, 1990, p. 69):

1. **Fitness,** due to modern methods of locomotion

2. **Initiative** and **enterprise,** due to the widespread disease of "spectatoritis"

3. **Memory** and **imagination,** due to the confused restlessness of modern life

4. **Skill** and **care,** due to the weakened tradition of craftsmanship

5. **Self-discipline,** due to the ever-present availability of stimulants and tranquilizers

6. **Compassion,** due to the unseemly haste of modern life

One way the leaders of early outdoor programs addressed the decline was by providing a "moral equivalent to war." In describing this concept, James (1967) said that war, while producing a host of immoral actions and destructive consequences, often produced behaviors that brought out the best in people faced with adversity. James believed the aims of society would be advanced if some mechanism could develop these moral and beneficial qualities without including the destructive and immoral aspects of war.

In response to the declines and the widespread needs of British youth, a second school opened on Eskdale Green in the mountains of England's Lake District in 1950. For the next

An early American Outward Bound group.

decade, several new schools sprang up around Britain. In 1958, the first school was built outside of Britain in Lumut, Malaysia. In 1962, the first American school opened in Marble, Colorado, and several more followed across the United States. Today, Outward Bound operates over 40 schools in 27 countries and works with all types of clients: at-risk urban youth, recovering substance abusers, business executives, and so on (Outward Bound International, 2005).

Kurt Hahn died in 1974, having remained active throughout his retirement. Credited with the legendary and innovative Salem Schule and Gordonstoun, Hahn's visionary thinking also led to several other programs: the United World Colleges, one on each continent, attended primarily by international students; the Round Square Schools Conference, supporting community-based service learning; and the Duke of Edinburgh Award, a high-school achievement scheme. Outward Bound, by far the most famous of his accomplishments, also helped shape the U.S. Peace Corps and numerous other outdoor adventure programs (Miner, 1990).

GROWTH OF ADVENTURE LEARNING PROGRAMS

As the Outward Bound movement in America expanded, the need for other types of adventure programs also grew. Paul Petzoldt, chief instructor with the Colorado Outward Bound School in 1964, identified the need to better prepare Outward Bound instructors through leadership courses. To meet the need, he proposed creating the Wyoming Outward Bound School. But Josh Miner, founder of Outward Bound in the United States, had his hands full running the Colorado school and trying to start new programs in Minnesota and Maine. In 1965, Petzoldt got together with another Outward Bound instructor, Ernest "Tap" Tapley, and created the **National Outdoor Leadership School** (NOLS) in Lander, Wyoming (Bachert, 1990).

One of the more notable programs adapted from Outward Bound is **Project Adventure.** In 1970 America, Outward Bound was beginning to influence educational reform. Educators were searching for a way to tap into the benefits of adventure learning for the mainstream high-school curriculum. Project Adventure began as an attempt to modify the monthlong Outward Bound experience into several high-school subjects: physical education, science, biology, social studies, history, drama, English, and counseling.

Jerry Pieh (son of Bob Pieh, who started the Minnesota Outward Bound) was a principal at Hamilton-Wenham High School in Hamilton, Massachusetts. In 1971, he received a three-year grant from the U.S. Office of Education to start Project Adventure as a collaborative venture between teachers and former Outward Bound staff. The key to its success was that everything was connected: lessons learned in team cooperation and problem solving during physical education were applied in group projects in other courses (Prouty, 1990).

In 1974, at the end of the three-year test period, an evaluation of Project Adventure showed it to have been successful and capable of producing significant changes in student self-concept and locus of control. That year, the Office of Education awarded Project Adventure the status of National Demonstration School. They touted the program as a model to be disseminated to other schools. Through annual dissemination grants from the National Diffusion Network, Project Adventure staff shared their work with over 400 schools across the United States during the next six years. Karl Rohnke, author of the early books on group initiative and ropes courses, and Dick Prouty assumed its leadership in 1981. Since the program had grown well beyond the expectations of the high-school administrators, Project Adventure separated from the educational system and incorporated as a nonprofit organization. In the decade that followed, Project Adventure branched out to work with youth agencies, psychiatric hospitals, government offices, treatment centers, colleges, universities, corporations, and job-training sites (Prouty, 1990). Today, it has two offices in the United States and representatives in Australia, New Zealand, and Singapore.

In 1976, Paul Petzoldt looked for a new medium through which he and others could establish outdoor leadership training programs. He then began leading groups of students from midwestern universities into the Wyoming wilderness. Through discussions with several university professors, the concept for the Wilderness Use Education Association came into being in 1977 (they later dropped the "Use" in the title to become the WEA). While NOLS was a facility-based school, WEA became a membership organization composed of departments from a few American universities such as Western Illinois University (Lupton, 1990). At the time of publication of this text, WEA is headquartered at Indiana University in Bloomington, Indiana. Thus, Petzoldt is credited with beginning both the National Outdoor Leadership School

(NOLS) and the **Wilderness Education Association** (WEA).

Another membership organization with roots in Outward Bound is the **Association for Experiential Education** (AEE). Outward Bound, Project Adventure, NOLS, and WEA have all been longtime members of AEE. In 1974, Outward Bound sponsored a conference on using outdoor pursuits in higher education at Appalachia State University. In 1976, after several more conferences at other universities collaborating with Outward Bound (including one in Canada), organizers formed the AEE and incorporated the organization the next year in Boulder, Colorado (Garvey, 1990).

At the time of publication of this text, AEE has over 500 organizational members and 2,000 individual members. AEE had an international scope by the 1990s and indirectly influenced the creation of several AEE-like organizations in other countries around the world. The organization holds international conferences yearly as well as seven regional conferences around North America every spring (Warren, Sakofs, & Hunt, 1995). AEE also publishes the *Journal of Experiential Education*. We highly recommend this publication as well as the *Journal of Adventure Education and Outdoor Leadership* from England as the foremost sources for leading-edge thinking and writing in adventure programming.

HISTORY OF OUTDOOR LEADERSHIP PREPARATION

We can trace the formal beginnings of outdoor leadership preparation to Great Britain. From this country, parallel programs developed throughout the United Kingdom, Australia, Canada, Europe, New Zealand, and the United States. Let's examine the development of these programs.

Great Britain

Note: This section updated by Peter Allison.

Great Britain was the first nation to institute a formal training program for outdoor leaders, and the program's evolution had three distinct stages: certification, qualification, and occupation standards. The influence of Outward Bound had brought about explosive growth in outdoors use by British youth and school groups. Coupled with this growth was an increase in accidents in poorly led groups of young people, which repre-

sented 65% of all mountain rescues in the decade following World War II (Jackson, 1972). Early in 1958, an initial meeting chaired by Lord John Hunt, leader of the first successful Mount Everest expedition and director of the Duke of Edinburgh Award Scheme, led to the formation of the Mountain Leadership Training Board in 1961 with the mandate to certify mountain leaders to care for groups in the outdoors (Parker & Meldrum, 1973). Thus began the first stage of certification (for more on certification, see page 37).

The Mountain Leadership Certificate Program trained and assessed leaders in the basic skills "required to take a party on walking and camping expeditions in mountainous areas of the United Kingdom under normal summer conditions. It [was] intended as an essential requirement for teachers, youth leaders, and other adults wishing to take young people on to the mountains and to show them how to enjoy their mountain walking with safety" (Langmuir, 1969, p. 63).

The curriculum of the early Mountain Leadership Certificate Program was decidedly hard-skill oriented. The summer certificate included navigation, hill walking, camping and expeditions, security on steep ground, river crossing, exposure (hypothermia), heat, weather, lightning, and mountain rescue. A winter certificate was added in 1972 in response to the "Cairngorms disaster" in which several school children died of hypothermia in the mountainous Cairngorms region of Scotland in 1971. It was intended for leaders of groups in winter conditions as found in the Scottish Highlands. The components of the winter certificate included snow and ice climbing, belaying on snow and ice, snow shelters, frostbite, snow cover and avalanches, and avalanche search and rescue (Langmuir, 1973). As a direct result of the Cairngorms disaster, the Hunt Committee on Mountain Training, again chaired by Lord Hunt, formed to look closely at the certification scheme. Thus began the second stage of qualification.

Published in 1975, the Hunt Report raised critical points. First, the committee stated they had "serious reservations about the value of confering [sic] certificates on large numbers of adults who are not professionally engaged in mountain training. Furthermore, certification in any sphere carries its own limitations, in that it tends to prescribe in a rigid manner the content of a course of training, making it more difficult to provide imaginatively for varying needs" (British Mountaineering Council [BMC], 1975, p. 1). Second, the committee saw the certificate as having an inflated value, given that it merely met a minimum standard in a field in which the maximum might be more appropriate. Third, the granting of a certificate appeared to attract people who otherwise might not have been interested in mountain activities. Fourth, requirement of the certificate by many agencies prevented the involvement of leaders who lacked the certificate, but who had greater experience than required by such a certificate. Fifth, local educational authorities and other groups used the certificate as an inappropriate guarantee of the leader's ability (BMC, 1975).

The Hunt Committee made three major recommendations. First, training programs should continue, but the approach should be more varied in content, flexible in nature, and responsive to individual needs. Second, certificates should be abolished and a reporting method instituted that would give the conditions under which assessment took place. Essentially, assessors would suggest further training for a candidate based on his strengths and weaknesses. Third, the Mountain Leadership Certificate Program should be renamed (BMC, 1975).

A year later, the Hunt reforms were adopted, and the British Mountain Leadership Training Board (BMLTB, the newly adopted name) now offered a qualification, rather than a certification, in outdoor leadership. This move was overlooked by many North American proponents of certification who recommended following the British success story. Yet, ironically, the British scheme no longer certified leaders! Instead, it provided the "opportunity to gain minimum technical competence for leading parties in the hills. It [did] not provide a professional mountaineering or instructing qualification, nor a professional qualification. The completion of a training course alone [was] in no way a qualification in itself" (Langmuir, 1984, p. 360).

Rather than certify the individual to be a leader, the program placed that responsibility on the candidates as well as on the agency that hired them. The BMLTB clearly stated that it was the "responsibility of the employer or organiser [sic] to decide whether a leader possessed the personal attributes needed for leadership" (Langmuir, 1984, p. 361). They also stated that in nonmountainous terrain, the qualification should not be a requirement, and that plenty of competent outdoor leaders may possess the informal qualities of leadership, but may not have obtained the formal qualification. In no way should the possession of a leader qualification absolve employers from the responsibility of evaluating job applicants.

Nonetheless, the curriculum remained relatively unchanged with the exception of new classes on access, conservation, and "party leadership." This latter component was an effort by Ken Ogilvie to inject soft skills into the profoundly hard-skill curriculum of the BMLTB. In response to a report on leadership in outdoor activities (The Sports Council, 1991) calling for greater development of interpersonal skills in leaders, Ogilvie (1993) wrote a text titled *Leading and Managing Groups in the Outdoors*. With chapters on aims and values, personal experience, thinking about leadership, leadership models and styles, leader awareness, leader attitudes and approaches, and leadership skills, this book was the first attempt to consider leaders as more than competent technicians. To date, these ideas have yet to be incorporated into the BMLTB scheme, which still remains hard-skill oriented.

In 1986, the British Department of Employment began reforming vocational qualifications for all professions in the United Kingdom. Three years later, the profession of sport and recreation came under consideration and the third and present stage of occupational standards began. A committee of experts was established to define professional standards (called National Vocational Qualifications, or NVQs) in five occupational areas: coaching, teaching, and instruction; facility management and operations; sport development; playwork; and outdoor education, training, and recreation. The framework of NVQs for the outdoor profession was completed in 1992 and applied to everyone working in the outdoors, from schoolteachers to social workers to staff of outdoor centers.

Although the NVQs specific to outdoor education, training, and recreation were still under development at the time of this text's publication, they considered more than just hard skills. One particular outdoor occupation—development training, which is the use of experiential methods with youth and corporations—has encompassed meta- and process competencies as well as technical ones (Doughty & Loynes, 1993). Despite this refreshing approach, many of the other outdoor occupations appear stale and rigid from a North American perspective. Only time will tell if this stage will bring about true improvements.

One of the most significant United Kingdom developments in the past decade resulted from the Lyme Bay canoeing tragedy of March 1993. A group of eight pupils and their teacher were accompanied by two instructors from an outdoor center on the south coast of England. As a result of a series of errors and circumstances, four of the teenagers drowned. The subsequent trial prosecuted the parent company and the center manager. This tragedy accelerated governmental discussions until Parliament passed the Young Persons Safety Act in 1995. The resulting Adventure Activities Licensing Authority (AALA), supported by the Health and Safety Commission, now inspects providers and issues licenses to ensure, in so far as is reasonably practicable, that pupils will be "safe."

The consequences of AALA have proved immense. The Young Persons Safety Act only applies to centers, companies, or individuals providing adventurous activities for children under 18 years. It does not apply to voluntary organizations providing activities for their members or schools providing for their own pupils. However, the governmental standards of AALA are also widely regarded as applying to any organization providing outdoor activities and would probably now be used as the standards in any court case.

Historically, five universities offered degrees in outdoor education (University of Bangor, Edinburgh, Liverpool John Moore's, St. Martins, and Strathclyde) but in recent years several other universities have started to offer undergraduate and postgraduate qualifications. This increasing number of courses has led to a flooding of entry-level staff members who are specialists in activity or recreation, but not necessarily in education or outdoor leadership.

Higher education has also contributed to the development of academic study and to increased doctorates and master's degrees in outdoor education. The resulting dissertations and theses have spun off further research and a few books as well as articles in the international *Journal of Adventure Education and Outdoor Learning*. Nevertheless, Higgins (2002) has noted a substantial reduction in residential provision in the United Kingdom and the decline of outdoor education centers in Scotland, moving "past the point of viability" (p. 158).

Other European Nations

Mountain leader training boards also exist in Ireland, Northern Ireland, Scotland, and Wales. These boards have close ties to the BMLTB, and their curricula have much in common. With the recent trade coalition among European nations, the BMLTB has begun to influence France, Spain, Germany, Italy, and many other countries. Before this influence,

however, the United Kingdom already had had far-reaching impact, directly and indirectly, on other British Commonwealth nations. Several new European nations are making novel adaptations to the leadership training (e.g., the Czech Republic) (see Martin, Leberman, & Neill, 2003).

Australia

Note: This section updated by Peter Martin.

Until recently, Australia has developed outdoor leaders at the state level. Several Australian programs exist in the states of Victoria, Tasmania, South Australia, and Western Australia. The Australian outdoor leadership movement began in 1969 when the Victorian Bushwalking and Mountaincraft Advisory Board offered its first course, which was based closely on the British Mountain Leadership Certificate Program. Over the years, the Australians adapted British training materials to suit local conditions (R. Lingard, personal communication, April, 1984).

Subsequently, other interested organizations in Tasmania, South Australia, and Western Australia copied the Victorian scheme. The majority of these schemes still offered a certificate, but it was a certificate of course completion and not a certificate of leadership (Pickett & Polley, 2001). The trend was away from certification and toward the qualification of having completed the initial training, as in the qualification stage in Britain (W. Tomalin, personal communication, May, 1984).

Programming in Western Australia, which is geographically separate from the other states, has taken a slightly different track. Its Expedition Leader Course was formulated on the belief that the "values and qualities for good judgment in a leader emerge from a continuing learning dynamic rather than from a training scheme using knowledge already created and stored" (Manfield & Pearse, 1991, p. ii). In addition to the technical (hard) and people (soft) skills, its curriculum focused on the integrated skills of problem solving, organization, group management, and instruction.

In the Western Australian program, leadership development took place over several years through the primary, secondary, and tertiary education system. Children learned basic outdoor skills throughout their schooling, and then as university students they "studied" to become leaders. We found a similar pattern, independent of government schemes, in exemplary college programs such as the one created at the Bendigo Campus of Latrobe University–College of Northern Victoria.

Recent developments have seen meetings by representatives of the different Australian states for developing a national leadership preparation scheme (McArthur, 1999). For example, the Australians have begun a National Outdoor Recreation Leadership Development (NORLD) project to develop a nationwide leadership preparation curriculum (National Outdoor Recreation Leadership Development [NORLD], 1994).

Development of outdoor leaders in Australia now occurs through three distinct pathways: community-based courses, formal university programs, and vocational education and training by either workplaces or technical colleges. The history of these three pathways is intertwined, but each path made distinct contributions to education in outdoor leadership.

Community-based courses, such as the bushwalking and ski-touring leadership courses run by the Victorian Bushwalking and Mountaincraft Training Advisory Board (BMTAB), are the foundation from which other pathways developed. The BMTAB was the first of such state-sponsored programs in Australia and started running leadership courses in 1969. By 2000 the BMTAB had graduated over 700 leaders with several hundreds more having completed basic training (Bushwalking and Mountaincraft Training Advisory Board [BMTAB], 2000). The ski-touring leadership program was added in 1983 and also had over 100 graduates (BMTAB, 2000). Perhaps the greatest strength of the BMTAB program, and of those that followed in other states, was its reliance on grassroots bushwalkers for staffing and content. The BMTAB built a strong reputation for practical leadership training, primarily aimed at educating teachers and youth leaders in the wisdom of bush leadership.

Other community-based programs now exist to cover most popular outdoor activities. Often, like the BMTAB, they were created in response to legal and community pressure following well-publicized outdoor accidents. Most Australian states now have community-based leadership programs in a range of outdoor activities. Some, like the Australian Climbing Instructors' Assoc. Inc. and Canoeing Australia, are nationally coordinated bodies that have grown out of state groups.

The second key pathway to outdoor leadership development in Australia is that offered by universities. Outdoor leadership training through degree courses is most common in Victoria, where outdoor education is a formal school subject to year 12, thus providing vocational outcomes for teachers trained in outdoor education leadership.

The oldest of these programs is the degree in outdoor education at LaTrobe University at Bendigo. The Bendigo program originated in 1975 and is now supported by the largest university faculty of outdoor education in the world. Several other universities around Australia are also now conducting leadership training as part of education or recreation degrees, but the curricula vary widely.

The most recent pathway in leadership training to emerge in Australia is through vocational education and training (VET) schemes. The VET schemes grew out of a move in the early 1990s to coordinate community-based leadership programs nationally (Outdoor Recreation Council of Australia [ORCA], 2003). The NORLD project, mentioned earlier, brought together key state-based activity groups to thrash out more coherent national outdoor leadership curricula, with the goal of enabling certification across state borders. The end result was a nationally endorsed Outdoor Recreation Training Package (Sport and Recreation Training Australia [SRTA], 2003). The Training Package is a competency-based syllabus with massive numbers of modules and units describing an extensive array of different outdoor activities.

The delivery of this nationally endorsed syllabus has now been taken up by many Colleges of Technical and Further Education (TAFE) across Australia as well as by some commercial training enterprises. Ironically, the proliferation of these TAFE courses, and their support by the government, has sounded the death knoll for some community programs such as the long-running BMTAB, which conducted its final program in 2003. It remains to be seen if these new competency-based programs can match the wisdom of the elders that was so characteristic of the community programs.

New Zealand

Note: This section updated by John Corcoran.

In 1977, organizers in New Zealand established the provisional Outdoor Training Advisory Board (OTAB). Funded for six years, the OTAB sought to develop a scheme for outdoor leadership preparation. A close look at the Hunt Report, published in Britain, and Australia's adaptations gave the board a unique direction for development (C. Abbott, personal communication, March, 1984).

The board decided to include several key points in their preparation program. First, the scheme would be open-ended, not presenting a certificate, which would imply the end of training. Second, the scheme would be flexible enough to respond to varying training needs of participants. Third, training would be offered at several levels. Fourth, a modular approach would enable people from a wide variety of outdoor activities to benefit from the training. Fifth, the scheme would be open to input from the many agencies involved in outdoor recreation in New Zealand and thus allow for idea exchange. And sixth, the responsibility for assessment would lie with the participant and not with a panel of experts (Abbott, 1981).

The aims of the board were simple: develop a framework for coordinated leader training, advise existing programs, and act as an information clearinghouse (Toynbee, 1982). The unique aspect of this board was its role as an advisory agency. It did not offer an outdoor leadership program of its own; rather, it assisted other agencies and outdoor associations with their own training programs. As an advisory board, they helped orient efforts toward securing resource personnel for courses, avoiding duplication of training courses, and recommending standards and course offerings (A. Trist, personal communication, February, 1984).

When government funding cutbacks failed to support the OTAB, a collection of active outdoor leaders formed the New Zealand Outdoor Instructors Association (NZOIA). NZOIA supports the "concept of continual training, updating techniques and experience on an ongoing basis while working within high professional standards both in terms of instruction and safety parameters" (New Zealand Outdoor Instructors Association [NZOIA], 1989, p. 3). NZOIA is careful to state that any assessment of a leader's competence is not a guarantee, but is instead simply an indicator of demonstrated expertise at a specific time, in a particular place, and under certain circumstances. The New Zealand Mountain Safety Council and the New Zealand Department of Education run similar leadership schemes for club members (recreational programs) and schoolteachers (educational programs), respectively.

While the skills of outdoor leaders have not changed much in the last couple of decades, New Zealand society itself has undergone profound change that has radically affected outdoor leadership training. New Zealand has seen the demise of government insurance agencies and the rise of litigation. They have experienced unparalleled growth of commercial recreation and adventure tourism.

In response to the subsequent need for well-trained guides, widespread development of Outdoor Recreation and Leadership courses occurred at Polytechnics (often in colleges in small towns proximate to areas of outstanding recreational opportunity). These courses demanded programs, syllabi, and qualifications, which were only in the developmental stage from existing volunteer providers such as NZOIA and the New Zealand Mountain Safety Council (NZMSC). Consequential to this was the rise of professionally qualified instructors in outdoor education centers and the combination of regional Outdoor Education Associations into a new organization, Education Outdoors New Zealand (EONZ), as a professional body for teachers.

Two major disasters raised the public profile and visibility of qualification, competency, and risk management during the nineties. These were the Mount Ruapehu disaster in 1990 and the Cave Creek incident in 1995. In the former, six soldiers participating in a mountaineering training program from the Army Adventurous Training School died in very adverse wintry conditions near the summit of Mount Ruapehu. In the latter, 18 people, mostly from an Outdoor Recreation Leadership class at Tai Poutini Polytechnic, perished when a Department of Conservation observation platform collapsed in Paparoa National Park. The outcomes of these two disasters made the public aware of the nature of the programs and increased demand for outdoor safety management. This was reflected in government legislation, such as the Occupation Safety and Health acts, the latest of which brought demands on voluntary as well as commercial organizations. The army had a court of enquiry that enlisted civilian experts from the NZMSC and resulted in changes in organization and skill base as well as in the employment of professional instructors alongside military ones who possessed commensurate qualifications.

Perhaps the pivotal development in outdoor leadership in the past 20 years has been the founding, development, and acceptance of the Sports, Fitness and Recreation Industries Training Organization (SFRITO). One of the national economic developments in recent years has been the government's promotion of industry-based training, under the aegis of the New Zealand Qualifications Authority. SFRITO's qualifications are competency based and developed by industry members. As such, it attempts to bring all the outdoor leadership players and organizations together for the benefit of the profession.

In the second quarter of 2003 a major development in outdoor education leadership took place when the Ministry of Education released its report on risk management in school-based outdoor education. A series of fatalities in water-based programs shocked the New Zealand community and involved all interested parties in a review. The review's outcome has big implications, particularly on appropriate qualifications for teachers in outdoor education and the responsibilities of principals and boards of trustees. The true impact of the review remains to be seen.

Canada

Note: This section updated by Jude Hirsch.

Outdoor leadership in Canada has been examined by three provinces: Nova Scotia in the east, British Columbia in the west, and Ontario in the center. Since 1979, Nova Scotia has operated a scheme based partly on the British scheme and partly on the New Zealand adaptations. Patterned after the advisory board in New Zealand, the Nova Scotia Outdoor Leadership Development Program (NSOLDP) consists of an information clearinghouse, a service program providing instructional resources, and an open-ended course in outdoor leadership training. Upon completing the course, graduates are not granted a certificate but are encouraged to continue developing as outdoor leaders (Nova Scotia Outdoor Leadership Development Program [NSOLDP], 1988).

British Columbia investigated outdoor leadership as early as 1978. In 1981, the Federation of Mountain Clubs of British Columbia (FMCBC), a representative body of 31 outdoor clubs and organizations, issued a press release stating their opposition to mandatory leadership certification (Federation of Mountain Clubs of British Columbia [FMCBC], 1981). A survey of outdoor leadership development in British Columbia undertaken by the Outdoor Recreation Council confirmed this belief, with only 16% of the 138 respondents preferring a certification scheme (Todd, 1983).

The Council of Outdoor Educators of Ontario (COEO) has wrestled with the issue of certification since 1970. A task force on certification recommended not developing their own certification program (Council of Outdoor Educators of Ontario [COEO], 1977). In a COEO-commissioned work, Rogers (1979) proposed a model for outdoor leadership development with certification of technical skills only as a partial requirement for leadership preparation. The proposal itself was noncertifying and consisted of three stages very similar to the British and Australian schemes.

Societal trends and industry standards are now much more similar in Canada and the United States than they were a decade ago. For example, a tragic accident at the University of Alaska and the university's resulting decision to invite the Wilderness Risk Management Committee to meet in Anchorage improved risk management and consequently outdoor adventure leadership all across North America.

Many technical activity standards and instructor training that were provincially based a decade ago are now managed by national governing bodies to ensure greater consistency across the country. Outdoor leadership development programs continue in Nova Scotia and Ontario, and most provinces support some type of guide licensing or training. However, many university programs for outdoor leadership have closed due to cutbacks.

United States

Note: This section updated by Jude Hirsch.

While a number of programs in the United States, such as the National Outdoor Leadership School and Project Adventure, provide certificates of completion of courses in outdoor leadership and adventure education, the only organization that purports to certify outdoor leaders is the Wilderness Education Association (WEA).

WEA administers the National Standard Program for Outdoor Leadership Certification within the existing context of university programs. WEA states that certified outdoor leaders "are able to teach others to use and enjoy the wilderness with minimum impact; safely lead others in the wild outdoors; exercise good judgment in a variety of outdoor environments and conditions; and demonstrate a basic standard of outdoor knowledge and experience" (Cockrell & LaFollette, 1985, p. 40). WEA states that their certification "allows potential employers, parents of youth taking trips into the wilds, insurance companies, wild lands administrators, or others interested in the protection of wilderness users and areas, to know that these certified outdoor leaders have been trained in decision making, safety, and conservation" (Wilderness Education Association [WEA], 1984, p. 1). While WEA has taken this stand on certification, the organization has many opponents, and its certification is not recognized by any government agencies at this time.

The Association for Experiential Education has chosen program accreditation as an alternative to leadership certification. AEE recognized that leadership was only one part of the strategy to increase risk management and decrease environmental impact in adventure programs. Even if leaders are certified or qualified to perform their roles, many other aspects of the program can prevent them from being safe or environmentally appropriate. For example, competent leaders without the correct equipment sent to the wrong location with an unprepared group could cause enormous damage, despite their best efforts to the contrary.

Program accreditation grew out of an in-house safety review begun by Outward Bound (Wade, 1983) and was perfected by the addition of a voluntary peer review process (Gray, 1990; Rubendall, 1992). Today, AEE offers program accreditation for its members, one aspect of which is staff qualification. In the last 15 years outdoor adventure leadership has been challenged by a variety of societal trends and the changes in industry standards that have accompanied them. The refusal of insurance providers to offer adequate, affordable coverage and access to appropriate insurance coverage has often resulted in a major challenge for adventure programming professionals. Accidents involving 15-passenger vans, legislative proposals to control the transportation industry, and the privatization of facilities and programs previously managed by government agencies have changed definitions of leadership competency. The sad reality that accidents continue to injure participants and cause death has invoked a need for defensible, comprehensive risk-management planning in which leadership competency is inextricably embedded. And, there is no question that the September 11, 2001, terrorist attacks on the World Trade Center have negatively impacted the economic and political fabric of the United States.

As a result, leadership development programs have experienced the gambit of expansion, diversification, downsizing, and strategic repositioning in one short decade in efforts to tailor services to a demanding industry. Accredited programs are increasingly favored by insurance providers and resource managers. In 2003, The Association for Experiential Education unveiled its Professional Member category, affording this level of membership the option of assessment for group insurance. Many activity-specific associations are revising instructor training to respond to public and organizational needs. For example, the American Camping Association offers online leadership training to its numerous and diverse member organizations. Professional lists and web portals provide access to information previously reserved for professional journals or technical publications. Today, outdoor adventure leadership exists in a different milieu then it did a decade ago and the programs and systems that support it have changed to reflect this difference. Because they are central to this book, let's discuss the trends and issues of leadership certification and program accreditation further.

CERTIFICATION VERSUS ACCREDITATION

As we have seen, the world has passed the point of deciding whether or not to prepare outdoor leaders. Increasing outdoor accidents and environmental damage, coupled with the associated rise in costs for search and rescue, insurance premiums, and resource user regulations, have combined to make competent outdoor leadership both appropriate and necessary (Attarian, 2001). A question facing the field in the past has been whether or not to certify leaders after preparation and, if certified, to what extent? Hunt (1985, p. 24) summed up this concern by stating that the key issue in the certification conflict was the "attempt to conflate [confuse] being safe with being certified!"

As we saw with the British programs, the concern revolves around beliefs that certificates guarantee competence and encompass all the critical components of outdoor leadership. "The Certification Workshop" on page 38), a true scenario, demonstrates some of the shortcomings of certification. Supply and demand can influence, if not determine, the training and assessment standards or curriculum content for certification. In other words, few available leaders with a need for more can make getting certified very easy for novices, while an overflow of leaders can make getting certified very difficult for experts.

Rogers (1979) was careful to point out that outdoor leadership is not a case of certification but is rather an ongoing process of preparation that never ends for the leader who aspires to be truly competent. Risk management rests on a leader's judgment; this has been a focal point of an intense debate on certification in years gone by. "Regardless of how extensive and thorough a certification system may be, it cannot [ensure] nor certify that leader's judgmental capabilities in a short time" (Swiderski, 1985, p. 20).

Certification of outdoor leaders will always be an issue, but it is no longer a trend (Priest, 1987; Wade, 2003). As we have seen, the history of outdoor leadership preparation in Australia, Canada, New Zealand, and the United Kingdom

The Certification Workshop

When I was a young camp director, I took some of my staff to a certification workshop. We needed to be certified as canoeing leaders. Although we were all keen to get a leader certificate (level 1—capable of teaching canoeing), if we were really competent, we could get a certificate as a leader trainer (level 2—capable of instructing other leaders) or even a master trainer (level 3—capable of independently running certification workshops like the one we were attending).

At the certification workshop, we were required to take one day of core lectures and then a day of examinations in three out of five activity sessions including canoeing, kayaking, power boating, rowing, and sailing. I signed up for canoeing, power boating, and rowing. My first choices of kayaking and sailing were full, so I was denied access because of their popularity. I elected to take the leftovers that had ample space available due to an enormous demand for certified leaders in these activities. Besides, we had a powerboat at camp, and I had been in a rowboat once before!

As you might expect, we all worked very hard in the canoe-handling tests, which were extremely demanding because high winds blew across the lake. Even with many years of experience, I almost missed passing, but luckily I was awarded a level 1 leadership certificate!

I had even more difficulty in the rowing test. We had to row directly toward the dock and pivot at the last minute to approach side-on. The maneuver required a complex stroke of oars in opposite directions. I had practiced this move unsuccessfully for about an hour when it became my turn. I nervously approached as slowly as I could with observers shouting for me to row faster! Expecting to crash head-on into the dock, I clumsily made my move and without realizing it parked my boat neatly beside the dock. The only one in the group to succeed on the first try, I was awarded a level 2 leader–trainer certificate in rowing despite never having rowed before!

Things were the worst in the powerboating test. I had trouble reversing engines and backing up. I bumped the dock repeatedly during practice. When the motor stalled and wouldn't restart, I pulled the cowl off and removed, cleaned, gapped, and replaced the spark plugs. After considerable effort, I finally managed to get the motor running, but time had expired, and I had missed my test. Imagine my surprise when I received by mail my level 3 master–trainer certificate in power boating and a note explaining how the tester had been impressed by my ability to troubleshoot engines!

---

prefers alternatives to certification. Probably the most visible American alternative is the accreditation of adventure programs practiced by the Association for Experiential Education (AEE). Clarifying the certification versus accreditation issue will help you understand the dynamics as well as future trends facing the field in these areas (Garvey, 2002; Medina, 2001).

Certification

Senosk (1977) defined certification as a process guaranteeing that certain minimum standards of competency had been met or exceeded by an outdoor leadership candidate as evaluated by a certifying agency. According to Ewert (1985, p. 17), certification was a "means to [ensure] that only qualified people may systematically engage in the formal teaching and/or leading of individuals in the outdoor adventure situation." Many experts have questioned certification as a valid means of determining the competency of an outdoor leader (Green, 1982). Yerkes (1985, p. 12) summarized the argument: "Some outdoor professionals thought that we should implement certification before the government did it for us. Other outdoor leaders proclaimed that it was an infringement on their professional domain and that no one had the right to regulate this change."

At least two sides of this controversy exist. Advocates of certification believe that it can protect the consumer and the environment, maintain public safety, establish a caliber of excellence, motivate outdoor leaders to higher standards, lower insurance premiums, and provide support in case of litigation (March, 1980; Rollins, 1983). Skeptics argue that certification is costly and time-consuming, establishes a "closed-shop monopoly" by excluding experienced but uncertified people, tests only specific skills, does not evaluate a leader's capacity for judgment, and may attract the wrong people for the wrong reasons (Cockrell & LaFollette, 1985; Green, 1982). Priest (1988) felt that a compromise was possible. Since research showed that proponents and opponents agreed that the hard skills of leadership were certifiable, yet that certification was not desirable for soft skills, "could the two groups have wanted the same end product, but referred to it in different terms? A solution to this long standing problem seems possible. . . . Let the certificate be one of skills and not one of leadership" (p. 42-43).

While some organizations have established in-house certification for their staff and outdoor leadership candidates, no certification process has been recognized or accepted by the adventure programming field in North America. Research (Bassin, Breault, Fleming, Foell, Neufeld, & Priest, 1992) has established that the profession favors program accreditation as an alternative to certification.

Accreditation

We can define **accreditation** as the recognition that a program or institution has met certain predetermined standards of operation. Wade (1983) first suggested accreditation as a viable alternative to certification, stating that "such a system of peer reviews has been in operation within the Outward Bound schools" (p. 6) in the United States for almost two decades. In a related step, Gray (1990) designed a voluntary peer review on a regional basis for AEE that was modeled after an Outward Bound safety review detailed by Wade and Fischesser (1988). Gray cited reduced insurance premiums, marketing advantages, and reduced program costs for accredited programs as immediate benefits beyond the expected improvements in educational quality, accident prevention, environmental impact, and ethical behavior.

In Virginia, Cockrell and Detzel (1985) found that 70% of adventure programming professionals supported the idea of accrediting outdoor adventure organizations rather than certifying individuals. A study of AEE organizations showed 62% supported adventure program accreditation as opposed to 38% who supported certification (Bassin et al., 1992). Respondents felt that "accreditation was the only viable alternative to certification because more professional credibility would be gained and there would be less dependence on the unpredictable human part of the equation" (p. 25) being responsible for safety. On the basis of this research, AEE chose to use voluntary accreditation conducted under external peer review.

In the accreditation process, the AEE reviews the program or institution as a whole in terms of meeting specific standards of operation. Accreditation is the final and critical step in verifying program quality. Earlier steps include self-evaluation and self-training, internal evaluation and internal training, conferences and external training, external consultation, and external peer review (Williamson & Gass, 1993).

The first step of **self-evaluation** and **self-training** occurs when outdoor leaders consider what took place during a particular aspect of the program and consciously adjust their own actions. For the second step of **internal evaluation** and **internal training,** which follows a program, the staff and administrators discuss how to improve programming. The third step, which consists of **conferences** and **external training,** is an opportunity for outdoor leaders to gain new experience and learn from others by interacting with peers, informally sharing ideas, attending outside courses, and going out on personal expeditions. The fourth step, **external consultation,** brings in authorities to formally train staff or create new program components, such as advertising and marketing, risk-management planning, or communicating. The fifth step, **external peer review,** invites outside experts to look at the program and give feedback on what could be changed before the sixth and final step of accreditation is undertaken.

The standards for accreditation address several topics, such as philosophical, educational, and ethical concerns; risk management; staffing; transportation, including land-, water-, and air-based travel; and environmental, emergency, and cultural skills. The *Manual of Accreditation Standards for Adventure Programs* (Williamson & Gass, 1993) devotes a chapter to each of these areas. Within each chapter, standards cover general issues, environmental understanding, human understanding, conduct for the activity, emergency procedures, clothing and equipment, and nourishment.

Program accreditation retains the strengths of leadership certification without being bound by its weaknesses. For example, accreditation provides adventure programs the ability to achieve

◄ EFFECTIVE OUTDOOR LEADERS ►

► Understand the history of the adventure programming profession and the outdoor leadership field. Rather than just know programs, people, places, and dates, they should comprehend the relationships among these facts.

► Understand how and why programs, people, and places have evolved over time, and how various programs have impacted one another. By knowing the influences of the past, leaders should be able to better predict the future.

► Understand the pros and cons of leadership certification and program accreditation.

► Understand that a certificate is not a guarantee of maximum competence, but is limited evidence of minimum competence, and bear this in mind when applying for work.

► Understand the five-step sequence of accreditation.

standards without losing the flexibility to determine how these standards are met. It allows you as a leader to deviate from those standards when doing so is clearly in the best interest of a participant's safety, growth, or psychological well-being. Accreditation takes a systemic view of adventure programming rather than dividing it into individualized categories such as leadership. In adventures, during which uncertainty prevails, your best judgment for safely conducting an activity could differ from the standard. In those particular instances, remember that standards are guidelines that you must apply to the spirit of the situation, not the mandated letter of practice under all circumstances (Gass & Williamson, 1995).

SUMMARY

Kurt Hahn established Salem Schule, Gordonstoun School, United World Colleges, the Round Square Schools Conference, the Duke of Edinburgh Award Scheme, and most importantly, Outward Bound. Many of Hahn's principles were based on his perceptions of social decline in youth. Outward Bound went on to operate over 40 centers in 27 countries and to influence the United States Peace Corps and numerous spin-off programs: Project Adventure (Outward Bound in schools), the National Outdoor Leadership School (Wyoming Outward Bound dedicated to developing leaders), the Wilderness Education Association (leadership certification through universities), and the Association for Experiential Education (a collection of adventure organizations and individual members). As the international body for adventure programming,

AEE holds conferences, distributes books, and publishes journals: all are excellent resources for professional development.

Since 1961, the influence of the "original" British Mountain Leadership Certificate Scheme has spread throughout Australia, New Zealand, Canada, and the United States. Begun originally as a certification scheme, the program operated by the Mountain Leadership Training Board is now a qualification scheme for aspiring outdoor leaders. Reforms resulting from the Hunt Report altered the format of the program. Today, the program no longer certifies outdoor leaders, and new developments in National Vocational Qualifications may bring new changes to leadership training.

Australia was the first to adapt the British programs, adding the concept of initial appraisal sessions and advisory panels for training and assessment. Several statewide leadership schemes are presently contributing to the development of a national strategy for outdoor leadership preparation. Looking to Australia as well as to the changes in Britain, New Zealand developed an advisory, rather than a certifying, role.

Today several groups offer independent leadership training programs. Noting the successful New Zealand scheme, Canadian programs in British Columbia, Ontario, and Nova Scotia are moving away from certification. Two programs in the United States still certify outdoor leaders; however, a nationally recognized program without certification has yet to arise in this country.

Outdoor leadership preparation is necessary. While certification will always remain a contentious issue, it is no longer a trend. Certification has several serious shortcomings that have moved the profession toward program accreditation instead of leadership certification. The Association for Experiential Education (AEE) has responded with a process for program accreditation composed of five steps: self-evaluation and self-training, internal evaluation and internal training, conferences and external training, external consultation, and external peer review.

QUESTIONS TO THINK ABOUT

1. What factors contributed to the development of Outward Bound?

2. Trace the path of Outward Bound's influence on adventure programming.

3. From these past influences, what future directions do you expect adventure programming in North America to take?

4. Identify examples from your own culture of Hahn's six areas of decline.

5. What factors contributed to the development of the British Mountain Leadership Training Board (BMLTB)?

6. Trace the path of the BMLTB's influence on outdoor leadership.

7. From these past influences, what future directions do you expect the field of outdoor leadership in North America to take?

8. Differentiate between certification and accreditation. Discuss situations in which one might be preferable over the other, and vice versa.

REFERENCES

Abbott, C. (1981). Flexible leader training: The history and philosophy of the New Zealand Outdoor Training Advisory Board. *Proceedings of the National Outdoor Education Conference* (pp. 52-55). Maroon, Australia.

Attarian, A. (2001). Trends in outdoor adventure education. *Journal of Experiential Education, 24*(3), 141-149.

Bachert, D. (1990). Historical evolution of NOLS: The National Outdoor Leadership School. In J.C. Miles & S. Priest (Eds.), *Adventure education* (pp. 83-88). State College, PA: Venture.

Bassin, Z., Breault, M., Fleming, J., Foell, S., Neufeld, J., & Priest, S. (1992). An AEE organizational member preference for leadership certification or program accreditation. *Journal of Experiential Education, 15*(1), 21-26.

Bushwalking and Mountaincraft Training Advisory Board (BMTAB). (2000). *Bushwalking and ski touring leadership.* Melbourne, Australia: Bushwalking and Mountaincraft Training Advisory Board.

British Mountaineering Council (BMC). (1975). *The Hunt committee report on mountain training.* Manchester, England: Author.

Cockrell, D., & Detzel, D. (1985). Effects of outdoor leadership certification on safety, impacts and program. *Trends, 22*(3), 15-21.

Cockrell, D., & LaFollette, J. (1985). A national standard for outdoor leadership certification. *Parks & Recreation, 20*(6), 40-43.

Council of Outdoor Educators of Ontario (COEO). (1977). *COEO task force report on certification.* Toronto: Author.

Doughty, S., & Loynes, C. (1993). *The training of development trainers: Proposed standards.* Ambleside, England: Lancaster University.

Ewert, A. (1985). Emerging trends in outdoor adventure recreation. In G. McLellan (Ed.), *Proceedings-1985 National Outdoor Recreation Trends Symposium II* (pp. 163-176). Atlanta: USDI National Park Service.

Ewert, A. (1989). The history of outdoor adventure programming. *Journal of Adventure Education and Outdoor Leadership, 6*(4), 10-15.

Federation of Mountain Clubs of British Columbia (FMCBC). (1981, May). *Mountain leadership certification press release.* Vancouver, BC: Author.

Garvey, D. (1990). A history of the AEE. In J.C. Miles & S. Priest (Eds.), *Adventure education* (pp. 75-82). State College, PA: Venture.

Garvey, D. (2002). The future of adventure education. *Outdoor Network, 40*(13), 1-4.

Gass, M.A., & Williamson, J. (1995). Accreditation of adventure programs. *Journal of Health, Physical Education, Recreation and Dance, 66*(1), 22-27.

Gray, D. (1990). *A pilot model for a New England peer review program.* Unpublished manuscript, Association for Experiential Education.

Green, P. (1982). *The outdoor leadership handbook.* Tacoma: The Emergency Response Institute.

Higgins, P. (2002). Outdoor education in Scotland. *Journal of Adventure Education and Outdoor Learning, 2*(2), 149-168.

Hunt, J.S. (1985). Certification controversy. *Camping Magazine, 57*(6), 23-24.

Jackson, J. (1972). *Notes on party leadership.* Manchester, England: Mountain Leadership Training Board.

James, W. (1967). The moral equivalent of war. In J.J. McDermott (Ed.), *The writings of William James* (pp. 668-669). New York: Random House.

Langmuir, E. (1969). *Mountain leadership.* Edinburgh, Scotland: Scottish Sports Council.

Langmuir, E. (1973). *Mountain leadership* (Rev. ed.). Edinburgh, Scotland: Scottish Sports Council.

Langmuir, E. (1984). *Mountaincraft and leadership.* Edinburgh, Scotland: Scottish Sports Council.

Lupton, F. (1990). WEA history. In J.C. Miles & S. Priest (Eds.), *Adventure education* (pp. 89-95). State College, PA: Venture.

Manfield, L.M., & Pearse, J.K. (1991). *A-WAY: For the expedition leader.* Albany, WA: Denmark Printing.

March, W. (1980). Assessing outdoor leaders: The catch-22 of wilderness leadership certification. *Foothills Wilderness Journal, 7*(2), 16-17.

Martin, A., Leberman, S., & Neill, J. (2003). Dramaturgy as a method for Experiential Program Design. *Journal of Experiential Education, 25*(1), 196-206.

McArthur, A. (1999). Best practice in outdoor education: What? Why? How? *Australian Journal of Outdoor Education, 4*(2), 10-13.

Medina, J. (2001). Types of positions, job responsibilities, and training backgrounds of outdoor/adventure leaders. *Journal of Experiential Education, 24*(3), 150-159.

Miner, J. (1990). The creation of Outward Bound. In J.C. Miles & S. Priest (Eds.), *Adventure education* (pp. 55-66). State College, PA: Venture.

National Outdoor Recreation Leadership Development (NORLD). (1994). News on the National Outdoor Recreation Leadership Development strategy. *Outdoor Update 2.* Hobart, Australia: Author.

New Zealand Outdoor Instructors Association (NZOIA). (1989). *Instructor's logbook.* Wellington, New Zealand: Hillary Commission for Recreation and Sport.

Nova Scotia Outdoor Leadership Program (NSOLDP). (1988). *Leadership development.* Halifax, NS: Author.

Ogilvie, K.C. (1993). *Leading and managing groups in the outdoors.* Sheffield, England: NAOE Publications.

Outdoor Recreation Council of Australia (ORCA). (2003). *The history of ORCA.* Retrieved June 23, 2003 from www.ausport.gov.au/orca/history.html.

Outward Bound International. (2005). *Outward Bound School locations.* Retrieved May 12, 2005 from www.outwardbound.net/locations.

Parker, T.M., & Meldrum, K.I. (1973). *Outdoor education.* London: Dent.

Pickett, B., & Polley, S. (2001). Investigating the history of outdoor education in South Australia. *Australian Journal of Outdoor Education, 5*(2), 49-53.

Priest, S. (1987). Outdoor leadership certification: Always an issue, but no longer a trend. *Bradford Papers Annual, 2,* 37-44.

Priest, S. (1988). Agreement reached on the issue of outdoor leadership certification? *Bradford Papers Annual, 3,* 38-43.

Prouty, D. (1990). Project adventure: A brief history. In J.C. Miles & S. Priest (Eds.), *Adventure education* (pp. 97-109). State College, PA: Venture.

Richards, A. (1990). Kurt Hahn. In J.C. Miles & S. Priest (Eds.), *Adventure education* (pp. 67-74). State College, PA: Venture.

Rogers, R.J. (1979). *Leading to share, sharing to lead.* Sudbury, ON: Council of Outdoor Educators of Ontario (COEO).

Rollins, R. (1983). Leadership certification revisited. *California Association for Health, Physical Education, and Recreation (CAHPER) Journal, 50*(1), 8-9.

Rubendall, R. (1992). *Heartland peer review practices.* Boulder, CO: Association for Experiential Education.

Senosk, E.M. (1977). *An examination of outdoor pursuit leader certification and licensing within the United States in 1976.* Unpublished master's thesis, University of Oregon.

The Sports Council. (1991). *Leadership in outdoor activities: Report of the interim working group.* London: Author.

Sport and Recreation Training Australia (SRTA). (2003). *Training package review.* Retrieved June 23, 2003 from www.srtaustralia.org.au/trngpkg/review.asp.

Swiderski, M.J. (1985). Stop going around in circles. *Camping Magazine, 57*(6), 20-22.

Todd, A. (1983). *Leadership development program: Summary of survey results.* Vancouver, BC: Outdoor Recreation Council.

Toynbee, P. (1982). Improving leadership training. In *Proceedings of the National Outdoor Education Conference* (pp. 132-136). Wellington, New Zealand.

Wade, I. (2003). Current issues in accreditation. *Outdoor Network, 48*(14), 1-4.

Wade, I.R. (1983). *Alternative to certification programs.* Unpublished manuscript.

Wade, I.R., & Fischesser, M. (1988). *The safety review manual: A guide to conducting safety reviews for assessing and upgrading safety in outdoor adventure programs.* Greenwich, CT: Outward Bound USA.

Warren, K., Sakofs, M., & Hunt, J.S. (1995). *The theory of experiential education.* Dubuque, IA: Association for Experiential Education.

Wilderness Education Association (WEA). (1984). *Pamphlet.* Driggs, ID: Author.

Williamson, J., & Gass, M.A. (1993). *Manual of accreditation standards for adventure programs.* Boulder, CO: Association for Experiential Education.

Yerkes, R. (1985). Certification: An introduction behind the growing controversy. *Camping Magazine, 57*(6), 12-13.

Individual Behavior and Motivation

To deliver your adventure program more effectively, it helps to understand individual behavior during adventure experiences. In this chapter, we explain some of the social psychology theories that have contributed to the present body of knowledge of human motivation in times of risk and adventure. To show you real-life applications of these theories, we include examples of common outdoor activities.

PHYSIOLOGICAL AND PSYCHOPHYSIOLOGICAL FACTORS

The uninitiated public often asks, "Why? Why would anyone in their right mind climb a mountain, paddle a river, descend a ski slope, or jump out of an airplane?" Mallory's historic answer, "Because it's there," made in reference to his plan to ascend Everest in 1924, sheds little light on what motivates people to take risks. The idea that some people are "adrenaline junkies" who are addicted to thrill seeking may seem somewhat humorous. On inspection, however, physiological studies suggest that thrill addiction may be closer to the truth than experts or laypeople originally suspected.

Endorphin High

Endorphins are hormone-like chemicals released into the bloodstream during times of stress. Their chemical structure resembles narcotic compounds such as opium, and they similarly affect the nervous system without producing the negative side effects that often accompany illicit drugs. The well-known "runner's high" that dulls pain and gives feelings of limitless strength or endurance to marathoners is just one positive example of endorphins in action.

We humans need a certain amount of stress in our lives to maintain the level of endorphin secretion we have come to expect. Some people experience enough stress in their daily lives. Others have greater needs and often fulfill their desires by consciously seeking stimulation through risk-taking adventures (Bunting, 1987; Schreyer, White, & McCool, 1978; Selye, 1974; Zuckerman, 1979). While this explanation of motivation is based in human physiology, other theories examining the social psychology of adventure (Garst, Scheider, & Baker, 2001) are presented in this chapter.

Optimal Arousal

In *Why People Play*, Ellis (1973) discusses his **optimal arousal theory of play,** asserting that the human brain is a continually active organ in need of ongoing stimulation. Deprived of external stimulation, for example, as it is during sleep, the brain manufactures its own arousal in the form of dreams. Optimal behavior is easily observed in children (most of Ellis' work was conducted in the children's play laboratories), who when without external stimulation from a parent or friend seek their own arousal in the form of imagined or other independent play. Since adventure is seen by some as a form of adult play (Carpenter & Priest, 1989), the optimal arousal theory of play may apply to adults as well.

The brain's level of arousal depends on the amount of information the brain is receiving. The more information received in a period of time, the higher the arousal; the less information coming in, the lower the arousal. People may be over- or underaroused by the conditions around them, and levels of arousal in the same situation differ for various people. These principles suggest that a unique level of optimal arousal exists for each individual. Ellis believed this was the point at which performance is at its maximum. Figure 4.1

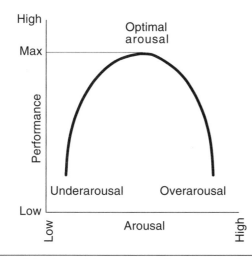

Figure 4.1 A graphic representation of optimal arousal theory.

Individuals seek out adventure for many reasons.

diagrams the relationship between performance and arousal.

For example, a mountaineer climbing an easy route may be underaroused to the extent that performance drops off. The mountaineer may also climb a difficult route, become overaroused, and experience a similar decrease in performance. Most mountaineers usually seek that particular level of difficulty that is optimally arousing, leading to the best climbing performance. The unique point to Ellis' theory is that people like to perform their best and purposefully seek out conditions that produce a state of optimal arousal. Since adventure is considered adult play, theories such as Zuckerman's (1979) identification of **sensation seeking** have been adopted as possible reasons why people test and push their limits by taking risks.

Flow State

M. Csikszentmihalyi (1975) wrote a book titled *Beyond Boredom and Anxiety* in which he observed and interviewed a wide cross section of the public, including chess players, poets, dancers, surgeons, and rock climbers. All subjects of his study experienced a similar state of being when fully involved in their chosen activity, which he later termed **flow**. "Flow describes a state of experience that is engrossing, intrinsically rewarding and outside the parameters of worry and boredom" (M. Csikszentmihalyi & I.S. Csikszentmihalyi, 1991, p. 150). Studies on flow suggest that people are motivated to participate in adventure experiences because of

the intrinsic feelings of enjoyment, well-being, and personal competence they achieve. These positive effects are the reasons people return to adventure programming to recapture the feelings.

M. Csikszentmihalyi and I.S. Csikszentmihalyi (1991) outlined six characteristics that make the flow-producing experience worthy of repetition:

1. People experiencing flow clearly know the goals they are trying to achieve and receive **immediate feedback** about how they are doing.

2. **Action and awareness merge** as they see themselves fully engrossed in the activity with pure, uninterrupted concentration.

3. This merging is made possible by their centering on a **limited stimulus field** in which they consciously screen out potential interruptions and unimportant information.

4. They experience self-forgetfulness by losing touch with physical reality or by gaining a **heightened awareness** of their inner workings.

5. They enjoy a **feeling of control** over personal actions and the environment during

which an awareness of control may be present or a worry over lack of control may be absent.

6. The flow experience is **autotelic:** so enjoyable and meaningful that participants desire to repeat the activities in hopes of reproducing such a state, regardless of their reasons for first trying the activity.

Participants can only experience flow when the opportunity to take action is balanced with the individual's capacity to act. Figure 4.2 illustrates this point.

For example, an expert paddler has a high capacity to act, while a novice paddler has a low capacity. Flatwater offers little opportunity to act, while difficult white water gives plenty of opportunity. If you place the expert paddler on flatwater, she experiences boredom, or underarousal, since her capacity for action exceeds opportunity. If you place the novice on white water, she experiences anxiety, or overarousal, since the opportunity for action far outweighs the capacity to act. M. Csikszentmihalyi (1975) asserted that states of flow exist between boredom and anxiety where opportunity and capacity achieve a synergistic balance. In this example, the novice paddler on flatwater and the expert in white water could each experience flow if their capacities matched their opportunities.

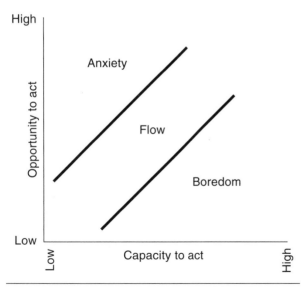

Figure 4.2   A graphic representation of flow theory.

Antecedents of Adventure

Mitchell (1983) noted the lack of important conditions or antecedents in Csikszentmihalyi's flow theory. He proposed adding several conditions that "constitute and potentiate [augment] the flow experience" (p. 154) to enhance M. Csikszentmihalyi's theory. These antecedents included freedom of choice, state of mind, intrinsic motivation, outcome uncertainty, and competence engagement.

First, Mitchell suggested that in order for an adventure to create the experience of flow, it must be completely voluntary, meaning individuals choose their level of involvement. One way leaders meet this condition in adventure programs is by implementing Rohnke's (1989) axiom of challenge by choice, under which no one is coerced into taking risks.

Second, adventures are individually specific because each person brings his own level of competence to the experience. Moreover, adventures are situation specific because each setting has a different level of inherent risk. As a result, adventures are experienced differently by different people: an adventure is a state of mind.

Third, people initially engage in adventure for a variety of reasons. But those motivated by intrinsic reasons (joy, happiness, independence, self-development) generally continue to participate year after year. Most people do not seek extrinsic rewards, such as status or money, in adventure experiences.

Fourth, Mitchell defined adventures as undertakings with uncertainty of outcome. Too much uncertainty is overarousing; too little is underarousing. Thus, unattainable goals can cause a participant to panic due to anxiety and goals too easily achieved can lead to complacency due to boredom. Neither of these situations results in flow or a positive learning experience; rather, they could create dangerous conditions. To make the best of an adventure, participants should feel challenged, yet in control of the situation. If a facilitator or friend gives away answers or rescues a participant by providing solutions, the amount of uncertainty changes, altering the experience (Goffman, 1981). Except in situations of safety, ethical adventure leaders avoid helping participants too much.

Fifth and last, the client must be actively engaged in her adventure with the opportunity to influence the outcome and resolve the uncertainty

Stages of Adventure

After 20 years of observing and interviewing participants in outdoor adventures, Mortlock (1984) proposed that there are four stages people can experience in any outdoor journey: play, adventure, frontier adventure, and misadventure. According to Mortlock, participants can be in any stage at any time, whether they are novice or expert, depending on the amount of fear present in the activity.

▶ Play is characterized by the absence of fear. We can describe play as pleasant or fun and as boring or a waste of time.

▶ Adventure is characterized by the presence of some fear. Participants are in total control of the situation but are being challenged.

▶ Frontier adventure involves a high degree of fear. Participants experience the risk of physical harm and no longer feel in complete control.

▶ Misadventure encompasses too much fear and often results in failure. The outcome of misadventure may be as simple as personal dissatisfaction or as serious as physical or psychological damage. Participants may experience a bruised ego, scrapes, and splinters, which we consider acceptable and recoverable outcomes, or may suffer fractures, emotional breakdown, or even death, which we consider unacceptable and unrecoverable outcomes.

Mortlock reserved play as the stage to learn new skills in. He felt that the outdoor experience must strive for adventure and especially frontier adventure, as they make life worth living. Last, the condition of misadventure was where people learned best from their mistakes, provided they were not permanently injured.

We cannot overstate the role of fear. Fear is the human response to risk and, as such, you should consider it a healthy and necessary reaction. Nonetheless, there are times when you must help participants deal with their fears of risky situations. Ewert (1989) suggested several strategies for coping with fear: desensitization, which is gradual exposure by building up to big risk through progressively riskier activities; flooding, which is careful and prolonged exposure to the risk once encountered; modeling, which is the observation of the techniques others use to manage their fear; and rehearsal, which is applying those techniques with repeated practice.

---

by applying personal competence to the risky situation. The approach some adventure programs use, in which leaders care for the client, removing him from the experience—as if in an amusement park—can negate the empowering effect of an adventure. The individual cannot learn unless she has an active role in the experience, including receiving the benefits and consequences of her actions. Of course, as a leader, you must intercede in truly dangerous situations.

Adventure Experience Paradigm

Martin and Priest (1986) combined ideas from previous works to develop their own model: the **adventure experience paradigm.** The adventure experience paradigm explains participants' behaviors using the variables of risk and competence. We can define risk as the potential to lose some-

thing of value and competence as the capability of individuals to deal with the demands placed on them by their environment.

In this model, the interaction of risk and competence creates the challenge. Challenge cannot exist without both situational risk and personal competence engaged in an effort to resolve uncertainty. Depending on the amount of risk and degree of competence interacting together in an adventure experience, five conditions of challenge are possible: exploration and experimentation, adventure, peak adventure, misadventure, devastation, and disaster (Priest & Baillie, 1987). Figure 4.3 diagrams this relationship between risk and competence.

This diagram illustrates that when a competent person performs a low-risk activity, the result is a condition of exploration and experimentation similar to Mortlock's (1984) play stage during which new skills are learned, tested, and honed. As com-

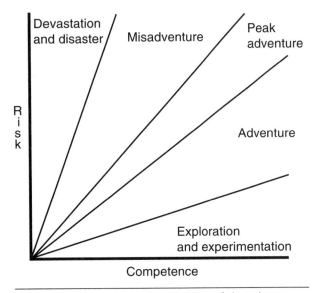

Figure 4.3 A graphic representation of the adventure experience paradigm.

petence decreases or risk increases or both, the participant moves into the adventure. When the two components are balanced and matched, peak adventure results, similar to M. Csikszentmihalyi's (1975) state of flow. As risk exceeds competence, the potential for misadventure arises; when risk becomes very high and competence is very low, devastation and disaster may occur.

Consider average skiers at the start of the ski season. They begin on the gentle bunny hills where the risk of falling is minimal and their skiing competence is maximal. This exercise is exploration and experimentation: the skiers can practice their turns and stops to gain confidence. When ready, they move to green (easy and beginner) runs where the risk of falling increases and their skiing competence may decrease. This is adventure, in which participants work harder at skiing and feel more challenged. On the blue square (moderate and intermediate) runs, they find peak adventure, at which their competence perfectly balances the risk of falling, and they feel "on the razor's edge" as they descend the slope, uncertain whether they will succeed, but confident they will ski their best. The black diamond (difficult and expert) runs provide a little misadventure for these average skiers, because the risk of falling outweighs their competence to ski at this advanced level. When they fall, they consider it to be a minor mishap from which they can recover. They may be bruised, embarrassed, and covered by snow, but they will not suffer permanent damage. Devastation and disaster would come in the out-of-bounds areas,

or the back gullies and avalanche slopes where a fall means a broken limb—or worse—death! Ethical adventure programs deal with the conditions up to and including misadventure (because people learn well from their mistakes), but devastation and disaster are not a purposeful part of ethical adventure programs.

Martin and Priest (1986) proposed that the goal of an outdoor adventure experience for an individual is to reach peak adventure (similar to Ellis' [1973] concept of seeking optimal arousal), since this is the realm that provides flow and the most positive benefits of adventure experiences. However, the "key to application of the adventure experience paradigm lies in the perceptions of the individual" (p. 19). Individuals can misperceive both the real risk and their actual competence and, as a result, overshoot or fall short of the goal of peak adventure.

By integrating the concept of misperception in their model, Martin and Priest identified nine types of individuals (see figure 4.4). Let's look closely at three of these: the astute, the timid and fearful, and the arrogant and fearless individuals.

The **astute** individual correctly perceives the level of risk as well as her competence to perform the activity and so possesses a high probability of experiencing peak adventure. The **timid and fearful** individual misperceives adventure in two ways: she overestimates the risk of the activity and underestimates her competence to perform the activity. The timid and fearful individual falls short of peak adventure and perhaps drops into exploration and experimentation, because the real risk is actually lower and the real competence is actually higher than perceived. In contrast, the **arrogant and fearless** individual misperceives adventure in ways opposite the timid and fearful individual: she underestimates the risk and overestimates her competence. The arrogant and fearless individual overshoots peak adventure and perhaps experiences devastation and disaster, because the real risk is actually higher and the real competence is actually lower than perceived. Figures 4.5 and 4.6 portray these latter two profiles.

Adaptive Dissonance

When a person has two different and conflicting thoughts, a cognitive, affective, or psychomotor condition known as **adaptive dissonance** results (Festinger, 1957; Walsh & Golins, 1976). A common example in outdoor activities occurs when participants look at a ropes course and focus on the

		Competence		
		Over-perceived	**Correctly perceived**	**Under-perceived**
R **i** **s** **k**	**Under-perceived**	Fearless and arrogant	Bold	Naive and innocent
	Correctly perceived	Assured	Astute	Insecure
	Over-perceived	Carefree and exaggerated	Overawed	Timid and fearful

Figure 4.4   The nine types of individuals, based on perceptions of risk and competence.

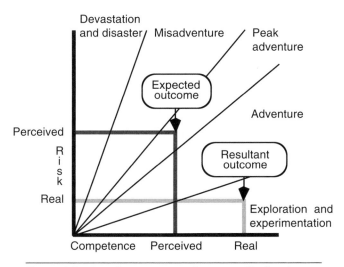

Figure 4.5   An adventure experience profile for the timid and fearful individual.

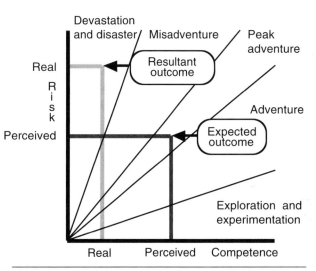

Figure 4.6   An adventure experience profile for the arrogant and fearless individual.

danger and difficulty while you as the outdoor leader explain the safety of the belay ropes and the ease of balancing when not looking down. In this instance, the participants are struck by the paradox of opposing views. Both seem sensible and correct, but the participants are unwilling to accept both as true and so are motivated to resolve the dissonance, perhaps by testing either view through an attempt to complete one element of the ropes course. The strength of their motivation to attempt the ropes course is partially a function of how big a gap exists between their expectations and your comments. We discuss other motivational influences later in this chapter. For now, let's focus on the role of adaptive dissonance.

Priest and Baillie (1987) have discussed the application of the adventure experience paradigm to facilitated outdoor learning. The purpose of their model is to help you lead timid and fearful or arrogant and fearless participants toward becoming astute. According to their model, the way to elicit astute behavior is to create situations with strong adaptive dissonance. In practice, this means presenting tasks that appear difficult to the timid and fearful, knowing that success is highly probable, and that appear easy to the arrogant and fearless, while carefully setting them up for failure. In essence, dissonance between client perceptions and the reality of the adventure increases the likelihood of a peak experience.

Adaptive Dissonance and Personality Types

For timid and fearful individuals, adaptive dissonance lies between their anticipated failure and your encouragement that success is imminent. The timid and fearful individual expects misadventure, while you as the leader must structure and control his experiences so that adventure results (see figure 4.7).

During the debriefing, you can ask participants about their initial perceptions of risk and competence. They might typically respond with comments like "It wasn't as dangerous as I had first thought" and "Maybe I can perform better than I give myself credit for!" Following these guided discussions, participants often shift their perceptions toward reality for the next experience. Overall, the adaptive dissonance is reduced (see figure 4.8).

In time, repeated and varied experiences coupled with subsequent debriefings help the perceptions of the timid and fearful participants merge with reality, and the participants become astute. Once they become astute, you should encourage them to review the overall process of change in light of how their new learning about themselves might apply to their real lives.

To illustrate, consider a timid and fearful man on a high ropes traverse. The facilitator has structured an experience in which she asks this man to walk across a tightrope 50 ft above the ground with only a rope strung from the far tree for balance and support. In his perception he is expecting a misadventure or, even worse, devastation and disaster! The real outcomes are quite different, since he is belayed. After considerable coaxing and assistance from the facilitator, he completes the traverse and feels elated. The facilitator helps him reflect on his adventure, and after some thought and discussion, he recognizes that the task was not so dangerous and that he was capable enough to complete it. This learning may later transfer to daily living, in which the man expresses timid and fearful behaviors when meeting new people. In the future, he may be able to take on new friendships with his newly learned confidence.

For arrogant and fearless individuals, adaptive dissonance lies between their apparent sureness and the leader's expression that success is doubtful for the activity. The arrogant and fearless expect adventure, but since the leader has structured or controlled the experience for gentle failure, misadventure results (see figure 4.9).

Occasionally, arrogant and fearless individuals' behavior results from repeated failures in life, and their demeanors are a coping mechanism

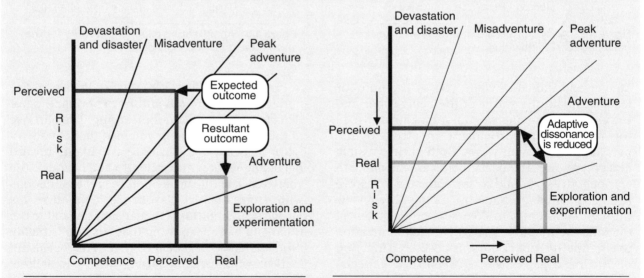

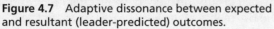
Figure 4.7 Adaptive dissonance between expected and resultant (leader-predicted) outcomes.

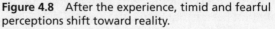
Figure 4.8 After the experience, timid and fearful perceptions shift toward reality.

for dealing with failure. Hence, you must be very careful not to further embarrass these individuals in front of others and reinforce this personality trait. If such a concern exists, the best approach may be to conduct the activity away from the group, debriefing the individuals separately and in advance of the shared group discussions. In this way, the arrogant and fearless may respond to questions about risk and competence with answers such as "It may be that that was more difficult than I first thought," and "Maybe I'm not as good as I think!" From these reflections, the arrogant and fearless participants can shift their perceptions toward reality for the next experience. Once again, adaptive dissonance is reduced (see figure 4.10).

With further experience and debriefing, the arrogant and fearless participants become astute as their perceptions merge with reality. In the unlikely instance that they convert to being timid and fearful from experiencing overwhelming failure, you can simply structure an easier task for the next activity. Once again,

after repeated activities, you can debrief the learning in relation to real life.

Let's consider an arrogant and fearless woman on a rock climb. The facilitator has structured an experience asking her to climb a particularly difficult route, which has previously been the topic of some bragging on her part. In her perception, she expects exploration and experimentation or, at best, mere adventure! In actuality, the real outcomes of her top roped experience are quite different because of the extreme difficulty of the climb. After considerable effort, she has fallen off the crux of the climb repeatedly and is exhausted. The facilitator now helps her reflect on her misadventure. After some thought and discussion, she recognizes that the task was indeed more difficult than she expected and that she really was not as good as she was saying. This reversal may later transfer to daily living, in which the woman expresses arrogant and fearless behaviors when working on projects as part of a small group. Perhaps next time, she will be more agreeable.

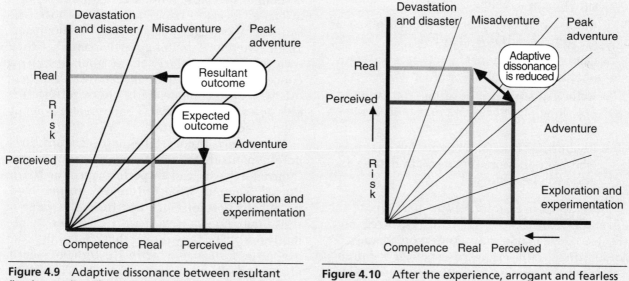

Figure 4.9 Adaptive dissonance between resultant (leader-predicted) and expected outcomes.

Figure 4.10 After the experience, arrogant and fearless perceptions move toward reality.

Ethical adventure programs debrief individuals' experiences, perhaps privately and then within a group. The debriefing helps participants reflect on past experiences, encouraging them to reassess their perceptions of risk and competence from their previous attempts. As they come to identify, accept, and change their shortcomings, their perceptions move closer to reality, and the individuals eventually become astute (Carpenter & Priest, 1989). With astuteness often comes improved self-concept and socialization (Garst, Scheider, & Baker, 2001). Indeed, interpersonal and intrapersonal relationships benefit from such facilitated experiences.

One caution regarding the facilitated adventure experience is that you must structure, control, and supervise the activity. The activity is structured, since you customize the level of challenge to the individual, and is controlled, because you manipulate the risks so perceived values are high while real values are low. As the leader, you are the key to the operation and must be sufficiently experienced and astute to accurately perceive the risks and the participants' competencies.

THEORIES AND MODELS OF MOTIVATION

Motivation comes from the Latin word *movere,* meaning "to move." In this sense, motivation is about why and how individuals move or don't move from one state of being to another. Factors influencing motivation include the following (Sage, 1977; Weinberg & Gould, 1995):

- Direction of effort, such as confronting a situation or avoiding a situation

- Intensity of effort, or how much effort a person expends in a situation

- Choice of behaviors, such as strategies people use to deal with a situation

- Ability to sustain motivation, for example, how long an individual persists in a situation

- Resulting behavior change, for example, whether behaviors that result from the situation will be sustained

Individuals are motivated to participate in adventure experiences for a variety of reasons (Festeu, 2002; Todd, S.L., Anderson, Young, & Anderson, D., 2002). In this section we present several theories and models addressing how motivation principles affect participants in adventure programming and enhance your ability to motivate clients toward their goals. Specifically, we discuss (1) goal theory, or how a person's commitment to a goal influences his actions; (2) expectancy theory, or how a person's expectations about achieving a goal influences his actions; (3) self-efficacy, or how a person's belief of whether or not she can accomplish a task affects motivation, and how you can implement

various strategies to enhance clients' success; (4) attribution theory and locus of control, or how individuals explain their successes and failures and the influence these attributions have on future actions and emotions; and (5) effectiveness and competence motivation, or how the effectiveness of completing tasks influences feelings of competence as well as how social and interpersonal factors are influenced—and were influenced—by these feelings. A final model combines all of the models presented in this chapter into one that outlines risk taking and competence effectiveness and how you can use the accuracy of participants' beliefs to influence success or failure in adventure experiences.

Goal and Expectancy Theories

As the facilitator, your ability to manipulate the risk and competence variables depends heavily on clients' personal commitments to attaining goals as well as on their expectations about being successful. **Goal theory** states that performance is determined by a participant's commitment to goals. These goals may be established by the individual or dictated by others. Participants who commit to specific and well-defined goals perform at higher levels of competence than those who set general or vague goals (Katzell & Thompson, 1990). Therefore, helping participants set their own goals, particularly those goals requiring concentrated effort to attain, can be an excellent motivational technique. Certainly, by setting their own goals, participants will have greater commitment to achieving the task.

Expectancy theory takes into account three determinants that motivate people: first, whether their efforts will lead to performance, or "Can I do it?"; second, what outcomes are involved, or "What's in it for me?"; and third, the value of those outcomes, or "Is it worth it?" People are motivated when they expect that effort will result in good performance, which will in turn be useful in attaining desired outcomes (Katzell & Thompson, 1990). Expectancy theory has useful application to outdoor programs as it helps define exactly how you can motivate individuals to experience peak adventures. Participants provided with sufficient training, emotional support, proper resources, and understanding of benefits will feel more confident about accomplishing a task. This confidence reduces their anxieties and enhances perceived competence, empowering them to tackle greater risks.

Self-Efficacy

Bandura's (1977) social learning theory defines **self-efficacy** as the certainty of an individual's belief under risk that she can successfully accomplish a task that tests ability. It is more than mere self-confidence; it is the individual's belief that he can successfully execute the behaviors necessary for accomplishing the "anticipated and desired" tasks (p. 192).

Self-efficacy expectations vary in at least three ways: magnitude, strength, and generality.

1. **Magnitude** refers to the degree of certainty associated with success and is heavily influenced by perceptions of risk and difficulty. For example, when working with clients who were afraid of snakes, Bandura offered three ways to confront the fear: looking at pictures of snakes, being in the same room with snakes, and actually touching snakes. Clients varied widely in magnitude, as some were 100% certain of being able to deal with the less risky task of looking at pictures, and others were only 10% certain of accomplishing the more risky task of actually touching snakes. Thus, although any two people may expect success for a given task, they may differ in the magnitude of their certainty of success.

2. **Strength** refers to how long a person holds on to expectations of success despite contradictory information. For example, a person with low strength may lose her belief that she can accomplish a task after a single failure. A person with high strength will be more likely to continue to attempt a task in the face of many failures. A history of succeeding after multiple unsuccessful attempts plays an important role in building up the strength of an individual's expectations.

3. **Generality** refers to the degree of transfer of self-efficacy beliefs from one situation to another. One person may limit efficacy expectations to the performance of identical or closely related tasks, while another may generalize these expectations for success to a wide range of situations. This transfer is more easily accomplished if the individual can see the connections among tasks (see Gass, 1985, 1991, 1993).

Self-efficacy is based on information interpreted and derived from four internal and external sources: past performance accomplishments, vicarious experiences, verbal persuasion, and physiological arousal. Researchers believe that information gained through success is the most influential and stable because it is based on actual experience (Paxton & McAvoy, 1998). Failures early in learning tend to be more influential than later failures. Moreover, failures that are overcome by increased effort can strengthen self-efficacy more than failures overcome by chance. Hence the importance of second tries at certain tasks.

Seeing or hearing someone else's vicarious pursuit of mastering a skill or overcoming a problem without negative repercussions can also enhance an observer's efficacy expectations. Observing others of similar competence and hearing stories of others' experiences are two positive means for directly enhancing clients' feelings of self-efficacy.

Although gathering efficacy expectations from verbal information is not as strong as acquiring expectations from actual experience, it can serve as a powerful mobilizing factor when combined with the manipulation of adaptive dissonance. Indeed, encouragement—without coercion—from you can enhance a participant's self-efficacy.

Since over- or underarousal usually interferes with performance, people experiencing high anxiety or boredom might have certain expectations. In addition, expectations of success or failure can further alter arousal levels, since anticipation can confirm positive or negative beliefs about performance. You need to defuse anxiety or boredom associated with setbacks, especially if either emotion becomes debilitating.

Bandura (1977) also suggested that the relationship between self-efficacy and performance is reciprocal: efficacy expectations influence performance and performance outcomes influence self-efficacy. The direction of reciprocity, increasing or decreasing self-efficacy, also depends on the degree of stress present in the situation. Selye (1974) described stress as occurring in one of two forms, either **eustress,** which is pleasant and desirable, or **distress,** which is unpleasant and undesirable, depending on the effect—in the form of emotions and feelings—exhibited by the person under stress.

Attribution, or Locus of Control

According to Weiner (1972), individuals attribute their performance outcomes to a variety of causes, including ability, effort, luck, task characteristics, and attention. Weiner classified these attributions according to a two-dimensional scale. The first dimension, **causality,** ranged from internally to externally attributed causes. The second dimension, **stability,** ranged from stable to unstable causes. As an example, Weiner classified ability as an internal and stable attribute and defined luck as external and unstable.

Later on, Weiner (1979) added a third dimension to his model: **controllability,** or the degree to which the individual perceives that the attribution is under his **locus of control.** This new dimension differentiated attributions, for example, defining effort as internally controllable and fatigue as externally uncontrollable. The way an individual perceives a specific attribution is far more important than how the attribution is generally classified (Russell, 1982).

Weiner, Russell, and Lerman (1978, 1979) found that causality plays an important role in differentiating various effects. Under success conditions, an **internal locus of control** was found to be associated with pride, confidence, competence, and satisfaction. Gratefulness and thankfulness were linked to an **external locus of control** under similar conditions. Under failure conditions, guilt was associated with internal control, while anger and surprise were linked to external control.

Using this research, Weiner (1985) developed his theory of achievement motivation and emotion. According to his theory, a person experienced an emotional reaction immediately after an achievement. This reaction could be either positive (e.g., happy) or negative (e.g., sad), and it was based on the individual's perception of success or failure. Weiner described these initial reactions as "outcome-dependent" since they were a function of outcome success or failure rather than a function of attributed cause and control. He found that following the general reaction, an individual carefully thought through the reasons that might explain the outcome cause and control. Once the individual established causality and control, she experienced secondary, specific emotions that were "attribute-dependent." This unique combination of general effects based on outcomes and

specific effects based on attributions influenced future motivation and risk taking (Newberry & Lindsay, 2000).

By way of illustration, the downhill skier who performs poorly in the moguls feels nonspecific, or general, negative emotions such as sadness, which are outcome-dependent effects. In trying to figure out why performance was so poor (or causality), the skier attributes failure to a lack of skiing ability, which is internal attribution, and decides that this ability will not improve due to a strong belief that she cannot change equipment, conditions, and body type, which is external attribution: fixed, stable, and uncontrollable. Thus the skier experiences specific emotions, such as frustration and defeat, which are attribute-dependent effects, and may decide to give up on the sport, which is a behavioral consequence. This example demonstrates the power of attribution to have a destructive, instead of a constructive, impact on motivation.

Effectance Motivation

In his theory of **effectance motivation,** White (1959) felt that individuals were intrinsically motivated to positively influence their environment. If people can successfully meet the demands of the environment through mastery attempts or performance tries, they experience feelings of "effectance," or positive effects and emotions. These positive effects, in turn, encourage future mastery attempts under similar environmental conditions. Figure 4.11 presents this model.

As seen in this model, behavior results from an urge to gain competence and affect the environment. Individuals try a task and, if successful, equate the success with improved competence at that task. This result makes them feel good (joy, pleasure, efficacy) and in control of their environment. In turn, these positive effects motivate them to try again. A very simple model, White's theory did not account for a number of extraneous influ-

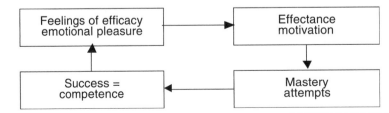

Figure 4.11 Effectance motivation (White, 1959).

ences, such as the opinions of significant others or the attribution of success, and did not consider the negative side of failure.

About 20 years later, Harter (1978) built White's framework into a theory of **competence motivation.** She expanded his model to include the effects of social and interpersonal factors as well as the effects of positive and negative experiences. She further hypothesized that the motivational process revolved around perceived competence. Subsequently, Harter (1986) suggested that perceived competence was influenced by many factors: success or failure after mastery attempts, perceptions of control, motivational orientation, positive or negative reinforcement from significant others, and characteristics of the task. Figure 4.12 presents her model.

But how does this model apply to real life? Suppose a kayaker decides to run a new set of rapids for the first time. If the route difficulty matches the kayaker's skill, then we can describe the task as optimally challenging. Achieving optimally challenging tasks has a greater impact on an individual's perception of himself. If the kayaker succeeds in the attempt, he will experience positive effects such as enjoyment or intrinsic pleasure. Moreover, his success can increase perceived paddling competence as well as enhance the likelihood that he will develop internal perceptions of greater control (see also locus of control discussion in previous section). In other words, the kayaker attributes success to internal sources, such as effort and ability. This successful attempt can also receive positive reinforcement and approval from signifi-

cant others, such as paddling friends. In this case, this information also results in internalized reinforcement, further enhancing internal attribution of feelings. Specifically, the kayaker develops an intrinsic motivational orientation, meaning that he chooses activities that provide personal satisfaction and meet personal standards of performance. In turn, an intrinsic motivational orientation further enhances perceived competence and internal locus of control. These positive perceptions of self augment affective reactions such as pleasure, and the combination of positive effects and perceptions of self increases motivational levels. Thus, the kayaker is likely to attempt the task again.

In contrast, failure to run the rapids can diminish motivational levels as the kayaker experiences negative effects and perceptions of self. Repeated failure eventually reduces perceived paddling competence levels, possibly leading to external perceptions of control. In other words, the kayaker may attribute the failure to external reasons such as the difficulty of the route or faulty equipment. In addition, the lack of reinforcement and approval from significant others may result in extrinsic motivational orientation. The kayaker may begin to choose routes that meet other peoples' expectations, striving to meet their external standards of performance. In turn, an extrinsic orientation tends to decrease perceived competence levels, thereby enhancing an external locus of control. Decreasing perceptions of self or negative effects, such as anxiety, further decrease effectance motivation. Thus, the kayaker may not attempt that route or similar ones ever again.

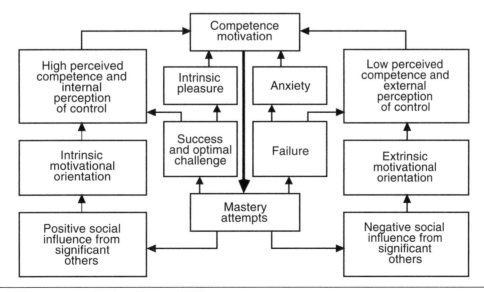

Figure 4.12   Competence motivation (Harter, 1978).

Risk Taking and Competence Effectance

Priest and Klint (Priest, 1993) have combined all the frameworks we've discussed so far into one theoretical model partially founded on research and partially rooted in experience. The model revolves around using **competence effectance** (the belief in one's personal competence if correctly perceived) to increase a client's chance of success in an adventure experience as well as to enhance the experience's possible ramifications.

The model is a series of loops connecting key constructs such as perceived risk, perceived competence, competence motivation, competence performance, arousal, intrinsic feelings, extrinsic influence, self-efficacy, attribution, and locus of control. The model is composed of three parts designated as neutral, positive, and negative feedback loops. Figure 4.13 shows the neutral loop.

The left side of the loop describes the three levels of risk that participants can select on the basis of their efficacy expectations. If people are feeling less competent, they are likely to select a lower level of risk; if they are feeling more competent, they are likely to select a higher level of risk;

and on rare occasions, they may select a level of situational risk that perfectly matches their personal competence. This latter condition results in peak adventure, optimal arousal, state of flow, or what is commonly expressed as "living on the razor's edge!"

Regardless of the level of risk they choose, people can either perform sufficiently or insufficiently. This evaluation is usually a subjective assessment of personal performance. If participants believe they have performed sufficiently for the level of risk chosen, then challenging conditions of adventure result (e.g., exploration and experimentation). If participants think their performances were insufficient to meet the risk, then the challenging conditions of misadventure, perhaps even devastation and disaster, are possible.

Following this decision, participants begin to attribute, or justify, the way things turned out. Obviously, your role in helping people correctly attribute their adventure outcomes is extremely important. If people attribute their successes or failures to external sources, that is, to something other than themselves, they may reevaluate their performances and possibly change their minds

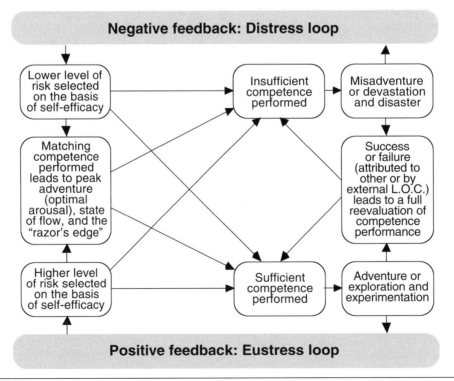

Figure 4.13   The neutral feedback loop of the risk taking and competence effectance model.

about whether they performed sufficiently or not. If they own their successes or failures by attributing them to internal sources, then they may enter into either of the other two loops. If people experience misadventure or devastation and disaster, they enter into the negative feedback loop, or distress. And if the challenge is one of adventure or exploration and experimentation, they enter into the positive feedback loop, or eustress. Figures 4.14 and 4.15 detail these two loops to help you better understand the model.

The negative loop of distress (see figure 4.14) begins with a perception of failure that results from misadventure and is attributed to internal sources such as personal performance. The fail-

ure can cause direct, negative intrinsic responses, such as feeling bad about yourself, or cause indirect, negative extrinsic responses, such as disappointment from significant others. Through a decrease in perceived competence, these negative responses can lower feelings of competence motivation. For example, people who believe they cannot accomplish a task experience anxiety when facing the same level of risk. Because of this, when emerging from the negative feedback loop, such participants tend to select a lower level of risk in the neutral loop.

The positive loop of eustress (see figure 4.15) follows a similar pattern, but, naturally, the effect on competence motivation is the reverse of the

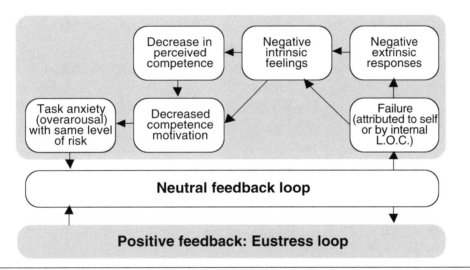

Figure 4.14   The negative feedback loop of the risk taking and competence effectance model.

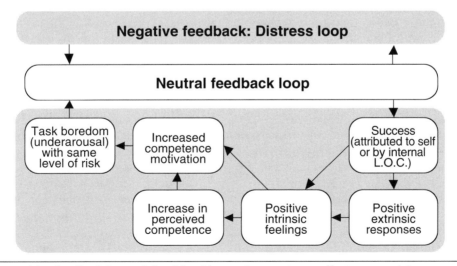

Figure 4.15   The positive feedback loop of the risk taking and competence effectance model.

negative loop. The positive loop begins with an internally attributed perception of success resulting from adventure. This success leads to direct, positive intrinsic responses, such as feeling good about yourself, and to positive extrinsic responses, such as approval from significant others, indirectly building on the good feelings. Through an increased perception of competence, these positive feelings generally increase competence motivation. For example, people who believe they can accomplish the task will experience boredom with the same level of risk. Because of this, when emerging from the positive feedback loop, such participants tend to select a higher level of risk in the neutral loop.

Consider a participant in an adventure experience who is timid and fears what lies ahead. The first task you, the facilitator, set for this individual is an easy rock climb that the participant initially views as unattainable. The discrepancy between the actual task and the client's perception of competence creates adaptive dissonance, or mental argument, within the participant's mind. Resolving this dissonance and attempting the task requires encouragement, rather than coercion, from you.

Assume that the individual overcomes the difficulty of a climb, performs with sufficient competence, experiences an adventure in the exploration and experimentation realm, and considers the experience successful. If the individual attributes the success internally to personal effort, then she enters into a positive feedback loop, or eustress. She experiences positive, intrinsic feelings and receives praise and congratulations from others, or a positive extrinsic response. This leads her to believe that her personal capability has improved as her perceived competence increases; thus, she is likely to desire to do better next time because competence motivation has increased. Since repeating the same climb would be underarousing for similar levels of risk, the individual will likely select a higher level of risk due to the self-efficacy belief that success is achievable where failure initially seems evident.

For this new level of risk, three performance scenarios are now possible. First, the individual may perform sufficiently and return to eustress—if an internal locus of control is in effect and if success is attributed to self. Second, competence may perfectly match the new risk, leading to the condition of peak adventure. In this case, the individual will attempt to maintain the condition for as long as possible, eventually falling off to one side or the other. The third possible scenario is that the individual may perform insufficiently and cross over to distress, or to misadventure, or even to devastation and disaster.

Consider the latter scenario. Insufficient competence performance for the new risk leads to misadventure—or worse, devastation and disaster—and the feeling of failure. If the individual attributes failure to himself, then he enters the negative feedback loop of distress. He has negative intrinsic feelings and may even receive sarcasm and blame from others, or negative extrinsic responses. This leads to the belief that personal capability has dropped, that is, his perceived competence decreases, and the desire to stop trying arises, that is, his competence motivation decreases. Since repeating the same climb would create anxiety, or would be overarousing for similar levels of risk, the individual will likely select a lower level of risk next time due to the self-efficacy belief that he may again fail at an activity for which he had originally expected success.

Say that this individual chooses a new level of lower risk. Once again, three performance scenarios are now possible. First, the individual may perform insufficiently and remain in distress, especially if he continues to attribute his failure to internal causes. Second, a perfect match of competence with the new level of risk may lead to the condition of peak adventure. As before, the individual may attempt to maintain this condition for as long as possible. Third, and more likely with the help of a competent facilitator, the individual may perform sufficiently and cross back to the positive side of eustress.

If the individual attributes success or failure to external sources such as the facilitator (which can happen if the participant is coerced or encouraged too much) or to sources such as equipment, luck, or weather (which are frequent complaints from novices), then personal contribution to the task must be reevaluated. This needs to be done so that the individual may recognize that he actually may have experienced a different type of challenge with potentially different outcomes. This change of mind may determine which loop is entered. With or without a facilitator, humans are likely to follow a sequence vacillating back and forth between the looped pathways until they become fully astute: accurate in their perceptions of both situational risks and personal competence.

◀ EFFECTIVE OUTDOOR LEADERS ▶

▶ Vigilantly monitor group members' arousal levels, are aware of the effect of over- or underarousal on performances, and ensure that clients are optimally aroused whenever appropriate and desirable.

▶ Help participants balance opportunities to act with personal capacity for action so that they experience states of flow and the related benefits.

▶ Ensure the antecedents of an adventure exist within each experience: freedom of choice, state of mind, intrinsic motivation, outcome uncertainty, and competence engagement.

▶ Understand the role fear plays in an adventure and help participants cope with their concerns through desensitization, flooding, modeling, or rehearsal.

▶ Understand the varying conditions of challenge that can arise from the interaction of risk and competence and help participants recognize these conditions in relation to the level of risk and competence present in an adventure.

▶ Understand the role of adaptive dissonance and structure and control adventure experiences to create healthy adaptive dissonance in clients.

▶ Help participants set their own goals to enable greater commitment, as well as provide sufficient training, emotional support, resources, and benefit comprehension to increase motivation.

▶ Are aware of the impact that past performance or physiological arousal can have on self-efficacy and share vicarious experiences or use verbal persuasion, but not coercion, to encourage participation.

▶ Monitor how participants attribute success or failure and assist them with proper attribution to either internal or external loci of control.

▶ Guide participants' reflection on their levels of competence and performance relative to their emotions and motivation to complete tasks.

▶ Note the impact of successful or failed attempts at mastery on participants' perceived competence and how this impact affects their motivation.

▶ Are aware of the impact that perceived competence and motivation have on participants' feelings of self-efficacy and on their selection of risk in an adventure experience.

SUMMARY

Ellis' play theory of optimal arousal suggests a reason for human engagement in adventure: people purposefully seek conditions of optimal arousal that permit maximal performance. M. Csikszentmihalyi's model of states of flow details what people can experience in an adventure: goal clarity, immediate feedback, merging of action and awareness, concentration on a limited stimulus field, self-forgetfulness, heightened self-awareness, personal control, and autotelic enjoyment. Mitchell lists the necessary antecedents of adventure as freedom of choice, state of mind, intrinsic motivation, outcome uncertainty, and competence engagement. Mortlock presents the stages in an outdoor journey based on the level of

fear present: play (no fear), adventure (some fear), frontier adventure (great fear), and misadventure (too much fear).

Martin and Priest's adventure experience paradigm combines the work of Ellis, M. Csikszentmihalyi, Mitchell, and Mortlock into a graphic representation of the relationship between risk and competence. Their paradigm explores how the combination of risk and participant competence in an adventure experience creates 1 of 5 conditions of challenge: exploration and experimentation, adventure, peak adventure, misadventure, and devastation and disaster. Priest and Baillie describe how adaptive dissonance can be used to create astute individuals within the adventure experience paradigm. Adaptive dissonance occurs when clients experience tasks they are unsure that they can accomplish. Accomplishing foreboding tasks generates a strong sense of mastery, leading to astute learners.

Motivation refers to why and how individuals move or don't move from one state of being to another. Factors influencing motivation include the direction of effort, intensity of effort, choice of behaviors, ability to sustain motivation, and resulting behavior change. Important motivation theories include goal theory, or how a person's commitment to a goal influences actions; expectancy theory, or how a person's expectations about achieving a goal influence actions; self-efficacy, or how the belief of whether or not a person can accomplish a task affects motivation and how you as an outdoor leader can enhance a client's ability to be successful; attribution theory and locus of control, or how individuals explain their successes and failures and the influence these attributions have on future actions and emotions; and effectance and competence motivation, or how effectiveness of attempts to complete tasks influences feelings of competence as well as how social and interpersonal factors influence—and were influenced by—these feelings. A final model from Klint and Priest combines all of these frameworks into one outlining risk taking and competence effectance, and how the accuracy of participants' beliefs influences the probability of success or failure in adventure experiences. The model uses Selye's concepts of distress and eustress to theorize how people change perceptions on the basis of experience and how astuteness develops through adventure experiences.

QUESTIONS TO THINK ABOUT

1. Can you recall a time when you experienced M. Csikszentmihalyi's flow state on an adventure experience? If so, describe what was happening and why it was occurring. How might you as an outdoor leader replicate such an experience for others?

2. Discuss the similarities between M. Csikszentmihalyi's six characteristics of flow and Mitchell's five antecedents of adventure. Create a list of conditions you would foster in adventure experiences to enhance the likelihood that your clients reach their goals.

3. Define and differentiate between the four sources of self-efficacy. Select an adventure activity (e.g., rock climbing, challenge

course) and use it to provide examples of methods for increasing self-efficacy in clients.

4. What does motivation mean to you? Choose one of the theories of motivation and use it to explain how you would create conditions to motivate a client.

5. Recall a time when you led a group on an adventure. Explain individual behaviors within the group by applying the adventure experience paradigm and competence effectance theory.

REFERENCES

Bandura, A. (1977). Self-efficacy: Toward a unifying theory for behavioral change. *Psychological Review, 84,* 191-215.

Bunting, C. (1987). Challenge activities and stress management. In J.F. Meier, T.M. Morash, & G.E. Welton (Eds.), *High-adventure outdoor pursuits: Organization and leadership* (pp. 28-35). Columbus, OH: Publishing Horizons.

Carpenter, G., & Priest, S. (1989). The adventure experience paradigm and non-outdoor leisure pursuits. *Leisure Studies, 8*(1), 65-75.

Csikszentmihalyi, M. (1975). *Beyond boredom and anxiety.* San Francisco: Jossey-Bass.

Csikszentmihalyi, M., & Csikszentmihalyi, I.S. (1991). Adventure and the flow experience. In J.C. Miles & S. Priest (Eds.), *Adventure education* (pp. 149-155). State College, PA: Venture.

Ellis, M.J. (1973). *Why people play.* Englewood Cliffs, NJ: Prentice Hall.

Ewert, A. (1989). Managing fear in the outdoor experiential education setting. *Journal of Experiential Education, 12*(1), 19-25.

Festeu, D. (2002). Motivational factors that influence students' participation in outdoor activities. *Journal of Adventure Education and Outdoor Learning, 2*(1), 43-54.

Festinger, L. (1957). *The theory of cognitive dissonance.* Evanston, IL: Row & Peterson.

Garst, B., Scheider, I., & Baker, D. (2001). Outdoor adventure program participation impacts on adolescent self-perception. *Journal of Experiential Education, 24*(1), 41-49.

Gass, M. (1985). Programming the transfer of learning in adventure education. *Journal of Experiential Education, 10*(3), 18-24.

Gass, M. (1991). Enhancing metaphor development in adventure therapy programs. *Journal of Experiential Education, 14*(2), 6-13.

Gass, M. (1993). *Adventure therapy: Therapeutic applications of adventure programming in mental health settings.* Dubuque, IA: Kendall/Hunt.

Goffman, E. (1981). Fun in games. In M. Marie-Hart & S. Birrell (Eds.), *Sport in the socio-cultural process* (pp. 40-91). Dubuque, IA: Brown.

Harter, S. (1978). Effectance motivation reconsidered. *Human Development, 21,* 34-64.

Harter, S. (1986). Cognitive-developmental processes in the integration of concepts about emotions and self. *Social Cognition, 4,* 119-151.

Katzell, R., & Thompson, D.E. (1990). Work motivation: Theory and practice. *American Psychologist, 45*(2), 144-153.

Martin, P., & Priest, S. (1986). Understanding the adventure experience. *Journal of Adventure Education, 3*(1), 18-21.

Mitchell, R.G. (1983). *Mountain experience: The psychology and sociology of adventure.* Chicago: University of Chicago Press.

Mortlock, C. (1984). *The adventure alternative.* Cumbria, England: England Cicerone Press.

Newberry, E.H., & Lindsay, J.F. (2000). The impact of social skills training and challenge course training on locus of control of youth from residential care. *Journal of Experiential Education, 23*(1), 39-42.

Paxton, T., & McAvoy, L. (1998). Self-efficacy and adventure programs: Transferring outcomes to everyday life. *Proceedings from The Coalition for Education in the Outdoors 4th Research Symposium* (pp. 32-39). Bradford Woods, IN.

Priest, S., & Baillie, R. (1987). Justifying the risk to others: The real razor's edge. *Journal of Experiential Education, 10*(1), 16-22.

Priest, S. (1993). A new model for risk taking. *Journal of Experiential Education, 16*(1), 50-53.

Rohnke, K. (1989). *Cowstails and cobras II: A guide to games, initiatives, ropes courses, and adventure curriculum.* Dubuque, IA: Kendall/Hunt Publishing Company.

Russell, D. (1982). The causal dimension scale: A measure of how individuals perceive causes. *Journal of Personality and Social Psychology, 42,* 1137-1145.

Sage, G.H. (1977). *Introduction to motor behavior: A neuropsychological approach.* Reading, MA: Addison-Wesley.

Schreyer, R.M., White, R., & McCool, S.F. (1978). Common attributes uncommonly exercised. *Journal of Health, Physical Education, and Recreation (JOHPER), 49*(4). Also in J.F. Meier, T.M. Morash, & G.E. Welton (Eds.), *High-adventure outdoor pursuits: Organization and leadership* (pp. 36-42). Columbus, OH: Publishing Horizons.

Selye, H. (1974). *Stress without distress.* New York: Lippincott.

Skow, J. (1983, August 29). Risking it all: The spirit of adventure is alive and well. *Time,* 52-59.

Todd, S.L., Anderson, L., Young, A., & Anderson, D. (2002, January). The relationship of motivational factors to level of development in outdoor adventure recreationists. *Proceedings from The Coalition for Education in the Outdoors 6th Biennial Research Symposium* (pp. 124-138). Bradford Woods, IN.

Walsh, V., & Golins, G. (1976). *The exploration of the Outward Bound process.* Denver, CO: Colorado Outward Bound School.

Weinberg, R.S., & Gould, D. (1995). *Foundations of sport and exercise psychology.* Champaign, IL: Human Kinetics.

Weiner, B. (1972). *Theories of motivation: From mechanism to cognition.* Chicago: Rand McNally.

Weiner, B. (1979). A theory of motivation for some classroom experiences. *Journal of Educational Psychology, 71,* 3-25.

Weiner, B. (1985). An attribution theory of achievement motivation and emotion. *Psychological Review, 92,* 548-573.

Weiner, B., Russell, D., & Lerman, D. (1978). Affective consequences of causal ascriptions. In J.H. Harvey, W.J. Ickes, & R.F. Kidd (Eds.), *New directions in attribution research* (Vol. 2). (pp. 59-90). Hillsdale, NJ: Erlbaum.

Weiner, B., Russell, D., & Lerman, D. (1979). The cognitive-emotion process in achievement-related contexts. *Journal of Personality and Social Psychology, 37,* 1211-1220.

White, R. (1959). Motivation reconsidered: The concept of competence. *Psychological Review, 66,* 297-333.

Zuckerman, M. (1979). *Sensation seeking: Beyond the optimal level of arousal.* Hillsdale, NJ: Erlbaum.

Group Development and Dynamics

Thirteen people signed up for the monthlong adventure experience. They arrived with many questions, fears, and uncertainties. Being unfamiliar with one another, they felt uncomfortable in this unfamiliar environment and kept to themselves. Conversations were characterized by small talk about conventional topics. As essential equipment and food were distributed, they started to interact and make simple decisions about packing gear and sharing loads. The start of the journey stimulated interaction as group members confronted and solved realistic problems and were challenged physically, socially, and emotionally.

As the journey became more demanding, requiring difficult decisions made during lengthy travel in extended darkness, group members became stressed out and exhibited anger, rebellion, confusion, and disillusionment, and the situation deteriorated into chaos. Members with common interests sought each other for comfort. At times, the group divided into subgroups. In some instances, members became upset at the leader for refusing to solve problems for them. Power struggles leading to conflicts were common during established routines such as camp chores or navigation.

As the expedition reached its midpoint, members were still establishing their group identity. They tried to deal openly with problems as they arose and to restore harmony by coming up with a behavioral contract. In time, as members spoke freely about themselves and others, the group became more open. Members began to seek help by directly asking for it or by indirectly expressing self-doubt. Leadership was shared among group members, and more supportive behaviors became common.

Because of a newfound independence, the group relied less on their appointed outdoor leader, navigated in a remote setting with the leader acting as a "shadow," accepted sole responsibility for their decisions or behaviors, and resolved their own crises and conflicts. The whole group worked together as a cohesive team, experiencing the success of high performance. Communication, trust, cooperation, and support prevailed. Group members felt positive, and all expressed a sense of satisfaction.

The final days of the expedition were hectic and filled with emotion, nostalgia, and a feeling of success. Some members experienced a loss of confidence, a fear of leaving, and anger or anxiety. Others reverted back to earlier behaviors, such as denying that the group was important to them, in attempts to salvage their egos. On completion, the group participated in closing activities designed to reinforce its sense of accomplishment. Following this closure, most members realized that their journey was nearly over. They returned equipment, debriefed, and celebrated the trip. The next morning they departed for home.

Adventure programs foster the development of groups (Glass & Benshoff, 2003). Groups tend to evolve through a series of progressive stages. While occasionally groups may skip, repeat, reverse, or even exhibit some stages simultaneously under certain conditions, these growth stages are generally predictable and sequential. Each stage exhibits specific and reoccurring characteristics with transitions between stages tending to be gradual rather than sharp.

STAGES OF GROUP DEVELOPMENT

Numerous researchers have tried to order, number, and name group stages; most theories contain five distinct stages (Cain, 2003; Kerr & Gass, 1987; Jensen, 1979; Tuckman & Jensen, 1977). As you see in the opening vignette, in the first stage, the group comes together and begins to sort out tasks and relationships. In the second stage, concerns arise in the way members relate to one another as they work together. In the third stage, the group begins to overcome its concerns, establishing ground rules for tasks and relationships. In the fourth stage, the group works efficiently as a team, accomplishing a high level of output in both tasks and relationships. In the fifth and final stage, the group closes down, or breaks up, and members move on to other tasks and relationships, perhaps within a new group.

Of the many labels used, the five-stage model of forming, storming, norming, performing, and adjourning has become widely accepted (Tuckman & Jensen, 1977).

1. **Forming** encompasses the discomforts, concerns, feelings, and doubts members experience in a new group.

2. **Storming** occurs when participants begin to meet the needs of the group, question authority, and feel more comfortable about themselves and their relationships.

3. **Norming** involves members addressing appropriate and necessary standards of behavior through which a greater sense of order prevails.

4. **Performing** finds the group concentrating on the tasks at hand with mutual support and interaction among group members.

5. **Adjourning** provides closure of the task, including the imminent end of relationships.

The main strengths of this model are that it is easy to use, it is widely applicable to different types of adventure programs, and it provides useful information concerning the progress of a group (Jensen, 1979).

Task and Relationship Dimensions for Each Stage

We can further divide group functions into the **task dimension,** or work undertaken by the group, called products, and the **relationship dimension,** or group members' interactions with one another, called processes. Examining how these two dimensions interact within the five stages of group development will help you apply leadership styles and strategies to suit client needs.

In the forming stage, the group comes together for the first time, and its members typically strive to become better acquainted with one another. The task dimension in this stage is characterized by members accepting the tasks without investing in common purposes. Members are not committed to the bigger picture or the group's direction and may prefer to work alone. At the same time, they are relatively dependent on you (the leader) for support and guidance. They attempt to discover the nature of a task and to determine what their roles may be in accomplishing that task. In terms of relationships, they tend to feel uncomfortable when they meet for the first time or anxious as they wonder how they will fit into the group. Individuals' past experiences with other groups, such as schools, churches, clubs, or sports teams,

Groups as small as two people, such as this climbing pair, can exhibit the five stages of development.

influence how the individuals view this new, small-group environment. Members are often reluctant to discuss personal views and opinions, so conversation tends to be superficial and stereotypical. Some quickly form impressions, deciding which strangers they will befriend or which they will avoid.

In the storming stage, the group works through tough times as interpersonal issues come to the forefront. Members begin to push the limits of acceptability as they try to figure out the "pecking order." Issues can include status, communication, and defining group values. Attempts at influencing one another begin, and power struggles often follow. The task dimension contains possible resistance to roles and confrontation with overlapping responsibilities. The underlying dysfunctional behavior, however, generally remains more of a relationship concern than a problem of the task dimension. Relationships are fraught with rebellion against influence (perhaps against you as the leader) and with conflict among member personalities—often because past frames of reference may not apply to the present situation. The group members may become polarized around decisions to the point of becoming very opinionated. This polarization, if allowed to run its course, may erode the group's efforts and lead to competition. At this point, members often reveal their personal agendas as they begin to assert and defend their individuality. Behaviors may be marked by jealousy, hostility, distrust, and defensiveness. Interactions may become disruptive, unhealthy, incompatible, and ineffective. Friction grows, anxiety runs high, disagreement abounds, and angry argument may be common. A pecking order often develops on the basis of power and influence.

In the norming stage, the group creates new ground rules characterized by renewed hope. Satisfied members comply to their roles, becoming more involved with the group task. They adopt and accept their workloads. An atmosphere of cooperation emerges as the group starts to openly collaborate on projects. Members genuinely offer help to others and willingly accept assistance in return. The group's purpose is clear, and a strong sense of team identity exists. Relationships in this stage include conflicts that resemble sibling-like rivalries and deeper emotions characteristic of close friendships. Members seem more tolerant of differences and ease into relationships that tend to be more cohesive and intimate. They have dealt with most of the previous resistance and have created a set of mutually accepted operating principles. Personality clashes typically have dissipated, and harmonious dialogue has replaced past arguments. An attitude of "we" instead of "me" often prevails as members become much less dependent on your leadership.

In the performing stage, the group tends to work very well together. Members competently accomplish tasks, resulting in productive outcomes. As a high-achieving team, members are preoccupied with getting the job done and done well. They are proud of the group and are committed to making relationships work. They may experience minor setbacks, but these rarely amount to lasting or real conflicts. They have fully established the pecking order; however, they have based it on members' skills and resources rather than on members' power and influence. Group members admire and respect the strengths and weaknesses of others, and their roles tend to be less rigid. They conduct their roles in a way that allows them to balance tasks and rela-

tionships—just as a leader might attempt to facilitate when leading a highly successful group.

In the adjourning stage, the group wraps up loose ends, bringing work to a close usually with adjourning anxiety. Members may begin to miss the deep focus they achieved in performing their work and may have trouble coping with closure. Members may also reflect on their effectiveness in accomplishing their tasks and may encounter difficulty facing unmet goals or planning for the future. In the adjourning stage, members must find new resources for meeting their own needs separate from the group. Members can find these resources in a positive manner, such as by reviewing experiences to summarize benefits and by incorporating growth into future interactions (Ewert, 1991), or in a negative manner, such as by denying that the experience is over or by regressing to previous negative behaviors seen in the storming stage. The relationship aspect of this stage follows a similar pattern. Members may begin to miss the deep connections they have made to others. Although members are disbanding, they frequently feel that they can stay in touch if needed, and modern communications make this departure easier. Nevertheless, some members may deny the end, especially if the group held emotional significance for them, and reunions may be necessary to ease the transition.

Leadership Style for Each Stage

As a leader, you play a critical role in the development of a group. We can arrange the various roles, or styles, you may employ to assist group development on a continuum from laissez-faire, in which you do nothing to control the group, to dictatorial, in which you exert total control over the group. Since neither of these styles has ever been considered appropriate for outdoor leadership, three styles between these two extremes are more acceptable: autocratic, democratic, and abdicratic (see chapter 18 for further details on flexible outdoor leadership styles).

Since leadership is a process of influence, these three outdoor leadership styles are defined by the amount of influence, or decision-making power, held by the group or by the leader. The **autocratic style** involves your making decisions and then convincing the group to follow you. In a **democratic style,** you and the group share various decision-making responsibilities. In an **abdicratic style,** you abdicate decision-making responsibility to the group, but remain closely involved in case you need to intervene.

The **conditional outdoor leadership theory (COLT)** predicts appropriate leadership style on the basis of the leader's concern for task, relationship, and conditional favorability (Priest & Chase, 1989). See figure 18.4, on page 248, for a detailed discussion of this model. As concern for task, or getting the job done, takes precedence, an effective leader utilizes an autocratic style. As concern increases for relationship, an effective leader employs an abdicratic style. An intermediary value or an equal balance of both concerns favors the democratic style. Changes in condition favorability (e.g., changes in environmental dangers, leader proficiency, group unity, member competence, and characteristics of the decision) can also shift the style in one direction or the other. Note that these conditions may sometimes be a greater determinant of appropriate leadership style than task and relationship.

Figure 5.1 details typical levels of leader concern for the task and relationship dimensions of each stage in group development (Attarian & Priest, 1994). Attarian and Priest suggested that the appropriate leadership style to use during each stage ranges from autocratic through democratic to abdicratic and back again.

During the forming stage, you should invest a great deal of time and effort into the group's tasks: setting goals, orienting members to new roles, and developing a sense of group identity. Your concern for relationship development should take on an important, yet less direct, role. Facilitate healthy interactions among members, encourage members to clarify their reasons or expectations for being in the group, and create a comfortable atmosphere of sharing. Devoting too much energy into informing the group as to how they should relate to one another can be patronizing and inappropriate. Instead, you should support members through "being" types of messages, such as "Glad you're here," and "Welcome to a program that can be a great experience for you" (Mitten, 1995). Concurrently, you must empower the group to determine its own path toward developing positive relationships. Given the direct concern for task and indirect concern for relationships, it is often appropriate to select an autocratic leadership style during the forming stage.

Group development stage (Tuckman & Jensen, 1977)	Task dimension	Relationship dimension	Leader's concern for task vs relationship	Conditional leadership style (Priest & Chase, 1989)
Forming	Acceptance Independence	Acquaintance Initiation	High vs Low	**Autocratic**
Storming	Resistance Confrontation	Rebellion Conflict	High vs High	**Democratic**
Norming	Compliance Involvement	Cohesion Intimacy	Low vs High	**Abdicratic**
Performing	Productivity Competence	Pride Commitment	Low vs Low	**Democratic**
Adjourning	Termination Separation	Transformation Satisfaction	High vs Low	**Autocratic**

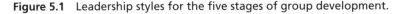

The interaction between leader's concern for dimensions of Task and Relationship

Figure 5.1 Leadership styles for the five stages of group development.

As the group enters the storming stage, conflicts tend to erupt and your concern for relationship should rise to balance your concern for task. At this stage, you should typically employ a democratic style, remembering that the conflict and confrontation that often occur are typical for groups progressing through an adventure experience. As a leader, you should not try to avoid or prevent the storming stage; rather, you should welcome it, using it to the advantage of the group. The storming stage permits members to express grievances, change inappropriate issues hampering the group's progress, and test that the group is truly sincere in its support. You should create an environment that permits members to speak their minds without fear of retribution or retaliation. You can create this atmosphere by explaining how conflict is a natural and important step in the evolution of a high-performing team. At the same time, you should not ignore the task dimension. Your concerns for task and relationship should be about equal: you need to adapt goals, restate priorities, adjust roles, and refocus efforts on getting the job done as well as address the troublesome interpersonal issues.

A comfortable calm often follows the "storm" as the group begins the norming stage. At this time, you should be primarily concerned with relationship, since operating principles are already well in hand. In this situation, it is helpful to apply an abdicratic style, simply supporting group members as they work out their ground rules for future behaviors. Since established norms are a key to success in this stage and to moving on to the next stage, you should facilitate group discussion, acting more like a peer or colleague whenever possible and appropriate. Subsequently, if new members join the group, you must introduce newcomers to the existing guidelines and encourage the group to reexamine their norms to include the new members.

As a high-performing team, the group "kicks into high gear" and produces top-quality work in the performing stage. Now the concern for task returns as productivity becomes important; however, both your concerns should be low because the group is in control. Once again, with concerns for task and relationship being relatively equivalent, a democratic leadership style is probably most appropriate. At this point, you should act as a resource and remind members that the group could not have reached this pinnacle of performance without passing through the earlier stages of development. You should focus most of your attention on maintaining the group in high-performance while remaining aware that past problems may reoccur or that new crises may appear. If these happen, the group could slip back 1 or 2 stages, and you will need to adjust your leadership style accordingly.

As in the forming stage, in the adjourning stage you should invest time and effort into the group's task of creating closure for the experience and into helping clients integrate what they've learned into the future, organize future reunions, and accept changes, as well as into facilitating ongoing communication. Your concern for relationship development should again take on an important, yet indirect, role. Remember that members may regress to earlier dysfunctional behaviors under the stress of closure. Once again, we recommend that you become more autocratic, focusing more on task and relatively less on relationship.

Leadership Strategies for Each Stage

Both understanding the five development stages and knowing the appropriate leadership style for each stage give you a framework for determining the best strategy to meet the goals of recreational, educational, developmental, or therapeutic groups as outlined in chapter 2. Recall that these goals are having fun, learning skills, and being entertained for recreation; understanding new concepts, enriching old ones, and becoming aware of needs for education; improving functional behaviors and training positive actions for development; and changing specific behaviors to remedy a social dysfunction for therapy (Ashby & DeGraaf, 1998). Let's consider strategies for meeting the needs of the different groups in each of the five stages of development.

Forming

For recreational groups, you must clearly specify program goals, objectives, and your expectations of members. When possible, encourage participation and group interaction. For example, at the beginning of a course on backcountry skiing, you should take the time to describe the course goals and activities. Following this explanation and using clients' input, you should determine if these goals and associated activities meet their needs and then make necessary changes to help individualize learning.

For educational and developmental groups, encourage exploration and involvement in relation to how the group wishes to approach its needs and goals. Clarifying goals and group expectations is often a major portion of this process. While you may typically use highly structured activities, you must encourage members to make sure that individual differences are permitted. For example, say some members of the group have stated that they have a very strong fear of heights. During an initial Trust Fall, you should adapt the exercise to respect these individuals' needs.

For therapeutic groups, you should begin by examining the goals and expectations of group members and their congruency with the goals assigned by the sponsoring or overseeing agency. You should help the group explore individual differences in conjunction with the options available to the group. Through this process of clarification, you should help members understand individual needs and the expectations of the sponsoring or overseeing agency. For example, a judicial system conducting wilderness programming for juvenile offenders expects leaders and participants to follow certain standards to increase the therapeutic value for each individual.

Storming

Recognize that conflict can be beneficial and present the conflict's relevance to the goals of the program. With recreational experiences, you should structure activities so that individuals are able to express themselves. Remain clear, however, about which decisions the group can make and which you will make.

With educational and developmental groups, you should allow potential group struggles to occur, yet ensure that the group atmosphere remains open and safe. In permitting group decisions, it is essential that you not intercede unless necessary. If you overrule group decisions, members may lower or invalidate their opinions of their decision-making abilities. This discounting can create an atmosphere in which members are less willing to express themselves. For example, if three members of the group are continually late to activities, you might initiate a discussion about how this affects the group, but you must allow the participants to generate their own possible solutions to the problem.

With therapeutic groups, you should clarify the storming (or power and control) issues in regard to the purpose of the group. For example, ask, "Why do you think the three of you are having such a hard time with this issue? Are there ways this issue relates to the one that brought you here? Are there exceptions to when you can deal appropriately with what is occurring?" With therapeutic groups, you have the added responsibility to help clarify appropriate and inappropriate behaviors as the group works through issues. You must enforce limits, but these limits should have relevant purpose for their existence. In other words, create rules that have purpose rather than rules for rules' sake.

Norming

In norming, you should support the group members as they establish their own set of operating principles. For recreational experiences, as participants gather more skill and competencies, members either become a group or remain a collection of individuals. For the group to attain a mutual reciprocity, a sense of cohesiveness must occur among individual members. If this process occurs, individuals will generally experience the benefits of each other's talents as they work together to achieve established goals. You should help the group set common goals that are well-defined and can help develop the skills of each individual in the group. For example, if a group learning white-water canoeing has decided to paddle a class III rapid, you should support the group in its team planning while also working on specific techniques with each person to develop individual skills, ensuring that each person remains safe throughout the experience.

In educational and developmental programs, you should encourage greater levels of responsibility. When appropriate, you should also be flexible in allowing participants to adapt goals and activities to their own needs. You should facilitate increased interdependency among members as well as personal independence, encouraging participants to become less dependent on you. In other words, you should encourage group members to see you more as a resource than as a leader. For example, if the group has agreed that its goal is to climb a particular mountain, you should help participants own their behaviors by providing feedback and clarifying issues as needed.

In therapeutic programs, you should continue diagnosing problem areas, offering new perspectives, and supporting positive achievements. Through clarification and confrontation, you and the group should jointly explore possible ways that individuals can meet their needs without compromising the rights of others. For example, if Jesse hits Sam, your questioning might include "Jesse, what did you want when you hit him? What is another way of getting Sam's attention? Which method gets Sam's attention and keeps your friendship? What are ways you have used in the past where you have been noticed and the group made you feel like you belonged?"

Performing

In the performing stage of recreational groups, you should help the group achieve its own goals by encouraging individuals to increase initiative and responsibility for their skill development. Effective leaders often monitor the group, supporting its inclination to work independently. For example, as our white-water canoeing group continues to develop, you should encourage members to take on increasing responsibilities in conducting experiences. For example, allow them to check out safety systems or scout white-water sections before entering them with a canoe.

With educational and developmental groups, you should also encourage members to take on increasing responsibility for their actions, until you eventually reach the point at which the group could achieve complete independence from you. Acting as a resource, you should help the group clarify its goals instead of directing the group toward its goals, and you should help it make minor adjustments to increase its likelihood of meeting its goals. For example, suppose two members fall far behind while ascending a mountain. Rather than reminding the group of its goals, you should ask the group to clarify the purpose of the activity and then encourage members to use a group process to resolve the issue.

In therapeutic programs, you should clarify what progress the group has made and then help individuals transfer this knowledge to other situations outside of the group. You should remain supportive but may begin to play the devil's advocate, perhaps representing the point of view of others outside of the group. An example in an at-risk youth program might be "As a group you've all agreed that it's alright to swear while we are in this group; but if I were a potential employer and heard you using that kind of language, what do you imagine I would think?" (Kerr & Gass, 1987, p. 45).

Adjourning

By the adjourning stage of recreational programs, group members should have achieved high or adequate levels of independent skill competency.

You should encourage participants to consolidate what they have gained as individuals working in the group and to apply what they have learned to other technical situations.

In educational and developmental programs, you should help group members by encouraging them to review and evaluate what the group has learned. Effective leaders often help the group summarize areas of progress, helping individual members to transfer newly acquired knowledge to other situations outside of the group. When appropriate, you may also provide alternatives for people to reconnect in the group. For example, follow-up strategies such as mentoring meetings, reunion socials, coaching schemes, and refresher programs may all maintain the momentum of change.

In therapeutic programs, you should focus on clarifying gains, encourage the transfer of learning, and help clients address the tendency to regress to previous dysfunctional behaviors. Regression during closure is particularly common with therapeutic populations. In addition, you should help members access helpful resources outside of the adventure experience. Consider a group of young offenders who have made excellent progress in their wilderness therapy program. When returned to their original, dysfunctional environment, they are likely to experience pressures to repeat old behaviors. Your challenge is to find a substitute for the therapy group that will work in the members' everyday environments and will counter any factors that may reverse the changes members have experienced. Often, helping members find suitable support networks of other rehabilitated offenders can go a long way toward preventing recidivism.

OTHER FACTORS AFFECTING GROUP DYNAMICS

Using small-group dynamics to attain recreational, educational, developmental, or therapeutic goals is central to adventure programming. Effective leaders often utilize the strength of the group to bring about individual behavior changes. In using small-group development as a tool for creating change, you must keep in mind several considerations:

1. *Individual needs.* While the model focuses on group development, you must also be aware of the unique needs of each partici-

◄ EFFECTIVE OUTDOOR LEADERS ►

- ► Know the five stages of group development and the various characteristics associated with each.
- ► Identify which stage of development their group is in and employ correct leadership style as well as leadership strategies to bring about change and growth.
- ► Differentiate how recreational, educational, developmental, and therapeutic

groups vary in their stages of development and identify strategies that develop members in these groups through the various stages.

- ► Identify factors that affect group dynamics as well as adjust for these factors within a particular group's development.

---

pant. Participants may have goals separate from the group that demand consideration. You should strive to blend individual and group needs so that the two forces interact to achieve the highest degree of success.

2. *Variation in development.* Remember that groups progress through the stages of development at different rates and directions. Moreover, individual members within the same group will grow at different speeds. This variation in development often makes allowing for different individual outcomes especially important. For example, some participants may progress to a point at which they feel comfortable while others may still question whether they are willing to commit to the group. You should recognize that members can regress as well as advance through these stages. For example, varying degrees of regression to earlier stages are often evident in therapeutic programs as participants approach the end and are not yet ready to separate.

3. *Group restructuring.* Inserting or removing members from a group will affect its development and the dynamics of every interaction within the group. Since everyone plays a role within the group, when a person is added or removed, the group will go through some form of restructuring. This restructuring can often result in regression to earlier stages of development.

4. *Members' unique characteristics.* Other member characteristics, such as age and gender, will influence group development. Intelligence, cognitive processing ability, and the capacity to integrate new learning

will also accelerate or delay group evolution. You should adjust the program to accommodate these needs. One example of an adjustment might be to use facilitation methods that are appropriate for the group or particular population (e.g., school children versus corporate executives—see chapters 14-17).

SUMMARY

In the past, leaders often relied on repeating past occurrences and on the "magic" of groups to reach their intended goals. By understanding group development, however, you can choose activities, leadership styles, and strategies that are appropriate for the needs of a group in a particular stage. When you accomplish this, your program will flow, or have a sense of natural timing that allows participants to get the most out of their experiences. While groups will develop regardless of your level of involvement, knowing how you can affect this growth will often be the difference between providing a valuable experience and simply helping people survive an adventure program.

Many theorists have postulated their own multistage models of group development. Tuckman and Jensen's (1977) model, most commonly used, lists five stages: forming, storming, norming, performing, and adjourning. These stages describe the coming together of individuals in a group and the conflict that leads to developing acceptable ground rules, which in turn permit a period of high achievement before the experience and the group relationships end.

You should apply one of the three common leadership styles (autocratic, democratic, and abdicratic) to each of the five stages, depending on the situation. The style you choose should be a function of your concern for task or relationship as well as for conditional favorability. By correctly identifying the group's stage at any particular time, you can employ the best style, thereby helping the group move to the next stage of development. Indeed, if you are familiar with the five development stages and the three leadership styles and their possible interactions, you can effectively guide a group through its evolution so it can ultimately reach and sustain top performance.

Use your knowledge of the development stages and leadership styles to determine the best strategy to help groups meet recreational, educational, developmental, or therapeutic goals. In forming, examine program goals and group expectations, and then alter the program as necessary in order to accommodate these. Help individuals clarify their similarities and differences and share their fears and concerns. In storming, recognize the benefits of conflict while not permitting it to occur at the expense of others. Draw attention to acts of danger while maintaining an open and supportive atmosphere by encouraging the group to solve its own problems. In norming, help the group establish its norms and see issues from new perspectives. Clarify and confront issues, encouraging members to consider ways they may meet their needs without compromising the rights of others. In performing, get the group to share its talents and to offset its strengths and weaknesses. Shift responsibility and accountability to the group but remain supportive by occasionally taking opposing sides or acting as a resource for advice and assistance. In adjourning, summarize the group's learning and progress and help members transfer what they have learned to their everyday lives (Larcher, 1999). Provide alternatives to the support the group offered to its members and use follow-up strategies to maintain changes.

The group development model does not account for individual development, the evolution of group dynamics at different rates and in different directions, the addition or subtraction of members, and the specific characteristics and competence of the group. Yet, by understanding group development, you will be equipped to select the best activity, express the correct leadership style, and apply appropriate strategies to help a group grow toward its next stage.

QUESTIONS TO THINK ABOUT

1. Describe a group (preferably one you were a member of) and its behaviors using the five stages of the group development model.

2. Discuss the style and strategies used by the leader of that group. Were the leadership style and strategies effective? How could the style and strategies have been improved?

3. What will you do differently in each of the five stages with the groups you will work with?

REFERENCES

Ashby, J., & DeGraaf, D. (1998). Re-examining group development in adventure therapy groups. *Journal of Experiential Education, 21*(3), 162-167.

Attarian, A., & Priest, S. (1994). The relationship between stages of group development and styles of outdoor leadership. *Journal of Adventure Education and Outdoor Leadership, 11*(3), 13-19.

Cain, J. (2003). Exploring the five stages of group formation using adventure-based activities. *Horizons, 21,* 23-28.

Ewert, A. (1991). Group development in the natural environment: Expectations, outcomes, and techniques. *Environment and Behavior, 23*(5), 592-615.

Glass, J.S., & Benshoff, J.M. (2003). Facilitating group cohesion among adolescents through challenge course experiences. *Journal of Experiential Education, 25*(2), 268-277.

Jensen, M. (1979). Application of small group theory to adventure programs. *Journal of Experiential Education, 2*(2), 39-42.

Kerr, P.J., & Gass, M.A. (1987). A group development model for adventure education. *Journal of Experiential Education, 10*(3), 39-46.

Larcher, B. (1999). Putting management team-building to work. *Horizons, 5,* 19-21.

Mitten, D. (1995). Building the group: Using personal affirming to create healthy group process. *Journal of Experiential Education, 18*(2), 82-94.

Priest, S., & Chase, R. (1989). The conditional theory of outdoor leadership style. *Journal of Adventure Education and Outdoor Leadership, 6*(3), 10-17.

Tuckman, B.W., & Jensen, M.A. (1977). Stages of small group development revisited. *Group & Organization Studies, 2*(4), 419-427.

PART

II

Practical and Organizational Skills for Outdoor Leaders

CHAPTER

6

Technical Skills

The day was perfect. A warm breeze blew across Maria's face as she stood on top of the cliff after setting up four independent sets of anchor systems for rock climbing. The progressions for climbing, based on the students' objectives, were in place for the day's lessons. She could see James, her coinstructor, briefing the group on the day's activities and laying out the risk-management procedures. The day progressed wonderfully and in the final discussion no one felt it could have gone much better.

The day was terrible. An unexpected ice storm settled over the mountain range, covering everything with 3 inches (8 cm) of ice. Several tents in the group had collapsed during the night, and the group had retreated into cramped, yet convenient, snow caves they had built earlier. Following the planned route to the summit was out of the question because of the unstable snowpack, so the group took a secondary route that required a less technical experience—but much longer and more arduous—encountering mundane "post-holing" conditions for several hours. Such a change required a number of program adaptations that the staff implemented with input from students. At the end of the day, while students and staff members alike agreed that the experience was a total drag, no one felt it could have gone much better.

As seen in both vignettes, technical skills serve as one of the foundations for conducting any adventure experience. Although technical skills are not always the product of adventure programs, they always serve as the process through which people grow. Without appropriate knowledge of such skills, you may find conducting adventure experiences to be dangerous—if not impossible. As a leader, you may be blessed with tremendous facilitation techniques or great organizational capabilities, but without technical skills to serve as the underlying medium for conducting adventure activities, other techniques and capabilities are useless.

In writing this chapter, as well as the other hard-skill chapters (7 and 8), we do not intend to detail the technical aspects of each skill area in adventure programming. Unfortunately, space does not allow for in-depth discussion, but you can find numerous books written on each skill. The list of books at the end of this chapter is a good place to start.

What we provide in these chapters are some of the key, specific competencies you should possess to effectively teach and lead certain adventure activities. Please note, however, that these competencies change according to geographic areas, client populations, client goals, and environmental conditions. These competencies only become valuable when they are guided by the accommodating judgment required of outdoor leaders.

GENERIC, METASKILLS, AND SPECIFIC COMPETENCY

In conducting adventure programs, no matter what the activity, you need to be capable in a variety of **generic competency** areas. These areas include those skills applicable to all adventure experiences. Examples of these areas include weather interpretation, first aid, trip planning, performance, skill, physical fitness, and mental awareness above and beyond the call of the activity, location, participants, and anticipated adversity.

Furthermore, you need to be capable in **metaskills,** or those areas that combine hard and soft skills into a workable design. Examples of these areas include leadership style, problem solving and decision making, experience-based judgment, effective communication, and ethical behavior (see chapters 18 through 23).

In addition, you need to be capable in several **specific competencies**—those skills unique to the activities chosen for the adventure program. For example, paddling and rope handling are two skills that you need only if you are actually going to be kayaking or canoeing and climbing or doing challenge courses. In this chapter, we outline the specific competencies needed for eight of the most popular adventure activities. We base our guidelines on three main works: *Safety Practices in Adventure Programming* (Priest & Dixon, 1990),

Manual of Program Accreditation Standards for Adventure Programs (Garvey, Leemon, Williamson, & Zimmerman, 1999; Williamson & Gass, 1993), and *Administrative Practices of Accredited Adventure Programs* (Gass, 1998).

SPECIFIC TECHNICAL-SKILL COMPETENCIES

The eight adventure activities in this chapter are backcountry travel, top-rope rock climbing and rappelling, mountaineering, challenge (ropes) courses, caving or spelunking, flatwater and white-water paddling, on-road and off-road bicycling, and cross-country skiing. The vast majority of these specific skills are technical, that is, they are related to activity performance. Although we mention some of the specific risk-management, environmental, and ubiquitous "other" competency skills here, we do not consider any of the generic risk-management or environmental competency skills until the next two chapters, or any of the metaskills until chapters 18 through 23.

One final reminder: competence in technical, risk-management, and environmental skills alone does not constitute effective outdoor leadership. Such competence is merely a start; you must build on your capabilities by adding the skills we discuss in later chapters. The organizational skills of trip planning (chapter 9) or risk management (chapter 10) are the same for most programs, regardless of the activity. Being properly skilled in all areas will give you a greater cushion of competence to fall back on in times of need!

Backcountry Travel

Activity: As a backpacking leader, you should know appropriate travel techniques, such as using the locking-knee rest step on uphill grades; switchbacking in steep, open country; and correct stride length and cadence on various slopes. You should know correct equipment selection, such as which packs, footwear, tents, and sleeping bags are appropriate for encountered conditions; equipment use, such as equally loading backpacks, adjusting suspension straps, erecting tents, and refueling and lighting stoves; equipment care, such as waterproofing boots; and equipment repair, such as fixing broken tents or packs and unclog-

ging stoves or water filters. You may also need to know how to improvise emergency rescue equipment, such as how to fashion a stretcher from pack frames or how to weave one with rope.

Risk management: Common backpacking injuries are joint strains and sprains. You should be aware of participants with weak leg joints or back or neck problems. You should know warm-up stretches for various body regions (e.g., legs, hips, neck, shoulders). Furthermore, you should understand the unique concerns that arise from all possible weather and terrain interactions, such as the concerns of crossing steep hills in freezing rain. Finally, you should have adequate plans for finding lost hikers and for supervising a group in wilderness conditions.

Environmental: For backcountry travel in wilderness areas, unique considerations may be necessary, such as obtaining land-use permits. You should be aware of local trail etiquette, for example, whether or not downhill hikers have the right of way. You should be especially aware of the potential impact of highly used camping areas on resources.

Other: When traveling off-trail, technical terrain can challenge leaders. This terrain may include steep slopes with scree or slippery snow. More injuries generally happen during the descent than the ascent, usually because people are tired and relaxed after having reached a summit. When appropriate, you need to be prepared for rock falls or avalanches, ensuring that everyone wears a helmet. You should anticipate the possibility of people slipping, perhaps spraining an ankle. Encourage people to use appropriate hiking techniques for the area, such as treading carefully, facing the hill, avoiding leaning too far into the slope (like climbing a ladder), digging the feet into the hillside without loosening debris, keeping one eye uphill for falling debris, and not lingering downhill from others moving above them. You may need to fix a hand line and use it with the appropriate procedures, including allowing only one person on the line at a time, since a sideways stumble can dislodge several others who might be holding on.

River crossings are occasionally part of backpacking. Crossing a slippery log high above the water or jumping along stepping-stones may be more dangerous than simply wading across a river. You should know how to combine various methods for fording a river such as human tripods, chains of people, upstream hand lines, third-leg poles, extra flotation, and Tyrolean traverses. For rocky fords, you may need to consider wearing shoes, sandals, or boots as well as helmets if the risk of head injury exists. In addition, you may need to prevent people from wearing baggy clothing that may fill with water, causing them to submerge. Generally, have everyone unbuckle waist belts and sternum straps and loosen shoulder straps so that a pack may be quickly removed in the water so it does not pin or drag someone under.

You must understand and "read" river-crossing characteristics, including downstream dangers, air and water temperatures, water murkiness, footing stability, water depth, flow rates, current speed, length of crossing, and obstacles. Moreover, you may need to pay particular attention to preplanning rescue attempts in case someone is swept downstream, remembering that ample visibility and danger-free river space are needed for floating, drifting, swimming, and reaching the nearest bank. Certainly, you should know group members' skill levels, especially swimming, strength, and balancing capacities, and make sure the members' skill levels match your chosen crossing. In addition, you need to carefully consider the time of day because, for example, snowmelt and runoff can be greatest in the afternoon; avoid fording rivers that might be beyond group capabilities. Remember: it may be better to wait for water levels to subside or find another location.

Addressing many other factors can make fording a river safer. When conditions warrant extra assistance on either bank, you should consider placing a person with a throw bag downstream from the crossing point. You may need to belay people from either or both banks. You might want to keep knives handy to cut any ropes that may tangle with people in the water. You may need to test all crossings before permitting any participants to cross, possibly leaving a qualified staff member to cross last. When river temperatures are cold, be prepared to deal with immersion hypothermia. Finally, you may need to think ahead about how to communicate over the noise of the river.

Top-Rope Rock Climbing and Rappelling

Activity: As a rock-climbing leader, you should know movement techniques, such as laying back,

jamming, chimneying, and using counterforce; belaying techniques, such as using the body or devices for friction and using backup belay systems; anchor systems, such as natural, artificial, solid, independent, equalized, and redundant; spotting for bouldering; knot tying; forming harness tie-ins and anchor clip-ins; and communication signals. You should know about selecting specific equipment for the conditions you may encounter, such as when to use dynamic or static ropes, webbing, carabiners, harnesses, and helmets; correct equipment uses, such as how to fit and dress in harnesses and helmets; equipment care, such as not stepping on nylon software or dropping aluminum hardware; and equipment replacement, such as regularly logging usage and making visual inspections for wear and tear. You may also need to know how to improvise emergency lowering and raising techniques, including litter lowering, Z-pulley raising, and knot jumping.

Risk management: Common injuries in rock climbing are joint dislocations. You should be aware of participants with a history of separated shoulders, elbows, or fingers. In addition, you should assess clients' overall physical fitness and psychological readiness to climb. Encouraging the removal of all jewelry (rings, bracelets, necklaces, earrings) and sharp objects from pockets (especially pens and pencils) to prevent shear injuries or impalements is an appropriate risk-management measure. You should know specific warm-up stretches for the body regions (e.g., arms, neck, shoulders, hips, knees). Furthermore, you should understand the unique concerns that arise from weather and terrain interactions, such as the dangers of exposing people on cliff faces during lightning. Moreover, you should have clear plans for supervising individual climbers and belayers as well as generally managing the group. Finally, you may need to inspect climbing sites for environmental dangers such as potential rock falls, loose holds, uneven ground, and sharp objects.

Environmental: For rock climbing, unique considerations may be necessary for site preservation, such as avoiding bird nests and rock paintings, and for conservation, such as keeping wire from brushing lichen and avoiding pulling plants from cracks, dragging ropes around trees, using too much chalk, excessive bolting, bashing pitons, glue-fixing holds, and chipping rock to make new holds. You should be aware of local rules for the climbing site, including bolting practices and whether you must boulder only in dedicated areas.

Other: If you work with clients on climbing walls, you should know if the wall construction follows acceptable standards. You may also need to know about the principles and technology of the facility you are using, noting safe working load, minimum breaking strength, anchor systems, base padding, wall materials, artificial holds, and regular risk-management inspection reviews.

Rappelling (or abseiling) can often be conducted as a stand-alone activity that is separate from top-rope rock climbing. The competencies we listed for climbing may also apply to rappelling. Competencies that usually differ from those for rock climbing include appropriate movement techniques, such as proper body shape, hand position, foot placement, and "free rappelling" past overhangs; equipment use and care of rappelling devices; and additional communication signals for rappelling. As a rappelling leader, you should use separate and independent rappel and belay systems when appropriate. One common example is a rappel device connected to the harness at a point different from the belay tie-in knot and rappel ropes and belay ropes each having their own separate anchor systems. In addition, you should know that common rappelling accidents include catching clothing or hair in ropes or devices and coming off the rappel rope (rappelling off the end of the rope). Accidents may also occur when anchors fail and equipment is damaged, such as when high-speed descents overheat friction devices and melt ropes.

Mountaineering

Activity: In addition to knowing some of the rock-climbing techniques, as a mountaineering leader you may need to know snow-climbing techniques, including post-holing, ice ax self-arrest, roped group travel, and glissading; ice-climbing techniques, including French and American cramponing and placing ice tools; and glacier travel techniques, including step cutting, walking in echelon formation, and crossing snow bridges and crevasses. You may also need to know belaying, including boot ax belays; anchors, such as bollards, buried "dead" objects, flukes, picket, and ice screws; knots, such as prepositioned Prussik and butterfly; and harness tie-ins to a chest harness in order to prevent inversion with a heavy pack on.

You should know equipment selection for the conditions you may encounter, including when to pack shovels, ice tools, crampons, crevasse rescue kits, altimeters, and eye protection from snow blindness or flying ice chips; correct equipment use, including how to walk in crampons and how to carry an ice ax and swing ice tools without injury; equipment care, including not stepping on nylon software with crampon spikes and checking anchors for melting under pressure; and equipment repair, including how to fix crampons and snowshoes. You should know how to improvise emergency lowering and raising techniques, such as crevasse rescue, Bilgeri lifts, Prussiking, and Z-pulley raising. You should know how to build emergency snow shelters, mark the return route with wands, and melt large quantities of snow for fluid intake.

Risk management: You should thoroughly understand mountain risk management. You should know snowpack or ice history (age, depth, layers, crystals), seasonal precipitation trends, spring runoff, freeze and thaw cycles, weather forecast, temperature, and time of day. This information can be critical to predicting the stability and characteristics of the routes you choose. You should also know how crevasses and snow bridges are formed, the likelihood of avalanches, and the impact of sun and temperature on snow-bridge, crevasse, and serac stability. In addition, you may need to know how to inspect on-site snow crystals and layers; ice strength, color, and water content; and the underlying foundation.

Injuries in mountaineering are most often associated with high altitude. Thus, you should be aware of high-altitude mountain sickness, hypothermia, frostbite, and cerebral or pulmonary edema. Furthermore, you should understand the unique concerns that come from possible weather and terrain interactions, such as the effect of altitude on high winds (e.g., winds can increase rapidly at higher elevations) and avalanches (see cross-country skiing). Moreover, you may need to inspect mountaineering sites for environmental dangers including potential avalanches, lightning, ice fall, and snow-bridge collapse. Certainly, you should assess clients' physical fitness and psychological readiness for the routes you choose. As with rock climbing, accidents are more likely to occur during the descent when people are tired and careless after reaching the summit.

Environmental: You need to understand the consequences of improper waste disposal such as dumping waste into crevasses. This practice is becoming less tolerated because of the large increase in wilderness use (see chapter 24).

Challenge (Ropes) Courses

Activity: As a challenge-course leader, you should know the difference between high elements, which require belaying, and low elements, which require spotting—not catching—as well as the differences in risk-management protocols for skills, such as dynamic belaying and static belaying with transfers between elements. You may need to know movement techniques such as ascending, crossing, and descending high elements; belaying techniques similar to rock climbing but also including using backup belay systems, dynamic and static belays, and transfer methods; anchor systems, including regularly inspecting permanent anchors in addition to knowing the rock-climbing anchoring techniques; spotting for low elements and group initiatives; knots; harness tie-ins; anchor clip-ins; and communication signals, including static transfers in addition to the rock-climbing communication techniques. You need to know equipment selection for the conditions you may encounter, such as when to use dynamic or static ropes and how to use spin static devices and shear reduction blocks; correct equipment use, including how to fit and dress in harnesses and helmets; equipment care, including not dropping aluminum hardware or stepping on nylon software; and equipment replacement, including regularly logging usage and visually inspecting for wear and tear. In addition, you need to know how to improvise emergency lowering techniques, such as performing cutaway rescues, evacuating physically injured people without an ambulance, and mobilizing people who are psychologically frozen by their fear.

Risk management: Injuries on challenge courses can include heart attacks (heart rates rise rapidly, often reaching their maximum), shear injuries, joint dislocations or hyperextensions from lifting people or participants being dropped, and minor cuts, scrapes, bruises, and splinters. You should be aware of participants with a history of cardiac risks, back concerns, and separated shoulders, elbows, or fingers. You should encourage the removal of jewelry, especially rings, bracelets, necklaces, and earrings, and the removal of any sharp objects from pockets. Encourage participants to wear long-sleeved shirts and long pants even on hot days and to tuck in loose clothing. You should know specific warm-up stretches for different body regions (e.g., arms, neck, shoulders, hips, knees). You should understand the unique concerns that come from all possible weather and terrain interactions, such as the dangers of people on wires during lightning and high winds. Moreover, you need to have clear plans for supervising individuals, such as first-time belayers, as well as generally managing the group, including dealing with congestion on elements and with horseplay. You should inspect the area for environmental dangers, such as sharp sticks, hanging limbs, exposed rocks, uneven ground, and equipment dropped from above. And, of course, you should assess clients' physical fitness and psychological readiness for participation.

Environmental: For challenge courses, unique considerations may be necessary for site preservation, including not disturbing bird nests or tree growth, and for conservation, such as avoiding through-bolting small trees, girdling trees with ropes or cables, and compacting soil around roots.

Other: You generally need to ensure that the course is properly constructed, meets appropriate standards, and is regularly inspected for dangers such as detached cables or ropes, loose clamps or strand vises, missing bolts or nuts, frayed cable or rope ends, split poles or planks, overexposure to ultraviolet light, weather damage, tree diseases, and root damage. You should know the principles and technology of the facility you are using, such as its safe working load, minimum breaking strength, ground-anchor integrity, guy line or belay cable fastenings, and regular risk-management inspection reviews. You should also recognize and repair—or not use—damaged elements. Finally, you may need to know how to secure the challenge course to avoid creating an attractive nuisance to trespassers.

Caving or Spelunking

Activity: As a caving leader, you should know horizontal- and vertical-movement techniques, such as walking, crawling, slithering, squeezing, getting unstuck, negotiating water hazards, rappelling, and ascending with ladders and with aid gear; belaying techniques; anchor systems; knots; harness tie-ins; anchor clip-ins; and communication signals. You may need to know equipment selection for the conditions you may encounter, which is similar to rock climbing but may possibly include a minimum of three different light sources per person and a rescue kit containing full-length static rope, wire ladders, ascenders, anchors, carabiners, and pulleys; correct equipment use, such as fitting and wearing special clothing and gear;

equipment care, including not stepping on nylon software and not dropping aluminum hardware; and equipment replacement, including regularly logging usage and visually inspecting for wear and tear. You may need to know how to improvise emergency lowering and raising techniques such as litter lowering, Z-pulley raising, and knot jumping.

Risk management: Common accidents in caving include head injuries, getting stuck in a tight place, and reacting to fear. Certainly, you must be aware of participants with a history of claustrophobia or fear of the dark. You need to consider using helmets as well as taking sufficient food and water for an extra 24 h stay. You should understand the unique concerns that potential weather and terrain interactions may cause, such as when heavy rains flooding deep passages can drastically alter the appearance and availability of routes. You should have plans for supervising individual cavers, such as those who may need extra help in tight squeezes, as well as for generally managing the group, such as how to keep everyone together in the dark. You may need to inspect caving sites for environmental dangers, such as potential rock fall, loose holds, and uneven ground. In addition, you should assess clients' physical fitness and psychological readiness to cave in the dark.

Environmental: Caving is often conducted in an especially sensitive setting. Unique considerations may be necessary for site protection, including properly removing and disposing all litter and human waste and leaving survey markers or prehistoric artifacts intact. You need to be aware of local rules for the caving site, such as no smoking, marking walls, contacting bats or other animals, touching or damaging cave formations, dumping spent carbide, or tampering with cave gates. You may need to secure special permission to enter caves, understanding that caves and cave-dwelling animals are protected by law in most areas.

Flatwater and White-Water Paddling

Activity: As a paddling leader, you need to know appropriate flatwater and white-water techniques, such as power strokes, turning strokes, corrective strokes, and braces; capsize techniques, including group, individual, boat-assisted self-rescue, and paddling a swamped boat; swimming techniques, such as drown proofing, treading water, and floating through rapids; boat dynamics

and maneuverability, including spins, forward, reverse, straight tracking, side slips, eddy turns or peel outs, bracing, U-turns, landings, rolling, and ferrying; boat transportation, such as rooftop or trailer tie-downs, turn signals, safe loading and unloading, and carrying; knots, such as the trucker's hitch; and river communication, including using whistles and signals. You need to know equipment selection for the conditions you may encounter, such as using helmets in white water, type III or V personal flotation devices (PFDs), dry bags, flotation devices, spray decks, bailers, sponges, foot pumps, repair kits, rescue kits containing haul ropes, pulleys, carabiners, anchors, and a knife for fouled lines and a saw for cutting through wood in strainers; correct equipment use, such as how to fit helmets, use throw bags, and wear PFDs while in a boat; equipment care, including appropriate waterproofing and securing of gear; and equipment replacement, such as regularly logging usage and visually inspecting for wear and tear. Clothing can be a special concern since people may remain wet for the entire day. You may need to recommend functional clothing such as wet or dry suits (when the sum of air and water temperatures is less than 50° C or 122° F) and footwear that allows for walking without interfering with swimming. You also may need to know how to improvise emergency rescue techniques, including securing people, securing equipment, dealing with pinned boats, Z-pulley dragging, and knot jumping.

Risk management: Common injuries in paddling are joint dislocations and reacting to fear. You should be aware of participants with a history of separated shoulders, elbows, or fingers as well as of how proficient each participant is in water. You should know specific warm-up stretches for different body regions (e.g., arms, neck, torso, shoulders). In addition, you should understand the unique concerns that come from all possible weather and terrain interactions, such as the dangers of wind and lightning on open water. You should have plans for supervising individual paddlers, such as watching for proper positioning for rapid running, as well as for generally managing the group, including maintaining visual contact on open water. You may need to inspect paddling areas, portages, and access or egress points for environmental dangers, such as moving water, submerged stumps, prevailing winds, water temperature, or uneven ground. As always, you should assess clients' physical fitness and psychological readiness to paddle.

Environmental: For paddling, unique considerations may be necessary for site preservation, such as avoiding beaver constructions, and for conservation, such as using existing portage trails, avoiding expanding damage around put-in and takeout areas, and preventing water contamination from poorly packed stove fuel. You should be aware of local rules for the paddling area, including river courtesy and whether or not fires must be only below the high-water line. You must avoid exceeding weight and personnel limits for boats as well as consider the effect that the equal or unequal distribution of supplies will have on those limits.

Other: When appropriate, you need to conduct swim tests and capsize drills before paddling flatwater, and rapid drills before paddling white water. For river trips, you should obtain recent information on river volumes and flow rates. As you probably well know, white water generally demands extra attention from leaders. You may need to scout rapids in advance, pair paddlers so that weak teams are not created, and stagger teams through the rapids, sending one craft at a time so that stronger teams may assist weaker ones and congestion doesn't lead to collisions. In addition, you may need to make room in eddies for other crafts that may want to enter.

High water combined with low bridges or narrow chutes can be very dangerous. As flow rate increases, so does the power of the river, making rescues more difficult and errors more serious.

Strainers or sieves permit water to flow through, but can trap crafts and people. The enormous water pressure can destroy a trapped craft and drown a trapped person. Hydraulic reversals (or souse holes) can happen when water drops over an object (usually a linear object like a weir, low-water dam, or rock ledge) and may depress the river surface. Top water can flow upstream into the hole in order to fill in the hole, thus forming a kind of vertical washing machine or whirlpool effect that is extremely difficult to get free from.

You must brief participants on what to do if they are thrown into white water: float with head up, look ahead for dangers, place feet downstream and in front to push off from obstacles, hold onto craft for extra flotation and visibility, remain upstream of the craft to avoid being pinned against obstacles, and do not stand up against the current; instead, wait for an eddy opportunity, kick toward shore, and abandon the craft if necessary. You should explain how to handle white-water and moving-water dangers on the river, such as fallen trees, strainers, hydraulics, undercut rocks, pinning, standing waves, eddies, chutes, waterfalls, weirs, dams, and shallows.

On-Road and Off-Road Bicycling

Activity: As a bicycling leader, you need to know on-road and off-road travel techniques, such as how to move in traffic; high-speed turning; single-file spacing; gear selection and cadence

Requiring participants to wear helmets is just one issue a bicycling leader needs to consider.

for inclines; weight distribution; front and back brake use; when to walk; jumping, hopping, ascending, descending, and falling safely; and communication techniques, such as those used to warn of traffic or obstacles. You need to know equipment selection for the conditions you may encounter, for example, ensuring that bikes are tough enough for the terrain and have adequate gear ratios, effective brakes, rearview mirrors, antenna flags, and ample water bottles, and that participants are wearing protective eyewear, footwear, brightly colored clothing, gloves, and helmets; correct equipment use, for example, how to fit the bike to the body size and how to pack, equally load, and suspend panniers; equipment care, including daily inspections of tire pressures, brake- or gear-cable tension, power-train lubrication, bottom brackets, pedals, headsets, wheel trueness, and bolts; equipment repair, including how to fix flats, adjust cables, true wheels, repack bearings, and pack a repair kit containing spare inner tubes and tires, pump, patch kit, screwdrivers, pliers, and adjustable wrench; and equipment maintenance, including regularly replacing tires, chains, and cables.

Risk management: Common injuries in bicycling are generally associated with collisions and repeated use or stress injuries. You should be aware of participants with a history of weak knees or hips and back or neck problems. You should demonstrate specific warm-up stretches for different body regions (e.g., arms, legs, neck, shoulders, hips, knees). You should understand the unique concerns that come with all possible weather and terrain interactions, for example, the dangers of combining rain with oil on the road or loose gravel with curves. You need to clearly plan for supervising individual cyclists, including how to maintain direct visual contact and how to make verbal contact to warn of dangers, as well as for generally managing the group, such as placing a support vehicle behind the group to warn approaching motorists on long road trips, in heavy traffic, or with beginners. You may need to inspect bicycle paths for environmental dangers, such as uneven surfaces, sharp objects, traffic volume, and shoulder width, and for safe places to rest, including places other than the shoulder. As always, you should assess clients' physical fitness and psychological readiness to bike.

Environmental: For bicycling, unique considerations may be necessary for site protection, such as avoiding startling animals or destroying vegetation by locking up and skidding the back wheel or by detouring, and for conflict resolution, such as warning others of approaching cyclists, sharing trails with other users, dismounting if necessary, and pedaling under control and at a reasonable speed. You need to be aware of local rules for the road, including traffic laws and regulations, or for the area, such as "no bikes in legally designated wilderness." You need to properly dispose of used rubber tires and conservatively apply chain lubricants, taking care not to spill any oil into the environment.

Other: If you bicycle in reduced-visibility conditions, such as at night, dawn, or dusk or in fog, wear reflective clothing and use bike lights and reflectors; be sure to carry spare batteries and bulbs. If you bicycle deep in backcountry areas, where breakdowns could mean a long walk for help, carry sufficient survival gear.

Cross-Country Skiing

Activity: As a skiing leader, you should know uphill and downhill techniques, such as diagonal striding, single and double poling, skating, telemarking, snowplowing, step turns, parallel turns, sidestepping, angular traverses, and herringbones; techniques for falling down and getting up with a heavy pack on; and waxing techniques for expected conditions as well as mohair or nonwax alternatives. You need to know equipment selection for the cold weather and steep terrain you may encounter, such as how to select durable skis, poles, boots, snow shovels, and saws; correct equipment use, including how to fit skis and poles to body height and weight; equipment care, including how to fix loose bindings, broken ski tips, broken poles, and scraped bases; and equipment repair, including carrying a kit containing wire, pliers, screwdrivers, and duct tape as well as spare ski tips, pole shafts, pole baskets, and bindings. You should understand the importance of using layered clothing when people frequently shift between standing still and heavily exercising and how to correctly fit hand- and footwear to prevent frostbite. You also should know how to build emergency shelters, such as snow caves, igloos, or quinzees; how to improvise evacuation sleds from skis and packs; and how to obtain adequate fluids by having enough fuel to melt snow.

Risk management: Common skiing injuries include joint dislocations or major bone fractures. You should be aware of participants with a history of previous fractures or separated shoulders, elbows, or fingers. You should know warm-up

◄ EFFECTIVE OUTDOOR LEADERS ►

► Understand the differences among as well as the interactions of generic-, meta-, and specific-skill competencies for the activities they lead, placing these competencies in the context of the geographic areas, client populations, client goals, and environmental conditions where they lead.

► Are specifically competent for the activities they lead.

stretches for the various body regions (e.g., arms, neck, shoulders, hips, knees). You should understand the unique concerns that come with all possible weather and terrain interactions, such as the dangers of deep snow-deposition zones created by high winds on leeward slopes. You should clearly plan for specifically supervising individual skiers, such as carefully observing descent areas where falls can result in greater injury, as well as for generally managing the group, especially in avalanche country. You may need to inspect skiing sites for environmental dangers, such as potential avalanches and uneven surfaces. You should also assess clients' physical fitness and psychological readiness to ski.

Environmental: For skiing, unique considerations may exist for waste disposal when the soil is covered by snow. You need to be aware of local rules, such as not disturbing the trap lines or caches of others.

Other: When crossing frozen lakes or rivers, you must check that the ice is thick enough to support the group's weight by spreading out, keeping ropes and long poles handy, not resting in large groups, and avoiding stream areas near the water's edge. You also need to watch for "bottomless" snow in the spring, in which water percolating beneath the snow has melted away the lower layers, creating a deep cavity beneath a thin surface.

Avalanches can be a major concern while cross-country skiing. You need to know how to identify potential avalanches by noting leeward hillsides, overhanging cornices, slope inclines and orientations, lack of ground cover, recent storms, sustained winds, new snowfall, temperature fluctuations, snow layering, and crystal types. You need to know how to avoid avalanche dangers by avoiding old slide paths, sticking to ridgetops and valley bottoms, crossing suspect slopes one person at a time, loosening equipment, zipping up clothing layers, not kicking deep steps, traveling quickly, and resting only in protected locations. In anticipated avalanche locations, you need to carry and know how to use transceivers or beacon locators; these must be turned on and worn on the body of each person. You also need to carry an appropriate number of snow shovels and a selection of avalanche probes—or ski poles and tent poles that can be converted to probes. Finally, you need to be competent at responding to avalanches. For example, you should designate an observer to watch for further danger, mark last-known locations of victims, hastily search downhill from those locations, probe suspect areas, locate beacons, and dig up all hits.

SUMMARY

Technical skills are a foundation for conducting adventure experiences. Although these skills are not always the product in adventure programming, they are always the process through which people learn. Without technical skills, you will be ineffective. To be an effective outdoor leader, you must possess a variety of generic competencies that apply to all adventure experiences, no matter what activity you lead. You also must have expertise in the specific competencies that are unique to the activity.

The specific competencies for the activities tend to be technical skills but also include unique risk-management and environmental skills. Competence in these specific areas alone is not sufficient for outdoor leadership but is definitely an important start. Refer often to the descriptions of appropriate practices for each of the eight activities we have described in this chapter as you strive to become an effective leader.

QUESTIONS TO THINK ABOUT

1. Select four activities that you are willing to lead and compare your competencies to the specific competencies listed for each activity.

2. Are you ready to lead these four adventure activities? Why or why not?

3. What will you do to make up for any shortcomings you have in these four areas?

4. You are going to lead a challenge (ropes) course on one day for a group of 13- to 14-year-old students and the next day for a group of 50-year-old corporate clients. How will your concerns for specific technical-skill competency differ between the two days?

5. Select one of the eight activity areas in which you feel knowledgeable. Give examples of how each of the following four factors—geographic areas, client populations, client goals, and environmental conditions—would change the specific technical-skill competencies listed in this section.

REFERENCES

Garvey, D., Leemon, D., Williamson, J., & Zimmerman, B. (1999). *Manual of program accreditation standards for adventure programs.* Boulder, CO: Association for Experiential Education.

Gass, M. (Ed.). (1998). *Administrative practices of accredited adventure programs.* Needham Heights, MA: Simon & Schuster.

Priest, S., & Dixon, T. (1990). *Safety practices in adventure programming.* Boulder, CO: Association for Experiential Education.

Williamson, J., & Gass, M.A. (1993). *Manual of program accreditation standards for adventure programs.* Boulder, CO: Association for Experiential Education.

ADDITIONAL RESOURCES

Backcountry Travel and Orienteering

Birkett, B. (2002). *The hillwalker's manual.* Milnthorpe, England: Cicerone Press.

Boga, S. (1997). *Orienteering.* Mechanicsburg, PA: Stackpole Books.

Burns, B. (1999). *Wilderness navigation: Finding your way using map, compass, altimeter, & GPS.* Seattle: Mountaineers Books.

Curtis, R. (1998). *The backpacker's field manual: A comprehensive guide to mastering backcountry skills.* New York: Three Rivers Press.

Drury, J., & Bonney, B. (1992). *The backcountry classroom: Lesson plans for teaching in the wilderness.* Guilford, CT: Globe Pequot Press.

Hall, A. (1998). *Backpacking: Woman's guide.* Blacklick, OH: McGraw-Hill.

Hall, A. (2001). *The essential backpacker: A complete guide for the foot traveler.* Blacklick, OH: McGraw-Hill.

Harvey, M. (1999). *The National Outdoor Leadership School's wilderness guide: The classic handbook.* New York: Fireside.

Hawkins, P. (2004). *Map and compass.* Milnthorpe, England: Cicerone Press.

Kjellstrom, B. (1994). *Be expert with map and compass: The complete orienteering handbook.* New York: Hungry Minds.

Langmuir, E. (1995). *Mountaincraft and Leadership: A handbook for Mountaincraft and Leadership: A Handbook for Mountaineers and Hillwalking Leaders in the British Isles.* Manchester, England: British Mountaineering Council.

Letham, L. (2003). *The GPS made easy* (4th ed.). Seattle: Mountaineers Books.

Long, J., & Hodgson, M. (2000). *The complete hiker.* Blacklick, OH: McGraw-Hill.

McNeil, C. (1997). *Teaching orienteering.* Champaign, IL: Human Kinetics.

Randall, G. (1999). *The Outward Bound map and compass handbook.* New York: The Lyons Press.

Seaborg, E., & Dudley, E. (1994). *Hiking and backpacking: Outdoor pursuits series.* Champaign, IL: Human Kinetics.

Townsend, C. (1997). *The backpacker's handbook.* Blacklick, OH: McGraw-Hill.

Van Tilburg, C. (1999). *Canyoneering.* Seattle: Mountaineers Books.

Rock Climbing

British Mountaineering Council. (2000). *Climbing wall manual.* Manchester, England: British Mountaineering Council.

British Mountaineering Council. (2000). *The handbook of climbing.* Manchester, England: British Mountaineering Council.

Cox, S.M., & Fulsaas, K. (Eds.). (2003). *Mountaineering: Freedom of the hills* (7th ed.). Seattle: Mountaineers Books.

Cinnamon, J. (2000). *The complete climber's handbook.* Blacklick, OH: McGraw-Hill.

Fasulo, D. (1997). *How to self-rescue.* Guilford, CT: Falcon Press.

Fyffe, A., & Peter, I. (1990). *The handbook of climbing.* London: Pelham Books.

Lewis, S.P. (1998). *How to rock climb: Top roping.* Seattle: Mountaineers Books.

Lewis, S.P. (2000). *Climbing from gym to crag: Building skills for real rock.* Seattle: Mountaineers Books.

Long, J. (1993). *How to rock climb: Climbing anchors.* Guilford, CT: Falcon Press.

Long, J. (1994). *Gym climb.* Guilford, CT: Falcon Press.

Long, J. (2000). *How to rock climb: Sport climbing.* Guilford, CT: Falcon Press.

Long, J. (2003). *How to rock climb* (4th ed.). Guilford, CT: Falcon Press.

Long, J., & Luebben, C. (1997). *How to climb: Advanced rock climbing.* (4th ed.). Guilford, CT: Falcon Press.

Loughman, M. (1981). *Learning to rock climb.* San Francisco: Sierra Club Books.

Luebben, C. (2004). *Rock climbing: Mastering basic skills.* Seattle: Mountaineers Books.

Pesterfield, H. (2002). *Traditional rock climbing: Surviving the learning years.* Wilderness Press.

Watts, P. (1996). *Rock climbing: Outdoor pursuits series.* Champaign, IL: Human Kinetics.

Mountaineering

Adby, T., & Johnston, S. (2003). *The hillwalker's guide to mountaineering.* Milnthorpe, England: Cicerone Press.

Chouinard, Y. (1978). *Climbing ice.* San Francisco: Sierra Club Books.

Cox, S.M., & Fulsaas, K. (Eds.). (2003). *Mountaineering: Freedom of the hills* (7th ed.). Seattle: Mountaineers Books.

Cinnamon, J. (2000). *The complete climber's handbook.* Blacklick, OH: McGraw-Hill.

Fyffe, A., & Peter, I. (1990). *The handbook of climbing.* London: Pelham Books.

Gadd, W., & Chayer, R. (2003). *Ice and mixed climbing: Modern technique.* Seattle: Mountaineers Books.

Lowe, J. (1996). *Ice world: Techniques and experiences of modern ice climbing.* Seattle: Mountaineers Books.

Luebben, C. (1999). *How to ice climb!* Guilford, CT: Falcon Press.

March, B. (1997). *Snow and ice techniques* (3rd ed.). Milnthorpe, England: Cicerone Press.

MacInnes, H. (1998). *International mountain rescue handbook.* London: Constable.

Powers, P. (1993). *NOLS wilderness mountaineering.* Mechanicsburg, PA: Stackpole Books.

Strong, M., & Doerry, E. (2001). *Glaciers: The art of travel and the science of rescue.* Guilford, CT: Falcon Press.

Tyson, A., & Clelland, M. (2000). *The illustrated guide to glacier travel and crevasse rescue.* Carbondale, CO: Climbing Magazine.

Wilkerson, J. (2001). *Medicine for mountaineering and other wilderness activities* (5th ed.). Seattle: Mountaineers Books.

Challenge (Ropes) Courses and Group Initiatives

Association of Challenge Course Technology. (2004). *ACCT Challenge Course standards.* Martin, MI: ACCT. Available: www.acctinfo.org.

European Ropes Course Association. (2004). Available: www.erca.cc/cms.php?id=1.

Outdoor Recreation Centre—Victoria Inc. (2004). Available: www.orc.org.au.

Panicucci, J. (2003). *Adventure curriculum for physical education: High school.* Beverly, MA: Project Adventure.

Professional Ropes Course Association. (2004). Available: www.prcainfo.org.

Rohnke, K. (1989). *Cowstails and cobras II: A guide to games, initiatives, ropes courses, and adventure curriculum.* Beverly, MA: Project Adventure.

Rohnke, K. (1989). *Silver bullets.* Dubuque, IA: Kendall/Hunt.

Rohnke, K., & Butler, S. (1996). *Quicksilver.* Dubuque, IA: Kendall/Hunt.

Rohnke, K., & Grout, J. (1998). *Backpocket adventure.* Needham Heights, MA: Pearson Custom Publishing.

Rohnke, K., Tait, K., Wall, J., & Rogers, D. (1997). *The complete ropes course manual* (2nd ed.). Dubuque, IA: Kendall/Hunt.

Ropes Course Developments. (2004). Available: www.rcd.co.uk.

Snow, H. (1997). *Indoor/outdoor team building games for trainers: Powerful activities from the world of adventure-based team building and ropes courses.* New York: McGraw-Hill.

Webster, S.E. (1989). *Ropes course safety manual: An instructor's guide to initiatives, and low and high elements.* Beverly, MA: Project Adventure.

Caving or Spelunking

Halliday, W.R. (1973). *American caves and caving.* Scranton, PA: Harper & Row.

McClurg, D. (1998). *Adventure of caving.* Huntsville, AL: National Speleological Society.

Rea, T.G. (1992). *Caving basics: A comprehensive guide for beginning cavers* (3rd ed.). Huntsville, AL: National Speleological Society.

Smith, B., & Padgett, A. (1997). *On rope: North American vertical rope techniques.* Huntsville, AL: National Speleological Society.

Swart, P. (2002). *Caving: The essential guide to equipment and techniques.* Mechanicsburg, PA: Stackpole Books.

Flatwater, White-Water, and Sea Kayaking Paddling

Bennett, J. (1999). *The essential whitewater kayaker.* Camden, ME: International Marine/Ragged Mountain Press.

Burch, D. (1999). *Fundamentals of kayak navigation* (3rd ed.). Guilford, CT: Globe Pequot Press.

Ferrero, F. (2002). *Canoe and kayak handbook.* (3rd ed.). West Bridgford, England: British Canoe Union.

Ferrero, F. (2002). *White water safety and rescue.* West Bridgford, England: British Canoe Union.

Gullion, L. (1987). *Canoeing and kayaking: Instruction manual.* Newington, VA: American Canoeing Association.

Gullion, L. (1987). *Canoeing: Women's guide.* Camden, ME: Ragged Mountain Press.

Gullion, L. (1994). *Canoeing.* Champaign, IL: Human Kinetics.

Hanson, J. (1998). *Complete sea kayaking.* Camden, ME: Ragged Mountain Press.

Jacobsen, C. (2000). *Canoeing and camping: Beyond the basics* (2nd ed.). Guilford, CT: Globe Pequot Press.

Johnson, S. (2001). *The complete sea kayaker's handbook.* Camden, ME: International Marine/Ragged Mountain Press.

Kalner, B., & Jackson, D. (1990). *The basic essentials of kayaking whitewater.* (2nd ed.). Guilford, CT: Globe Pequot Press.

Rounds, J. (2003). *Basic canoeing.* Mechanicsburg, PA: Stackpole Books.

Schman, R., & Shiner, J. (2001). *Sea kayak rescue: The definitive guide to modern reentry and recovery techniques.* Guilford, CT: Globe Pequot Press.

Seidman, D., Cleveland, P., & Erikson, C. (2000). *The essential wilderness navigator* (2nd ed.). Camden, ME: International Marine/Ragged Mountain Press.

Seidman, D. (2000). *The essential sea kayaker: A complete guide for the open water paddler* (2nd ed.). Camden, ME: International Marine/Ragged Mountain Press.

Washburne, X. (1998). *The coastal kayaker's manual: The complete guide to skills, gear, and sea sense* (3rd ed.). Guilford, CT: Globe Pequot Press.

Wyatt, X. (2001). *The basic essentials of sea kayaking* (2nd ed.). Guilford, CT: Globe Pequot Press.

On-Road and Off-Road Bicycling

Australian Cycling Federation. (2004). Available: www.cycling.org.au.

Bicycling Magazine. (1994). *Mountain biking skills.* Emmaus, PA: Rodale Press.

Bridge, R. (1979). *Bike touring: The Sierra Club guide.* San Francisco: Sierra Club Books.

Canadian Cycling Association. (2004). 702-2197 Riverside Drive, Ottawa, Ontario K1H 7X3 Available: www.canadian-cycling.com.

Coello, D. (1985). *The mountain bike manual.* Salt Lake City: Dream Garden Press.

Cuthbertson, T. (1979). *Anybody's bike book.* Berkeley, CA: Ten Speed Press.

Davis, D., & Carter, D. (1994). *Mountain biking.* Champaign, IL: Human Kinetics.

International Mountain Bike Association. (2004). IMBA, PO Box 7578, Boulder, CO 80306 Available: www.imba.com.

Lovett, R.A. (2001). *The essential tourist cyclist: A complete guide for the bicycle traveller.* Camden, ME: Ragged Mountain Press.

Mountain Bike & Bicycling Magazines. (1996). *Mountain Bike Magazine's complete guide to mountain biking skills.* Emmaus, PA: Rodale Press.

New Zealand Mountain Biking Association. (2004). Available: www.mountainbike.co.nz/nzmba.

Strassman, M. (1989). *Mountain biking.* Guilford, CT: Globe Pequot Press.

USA Cycling. (2004). Available: www.usacycling.org.

van der Plas, R. (1988). *The mountain bike book.* New York: Velo Press.

Zinn, L. (2001). *Zinn and the art of mountain bike maintenance.* New York: Velo Press.

Cross-Country Skiing and Winter Camping

Cliff, P. (1987). *Ski mountaineering.* Guilford, CT: Globe Pequot Press.

Ferguson, S., & LaChapelle, E. (2003). *The ABCs of avalanche safety.* Seattle: Mountaineers Books.

Gillette, N. (1979). *Cross country skiing.* Seattle: Mountaineers Books.

Gorman, S. (1999). *Winter camping* (2nd ed.). Boston: Appalachian Mountain Books.

Lanza, M. (2003). *Winter hiking and camping: Managing cold for comfort and safety (Backpacker).* Seattle: Mountaineers Books.

McClung, D., & Schaerer, P. (1993). *The avalanche handbook.* Seattle: Mountaineers Books.

Moynier, J. (2001). *Basic essentials of cross country skiing.* Guilford, CT: Globe Pequot Press.

O'Bannon, M., & Clelland, M. (2001). *Allen and Mike's really cool backcountry ski book.* Guilford, CT: Globe Pequot Press.

Rutstrum, C., & Kouba, L. (2000). *Paradise below zero: The classic guide to winter camping.* Minneapolis, MN: University of Minnesota Press.

Townsend, C. (1994). *Wilderness skiing and winter camping.* New York: McGraw-Hill.

Vivies, J. (1998). *Backcountry skier: Your complete guide to ski touring.* Champaign, IL: Human Kinetics.

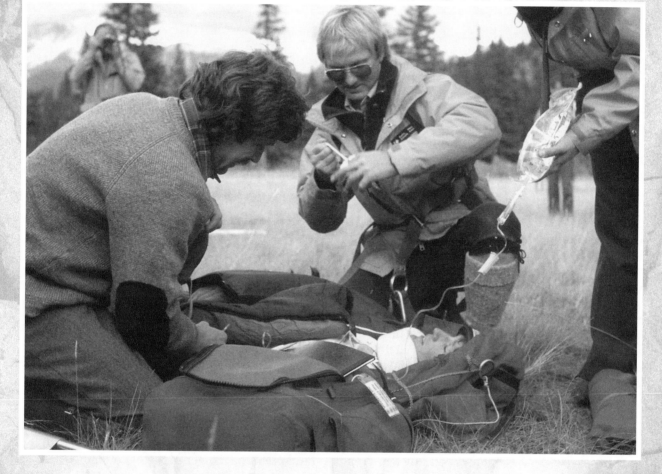

Safety and Risk Management

The weather had badly deteriorated. The wind blew horizontal sleet, and the group members were drenched and shivering in their cotton T-shirts as the leader pressed on. Base camp was only a few miles away, and although they were tired, the group believed it could make it home. Besides, the camp would have a hot meal waiting and dry sleeping bags to finally rest in. As the skies darkened, the group members fumbled around in the only day-pack they had brought with them (on what was to have been a short hike) and found a single flashlight. As the dim beam barely projected their way down the narrow trail, the members stumbled their way back to camp, often falling. Not until several members had been treated for hypothermia did the leader notice that one member was missing: still lost on the trail!

Raffan (1984) described the outdoor leader's role in risk management as similar to a slot machine. Every time you take a group outdoors, the slot machine spins and brings up a "lemon" or two in the form of dangers. When a sufficient number of dangers have accumulated—and if you have not attended to these lemons—the "jackpot" pays off with an accident. How many potential lemons can you count in the opening scenario?

Note the title of this chapter can be misleading. Nothing is ever truly safe. Crossing the street, driving a car, climbing the stairs, or getting out of bed in the morning all possess both positive benefit and negative consequence. Risk is an integral part of being human, and we usually assess the risk level in an experience before deciding to become involved in it. In many ways, this is one of the main goals of risk management: to make an informed and educated decision on choosing to participate in an experience given its potential positive and negative consequences.

Risk management in outdoor experiences is quite similar to other industries (e.g., airline and automobile industries). Regardless of the field, professionals design experiences and products based on a variety of factors, one of which is the level of actual risk. In fact, adventure experiences are typically less risky than most commonly accepted human activities. For example, Cooley (2000) found wilderness adventure experiences were about 18 times less likely to result in injury than high school football practices or cheerleading and were half as responsible for deaths resulting from motor vehicle accidents for 15- to 19-year-olds.

These comparative statistics don't mean that outdoor leaders should be complacent about leading experiences. Deaths in the outdoors, particularly with youth, tragically affect many people. It is critical that outdoor leaders minimize risks and the injuries resulting from the hazards associated with these risks while maintaining the value of the adventure experience (Ajango, 2000).

As in chapter 6, "Technical Skills," our purpose in this chapter is not to provide a detailed how-to for risk management in every skill area in adventure programming. What we provide are some of the guidelines you as an outdoor leader should follow regarding risk-management procedures and protocols of adventure experiences. Please note, however, that these competencies change according to geographic areas, client populations, client goals, and environmental conditions.

RISK IS ESSENTIAL

The activities conducted by adventure programs involve risk and danger, but so does everything else in life! Danger gives rise to risk, and risk is one of the critical components that make adventure programming popular and successful. State-of-the-art risk-management procedures reduce real dangers, yet keep desired perceived risks high. Balancing the amount of risk in an adventure experience is a central paradox for outdoor leaders: with too much risk the danger of the experience becomes unreasonable; with too little risk the adventure program fails to remain adventurous.

The general public considers adventure activities to be dangerous even when appropriate safety procedures are used, typically because they have difficulty differentiating between real and perceived risk. Yet, research has repeatedly shown that adventure activities are significantly safer than most other traditional physical activities. For example, a 20-year safety study conducted by Project Adventure (Furlong, Jillings, LaRhette, & Ryan, 1995, p. 5) reported an injury rate of 4.33 accidents/million hours of Project Adventure activities, which consisted primarily of initiatives and challenge-course experiences.

This report also showed that Project Adventure programs had injury rates comparable to the fields of real estate, insurance, and finance (which experience a rate of 4.5 accidents/million hours of activity) and lower rates than educational services (8 accidents/million hours) or amusement and recreational services (19 accidents/million hours). The U.S. National Safety Council reported that traditional physical education classes experience an accident rate nearly twice that of Project Adventure activities (9.6 accidents/million hours) (Project Adventure, 1987). Higgins (1981) found that Outward Bound courses had a lower ratio of disabling injuries (37.5 accidents/million hours) than either automobile driving or college football (more than 60 accidents/million hours). Meyer (1979) also reported that fewer deaths are due to outdoor adventures than to automobile accidents. These comparisons show that adventure experiences are actually less risky than traditional life activities as well as less risky than the average person perceives them to be.

Even with these statistics, however, as outdoor leaders, we still have difficulty convincing the public of adventure program safety and defending the job of deliberately placing people at risk. Thus, you need a clear understanding of the benefits of risk taking in order to determine whether these benefits outweigh the risks. In the unlikely event of an accident, a court of law may come to the same conclusion, based on accurate statistics, with the aid of your professional experience, knowledge, or understanding. Juries, however, may base their decisions on misguided, yet common beliefs, which are often developed by the infrequent, but spectacular, publicity outdoor accidents generate. Such incorrect perceptions are also common in other industries. For example, the general public fears flying after learning of a few air crashes—despite the fact that many more people regularly die in home or traffic accidents!

ACCIDENT THEORY

As we stated in chapter 2, **risk management** refers to all those procedures put into effect to reduce the possibility of accidents. We can define **accidents** as unexpected occurrences that result in an injury or loss. Such losses can be **physical,** such as suffering fractures or death; **social,** such as being embarrassed in front of peers; **emotional,** such as fearing a situation; or **financial,** such as not getting your money's worth or losing equipment.

A first step to implementing risk management is understanding how accidents happen in adventure programming and how they can be minimized (Ajango, 2000). Probably the first and most common model explaining factors associated with accidents is the one created by Jed Williamson and Dan Meyer in the late 1970s (Meyer, 1979). While other models examine the interacting influences that increase the chance for accidents (Brackenreg, 1999; Haddock, 1993; Hale, 1983), the Williamson and Meyer model states that most accidents occur when three types of dangers combine to create an **accident potential:** (1) unsafe conditions created by the outdoor environment, (2) unsafe acts performed by participating clients, and (3) unsafe errors made by instructors (see figure 7.1).

The idea of this accident model is that as each of these sources grows in strength or quantity, its "circle" moves closer to the middle, creating a greater overlap and greater potential for an accident. Obviously one incident could result in an accident, but generally, it is the interaction of all three sources that leads to accidents.

Let's take transportation for an example. Potentially hazardous environmental conditions include an icy road at night with a 15-passenger van fully loaded with a roof rack and a trailer full of equipment. Unsafe acts by clients could be not wearing safety belts and distracting the driver. Judgment errors include driving with minimal van-driving experience, driving too fast, and driving while tired. You can see how each of these factors could create an accident, but the chance of an accident decreases if these factors are reduced or eliminated.

Sources of hazards obviously extend beyond this example. In an effort to identify potential hazards in each of the three categories, Schimelpfenig (1996) compiled the following list:

Unsafe Conditions From Environmental Hazards (Environmental Dangers)

altitude	falling trees	strainers in rivers
animals	flash floods	
animal traps	illness	uneven terrain
avalanche	insects	underfoot
cold water	lightning	vehicles
currents, tides, and surf	loose rock & boulders	visibility
deadfall	moving water	weather
deep snowpack	rockfall	wet or slippery terrain
deep water	stoves and fires	

Figure 7.1 The accident equation (modified from Williamson and Meyer).

Adapted from Williamson and Meyer, 1978.

Unsafe Acts by Clients (Client Dangers)

cooking

exceeding ability

failure to follow instructions

fall

fall on rock

fall on snow games

haste, rushing to meet schedule

inadequate supervision

inappropriate role modeling

ineffective instruction

lost

planning errors

poor hygiene

poor position

poor technique

spilled hot water

stove fire

technical system fails

unsafe speed (fast or slow)

overconfidence

peer pressure

poor communication

poor conflict-resolution skills

poor decision or indecision

poor expedition

poor leadership

seeking novelty out of routine

summit fever

tunnel vision

unaware of hazard

unrealistic schedule

unresolved discrepancies

Unsafe Errors by Leaders (Leadership Dangers)

assumption

attitude toward risk

carelessness

denial

distraction

erratic behavior under stress

fatigue

flexibility or resistance to change

goals or preconceptions

complacency

health status

ineffective supervision

lack of experience

lack of knowledge or skill

lack of respect for hazard

Danger Classification

Since the interaction of client, instructor, and environmental factors increases the chance of an accident, let's take a closer look at two aspects of danger. As we mentioned in chapter 2, we can classify **dangers** as either perils or hazards. **Perils** are the sources of injury or the causes of loss, such as a lightning bolt. **Hazards** are conditions that accentuate the chance of an injury or loss, such as a storm. The presence of a danger, whether a peril or a hazard, gives rise to risk. For example, the risk of electrocution (accident) is created by two dangers: a storm (hazard) that increases the probability of lightning bolts (peril) striking a person.

By differentiating between perils and hazards and being able to identify them in the field, you may reduce the chance of your group encountering undesirable risks. Consider mountaineering involving glacier travel to a summit. Crevasses (cracks in the moving ice) and seracs (towers of ice moving along with a glacier) are obvious perils to the mountaineer. You may avoid them by skirting the section of the glacier where they are most prevalent. But when the route goes through such an area, sometimes you simply cannot avoid these perils. Instead, you should deal with them by also considering the hazards associated with these perils.

Temperature, which of course varies with the time of day, sunlight, and other climactic conditions, is a hazard that increases the likelihood that the ice will move as it warms up. Experienced mountaineers attempt to avoid the risk of injury from the peril of moving ice by choosing the correct time to encounter that peril—when hazards are minimal. One common practice begins a summit bid in the dark around midnight, using headlamps, reaches summit for dawn, and returns to camp by noon—all before temperatures rise. In the heat of the afternoon, the mountaineers may then relax, eat lunch, and watch the glacier come apart far above them, knowing that they have reduced the likelihood of danger by addressing perils and hazards. In summary, perils will always

be present in adventures. Knowing how and when these perils are impacted by hazards can help you reduce the cumulative dangers on either side of the accident equation.

Danger Analysis

You've seen how to deal with the specific perils and hazards of ice melting, but how do you generalize danger analysis from this one situation to other situations? Use the following 10-step procedure of **danger analysis** as one way to reduce the chance of an accident or to minimize an accident's consequences to acceptable and recoverable levels (Priest & Baillie, 1987).

The 10 steps, summarized in figure 7.2, include the following:

1. **Plan ahead.** Admit it can happen to you! If you have the attitude that it can't happen to you, you are fooling no one but yourself. It is highly likely that sometime in your career as an outdoor leader an accident will occur despite your best efforts. The matter is not *if*, but *when!* The key is being ready to deal with almost anything that can happen and keeping a humble attitude as a leader. Preplanning is essential! Know what you will do for each potential accident *before* it happens.

2. **Search for dangerous situations and conditions.** Maintain a continuous search for dangers,

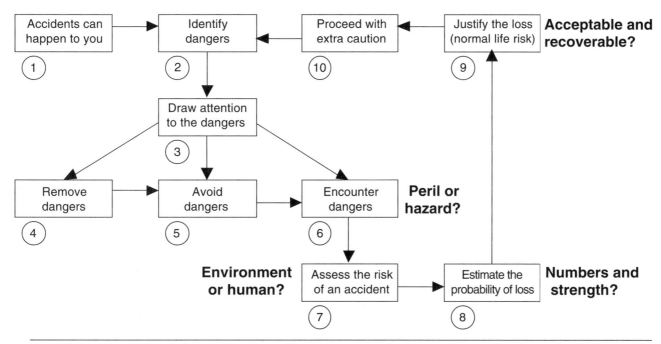

Figure 7.2 Ten steps for analyzing dangers in adventure programs.

Adapted, by permission, from S. Priest and R. Baillie, 1987, "Justifying the risk to others: The real razor's edge," *Journal of Experiential Education 10*(1), 16-22.

remaining vigilant in any situation. Imagine what might happen at any time. This is often accomplished by keeping an eye open for all suspect circumstances and by always being prepared to ask, "What if?" When many dangers are present, be extra alert and cautious. Always take the appropriate actions for dealing with dangers.

3. **Point out potential dangers.** Once you identify dangers, draw clients' and coleaders' attention to them. For example, making clients aware of wet and slippery ground, an environmental danger, and of horseplay, a human danger, can reduce the likelihood of an accident because recognizing the potential for an accident is often enough to change behavior.

4. **When appropriate, remove elements that contribute to dangerous situations.** If drawing attention to danger doesn't deal with it, then remove the danger as long as removal does not increase the risk of it or another danger occurring. For example, removing a loose rock, an environmental danger that could fall on a person or be tripped over on the trail, makes good sense, provided you don't throw the rock carelessly and hit someone else or start an avalanche of many loose rocks. You may at times view the actions of one client, a human danger, as creating a potential accident risk to the other members in the group and choose to remove that individual, provided such removal does not place the group or person in any further danger.

5. **Avoid dangerous situations.** If you cannot remove the danger, then attempt to avoid it. This may mean rerouting an expedition, adapting the old route; changing an activity altogether, adopting a new plan; or calling a halt and canceling the program, aborting the activity. Note that the purposeful encountering of dangers is occasionally necessary and sometimes desirable. Beyond the obvious dangers adventurers seek to challenge themselves, some potential dangers have benefits. For example, the human danger of horseplay is sometimes good: consider water fights helping cool people on a hot day during a river trip. The environmental danger of hot sun helps warm people on a cold winter's day. These potential dangers can be positive, provided you encounter them while avoiding combining them with other dangers. For the examples noted, you should have personal flotation devices and sunscreen available to prevent dangers from combining.

6. **Identify and classify dangerous situations.** If you cannot remove or avoid the danger, then you will have to encounter it and therefore must classify the danger as either a peril (source of

loss) or hazard (condition that influences probability of loss). This classification should enable you to encounter the peril when hazards are at a minimum, thereby reducing the risk of an accident (e.g., traveling in areas of ice fall when the sun does not increase the likelihood of falling ice). This information can often be obtained by addressing the question: "What hazards (the sun in this case) will accentuate the perils (ice fall) that may be encountered?"

7. **Assess risk and reclassify danger.** If you cannot avoid the danger, then assess the risk of a potential accident. Reclassify the danger as either environmental, based in the surroundings, or human, based in the group. This reclassification enables you to recognize if the potential for overlap of the two forces and the risk of an accident exist. Ask yourself the question: "What is the likelihood that the human and environmental dangers will overlap and combine to create an accident potential?"

8. **Estimate potential losses.** If a combination of human and environmental dangers appears imminent, then estimate the probability of loss. Answer these two questions: "How much overlap can be expected? How probable is it that this combination will lead to an accident?" Recall that more numerous and stronger dangers lead to a greater likelihood of an accident. Therefore, you should assess the number and strength of dangers in the human and environmental categories. Absolute numbers do not necessarily mean that accidents are proportionately likely; it's simply that the more dangers are present, the more combinations among these dangers are possible, and the more likely it is that an accident will occur. In some cases, the dangers will not combine at all. For example, lost tent poles and excellent summer weather indicate minute probabilities. In other cases, the dangers cannot help but combine. For example, a novice skier and a rocky hillside may be an almost certain accident waiting to happen.

9. **Minimize losses.** If the risk of an accident appears probable but still not an absolute certainty, then choose a course of action for which the outcome of an accident is more likely to be both acceptable and recoverable. If leaving behind climbing protection and ropes will enable your group to back off of a life-threatening mountain storm, lose the gear or go back to recover it at another time or accept the fact that the losses are merely financial and not more costly.

10. **Make appropriate adjustments.** If loss from an accident occurs (e.g., an injury), make

preplanned, appropriate adjustments (e.g., evacuation). Before you can adjust, you have to do that preplanning! Decide on your countermeasures before an accident occurs. Once you employ these measures, proceed with appropriate caution, continuing to search for new dangers that may arise and combine with the already existing dangers.

Please note that outdoor leaders need not use all 10 steps to reduce risk—the most preventive trip may be the one that discovers in planning ahead that the adventure experience isn't appropriate given the environmental conditions and the client populations. Following these steps does not guarantee that a severe accident will not happen. But knowing how to quickly and accurately use the preceding steps (without having to lug this book along on the trip!) is one method of creating safe experiences.

Inhibiting Factors

Figure 7.3 shows six factors that can inhibit your ability to analyze danger. These inhibiting factors include new or unexpected situations, inappropriate attribution, relaxed concentration, smelling the barn, risky shift phenomenon, and poor or unsound judgment.

1. **New or unexpected situations** mean that you are less likely to competently address situations because you have no or limited experience in dealing with them. Examples include using routes for the first time; changes in group dynamics through regrouping, new leadership structures, or new supervision; leading activities for the first time; and conducting experiences in new course sites or areas (Meyer, 1979). One reason for the value of presite investigation, which is scouting new areas before bringing in participants under similar conditions, is that it decreases the chance of surprise as well as informs you of potential teachable moments.

2. **Inappropriate attribution** refers to the tendency of some outdoor leaders to take credit for good happenings, internally attributing them to personal skills, and when things go wrong, to externally attribute problems by blaming bad weather or faulty equipment. Leaders do this often because of exaggerated pride or the need to please others, look good, or live up to real or perceived expectations. But beware! Such behavior can prevent you from taking the first step in danger analysis; you may simply refuse to consider that an accident could happen to you!

3. **Relaxed concentration** involves outdoor leaders who drop their guard because of fatigue,

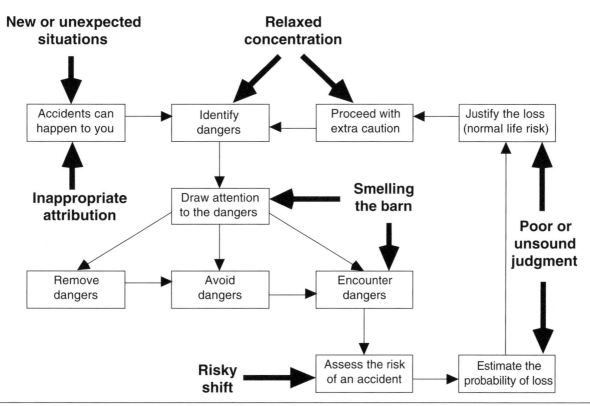

Figure 7.3 Six inhibiting factors at work in danger analysis.

distraction, or carelessness. With your guard down, you are less likely to constantly look for dangers and will not be sufficiently alert to proceed with caution. We have often seen this behavior in parties descending from mountain peaks; in groups egressing from a river run when, once the paddling is over, sprained ankles on the carry-out may be more common than at the carry-in when people are more attentive to dangers; and on ropes courses or during group initiatives when some spotters relax their concentration once someone reaches the top of a wall or climbs down a ladder. Familiarity with dangers can also breed contempt as you become desensitized to ongoing dangers. For example, spending all day skiing in potential avalanche conditions without evidence of any slides may incorrectly and positively reinforce the belief that these slopes are not really that dangerous.

4. **Smelling the barn** and rushing to get back is a behavior shared by some horses and outdoor leaders. When you attempt to maintain a time schedule—despite falling behind—or see that the end is in sight, you may forget to point out dangers to others or may encounter dangers that you might normally put more energy into removing or avoiding. Given the peer pressure to get home to a warm shower or a hot meal, you must resist the temptation to allow these goals to become more important than appropriate practices.

5. **The risky shift phenomenon** addresses the idea that when people are in groups, particularly when they are inexperienced, they tend to make riskier decisions than when they are by themselves (Meier, 1981). This can sometimes be seen in novice group members when they are reluctant to express their fears, especially when courage is socially desirable, and they go along, participating in higher risks than they would on their own. This shift can also be seen when some members abandon personal responsibility, choosing to transfer the responsibility for taking risks to other group members or to you—generally without informing you. When this occurs, you might find the group making decisions it really does not want to pursue: no one wishes to appear cowardly and many are reluctant to admit being in too far over their heads! For reasons such as these, you may underestimate the group's level of risk. You must be aware of this possibility, especially when peer pressure among group members is present.

6. **Poor or unsound judgment** always inhibits many aspects of outdoor leadership, and risk management is no exception. One common source of poor or unsound judgment is when you misperceive what is occurring (for example, overlooking the true risks associated with an adventure experience in your eagerness to have students experience a wonderful learning activity). Such misperception inhibits your ability to estimate the probability of loss and to justify that loss in terms of everyday living. Since good judgment is so vital to risk management in adventure programming, you should continually evaluate your judgment (see "Questions to Think About"). As you evaluate yourself, you should also consider the open and honest critiques of colleagues. Although you may find the process threatening, your judgment can be greatly improved by gathering with small groups of leaders to truthfully discuss close calls, near misses, epic journeys, and embarrassing mistakes without fear of retribution from adventure program administrators.

RISK-MANAGEMENT COUNTERMEASURES

Despite a thorough danger analysis and attention to factors that inhibit your judgment, accidents can and do happen! In the event of such an accident, a sequence of countermeasures may prove useful as you attempt to minimize the impact of the accident. We can divide risk-management countermeasures into three categories based on the timeliness of their application: proactive or primary, active or secondary, and reactive or tertiary.

1. **Proactive or primary procedures** refer to all practices carried out before a program to avoid an accident or at least to prepare a suitable response to one. Examples of preventive or proactive measures include equipment inspection, risk-management briefing, skills training for staff, completion of legal paperwork, review of potential environmental and human dangers, and close inspection of client health forms.

2. **Active or secondary procedures** refer to all actions taken during the program, usually as a result of an accident. Examples of responsive or active measures include first aid, search and rescue, evacuation, on-site recording of injury data, and response procedures.

3. **Reactive or tertiary procedures** refer to all actions that occur after an accident. Examples of follow-up or reactive measures include informing next of kin and the sponsoring organization, completing final accident documentation, contacting

legal counsel or insurance representatives, and scheduling visits to the injured client at home or in the hospital.

Program Risk Management

Program risk management includes those policies, practices, and procedures used by your program to appropriately address potential personal injury and financial losses, to protect your adventure organization from the economic cost of being sued, and to reduce your organization's financial obligation if a suit is successful. These concepts are probably best implemented into practice by a program's **risk-management plan.** As identified by van der Smissen (1990), the specific objectives of a risk-management plan are "(a) preventing damage or destruction to property, (b) reducing or preventing possible injury or suffering to individuals, (c) instituting loss reduction and prevention programs, and (d) shifting through transfer mechanisms those losses which cannot be controlled by other means" (p. 3).

Risk-management plans should be developed by adventure programs with specific guidelines to suit their particular situations. Such plans may contain a philosophy statement, program goals, learning objectives, the methods to evaluate behavioral outcomes, and an explanation of how these all relate to risk management (Brown, 1998; Priest & Dixon, 1990). Program policies and guidelines should be written in a staff manual. The guidelines should apply to both staff and clients alike, or if reason exists for different risk-management policies, these should be noted.

In turn, as an outdoor leader, you need to be familiar with the policy and procedures in the staff manual. Then you should help clients understand that they are responsible for contributing to their own well-being as well as to the well-being of others taking part in the activities. Make sure clients understand that because of the nature of adventure activities, everyone has a role to play in maintaining appropriate behavior and practices through awareness and a responsible attitude. Such an attitude includes being cautious about risk and developing the ability to ask questions when in doubt. Awareness includes looking out for one another's best interests and for client, instructor, and environmental dangers. Sharing the concepts of accident theory (see figure 7.1 on page 94) can help empower clients in their own responsibility for risk management.

Constructing risk-management plans can be daunting at first, yet it is a critical step in offering quality programming. Based on the principles of the Association for Experiential Education's Accreditation Program (Garvey, Leemon, Williamson, & Zimmerman, 1999), the following 20 items are offered as a beginning checklist to assist the construction of a risk-management system.

1) Do you have a written set of policies and procedures?

Program documents communicate to staff expected practices and standards for activities posing risk to the health and well-being of participants and staff. This documentation can be written by and for the program or adapted from other reputable sources. It may include policies or protocols governing practices or guidelines on accepted practices as curriculum or test materials.

All staff should be familiar with and have access to written risk-management procedures and associated guidelines. These procedures are part of a larger risk-management plan. Policies and procedures should apply to staff and students alike.

2) Do you have a written emergency action plan for all activities?

An emergency action plan includes but may not be limited to the following:

a) A brief, educational rationale for the activity

b) Site-specific considerations (e.g., details on the activity times and places, proposed itinerary with anticipated dangers and expected countermeasures)

c) Search-and-rescue protocols (e.g., route map with escape plans)

d) Location and contact information for emergency medical facilities

e) Emergency care and first aid protocols (e.g., summary of health information for all group members)

f) Notification protocols (e.g., rescue groups, next of kin, contact person, local authorities, media person)

g) Relevant associated information (e.g., budget of expenses, list of personal and group supplies and equipment)

Staff members should take copies of the plan on the trip as well as leave copies with responsible people who will take the necessary action and contact authorities in case the group is overdue.

Also see chapter 9, "Trip Planning," and chapter 10, "Legal Liability," for further information.

3) Does your program have a designated and functioning Risk-Management Committee?

The committee is a representative mix of individuals, including outside advisers, that meets regularly to review all facets of the program. Part of its responsibility can be to collect, analyze, interpret, and act on incident and accident data reported by staff. Such a committee is often composed of program staff, technical experts, and outside advisers. The committee's purpose is usually to regularly review and endorse the program's risk-management practices and to collect, analyze, interpret, and act on their findings.

4) Does your program prepare an annual risk-management report? Does your program make changes based on this report's findings (e.g., trends, training needs, close calls as predictors)?

The program has a system for managing risk and for sanctioning practices. Incident data are collected, analyzed, acted upon, and reported. For the benefit of the field, your program should submit this data to a professional organization (e.g., Association for Experiential Education, your governing agency) on an annual basis.

5) Does your program engage in periodic internal and external risk-management reviews?

In risk-management reviews, all aspects of a program are looked at and a written review is presented for discussion with program personnel and supervisors. A final written report is prepared with recommendations, suggestions, and observations on any necessary or suggested program changes aimed at increasing quality and managing risk. One copy of each internal and external risk-management report should be made available to your insurance company. For more information on how a program review is conducted, see the "Program Review" section later in this chapter.

6) Does your program send all staff and participants through an appropriate admissions and medical screening?

Programs should require information from staff and participants to facilitate medical screening so informed decisions can be made regarding their ability to participate. No participants or staff should be allowed to participate in activities likely to harm themselves or others because of a medical or physical condition. Medical forms should clearly state that failure to accurately complete all portions of a form could result in or compound an injury.

7) Does your program ensure that additional participant health concerns, specific to each activity, are addressed if necessary?

Certain health concerns make participants more susceptible to injury or sometimes contraindicate actual preventive efforts. For example, when going into a stream, lake, or ocean during or following a run as part of an adventure experience or to cool off, staff should consider changes in heart rate, especially with older participants and those with identified heart conditions. If a participant is on psychotropic medications, the interaction with certain environmental conditions (e.g., the body's heat regulation systems to appropriately adapt to heat or cold conditions) should be understood.

8) Does your organization inform participants of the nature and goals of the program, its requirements for physical conditioning and behavior, and the consequences of not meeting these requirements? Does your program inform participants of potential risks and have participants acknowledged and assumed the program's inherent risks?

Programs should take steps (written and verbal) to disclose the nature of the program, its physical requirements, and the rules of behavior. These conditions must be accepted, agreed upon, and followed.

Programs should have participants (and parents or guardians of minors) sign a document or documents stating that risks associated with the program are identified, acknowledged, and assumed. These risks include inherent risks (e.g., perils, hazards) that can reasonably be anticipated. Such provisions may appear in an assumption and acknowledgment of risk form or may be part of a release or waiver.

9) If your organization allocates legal liability for injuries or losses suffered by participants, does it do so with appropriate agreements?

Programs should allocate responsibility and liability for injuries or losses related to program activities. Note government statutes or regulations may limit the use of these documents. Releases and related documents should be reviewed and approved by the program's legal counsel for enforceability and consistency with the program's philosophy and intent. (For example, the program may choose not to be released for its negligence.)

Specific examples of these agreements include but may not be limited to the following:

    a) Release of liability

    b) Acknowledgment and assumption of risk

    c) Waiver of claims

    d) Agreement to indemnify or defend

    e) Other documents

10) Does your program maintain adequate insurance coverage?

Whether a commercial policy or self-insurance, your coverage must adequately meet local, state, and national requirements where your programs operate. Policies should be reviewed periodically by a knowledgeable insurance professional.

Specific examples of policies include but may not be limited to the following:

    a) General liability

    b) Auto

    c) Marine

    d) Property damage

    e) Workers' compensation

    f) Professional liability

    g) Medical professional liability

    h) Sexual abuse liability

    i) Staff medical coverage

11) Does your program have a policy forbidding the use of alcohol or drugs (other than those prescribed by a physician and used accordingly) during program activities by participants as well as by employees on duty?

There is no defense against the use of alcohol or other inappropriate drugs during adventure experiences.

12) Does your program have an emergency medical protocol and an established system for calling emergency medical services in the event of a serious or life-threatening injury or illness? Is your staff skilled in carrying out these protocols?

Programs need established and reliable emergency medical protocols (including a communications plan with phone numbers for area emergency medical services) in the event of an accident requiring outside expertise for medical care. Working methods for communication in the particular programming area must be used. These may include satellite phones, two-way radios, cellular telephones, CB radios, or locator devices. In remote areas where these methods are impractical or where a program chooses not to use them, participants should know, understand, and agree to this condition.

13) Does your program have a search-and-rescue protocol and an established system for calling rescue services, if needed, in the event of a lost or missing person? Is your staff skilled in carrying out this protocol?

Programs need to have procedures to prevent participants from becoming lost or separated from the group and a plan of supervision for when separation happens. Staff and participants must know what to do if participants become lost or separated from the group. Staff members must know what to do if they need a level of rescue that is greater than can be reasonably expected of the program. Staff must know how to implement the program's protocol for such search-and-rescue procedures, which may include air- or watercraft assistance.

Elements of this protocol may include but may not be limited to the following:

    a) Instructions to participants to prevent becoming lost or separated

    b) Instructions to participants for what to do if lost or separated

    c) Procedures for organizing a search (including locations, methods, boundaries, rendezvous times, communications)

    d) Documentation

    e) Criteria for determining the need for outside assistance

    f) Procedures for hasty, general, and fine searches

    g) Procedures for what to do if the entire group is delayed or behind schedule

Note that in case of an injury, the group has a response plan that includes but may not be limited to the following:

    a) Sending out a competent party for assistance while a competent group stays with the injured

    b) Treating the injured person with appropriate first aid or emergency care

    c) Evacuating the injured person

For example, with solo learning experiences, emergency notification and periodic check-in systems are in place. Each solo participant has signaling capabilities (e.g., a whistle) for emergency notification and knows the proper protocols for their use. Other participants are also aware as to how they should respond if the notification system is put into use. For longer solos, a visual check-in system should be established and followed according to predetermined procedures. While risk-management measures help prevent participants from becoming separated or lost, the program also has a contingency plan in place.

14) Does your program have an evacuation protocol? Is your staff skilled in carrying out this protocol?

Program staff needs to know how to evacuate under any circumstance the activity demands or how to have others evacuate a victim in need of higher care. Appropriate equipment for evacuation should also be available. This protocol may include procedures for initiating and carrying out evacuations by fixed-wing aircraft, helicopters, and watercraft as appropriate.

For example, if aircraft are used for evacuations, staff members are trained in selecting appropriate landing zones by keeping the following in mind:

   a) Appropriate size
   b) Limited slope level
   c) Potential obstacles
   d) Limiting loose debris
   e) Wind direction
   f) Approach and departure areas
   g) Loading and unloading procedures
   h) Maintaining minimum distance between personnel and the landing zone
   i) Maintaining appropriate supervision during evacuation

15) Does your program have a notification protocol to be used for an emergency or accident?

Program staff must understand the notification protocol for an emergency or accident (e.g., communications with family, officials, news media).

16) Are appropriate and adequate emergency and rescue equipment available at the site of each activity?

Adequate emergency care and rescue equipment should be present for all activities. Emergency care kits and emergency equipment should be available

and routinely checked. Repair kits and appropriate spare items should be available for trips beyond the facility or roadhead. Clothing, shelter, and food should be provided for activities conducted beyond the facility or roadhead. In the event of an injury, illness, or extreme change in weather, staff should have the skills and equipment to survive until they can return to the roadhead.

17) Are participants properly prepared for emergencies and taught emergency skills and procedures for each activity?

All participants should be informed of the risk-management and emergency procedures for each activity (e.g., evacuation routes, contingency plans, available rescue, and medical support). Emergency skills and procedures are taught to participants so they understand what to do in the event of an emergency.

18) Does your program use the staff–participant ratios designated for each activity?

There are accepted staff–participant ratios for all activities based on the activity, the participant profile, and the environment. Programs should provide appropriate staff–participant ratios depending on the designated ratios and other relevant factors.

19) Does your program make reasonable efforts to conform to all applicable government laws and regulations?

Specific examples of these laws and regulations include but are not limited to the following:

   a) The Americans with Disabilities Act
   b) Hazard communication and exposure control for blood-borne pathogens
   c) Laws and guidelines pertaining to facilities (e.g., programs complying with appropriate codes and regulations governing their facilities)

20) Do appropriate forms and documents exist and are they properly located?

Paperwork is a necessary part of risk management. Appropriate forms and documents should exist and you should complete and review them when appropriate, as understanding this information is part of risk management. Specific examples of these forms and documents include but may not be limited to the following:

   1. Administration
      • Mission, goals, and objectives
      • Marketing materials

- Licenses and permits
- Participant information
- Admission and orientation
- Releases and related documents
- Personnel policy and procedures
- Personnel files (for resumes, applications, documentation of staff training, copies of certifications, evaluations, and so on)
- Equipment purchase and maintenance logs
- Equal Opportunity Employment statement (appropriately posted)

2. Health
   - Staff medical history and data
   - Participant medical history and data
   - Release for emergency medical treatment
   - First aid supplies list

3. Emergency
   - Accident or incident report form
   - Program notification protocol
   - Media protocol
   - Search and rescue form, evacuation report form, missing person report form
   - Staff notification of next of kin information
   - Participant notification of next of kin information

Accident Response

In response to an accident, you may wish to follow the sequence of procedures outlined in figure 7.4. The sequence is based on eight steps of response: A = airway, B = breathing, C = circulation, D = diagnostic exam, E = evacuation plan, F = find resources, G = get assistance, and H = helicopter usage (Priest & Dixon, 1990).

The most qualified person is usually the individual in charge of the accident response. This person is usually the senior outdoor leader unless her expertise is required elsewhere. Response measures are generally organized and issued by this person. Given enough people, you should organize the group into three subgroups: a trauma team, which gives first aid and comforts and stabilizes the victim; a travel team, which alerts and directs outside resources to assist with the injured person;

and a transport team, which plans rescue and evacuation procedures as well as helps the individual in charge monitor the well-being of rescuers.

The trauma team is generally composed of the group members most competent at first aid. The team is responsible for the following:

1. Assessing the situation, asking, "Who is injured? What are the dangers present?"
2. Approaching the victim, asking, "Will the person giving first aid be placed in any danger by doing so?"
3. Neutralizing any dangers present by drawing attention to, avoiding, or removing them if possible.

Of course, this team is also responsible for providing first aid, checking and readjusting or removing obstructions to breathing and rechecking for further obstruction (A = Airway); performing artificial respiration if necessary and continuing to monitor (B = Breathing); and taking pulse and performing cardiopulmonary resuscitation (CPR) if necessary (C = Circulation). They also conduct a thorough exam (D = Diagnostic), looking for signs of consciousness, arterial bleeding, spinal damage, shock, fractures, and minor bleeding. In short, they treat the victim as necessary, double-check the examinations, and continue to monitor and record vital signs until a person with a higher level of medical training arrives. Even after help arrives, trauma team members may continue working with the injured parties to ensure medical continuity.

The transport team is responsible for evacuating and transporting the victim (E = Evacuation plan). One part of the team locates and marks the evacuation route in coordination with the travel team, while the other part collects needed materials for evacuation and transport (F = Find resources). When appropriate, they are responsible for the arduous task of littering the victim to the pickup zone or out of the wilderness. This task requires great physical effort and constant vigilance for the victim's well-being. Some members of the trauma team may double as transport team members when possible. The transport team also oversees the well-being of the entire group, ensuring that no more participants become victims. In this way, they are also the "temperature" team, responsible for continually monitoring the rescue team's body temperatures, lighting a stove to boil water for hypothermia, or locating a source of cool water for hyperthermia.

If outside assistance is needed, a separate travel team may be sent ahead of the transport and trauma teams. The travel team alerts and directs

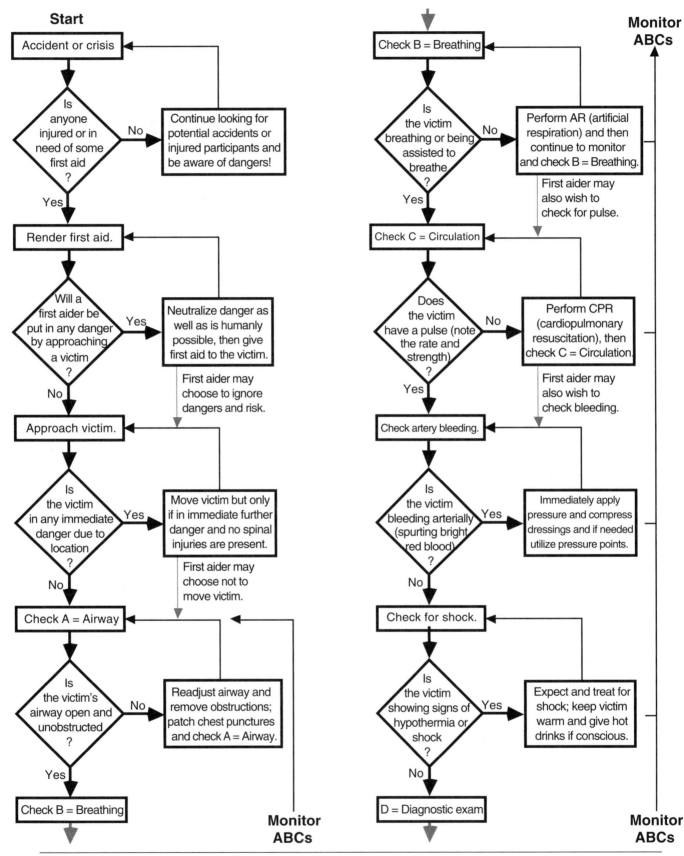

Start

Accident or crisis

Is anyone injured or in need of some first aid? — No → Continue looking for potential accidents or injured participants and be aware of dangers!

Yes ↓

Render first aid.

Will a first aider be put in any danger by approaching a victim? — Yes → Neutralize danger as well as is humanly possible, then give first aid to the victim.

First aider may choose to ignore dangers and risk.

No ↓

Approach victim.

Is the victim in any immediate danger due to location? — Yes → Move victim but only if in immediate further danger and no spinal injuries are present.

First aider may choose not to move victim.

No ↓

Check A = Airway

Is the victim's airway open and unobstructed? — No → Readjust airway and remove obstructions; patch chest punctures and check A = Airway.

Yes ↓

Check B = Breathing

Monitor ABCs

Check B = Breathing

Is the victim breathing or being assisted to breathe? — No → Perform AR (artificial respiration) and then continue to monitor and check B = Breathing.

First aider may also wish to check for pulse.

Yes ↓

Check C = Circulation

Does the victim have a pulse (note the rate and strength)? — No → Perform CPR (cardiopulmonary resuscitation), then check C = Circulation.

First aider may also wish to check bleeding.

Yes ↓

Check artery bleeding.

Is the victim bleeding arterially (spurting bright red blood)? — Yes → Immediately apply pressure and compress dressings and if needed utilize pressure points.

No ↓

Check for shock.

Is the victim showing signs of hypothermia or shock? — Yes → Expect and treat for shock; keep victim warm and give hot drinks if conscious.

No ↓

D = Diagnostic exam

Monitor ABCs

Figure 7.4 Part 1 of an accident response sequence (Priest and Dixon, 1990).

104

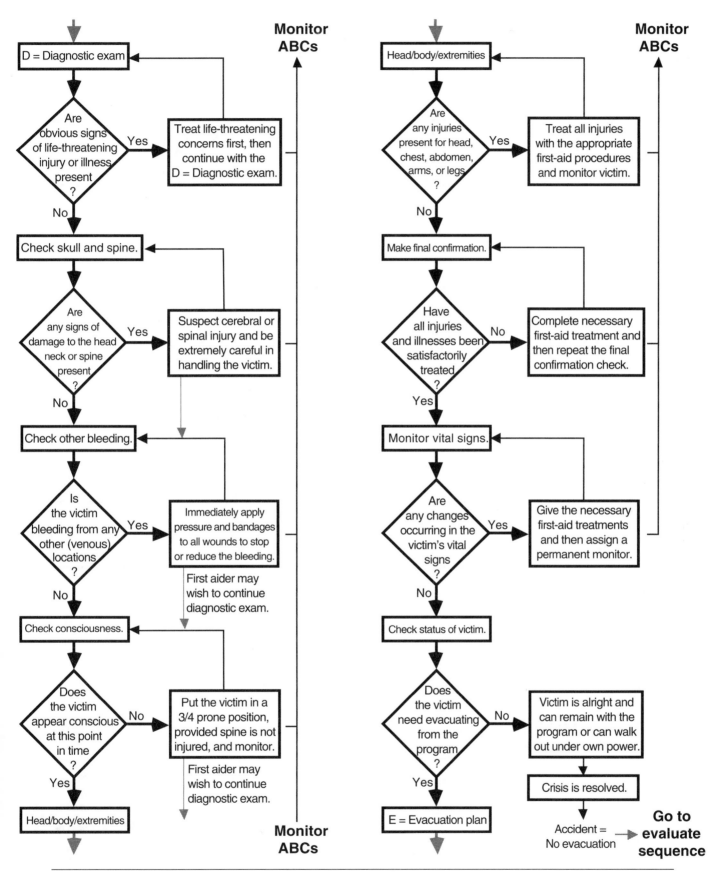

Figure 7.4 *(continued)*

105

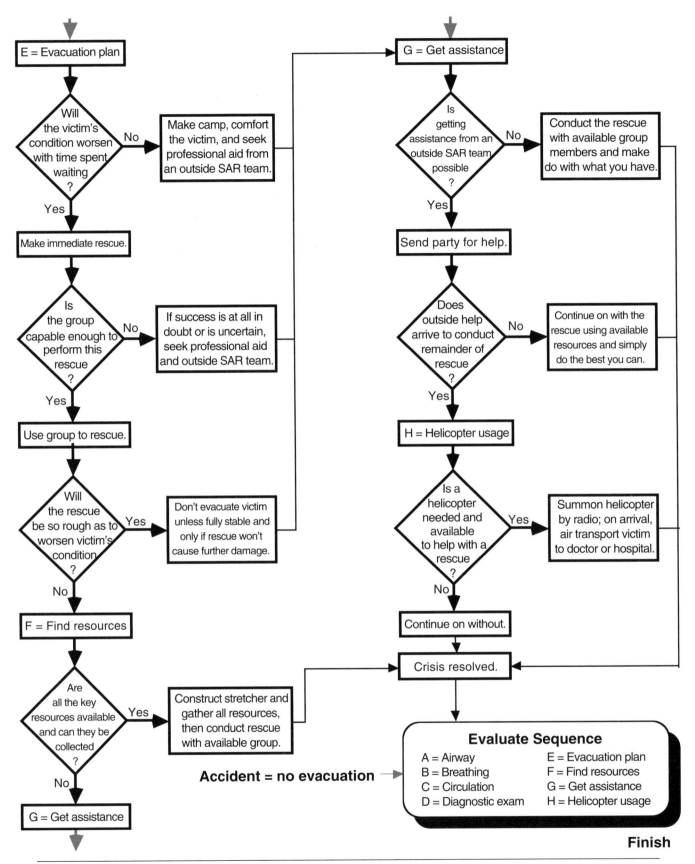

Figure 7.4 *(continued)*

Failure to anticipate and manage dangers appropriately can lead to the need for professional rescue services.

outside resources, such as additional medical help, evacuation assistance, external program personnel, or police. This may include activating a cell phone, radio, location device, signal flare or fire, or the like. If necessary, this team must summon an ambulance for evacuation from the accident site (G = Get assistance) or air support for emergency medical evacuation (H = Helicopter usage). If such messages need to be sent out on foot, written directions and a copy or summary of the accident report should accompany the party going for help. The party should consist of at least three, preferably four, people in case one of them gets injured along the way. The party going for help should be self-sufficient, stay together, and carry its own accident response kit. The party may also be responsible for flagging the return route for the search-and-rescue (SAR) team and marking it on a grid-referenced map, maintaining an evacuation report, and attaching a copy of the victim's health form to the victim. This form will greatly assist the SAR team and hospital medical staff. In addition, the SAR team providing the assistance will need to know the extent of the victim's injuries and the intended evacuation route. When possible, returning with the SAR team can be extremely helpful.

In the event of an obvious fatality, do not disturb the victim's body—only a coroner or appointed police officer may give permission to remove it.

Accurately flag and document the accident scene, disturbing it as little as possible. If a camera is available, take photographs and measure any relevant distances, depths, or heights. Triple-check all measurements. Contact the program's director and the local authorities (in that order), avoiding all speculation or admission of guilt and sticking to facts.

Do not discuss the matter with any media, referring all inquiries to an appointed program representative. This person will deal with public relations, including notifying relations and making follow-up telephone calls. This representative will also deal with the hospital or the morgue, prepare a press statement (the victim's name is not released until the next of kin has been contacted), and screen subsequent inquiries and requests for interviews.

Program Review

A program review is an accepted method of checking your program's risk-management procedures. Your risk-management committee can perform this review as a proactive measure before an accident or incident or as a reactive measure after an accident or incident. In general, the review provides a fresh perspective on risk-management procedures through involving external peers who can provide truthful and critical advice in a supportive manner. In best-case scenarios, programs utilize two risk-management reviews: an internal review from ongoing efforts of the in-house risk-management committee and an external review by periodic involvement of outside experts or peers. The purpose of these two reviews is to compare the program's performance with known state-of-the-art procedures and common practices (Wade & Fischesser, 1988).

With external program reviews, a small team of people generally observe the program in action as well as behind the scenes. During observation, they collect data concerning the risk-management practices and procedures. From these data they infer whether the program under review is operating within risk-management guidelines and what changes might improve the overall risk management, using their experience from working with a variety of other programs. They discuss their findings with the appropriate program representative or the risk-management committee, providing a chance for feedback. At the end of the visit, the committee generally presents a written report, summarizing the review methods, results, and recommendations for changes.

Some of the areas an external review committee may examine include the following: philosophy statement, program goals, learning objectives, methods to evaluate behavioral outcomes of clients, educational rationale for the activities, communication, transportation, specific details related to the activity times and places, proper emergency contact numbers, a proposed itinerary with anticipated risks and expected countermeasures, a route map with escape plans, a summary of health information, a budget of expenses, a list of participants and their supplies and equipment, a schedule for monitoring and maintaining equipment, litigation protection, liability or accident insurance, health care procedures, accommodation, food service, procedures for screening participants, activity and site selection, staff recruitment, staff supervision, staff training, staff assessment, staff–participant ratios, and the involvement and influence of the risk-management committee—with particular emphasis on the collection, analysis, interpretation, and action taken

---

General questions:

Does the program clearly state philosophy, mission, goals, and objectives in a safety policy?

Does that safety policy explain the educational rationale behind putting people at risk?

Do program guidelines apply to staff and participants alike or is there a double standard?

Are safety-management (risk-management) plans completed for each adventure activity or field trip?

Do safety plans contain the necessary safety preparations and emergency information?

Are accident response kits (including first aid) present for all activities?

Are emergency communication links available between field staff and outside medical help?

Are drivers licensed to drive vehicles and transport passengers? Are safety practices, such as wearing seat belts and equipment checks, in place for transportation?

Is equipment tested and used properly in the program? Is a repair and maintenance log kept?

Are participants warned and informed of the risks and responsibilities before acceptance?

Are the preenrollment orientation materials that are sent to participants accurate and adequate?

Do participants complete an appropriate health and medical disclosure and waiver or release?

Is staff competent in dealing with participants' typical and emergency health care?

Is there a policy statement concerning the use and abuse of alcohol and other drugs?

Are participants screened for health concerns or do they take a preenrollment medical exam?

Are activities or sites chosen for their potential to meet program goals and educational objectives?

Are participants properly briefed and progressively prepared for each activity or site?

Are participants coerced or forced into a particular activity or are they challenged by choice?

Does the program conform to local resource regulations and correctly apply for permits?

Do on-site and local facilities adhere to the public laws governing their proper operation?

Does the program have a safety committee? Does the committee monitor and sanction safety practices?

Are accident and incident data reported, compiled, analyzed, and acted on accordingly?

Do job contracts include procedures for training and assessing staff? Are these procedures followed?

Do acceptable staff–participant ratios exist for all adventure activities and sites?

Does staff have the necessary combination of hard, soft, and metaskills required for the job?

Is staff competent at the adventure activities and familiar with the sites?

Does staff anticipate dangers and is it capable of responding to accidents while in the field?

Is staff appropriately qualified or certified in first aid and CPR? Is such evidence on file?

Are written procedures in place to handle the most commonly expected emergency accidents?

Before the review:

Establish guidelines for conducting the review: who, what, where, when, why, and how much?

Appoint a representative liaison between program or safety committee and safety review team.

Select mutually acceptable team members, avoiding controversial or political appointments.

Examine existing paperwork, including brochures, reports, reviews, forms, manuals, lists, and logs.

Inform staff of pending interviews and encourage open and honest sharing of concerns.

During the review:

At the introduction, discuss particular areas of safety concern and attempt to ease anxieties. Maintain professional, diplomatic, and tactful behavior throughout the safety review.

Explain the review to participants who ask; avoid public criticisms that may be overheard. The review may be patterned after items on this list or may include other items. The team may wish to divide responsibilities for observing, interviewing, reading, and so on.

After the review:

Orally present findings in private to key program personnel, including safety committee.

Make sure statements about safety practices or observed behaviors are factual, not opinionated.

Exchange new ideas for improving safety through two-way communication with feedback.

Balance negatives with positives; permit personnel to explain any disagreements.

Submit a written report giving requirements, recommendations, suggestions, and observations.

Figure 7.5   Questions to ask for a risk-management review.

regarding incident and accident data (see also figure 7.5; Priest & Dixon, 1990).

Note that programs with a long-standing history of established risk-management procedures and reviews may wish to pursue external recognition through program accreditation by a governing body or association, such as the Association for Experiential Education.

RISK-MANAGEMENT SKILLS

Last, but not least, you should possess risk-management skills for the particular adventure experiences you provide. Examples of risk-man-

agement skills include weather interpretation, body temperature regulation, navigation, survival, water, first aid, and search, rescue, and evacuation.

Weather Interpretation

You should be able to predict weather using current weather reports, perhaps obtained by radio; your observations of present conditions, including clouds, precipitation, wind speed, wind direction, and temperature; and your familiarity with local prevailing patterns. You should be capable of dealing with weather extremes, especially thunderstorms and lightning.

Body Temperature Regulation

You should be able to prevent and treat hypothermia and hyperthermia, know the five pathways of body heat loss and their regulation, understand human thermophysiology (areas of high heat loss and metabolic effects of food, water, drugs, alcohol, and tobacco), and recognize the signs and symptoms of hypothermia (stumbling, incoherence, disorientation, shivering, or no shivering at all) and hyperthermia (headaches, nausea, cramps, excessive sweating, or no sweating at all). Most importantly, however, you must be capable of treating the different phases of hypothermia and hyperthermia by learning proper techniques of decreasing or increasing heat loss and of warming or cooling victims as necessary.

Navigation

You should be able to navigate in the worst possible terrain that you expect to encounter during an adventure activity. This means being able to read a map; measure distances by scale ratios and from bar scales; cite grid references; convert among map north, true north, magnetic north, or grid north directions; and interpret colors, symbols, contour lines, and other features. You should be able to use a compass, take map and field bearings, convert between these by accounting for local magnetic declination, travel on that specific bearing, and triangulate locations with two or more bearings. You should be able to orienteer, aim off, use attack points and steer marks, avoid obstacles, use back bearing, and use catching features and handrails. You should be able to find routes, note checkpoints along the path of travel, contour between points of similar elevation without losing altitude, and choose routes based on expected terrain, vegetation, party strength, or other variables.

Survival

You should be able to cope under the worst possible conditions in the event that you are lost, injured, or caught out in the elements during an adventure activity—with or without your group. You need to have a positive survival attitude, including being able to admit you're lost, keep from panicking, comfort others, and prioritize needs: protection from the elements, finding sustenance, and being found. You should be able to light fires with wet wood or insufficient fuel supply; build shelters that are easily constructed, insulated, and ventilated; signal for help using international distress and ground-to-air signals; and secure nonpoisonous food and water in various settings. Remember the food rule: If unsure, don't consume!

Lifesaving and First Aid

You should be able to swim and provide CPR and first aid. These are areas in which certification is welcomed and accepted by most adventure programs. You may wish to obtain your certification as a lifeguard and as a wilderness first aid provider or emergency medical technician (EMT). For white-water activities, we recommend that you seek training for risk-management and rescue techniques in moving water. Knowing how to use an accident response kit, including a first aid kit, is critical for every outdoor leader.

◄ EFFECTIVE OUTDOOR LEADERS ►

► Understand accident theory and danger classification.

► Are able to execute the 10-step procedure for danger analysis and avoid the six inhibiting factors that may interfere with the procedure.

► Are able to execute an accident response procedure, completing the appropriate documentation.

► Establish preventive measures, such as trip planning, risk-management policies, review committees, and program accreditation.

► Are skilled in weather interpretation, temperature regulation; navigation; survival; swimming and lifesaving; first aid; search, rescue, and evacuation; and, if insufficiently skilled in any of these areas, seek training.

Search, Rescue, and Evacuation

You should be able to locate missing people and remove them from danger. You should be capable of designating an appropriate base camp; interviewing people to obtain pertinent information and recording their comments; performing quick searches of high probability areas such as nearby trails, rivers, or meadows; performing coarse or fine searches walking side by side through a square grid; constructing stretchers appropriate for carrying, lowering, or raising; and lastly, recognizing when the search is beyond your resources and deciding to seek a professional SAR team.

SUMMARY

When leading outdoor trips, the safety of participants cannot be guaranteed. However, when guided by risk-management practices and systems, the relative danger of adventure experiences is no greater and sometimes less than that of other life experiences. Key to minimizing risks is understanding sources of perils and hazards in outdoor experience, understanding how risks interact with one another, reducing inappropriate risks with professional practices, and having risk-management systems to reduce accident potential while still maintaining a sense of adventure in the experience.

Adventure programs deliberately employ risk to bring about change. Balancing risks and safety is a central paradox for outdoor leaders: with too much risk the danger of the experience becomes unreasonable, and with too much safety the adventure program fails to remain adventurous. The general public considers adventure activities to be dangerous even when you use appropriate procedures, typically because they have difficulty differentiating between real and perceived risk in these experiences. Statistics show that adventure experiences are actually less risky than traditional physical activities as well as less risky than the average person perceives.

Safety management, or the practices used for protecting participants, is part of risk management, or the procedures for protecting the adventure organization from liability. Risk management includes the policies, practices, and procedures a program uses to address potential personal injury and financial loss, protecting the adventure organization from the economic cost of being sued

and reducing its financial obligation if a suit is successful. Specific objectives of a risk-management plan are preventing damage or destruction to property, reducing or preventing possible injury or suffering to individuals, instituting loss reduction and loss prevention programs, and using transfer mechanisms to shift those losses which cannot be controlled by other means. Four approaches program staff can take for controlling risks are elimination, transfer, retention, and reduction.

Risk management aims at client protection and is a collection of procedures designed to reduce accidents that might cause injury or other loss. Most accidents occur when client, instructor, and environmental dangers combine and interact at the same moment to create an accident potential, or the probability of risk. This is the likelihood that an accident will happen, not the certainty that one will occur. More dangers generally lead to a greater risk of an accident. We can classify dangers as perils or hazards. Perils are the sources of loss, and hazards are the conditions that accentuate the chance of a loss. When you must encounter perils, you should do so when hazards are low and therefore the least influential.

A 10-step procedure for danger analysis may help you reduce the risk of an accident or minimize the accident's impact. First, admit it can happen to you! Second, continually seek to identify dangers. Third, draw attention to identified dangers. Fourth, remove the dangers. Fifth, avoid the dangers. Sixth, encounter dangers in a controlled manner if you cannot remove or avoid them. Seventh, assess the risk of an accident from combining dangers. Eighth, estimate the probability of loss resulting from an accident. Ninth, justify that the outcome of the potential accident will be acceptable and recoverable. Tenth, proceed with caution! Six factors that can inhibit these 10 steps include new or unexpected situations, inappropriate attribution, relaxed concentration, smelling the barn, risky shift phenomenon, and poor or unsound judgment.

The concepts of risk management are probably best implemented by a program's risk-management plan. Constructing risk-management plans is a critical step in offering quality programming.

If an accident occurs within a group, follow a sequence of eight response steps: A = Airway, B = Breathing, C = Circulation, D = Diagnostic exam, E = Evacuation plan, F = Find resources, G = Get assistance, and H = Helicopter usage. The group, led by the most senior outdoor leader, breaks into three teams: trauma, travel, and transport and temperature teams.

If and when things go wrong, you should have proactive, active, and reactive risk-management countermeasures in place, ready to use. Filling out paperwork can be part of these countermeasures, possibly including filling out accident report forms, incident report forms, and risk-management plans. Program policies help guide adventure programs with risk management. A risk-management committee monitors and sanctions program practices according to the organization's policy, and the committee collects, analyzes, interprets, and acts on incident and accident data collected on the forms. The committee also plays a role in conducting internal and external program reviews for comparing program procedures with state-of-the-art or common practices.

QUESTIONS TO THINK ABOUT

1. List all the lemons (potential risk-management issues) in the introductory vignette.

2. Explain the overlapping circles diagram of accident potential (figure 7.1) and the difference between hazards and perils.

3. Apply danger analysis to a real outdoor activity, describing its strengths and weaknesses in regard to your performance in that activity.

4. Relate a time when an inhibiting factor has interfered with your analysis of danger.

5. Differentiate among the three forms of risk-management countermeasures: primary, secondary, and tertiary.

6. Use the accident response procedures (A through H) to respond to a simulated accident exercise and discuss their effectiveness in successfully resolving the accident. Identify the roles of the three subteams, noting how their roles may vary with conditions and geographic areas.

7. Plan your next trip, completing the necessary risk-management documentation.

8. Review an adventure program using the questions listed in figure 7.5.

9. As an outdoor leader, assess yourself in all of the risk-management skills, detailing how you intend to improve on any shortcomings in each skill.

REFERENCES

Ajango, D. (2000). Lessons learned: A guide to accident prevention and crisis response. Anchorage, AK: University of Alaska.

Brackenreg, M. (1999). Learning from our mistakes—before it's too late. Australian Journal of Outdoor Education, 3(2), 27-33.

Brown, T.J. (1998). Risk management: Research needs and status report. Journal of Experiential Education, 21(2), 71-83.

Cooley, R. (2000). How big is the risk in wilderness treatment of adolescents? International Journal of Wilderness. 6(1), 22-27.

Garvey, D., Leemon, D., Williamson, J., & Zimmerman, B. (1999). Manual of program accreditation standards for adventure programs. Boulder, CO: Association for Experiential Education.

Hale, A. (1983). Safety management for outdoor program leaders. Unpublished manuscript.

Haddock, C. (1993). Managing risks in outdoor activities. Wellington, New Zealand: New Zealand Mountain Safety Council.

Higgins, L. (1981). Wilderness schools: Risk vs. danger. The Physician and Sportsmedicine, 9(3), 133-136.

Meier, J. (1981). Ideas for improving safety in high adventure programs. Unpublished manuscript available from the author, Department of Recreation, Indiana University.

Meyer, D. (1979). The management of risk. Journal of Experiential Education, 2(2), 9-14.

Priest, S., & Baillie, R. (1987). Justifying the risk to others: The real razor's edge. Journal of Experiential Education, 10(1), 16-22.

Priest, S., & Dixon, T. (1990). Safety practices in adventure programming. Boulder, CO: Association for Experiential Education.

Project Adventure (1987). Fifteen year safety study. Beverly, MA: Project Adventure, Inc.

Raffan, J. (1984). Images for crisis management. Journal of Experiential Education, 7(3), 6-10.

Schimelpfenig, T. (1996). Teaching safety awareness. Proceedings of the Risk Management in the Outdoors National Conference, Tasmania. 20-22 May. ORCA Publishers.

van der Smissen, B. (1990). Legal liability and risk management for public and private entities. Cincinnati, OH: Anderson Publishing Company.

Wade, I.R., & Fischesser, M. (1988). The safety review manual: A guide to conducting safety reviews for assessing and upgrading safety in outdoor adventure programs. Greenwich, CT: Outward Bound USA.

CHAPTER

8

Environmental Skills

The group marched in single file across the meadow to reach the moss-covered high ground. On arrival, the members pitched their tents close together in the small area beside the lake and began digging trenches to drain expected rainwater away from the tent sides and into the nearby marsh. Once camp was established, the leader designated tasks to the group: collecting rocks for the campfire ring, cutting trees with a hatchet for firewood, and digging a meter-deep hole with a shovel to serve as a group latrine. That night, the group members burned their garbage in a large bonfire and what they couldn't burn, they buried in the latrine along with their leftover evening meal. They cleaned their dishes in the lake!

While such misuses and abuses of the natural environment have occurred since the beginning of humankind, the consequences of such actions have only recently reached catastrophic proportions, particularly in areas that are the most sensitive to human intrusion, such as wilderness areas. One of the main reasons for this calamity is the large increase in the world's population combined with the exponential growth of human use of wilderness areas. In summarizing the growth of participants in outdoor areas of adventure programming, the Outdoor Industry Association (2004) reported several key findings in America alone:

▶ The number of people participating in outdoor experiences has grown steadily over the past six years to 145.7 million Americans, two-thirds of the national population.

▶ 16 million additional participants are recreating the outdoors, and participants tend to be younger, more diverse in terms of culture and race, and more dedicated in their outdoor pursuits with more frequent and dedicated outdoor use.

▶ A marked increase in adventure/sports travel has occurred, involving 55 million participants in 2003.

In another vein, another indicator of the growth in adventure activities is the measure of retail sales of outdoor gear. In 1996, the sales of outdoor adventure specialty gear were projected to total nearly $10 billion, reflecting a strong record of stable growth over the past 10 years. Experts predict continued growth in the future (Outdoor Retailer 1997 Media Kit, 1996).

Given the enormous number of people seeking adventure in the outdoors, you and your groups can no longer afford to travel and camp in ways that greatly damage the environment. With anticipated increases in these already enormous numbers, such damage to the environment will inevitably destroy the very beauty that produces outdoor enjoyment. Since every action in the outdoors has some small impact, it is becoming imperative for all of us to find ways to "leave not a trace" or at least to minimize these impacts when traveling, camping, or adventuring in the outdoors. Besides guiding participants in adventure settings, teaching minimum-impact techniques to groups is essential to indoctrinate clients into similar belief systems and behaviors when they return to outdoor settings independently.

Probably one of the strongest evolutions toward protecting outdoor areas has been the establishment of the Leave No Trace (LNT) organization in North America. The mission of this organization is to "educate wildland user groups, federal agencies, and the public about minimum-impact camping" (Leave No Trace [LNT], 2004, p. 1). The LNT organization publishes the following pamphlets addressing specific environmental areas and conditions: *North America, Rocky Mountains, Southeastern States, Backcountry Horse Use, Western River Corridors, Temperate Coastal Zones, Desert & Canyon Country, Pacific Northwest, Rock Climbing, Alaska Tundra,* and *Northeast Mountains.* LNT's guidelines encompass six principles adapted for varying environmental areas and conditions: (1) plan ahead and prepare, (2) camp and travel on durable surfaces, (3) pack it in, pack it out, (4) properly dispose of what you can't pack out, (5) leave what you find, and (6) minimize use and impact of fires (LNT, 2004). We encourage you to contact this organization for guidelines addressing specific environmental areas and conditions.

As with chapter 6, "Technical Skills," and chapter 7, "Safety and Risk Management," our purpose in this chapter is not to provide detailed how-to procedures for every environmental skill in adventure programming; you should get these details from other sources, such as the LNT. What we provide in this chapter are some of the general guidelines you should follow to implement minimum-impact procedures during outdoor travel. We have divided these general guidelines into several categories: planning, hiking and travel, and camping and campsite behavior. Please note that these guidelines change according to geographic areas and environmental conditions. What will be appropriate in one type of area may not be called for in another setting.

But before we get into the specifics, let's consider a philosophy that should override all other guidelines: "A thing (an act in the outdoor environment) is right when it tends to preserve the integrity, stability, and beauty of the biotic community. It is wrong when it tends to do otherwise" (Leopold, 1966, p. 222). The principles of Leopold's "land ethic" should serve as the foundation for your program's environmental policies and procedures, which should include written lists of acceptable and unacceptable behaviors in the environments you commonly use. These policies should extend beyond the treatment of environments by also addressing the various cultures, whether native, urban, rural, or wilderness, that your groups may interact with during your adventures. Specifically, these policies might dictate the way participants interact with and respect others. Example policies include honoring native traditions by wearing local clothes, leaving farm gates as found, and remaining quiet in the wild.

PLANNING FOR AN ENVIRONMENTALLY APPROPRIATE EXPERIENCE

Outdoor leaders have always known that properly planning before entering an outdoor environment with a group is one of the key elements in leading a successful trip. The same holds true in setting up an environmentally sound trip. For example, forgetting a stove may necessitate lighting a wood fire; leaving the tent poles at home may require cutting vegetation for replacement.

Leave No Trace lists several aspects to consider when preparing an environmentally sound outdoor experience (LNT, 2004):

1. Know the area and what to expect. Know the area for risk-management and educational purposes and know how populated your wilderness experience will be to prevent overuse. Try (a) working with local experts, such as park employees, landowners, and regional outdoor enthusiasts, to learn about the sensitivity and popularity of the area you intend to travel through; (b) obtaining appropriate permits or permissions before the trip; (c) planning to camp in appropriate places; (d) considering whether you need to travel off-trail, and, if you do travel off-trail, following practices that minimize your impact on the land; and (e) traveling in areas that handle hiking and camping abuse better than others, such as using dry trails instead of wet and muddy ones and remembering that low-altitude zones are often less sensitive than alpine zones and that forested or sandy areas handle groups better than certain meadows or other areas of fragile vegetation.

2. Stick to an appropriate group size because large groups—those greater than 10—can have a greater impact than smaller ones.

3. Select appropriate equipment. Certain equipment, such as lightweight stoves, freestanding tents, and collapsible water carriers, creates less impact on the environment than the alternatives of building fires, making shelters from natural materials, and camping next to a water source. Buying earth-toned equipment can reduce visual impact on the environment.

4. Repackage food before leaving for the outdoors to reduce litter, broken glass, and surprise openings and spillage in clients' packs. Remove food from cardboard boxes and place it in reusable zipped plastic bags, empty contents from glass containers and place them into reusable plastic containers, and so on.

HIKING AND TRAVELING WITH MINIMAL IMPACT

The axiom "Leave nothing but footprints; take nothing but photographs; kill nothing but time" is an excellent guide for traveling in outdoor environments. But it may not be enough. Even footprints can be damaging. Footwear with hard soles, whether boots, shoes, or sandals, can tear the fragile surface of a meadow and accelerate erosion on hillsides. Reduce the effects of human intrusion on specific areas by avoiding trampling vegetation when moving off-trail, traveling as a dispersed group rather than as a mass, and hiking on surfaces that are durable or highly resistant to human impact.

Other principles advanced by LNT (2004) include the following:

1. Stay on the trails, for example, walk on planks or rocks in muddy places and don't shortcut switchbacks;

2. in alpine and subalpine areas, walk on trail or exposed rock;

3. when resting, do so on durable surfaces, such as exposed rock or bare ground; and

4. if going off-trail is necessary, keep your group small (less than six), walk only on durable surfaces, spread out if appropriate to diminish trampling and prevent creating new trails, and avoid fragile areas, such as alpine areas and marshes.

CAMPING AND CAMPSITE BEHAVIOR

Nowhere is the potential for environmental impact greater than at a campsite. When a group is situated in the same area for a prolonged time, its inadvertent or careless misuse of resources can bring about irreparable damage. You and your group should be able to camp in outdoor environments and leave only minimal traces of your visit. Furthermore, you should all be prepared to teach no-trace camping to others.

Many factors enter into campsite selection: flat and dry ground, shelter from the elements, lack of insects, proximity to drinking water, ground cover, and the absence of danger. In environmental terms, the most important decision is whether to use an existing campsite or establish a new one. Ultimately this choice forces you to judge the anticipated impact of the group and its size. Large groups may do better to use existing campsites, while small ones may make less overall impact at a new site.

Although your decisions will vary depending on conditions, as a general guideline use established sites to reduce impact. If such sites do not exist, stay at least 50 m (164 ft) from creeks, rivers, and trails and at least 100 m (328 ft) from ponds or lakes. In some regions, the guidelines for these distances may be as great as 1/3 km or 1/4 mi away from water sources, trails, or private property. Also consider how the layout of a campsite might create new trails between tents and toilet areas and how the cooking area may be repeatedly trod-den by people hanging around and shuffling their feet to keep warm while waiting for meals. Rotate areas of congestion to disperse wear and tear; this may mean moving sites if appropriate.

Pitch tents on sand, duff, or mineral soil, avoiding vegetated areas. When erecting a tent or other shelter, do not dig drain channels around its base as these channels can leave permanent scars. Instead, pitch tents on elevated sites to eliminate the need for trenching. Don't sweep away vegetation or organic material to get to the ground; set up the tent on top of these natural cushions.

When breaking camp, completely remove any string tied to vegetation for supporting the tent. Fill in tent-stake holes, replace any rocks or logs that you moved, and scatter a little ground duff or cover over any compacted areas. LNT also recommends brushing out footprints or matted grass with a stick (LNT, 2004). Perform a final check for any lost equipment or leftover litter, then bag trash and carry it out.

Waste Disposal

LNT suggests four guidelines for disposing of fecal matter: avoid polluting water sources, eliminate contact with insects and animals, maximize decomposition, and minimize the chances of social impacts (LNT, 2004). The technique most often recommended for disposing of human wastes (fecal matter, liquid food, or dishwater) is to use individual "cat holes." Dig a small pit about 6 in. (15 cm) into the topsoil layer rich in humus and bacteria. Then, normally, bury fecal matter in the top few inches of the humus layer where bacterial action can speed degradation. Leaving fecal matter on the surface of hot and dry or cold and wet ground in remote areas sometimes aids a faster breakdown than burying it. Locate cat holes at least 100 m (328 ft) from any water or trail, remembering that this distance should be greater in some circumstances. Consider using natural alternatives for toilet paper, such as snow or stones and sticks. If toilet paper and feminine hygiene products are used, carry them out in doubled plastic bags. For certain activities or places, special practices will supersede those we have outlined. For example, carry out all human wastes when spelunking in caves.

Cat holes are not necessary for urination. While posing little threat to human health, the odor of urine can be unpleasant, and the salts in urine can cause animals to dig up the ground. LNT generally recommends urinating on rocky or sandy areas away from camp and water sources (LNT, 2004).

Fire Building

Before building a fire, ask yourself if it is needed. Stoves can provide the needs of people traveling in the outdoors.

If, however, you want a fire for cooking or need one for survival, use an existing fire pit or carry a

The complexities of protecting natural environments include how we move through the environment and what we leave behind.

fire pan, a large tin can with holes in it. Use only "dead and down" wood as fuel. Don't break or cut the branches off living trees. Do not build the fire near any combustible items, such as tree roots, logs, or tents, and keep a large supply of water on hand to extinguish any runaway flames. If you build the fire in a pristine area without any previous scars, avoid leaving any trace by making a platform, or mound, fire on bare, flat rock with a deep layer of sand and gravel spread over the exposed rock to prevent charcoal staining. LNT (2004) generally recommends using these fire structures over pit fires. Of course, clean up mound fires as you would any others.

Washing and Cooking

Using soap to wash hands, bodies, or dishes is rarely necessary. Sand is an effective scouring substitute. If soap is absolutely necessary, use it sparingly since high concentrations of soap left on dishes can cause diarrhea. Pick a biodegradable soap with a low phosphate content. Lather first and then rinse over deep mineral soil situated well away from water. Soaping, brushing teeth, or washing clothes should take place 100 m (328 ft) away from water or camp. Dig a dump hole only for dishwater or for other liquids but not for solid foods—you should carry them out.

Cook and handle food well downwind from camp as the aroma will likely attract bears or other local animals, and securely store food in animal-proof containers hung high among the trees. If possible, use leftover food in the next meal. Don't bury it in the ground as animals may dig it up and eat it. Pack and carry out all that you packed and carried in! Don't burn or bury litter and leftover food. Use stoves, packing an ample fuel supply, instead of open fires, which consume wood. In many areas, this fuel supply is diminishing, and its use can interfere with biological or degradation processes that are integral parts of the local ecosystem.

Nonintrusive Behaviors

Since people seek solitude almost as often as they seek nature, social impacts are also important while adventuring in the outdoors. Consider the visual impact of brightly colored equipment and clothing in the outdoors. Except in emergencies and hunting seasons, avoid neon colors; instead, use more subtle earth tones. Unless it is to avoid a potential accident, don't flag trails with brightly colored surveyor's tape. Noise as well as bright colors can "pollute" others' experiences. Select campsites that won't interfere with the view and privacy of other campers.

SUMMARY

Being properly connected to natural environments can positively affect humans (Hunt, 1999; Mittelstaedt, Sanker, & VanderVeer, 1999; Simpson, 1999; Slattery, 2001). However, in this connecting process we risk damaging the environment that produces such positive changes within and between us. Minimum-impact travel avoids or reduces the damage humans cause by moving through an environment. For the most part, minimum-impact travel means carrying out litter, solid-food waste, and sanitary products as well as burying fecal matter, liquid foods, and dishwater. You should also keep in mind the social impacts of noise, visibility, and intruding on privacy. Your program should respect the environment and its indigenous populations.

No-trace camping avoids or reduces the damage caused by periodically stopping in an environment. Give special consideration to using existing campsites or carefully creating new ones. Remember to set up camp well away from water. Locate toilet, cooking, and washing areas well away from camp and water. Avoid fires but if you must use one, avoid inappropriate fuel consumption, fire spreading, and charcoal scarring. Finally, erect tents without disturbing vegetation or ground cover.

QUESTIONS TO THINK ABOUT

1. Identify all the environmental impacts in the introductory vignette.
2. Comment on the minimum-impact travel techniques used on the last trip you took as a participant.
3. Detail the no-trace camping techniques you will use on the next trip you take as a participant.
4. As an outdoor leader, how will you teach group members to use these techniques?

REFERENCES

Ewert, A. (1989). *Outdoor adventure pursuits: Foundations, models, and theories.* Worthington, OH: Publishing Horizons.

Hunt, G. (1999). Get out often—The importance of being in the environment. *Australian Journal of Outdoor Education, 4*(4), 17-23.

Leave No Trace (LNT). (2004). Leave No Trace, PO Box 997, Boulder, CO 80306. Phone: 800-332-4100, Fax: 303-442-8217. Available: www.lnt.org.

Leopold, A. (1966). *Sand County almanac, with other essays from Round River.* New York: Oxford University Press.

Mittelstaedt, R., Sanker, L., & VanderVeer, B. (1999). Impact of a week-long experiential education program on environmental attitude and awareness. *Journal of Experiential Education, 22*(3), 138-148.

Outdoor Industry Association. American outdoor recreation participation continues six-year ascent (2004, July 28). Retrieved January 7, 2005 from the World Wide Web: www.outdoorindustry.org/press.oia.php?news_id=708&sort_year=2004

Outdoor Retailer 1997 Media Kit. (1996). Outdoor Retailer, One Penn Plaza, 10th Floor, New York, NY 10119-1198. Phone: 800-950-1314, Fax: 212-279-4453.

Simpson, S. (1999). A simple lesson in experiencing nature. *Journal of Experiential Education, 22*(3), 118-122.

Slattery, D. (2001). What can environmental history offer outdoor education practitioners? *Australian Journal of Outdoor Education, 5*(2), 28-33.

Trip Planning

As an extremely competent outdoor leader, Anthony relied on his judgment and experience to organize expeditions. He was a master of logistics, but when his group arrived at the first campsite, the tent poles were nowhere to be found. Luckily, the weather was mild and he was able to improvise poles from nearby deadwood. In retrospect, he remembered that the tent bodies and flys were stored separately from the poles in his equipment room, and he resolved to change this procedure on return. He also realized that juggling all the trip logistics in his memory had led to a forgotten item. He asked himself, "What else would go wrong?"

Relying on experience alone was an error in this case. Reserve judgment based on experience (see chapter 20) for times of uncertainty and improvisation, such as when deciding how to replace lost equipment. In situations for which the tasks are common and repetitive, such as trip organization, use checklists to reduce mistakes and the chances that you'll leave anything behind. Many of the ideas in this chapter are based on prominent practices of leading adventure programs, like those found in the *Administrative Practices of Accredited Adventure Programs* (Gass, 1998).

We have written this chapter as a checklist, and we encourage you to customize the list by adding your own local operating procedures or by changing the order of items. We also discuss planning and organization during the trip—while traveling and at camp—as well as after the trip. So let's get packing!

BEFORE THE TRIP

Generally, when planning a trip, you should consider 14 items in the following order: rationale, activities, locations, routing and scheduling, participants, groups, staffing, equipment, food and water, accommodations, transportation, communication, budgeting, and safety and risk management. Triple-check each item for any errors or omissions.

1. Rationale

The first item to consider for any trip is the reason for going. A trip should usually respond to the clients' specific needs for recreation, education, development, or therapy through adventure (see chapter 2). Next, identify and write down the purposes, goals, and objectives for the trip. You should base the remaining trip planning on these.

2. Activities

You should choose activities for their ability to meet client goals and learning objectives and to fit the trip rationale, and not because you and the rest of the staff enjoy doing them! Choose activities that are consistent with the clients' readiness within an overall program, taking into account several factors, including emotional maturity, physical skills, social development, and cognitive abilities. Pick activities that are risky enough to provide an adventurous learning experience and engaging enough to challenge participants while reducing the actual risks. Activities should fit within a progression of learning through which subsequent experiences build on previous ones. Sequence activities so that their difficulty, complexity, required preparation, and prerequisites increase over time. Consider how well these activities foster independence from you rather than dependence on you. Have backup activities in mind in case drastic weather prevents the trip from going as planned. Be prepared to change activities if risk management is a concern.

Check: Does the chosen activity match the needs established by the trip rationale? If not, modify the activity and recheck its compatibility before continuing.

3. Locations

You should choose locations for their ability to meet program goals and learning objectives, and not because you enjoy visiting those specific sites. Review locations conducive to the selected activities. Obtain information from maps, aerial and satellite photos, guidebooks, club newsletters, and other appropriate sources. Areas should feature scenery, terrain, vegetation, weather, risks, routes, and campsites that complement the needs of the trip. Compare and contrast the suitability and practicality of each area by considering the

(a) time and distance needed to travel there, (b) time and distance needed to obtain emergency services, (c) ease and cost of obtaining permission to visit the area, (d) user regulations, (e) capacity of the local environment to handle the group size and type, and (f) possible crowding or conflicts with other groups.

Select the best location and conduct a site reconnaissance, or presite investigation. This recon decreases your chance of getting lost, increases the quality of your decisions, enhances accident response, and improves participants' learning through you and your coleaders' intimate knowledge of the best teaching sites. When using recon information to plan a route or schedule times, remember that leaders generally move faster than participants and that available daylight and weather may vary with other seasons. After you have confirmed the location, secure the necessary permits and permissions to park, enter, travel, and stay overnight in the area. Be prepared to change locations if risk management becomes a concern, having backup plans in place.

Check: Does the chosen location match the needs established by the trip rationale? Is it compatible with the selected activities? If not, modify the activity or location and recheck compatibilities before continuing.

4. Routing and Scheduling

Map a route connecting places of interest, such as teaching sites, camps, and viewpoints. In doing so, consider the route length, daily distances, available campsites, access and egress points, best direction to travel, order of site usage, and escape routes, including for inclement weather, injurious accident, or getting lost. Build in contingencies, such as rest days, long breaks, obstacle delays, shortcuts, and side trips. For example, plan a canoe circuit so that you can drop extra loops from the route if the group is delayed or add loops if the group is ahead of schedule.

Determine the trip duration, then select from available dates. Prepare a flexible itinerary. Often, it helps to work backward from the expected time of return. Calculate times for travel on all routes, including driving time to and from the trip area. Consider the influence that the following will have on travel speed: distance, terrain, elevation change, route width and linearity, route conditions, vegetation cover, weather, temperature, season, time of day, available daylight, group size, pack weights,

and participant fitness or competence. Although the group may not stick to the route or schedule, this itinerary can guide adjustments, since performance during early days often dictates changes in expectations in later days.

Check: Do the chosen route and schedule match the needs established by the trip rationale? Are they compatible with the activities and location? If not, modify the routing, scheduling, activities, or location and recheck their compatibilities before continuing.

5. Participants

Since the overriding concern in any adventure program is the participants' needs, you should check that the participants are sufficiently prepared for the activities, locations, routing, and scheduling. Do not accept participants unless they meet the criteria, carefully considering, for example, those who may be forced into the trip by a program eager to fill vacancies.

Consider whether these prerequisites provide appropriate criteria for participant acceptance: the completion of prior courses or tests, such as a swim test before canoeing; emotional and social maturity, such as compatibility with others or attitude toward the environment; health and fitness, including strength, flexibility, balance, agility, coordination, and cardiovascular endurance; and competence, including ability, skill, experience, and confidence. If appropriate, arrange for pretrip training and informational sessions in similar settings to eliminate any weaknesses in technical, risk-management, or environmental skills. Also consider the participants' number, planning for a range and expecting a few to add or drop; gender and ages, recognizing that legal restrictions may apply; interests, striving to correlate with motivation and energy; and special needs, disabilities, or medications.

Ensure that participants are well-informed before the trip. Provide written information well in advance and offer an orientation meeting when appropriate; you may wish to invite the parents or guardians of child participants. In the written information, include program philosophy, trip details, and any prerequisites or preparations that prospective participants should complete. In orientation meetings, introduce leaders and other participants. Explain the trip's activities, nature, reason, and purpose. Address potential fears by openly discussing risk-management procedures and possible risks. As other trip details become available, pass them on to participants by mail, phone, fax, e-mail, or another meeting.

Distribute, complete, and collect important paperwork, such as legal or medical forms. Recommend additional personal accident or medical insurance to those who need it. Screen participants' health histories, having participants with health issues, such as cardiac concerns, undergo an appropriate medical exam or seek a physician's permission before their involvement. Pay close attention to participants at risk for a heart attack, such as those who have a personal or family history of attacks; have high blood pressure; are over 40; are obese, smoke, or are sedentary; and if in doubt, consider preventing their participation.

Designate and inform participants of a responsible contact person who will act as an intermediate between the group members and their friends and family. If the group is overdue, it can let the contact know about the delay, and concerned family and friends can phone the contact to get the latest news.

Check: Do the participants match the needs established by the trip rationale? Are they compatible with the routing, scheduling, activities, and location? If not, modify the appropriate trip components and recheck their compatibilities before continuing.

6. Groups

Pick group size to maximize learning opportunities, optimize relationships among members, and minimize environmental impact. Typical groups range from 6 to 16, averaging about 10 or 12. Bigger groups are generally more difficult to supervise or manage, allowing some members to hide in the crowd. Smaller groups generally have fewer interactions to generate valuable dynamics. Groups may be restricted to as few as 4 to 6 people in some heavily used areas to protect nature. A minimum size of four makes sense in case of an injury. While one person stays with the injured, two others can go for help. Sending two people for help is good in case one gets injured on the way out.

Once you have formed groups, outline the ground rules and regulations, overview the routing and scheduling, detail probable dangers and risk-management procedures, discuss possible environmental impacts, distribute food and equipment lists, and assign roles or duties for the trip. Plan for plenty of time to allow the group to form

(see chapter 5) and to appropriately facilitate experiences.

Check: Do the groups match the needs established by the trip rationale? Are they compatible with the participants, routing, scheduling, activities, and location? If not, modify the appropriate trip components and recheck their compatibilities before continuing.

7. Staffing

Select a staff that works well together under all expected conditions, including adverse ones. Maintain an acceptable leader–participant ratio. This ratio will vary according to the risk expected on the trip, the competence found in the group, and the purpose of the outing. To start with, a minimum of two leaders per group is good. This permits you to bracket the group with one of you scouting at the front and the other sweeping up the rear. In an accident, if the victim is a leader, another leader remains to take control and respond as needed.

Designate leaders and assistant leaders for each group, then clarify their roles to prevent conflict that can polarize or split the group. As a leader, you must see the bigger picture and take overall responsibility. Your assistants should attend to smaller details and fill in the missing pieces. You oversee the tough decisions, while assistants serve as a valuable sounding board for ideas. For example, you should typically oversee emergency situations while your assistants deliver messages, monitor the victim, supervise the remaining group, or accompany the victim during evacuation. If you share leadership, agree on roles and responsibilities well in advance of the trip. Of course, you must communicate effectively during the adventure as well.

Check: Do staff members match the needs established by the trip rationale? Are they compatible with the groups, participants, routing, scheduling, activities, and location? If not, modify the appropriate trip components and recheck their compatibilities before continuing.

8. Equipment

Prepare three equipment and clothing lists: individual, group, and risk management. On the individual list, include not only items to bring but also those not to bring, such as watches, hair dryers, loud radios, drugs, and alcohol. Check that partici-

Trips where one way or circular routes are possible present a whole set of considerations not found in two way or return trips.

pants have the right gear, especially clothing and other appropriate essentials. Have them bring in their own equipment to inspect it and determine proper fit. Explain the layering concept to participants, then check that they have adequate layers (wicking, insulating, and protecting) for both average and worst conditions.

Obtain and inspect group equipment. Decide what pieces of equipment you and your coleaders will carry. Remember to carry extra food and spare clothing for emergencies. Divide the remaining gear among group members by considering their relative fitness and available pack space as well as the weight and volume of the equipment. People may wish to weigh their packs to ensure that they carry less than a third of their body weight. Obtain specialized equipment, such as that needed for canoeing or mountaineering, and teach participants during the pretrip training how to use such equipment. Keep abreast of innovations in outdoor equipment in order to better inform participants of what works and what does not.

Check: Do the equipment lists match the needs established by the trip rationale? Are they compatible with the staff, groups, participants, routing, scheduling, activities, and location? If not, modify the appropriate trip components and recheck their compatibilities before continuing.

9. Food and Water

Count the total number of meals and categorize them as breakfasts, lunches, dinners, or snacks. Prepare a menu for each meal in each category. Consider the nutrition, taste, palatability, perishability, cooking ease, and cleanup for all meals. Keep in mind the number of stoves and the amount of fuel required to prepare the meals. Recognize that melting snow, cooking at higher altitudes, or boiling without a pot lid will all require more time and fuel.

For each meal, calculate the amount of food needed to feed the participants in each group. Combine these menu contents into a single shopping list. Purchase this food and then repackage it to minimize waste (remove food from cardboard boxes and place in reusable ziplock bags, empty contents from glass containers and place into reusable plastic containers, and so on). Label and distribute food among group members. Try to keep a single meal's contents together with the same person. If the total volume or weight is extreme, consider arranging a food drop or cache at one or more points during the trip.

Decide on water purification. Boiling requires extra fuel and time to purify. Chemical treatments involve iodine tablets or crystals, of which some people do not like the taste. Filtering may demand a system that deals with both bacterial and viral components, and good systems are often expensive and occasionally troublesome. Carry sufficient water at all times—extra for arid areas.

Check: Do the food and water provisions match the needs established by the trip rationale? Are they compatible with the equipment, staff, groups, participants, routing, scheduling, activities, and location? If not, modify the appropriate trip components and recheck their compatibilities before continuing.

10. Accommodations

Accommodations can range from hotels, such as on the road to and from the trip location, to huts and shelters in more popular and less wild areas to campsites, which are the norm for most backcountry outings. Some of these facilities may require advance reservations and can cost money. Book and pay for obligatory accommodations in advance.

Check: Do the accommodation arrangements match the needs established by the trip rationale? Are they compatible with the food, equipment, staff, groups, participants, routing, scheduling, activities, and location? If not, modify the appropriate trip components and recheck their compatibilities before continuing.

11. Transportation

Traveling to and from the trip site is usually the most dangerous aspect of any outing. Therefore, focus on risk management for all transportation. Arrange for transport vehicles, taking into account insurance requirements, shuttling services, and parking arrangements. Keep photocopied records of all drivers' licenses and any rental agreements. Have staff take a defensive driving class.

Ensure that drivers are correctly licensed for the vehicle and number of occupants they drive. Be certain they are experienced at driving and backing up the vehicle and any trailer that may be attached. Give them a map, directions, and a list of meeting places, making sure these places have phones for reaching the contact person if a delay occurs. Remind them of the rules of the road (e.g., wear seat belts, obey speed limits, make frequent rest stops) and of what to do in case of a traffic accident. Decide whether several vehicles will travel independently, catching up at meeting places, or together in a convoy.

Do not operate vehicles filled with more people and equipment than their designed capacity, which you can determine by the number of seat belts and by the manufacturer's carrying capacity information. Require passengers to wear a seat belt while the vehicle is in motion. Do not allow passengers to distract the operator of the vehicle while in motion. Consider using headlights during the day as well as at night. Have guidelines for diminished driving conditions; for example, if visibility is limited to less than 100 yd (91 m), the driver pulls the vehicle over at the first appropriate spot, turns on the four-way flashers, and waits until visibility increases. Rotate drivers to reduce fatigue. For example, do not allow anyone to operate a vehicle for more than 5 h at a time or for more than 3 h if the operator was vigorously active for more than 8 h that same day.

Check that all vehicles contain the correct equipment, such as first aid kits, repair tools, fire extinguishers, chains, flares, reflectors, and spare tires, and check that attachments, such as roof racks, hitches, trailers, lashings, and equipment, are secured. Make sure staff members know how to use the equipment, such as how to use it to correctly change a tire. Stow any gear carried inside the vehicle so as to avoid creating projectiles in a crash situation. Before the trip, check tire pressure, lights, fluids, brakes, belts, cables, hoses, and gauges, and discuss loading, unloading, and onboard rules and risk management with participants and staff. Count heads before leaving any meeting place.

Unload and load the vehicle in an orderly fashion. Have appropriate protocols for loading, such as allowing only two people to load or unload the roof rack at any one time. Unload vehicles on the side of the road only in an emergency; try to unload or load in parking lots or on appropriate side roads.

When parking vehicles, remove all valuables, leave nothing in view, and place the vehicle out of the way of other vehicles. Decide whether to hide keys nearby or take them along. A spare set of keys permits both options. When shuttling, attempt to leave at least one vehicle at each end of the trip so that a retreat, such as one due to weather or accident, places a vehicle at your disposal.

Check: Does the transportation match the needs established by the trip rationale? Is it compatible with the accommodations, food, equipment, staff, groups, participants, routing, scheduling, activities, and location? If not, modify the appropriate trip components and recheck compatibilities before continuing.

12. Communication

In the event of a serious accident, communication with outside medical expertise is critical. Communication can range from CB walkie-talkies or radios with dedicated frequencies to cellular phones to sending people out to get help. When other forms of communication fail, the latter is an excellent fallback option. Unless the group is very small, try not to send only one person for help in case that person is injured while alone.

Communication may also be useful for getting up-to-date information about weather or fire dangers, for breaking a large group into several smaller subgroups, and for changing outside arrangements, such as pickup times and places. When choosing communication, consider cost, including monthly rental and annual licensing fees; maintenance, including replacing parts or recharging batteries; limitations, such as line of sight versus repeating stations; function, including the possibilities of loosing connection or freezing up in cold weather; and care, such as battery life or moisture encroachment. Above all, ask, "Are the batteries charged?"

Note that easy access to the outside world can severely reduce the wilderness state of mind common to many outdoor adventures. Ready contact can also encourage groups to overextend themselves, confident that these communications will help them. You may wish to not announce the possession of communications as well as have communications fail once in a while!

Check: Does communication match the needs established by the trip rationale? Is it compatible with the transportation, accommodations, food, equipment, staff, groups, participants, routing, scheduling, activities, and location? If not, modify the appropriate trip components and recheck compatibilities before continuing.

13. Budgeting

Budget for vehicle costs, including rental, gasoline, oil, tolls, extra mileage, shuttle drivers, and parking; food per person per day; equipment, including purchase, rental, and repair; permits, including camping and user fees; staff costs, including salaries, benefits, and personal expenses; and miscellaneous, such as advertising, facility rental, maps, telephone, and faxes. Balance these expenses against any expected income. Since the number of participants can fluctuate, build in an appropriate buffer to account for that extra person who might necessitate renting a more spacious vehicle or hiring an extra leader. Always have enough spare cash to pay for expenses during the trip and carry a credit card for unexpected emergencies.

Check: Does the budget match the needs established by the trip rationale? Is it compatible with the communication, transportation, accommodations, food, equipment, staff, groups, participants, routing, scheduling, activities, and location? If not, modify the appropriate trip components and recheck compatibilities before continuing.

14. Safety and Risk Management

Complete a risk-management plan for every trip, possibly including (a) a brief educational rationale; (b) specific details on the activity times and places, a proposed itinerary with anticipated dangers and expected countermeasures, a route map with escape plans, and emergency contact numbers, including police, hospital, and rescue; (c) a summary of participant qualifications, health information, and completed emergency contact and next of kin forms for staff as well as participants; (d) signed legal forms; (e) an expense budget; (f) locations of nearest phones, medical facilities, and important emergency agencies and their phone numbers, including search-and-rescue services and the nearest park service office; (g) appropriate information, systems, and forms for staff when it needs them, such as search-and-rescue procedures, missing person reports, crisis and fatality response forms and guidelines, and accident incident response forms and guidelines; (h) blood-borne pathogens handling procedures; (i) alcohol and drug policies; (j) media and information dispersal instructions; and (k) individual, group, and risk-management lists of clothing and equipment. Obtain the necessary approval from the supervising organization and double-check insurance coverage for all aspects of the trip.

Leave copies of the plan with the designated contact person who will inform the authorities, respond to inquiries from participants' families and friends, and take necessary actions if the group is overdue or in trouble. Give a copy of the plan to each leader on the trip as well.

Check: Do the safety and risk-management plans match the needs established by the trip rationale? Are all 11 pieces (a-k) of information included in the plan? Are they compatible with the budget, communication, transportation, accommodations, food, equipment, staff, groups, participants, routing, scheduling, activities, and location? If not, modify the appropriate trip components and recheck compatibilities before continuing.

Triple-Check

Immediately before departure, get the latest weather forecast or tidal charts and check the local conditions for icy roads, muddy trails, river flow rates, snow depth, and the like. Encourage participants to telephone one another to prevent oversleeping their alarms. Let them determine their own car pool arrangements to the initial meeting place.

Double- and triple-check: check all 14 steps forward and backward. Is everything compatible? Make the final decision to go or alter, adapt, abandon, or abort the trip! Last, establish and continually refine criteria for determining if the plan needs changing in midstream. Stay flexible!

DURING THE TRIP

While on the trip, you hold responsibility for the risk management of your groups and for balancing this risk against the groups' inevitable impact on nature and against the learning that comes from encountering risks. Attend to these concerns in order of priority: risk management, nature, learning, enjoyment, and completing the trip as planned.

Trying to stick to a route or time schedule is one of the major causes of fatal accidents. You must be prepared to alter, adapt, abandon, or abort a trip according to your judgment. Participants enjoying themselves is an added bonus on any trip but not if it is at the expense of learning, nature, or safety!

When it comes to learning, you must ensure the participants' receptivity, recognition, response, and reflection (Priest, 1988). To create learning opportunities, set behavioral learning objectives that are within the reach of each participant. Preparing ahead of time, including holding pretrip sessions on terminology and basic concepts, may be appropriate. Keep activities exciting and enjoyable to motivate participants. Keep participants well fed and watered and at stable body temperatures. When clients aren't cold, hungry, hot, or thirsty, they are receptive to learning. Keep an eye on group development and how it influences group and individual behavior.

Reflection is a key component in a client's learning progress. Build in plenty of time for reflective debriefing discussions and implement some other forms of reflection, such as writing in a journal, discussing in pairs or trios, drawing, painting, dramatizing, composing poetry, telling stories, dancing, or soloing (self-introspection).

When it comes to nature, you must protect the environment. This means clearly communicating appropriate behaviors, such as respecting private property, not littering, staying on trails, avoiding shortcuts on switchbacks, and traveling quietly so that others might see wildlife. Consider the area's carrying capacity by using stoves instead of fires, not creating new campsites, burying sanitary wastes in the topsoil layer, sharing resources with others, leaving no trace, and cleaning up the mess left by less considerate users.

When it comes to risk management, you must ensure the health of participants. This means continually monitoring weather, terrain, route, and participants' locations, body temperatures, morale, and energy. Make sure everyone knows where the accident response kit (ARK) is kept. Conduct ongoing danger assessment and accident analysis. Brief participants on impending dangers. Examine dangers by scouting rapids, digging avalanche pits, or crossing rivers before participants. Immediately stop any inappropriate actions, such as horseplay. Anticipate inappropriate actions that may occur when an initial explanation may not have been clear to some people.

Traveling

Frequently count heads while traveling on trails, over open water, down rivers, into caves, or across mountain slopes. Before beginning activities, discuss with participants what to do in emergencies, such as if they're injured or lost, and conduct stretching or warm-up sessions to prevent injuries and reduce the potential for fatigue. As people begin to exercise they can get warmer, so plan an early stop to adjust clothing. Before beginning, share with clients how the route is marked, whether by tree blazes, paint spots, metal signs, or rock cairns, and what special markings indicate junctions or changes in direction.

Review the first leg while participants follow along on their own maps. Remind them what to do if they become lost or separated from the group. Use a buddy system when appropriate, such as pairing weak participants with strong, and encourage participants to keep tabs on their buddies while traveling. Instruct participants to leave their packs or some other item on the route in plain view if they leave the route for any reason, such as photography or sanitation needs.

Discuss sanitation procedures. Model desirable behaviors, such as picking up litter and not taking shortcuts.

Pace the group by traveling at the speed of its slowest member. Develop a group consciousness about accommodating varying speeds of members by placing slow people near the front, fast people at the back, and redistributing carried loads. Travel single file unless route conditions permit different configurations. Keep the group between a designated scout (first group member) and sweep (last member), having ways to communicate if a stop is needed. For example, have scout and sweep stay close enough to see each other or call one another by whistle or voice.

Rest regularly to recover breath, adjust clothing, eat and drink, gather the group together, discuss the previous leg, plan for the next leg, or view scenery. At rest stops, allow all your clients time to rest and do not strike out on the next leg until the newest arrivals are rested. Perform a site check of the area, counting people, looking for dropped gear, or rechecking for litter before leaving.

Break large groups into smaller ones, maintaining reasonable spacing and contact between subgroups. Assign a scout and sweep to each subgroup and give each subgroup appropriate equipment, such as a first aid kit, spare rope, or radio. Stagger subgroups through obstacles and dangers, such as rapids, avalanche slopes, and river crossings, so that they may assist one another.

Stop at trail intersections or places of possible confusion. Count heads before continuing. When appropriate, such as in a well-known area with a competent group, leave one person at each intersection to wait for the next person. On arrival, that next person waits while the other continues. You and your coleaders can then move throughout the line, taking different positions in the group, alternating scout, sweep, and observer roles. Each position has its pros and cons.

Scout from the front when finding the route is difficult, when you expect danger, or when a runaway group needs holding back. Be aware that a front position, however, can cause the group to become too dependent on you, lose track of where it is, or be unaware of existing dangers. It may also lose motivation if a scouting leader exerts too much control.

Sweep from the rear when the group spreads out, when tired or straggling members need extra motivation and encouragement, or when others might benefit from navigating at the front. Be aware that a rear position, however, can cause the group to become too independent of you, allowing some members to get far ahead or even lost or into other trouble. They may be frustrated by too little control from a sweeping leader.

From the front or the rear, you may have difficulty seeing what is going on in the group. Observe from the middle when noting group interactions, such as cliques or conflicts; when checking on participant health concerns, such as fatigue or temperature; or when encountering difficult obstacles, such as avalanche slopes or river crossings. The middle position allows you to move freely and unobtrusively through the group as well as to be relatively close to everyone in the event of an accident. As an observer, you can also stop at any obstacle and assist or advise participants as they pass it. When in the middle, be careful not to let members spread out too far ahead or too far behind.

Camping

Select a campsite based on the following conditions:

- ▶ Environmental appropriateness, following the Leave No Trace organization's guidelines (see chapter 8)
- ▶ Flatness, remembering that a slight incline may be desirable
- ▶ Risk-management concerns, avoiding avalanche zones or hanging dead branches
- ▶ Drainage, not digging any trenches
- ▶ Surface, not damaging vegetation or moving soil
- ▶ Lack of insects, keeping in mind that a breeze can discourage them
- ▶ Proximity to water, not coming so close as to pollute it
- ▶ Protection, using trees for shelter from rain or wind
- ▶ Shade or sunshine, noting the direction of sunrise and sunset
- ▶ Aesthetics or scenic views
- ▶ Proximity to other groups who may detract from your group's need for solitude and privacy

Double-check that tents are correctly situated and erected to shelter participants from the elements.

Identify dangerous areas to avoid. Designate procedures and places for food storage, cooking, eating, and disposal and for sanitary concerns.

Encourage people to use flashlights as night falls. Manage gear by keeping the campsite tidy and organized, especially before going to bed. Disorganized equipment can be lost if covered by overnight snow. If possible, hang extra food between two trees well above ground to avoid animal inquiry and avoid taking food into the tent when in bear country. Clean up on departure and pack out all trash.

Difficult Conditions

Effective leaders normally keep an eye on their back routes by frequently looking behind. They often do this in case the forward passage is blocked and retracing steps becomes necessary. In selecting routes, consider the dangers of traveling in dry canyons prone to flash flooding, river valleys with obligatory crossings, mountain ridges with cliff bands and lightning hazards, snow slopes with avalanche or slips potential, glaciers with serac or crevasse movement, and scree slopes with rock fall or a high chance of twisted ankles.

If traveling at night, carry emergency lighting, wear eye protection for unseen sharp branches, wear reflective clothing if helpful, and plan for diminished vision. In reduced visibility, such as under fog or in a snowstorm, familiar terrain can quickly become unfamiliar and supervising a group can be extremely difficult. In appropriate circumstances, rope the group together to prevent separation. On poorly indicated routes that may occur in reduced visibility and when marking is sparse, let a route finder go out on a rope, looking for the next marker, while the group waits at the last known marker. If the next marker is found, the group can follow the rope and leave the security of the last marker. You should have the group repeat this process until the situation changes for the better.

BACK HOME AND OTHER PLANNING

Evaluation is valuable, and you should plan for it in advance rather than leaving it to the last minute. Provide opportunities for participants and coleaders alike to give you written and verbal feedback. Prepare a written report from the evaluations

◄ EFFECTIVE OUTDOOR LEADERS ►

► Are familiar with trip planning. Planning procedures typically include rationale, activities, locations, routing and scheduling, participants, groups, staffing, equipment, food and water, accommodation, transportation, communication, budgeting, and safety and risk management.

► Write risk-management plans, covering the following:

1. A brief educational rationale

2. Specific details on the activity times and places, the proposed itinerary with anticipated dangers and expected countermeasures, a route map with escape plans, and the emergency contact numbers (e.g., for police, hospitals, rescue services)

3. A summary of participant qualifications, health information, and emergency contact or next of kin forms, completed for staff as well as participants

4. Signed legal forms

5. An expense budget

6. The location of the nearest phones, medical facilities, and important emergency agencies (e.g., search-and-rescue services, park service office) and their phone numbers

7. Appropriate information, systems, and forms for staff (e.g., search-and-rescue procedures, missing person report forms, crisis and fatality response forms and guidelines, accident incident response forms and guidelines)

8. Blood-borne pathogens handling procedures

9. Alcohol and drug policies

10. Media and information dispersal instructions

11. Individual, group, and risk-management lists of clothing and equipment

► Are practiced in these procedures so that trip planning flows smoothly and the trip proceeds appropriately.

composed of a summary of what took place, being especially sure to note deviations from the original safety and risk-management plan and any recommendations for changes next time. Complete any additional paperwork, such as accident and incident reports.

Wash, dry, and return equipment after the trip. Appropriately dispose of leftover food and equipment. Return vehicles. Balance the budget and submit receipts or remaining moneys. Last, plan a reunion, perhaps a potluck dinner with a video or slide show, or a follow-up meeting.

For this checklist, we have purposefully omitted those aspects of programming that are not necessarily a leader's responsibility. For example, advertising or marketing and the financial or fund-raising tasks typically fall to program administrators. Hiring staff, budgeting, and using computers are roles for administrators, programmers, and leaders. But such program management topics are the subject for another book. Although operating an adventure program falls to managers rather than leaders, you may still wish to learn the responsibilities that lie beyond trip planning.

SUMMARY

Proper trip planning is vital for any adventure programming experience (Kanangieter, Sawyer, Gookin, & Johnson, 2004). When trip planning is routine, checklists can serve as an invaluable tool. A trip checklist covers the trip rationale, activities, locations, routing and scheduling, participants, groups, staffing, equipment, food and water, accommodation, transportation, communication, budgeting, and safety and risk management. Triple-check every aspect of preparation before the trip. But don't stop there! You have further responsibilities during the trip to risk management, nature, learning, enjoyment, and completion (in that order); while traveling on the route to pace, control, rest stops, and leader position; at the camp to site selection and organization; in difficult conditions; and after the trip to evaluation and cleanup.

QUESTIONS TO THINK ABOUT

1. What are the guiding principles of trip planning?
2. What are the key contents of a safety and risk-management plan?
3. Under what circumstances would you reprioritize the leader's responsibility for risk management, nature, learning, enjoyment, and trip completion?
4. What is the best line position for you to take in a traveling group and why?
5. How will you plan trips differently after having studied this chapter?
6. Plan a trip from start to finish. Present your trip to the class and then have them critique it, stressing the positive aspects and the areas you may want to improve.

REFERENCES

Gass, M. (Ed.). (1998). *Administrative practices of accredited adventure programs.* Needham Heights, MA: Simon & Schuster.

Kanangieter, J., Sawyer, E., Gookin, J., & Johnson, M. (2004). Creating a positive culture and learning environment on NOLS courses. In J. Gookin & S. Leach (Eds.). *The NOLS leadership educator notebook: A tool box for leadership educators* (pp. 19-21). Lander, WY: National Outdoor Leadership School.

Priest, S. (1988). The ladder of environmental learning. *Journal of Adventure Education and Outdoor Leadership, 5*(2), 23-25.

CHAPTER 10

Legal Liability

A client is on the final pitch of a rock climb of a major peak. The outing is recreational and is led by a certified mountain guide. The client has been correctly instructed in the techniques necessary for the climb and has completed and signed the usual medical and legal paperwork. After several failed attempts at the overhang crux, with each failure requiring the guide to lower the client for a brief rest, the client fails once more and somehow the rope becomes undone from the client's harness. Death results from a long, unprotected fall, and the client's widowed spouse sues the guide, recreational company, and harness manufacturer. The lawsuits are settled out of court.

As an outdoor leader, what legal responsibility do you have to prevent accidents such as this one? How can you protect yourself and your adventure program from being sued? In this chapter, we examine your role in managing the risks and the role of legal liability in conducting adventure programming.

LEGAL LIABILITY

Liability refers to the legal responsibility or obligation that people or programs have for repairing damages (often by paying money) for injuries to participants. Typically, four kinds of liability exist: contractual, criminal, human rights, and tort. Of these four, tort liability is the most common concern of outdoor leaders and falls within the domain of civil wrong, or injury (Cloutier, 2000). Tort liability includes three categories: intentional acts to harm, unintentional acts that harm, and strict liability or liability without proof of fault (van der Smissen, 1990, 1.41, p. 47). Most often the category of unintentional acts that harm (i.e., negligence) will concern you and your outdoor program.

FOUR CONDITIONS OF NEGLIGENCE

Negligence is an "unintentional breach of legal duty causing damage reasonably foreseeable

---

Disclaimer: In this chapter, we look at legal systems and insurance schemes in relation to outdoor leadership and adventure programming. But please do not take the concepts we discuss as legal advice. Laws vary for different countries, states, and provinces (Camargo, 2003; Dickson, Chapman, & Hurrell, 2000; Garvey, 1998), and the legal aspects pertaining to adventure programming constantly change (Brown, 1998; Dougherty, 1998). Programs should consult a lawyer and other appropriate personnel for advice.

---

without which breach the damage would not have occurred" (van der Smissen, 1990, 1.42, p. 65). Four main elements constitute negligence, all of which must be established or proven in order for a person to be guilty of negligence. These four elements are "(1) a duty is owed to protect the injured from unreasonable risk of harm, (2) the act breaches the standard of care required to protect the participants, (3) this breach of duty is the proximate cause of the injury, and (4) damage does, in fact, occur" (van der Smissen, 1998, p. 12).

APPLYING THE FOUR CONDITIONS OF NEGLIGENCE IN COURT

Proving negligence falls to the lawyers of a plaintiff, or the person who claims to have been harmed and brings a lawsuit. To gain restitution for a loss caused by negligence, the plaintiff and lawyer must prove the four conditions: duty owed, breach of duty, proximate cause, and actual terms. In other words, the defendants (people alleged to be liable) must have owed the plaintiff a duty of care. That duty of care must have been breached or have been below the acceptable standard of care. The breach or substandard performance must have caused the plaintiff to be injured, and the injury must have resulted in loss. The amount of money sought as compensation must match the actual damages caused by the injury.

If all four conditions are true, then negligence is present. If any one condition cannot be proven, then negligence is absent. While all four conditions must be established, the debate of negligence is not equally divided among these four areas. The major contention in most courtroom interactions revolves around the question of "Did the outdoor leader provide the appropriate standard of care?"

STANDARD OF CARE: BEING REASONABLE AND PRUDENT

In outdoor leadership, courts measure the **standard of care** as that of a reasonable and prudent professional (Hansen-Stamp & Gregg, 2001). Two points are important to stress. First, whether or not you are a professional, the court will hold you to the standard of care of what a professional would do in the adventure experience. "The standard of care would be measured by the moral qualities, judgment, knowledge, experience, perception of risk, and skill that a person in the capacity of a professional would have" (van der Smissen, 1990, 2.22, p. 43). Second, the court will hold you to and judge you by the quality of being reasonable. As explained by van der Smissen, "What is reasonable is situational. Reasonableness is usually determined by three situational elements—the activity, the environment conditions, and the participants" (2.22, p. 44).

There are three breaches of the standard of care: malfeasance, nonfeasance, and misfeasance. Malfeasance is doing something illegal, such as

Adventure experiences require reasonable and prudent actions.

drinking alcoholic beverages while driving with other people in the car. Nonfeasance is failing to do something a reasonable and prudent outdoor leader would normally do, such as not belaying novices on a first rappel. Misfeasance is incorrectly doing something a reasonable and prudent outdoor leader would do right, such as incorrectly teaching belaying methods. Malfeasance is an act of commission, or actively doing something wrong; nonfeasance is an act of omission, or passively forgetting to do something required; and misfeasance may be an act of commission, such as being warned that someone is belaying incorrectly and not checking it out, or of omission, such as teaching belaying incorrectly, resulting in an accident.

The standard of care in court would probably be determined from the opinions of one or more practicing (and likely expert) outdoor leaders and possibly from publications that describe established risk management practices in adventure programming. Regarding such practices, the standard of care for outdoor leaders may include the following: to anticipate, identify, draw attention to, remove, or avoid dangers; to assess risk of accidents; to warn and inform participants about those risks; to implement safety countermeasures; and to respond to accidents, give first aid, and evacuate injured participants. As we saw in the definition of reasonableness, however, the standards vary with the type and kind of activity. A greater degree of care is required for whitewater boating, which is usually viewed as more risky than flatwater boating. Standards also vary with the environmental conditions, about which the court may ask, "Did they suit the activity or not?"; and standards vary with the participant. A greater degree of supervision is generally required for children, who are typically seen as being less cautious and mature than adults.

DEFENSES AGAINST NEGLIGENCE CLAIMS

As a defendant, aside from the bad publicity of injuring clients and the cost of time and money to defend yourself even if innocent, you're sure to suffer at the thought of being found negligent. Thus, to protect defendants, outdoor leaders and adventure programs have several means of proactively reducing the chances of being successfully sued (see Cloutier, 2000).

Van der Smissen (1998) identifies three types of defenses against negligence:

1. Immunity—where volunteers, landowners, individuals offering certain activities, and governmental entities are immune, or protected, from ordinary negligence claims
2. Contract—where liability is transferred to another individual or organization through a contract such as a written agreement or participant waiver
3. Challenging the elements of negligence—where the defendant claims certain critical elements were or were not present and that therefore the claims of negligence are invalid

Key to all three of these defenses is appropriate risk-management and legal procedures. Programs with up-to-date and appropriate procedures will incur fewer and less severe accidents to start with. This in turn will likely decrease the chance of being sued. This is one reason we have highlighted many such procedures throughout this book (see chapters 6, 7, and 9).

When it comes to legal procedures regarding contracts and challenging negligence, your initial line of defense is to combine warning and informing with appropriate participant forms. Specifically, verbally warn and inform participants of the risks and responsibilities associated with participating in the adventure program. Be certain participants know what they will be getting into. Make sure you discuss that the program is not perfectly safe, that you cannot guarantee safety, and that they must assume responsibility for their own safety and the safety of others. Mention examples of the activities and settings they will experience, paying particular attention to the probable distance from medical aid. Verbally list the potential dangers associated with adventure programs and the key safety procedures they will be expected to perform. Emphasize that accidents are always possible. Describe a wide spectrum of possible accidents from minor bruises through moderate hypothermia to fatalities.

WRITTEN FORMS

As important as it is to verbally inform clients of risks, having the participants read and sign a form that alerts them to dangers is equally important. Written forms range from ones that provide some assistance in case of legal action, such as agreements to participate, to others that may lend tremendous support in a lawsuit, such as waiver and release forms with indemnification clauses. Some of these forms state that if clients are injured by an act of ordinary negligence by outdoor leaders they may not sue, which is known as an **exculpatory agreement.** Van der Smissen (1990) and van der Smissen and Cotton (1995) described eight examples of written documents that can help support professionals. We have listed these eight documents by increasing assistance, that is, the further down on the list, the more support they generally give you. In addition, forms further down on the list generally contain elements from forms higher up. Also note that the first four forms are based in tort law and the last four forms in contract law.

1. No document
2. Agreement to participate, which formalizes the fact that clients are agreeing to participate
3. Informed consent, used only with adults, which states that they were informed about the nature of the activity, outcomes, and potential consequences
4. Parental permission with minors, which is a signed statement saying parents agree that their child can participate
5. Covenant not to sue, used only with adults, which is a contract stating no legal actions will be brought forward
6. Waiver to sue, used only with adults, which is an agreement not to sue even if ordinary negligence is the reason for client losses
7. Release, used only with adults, is similar to a waiver but releases you from already existing liabilities
8. Indemnification clauses, or "save harmless" clauses, used only with adults, which shift financial responsibility of any award to someone else other than the outdoor leader or program

Note that waivers and releases possess some form of exculpatory agreement. Some courts uphold these agreements; however, your program should not rely solely on exculpatory clauses to protect against liability. Also note that some professionals have questioned the ethical use of such agreements.

In 1994 in Washington, D.C., professionals from the recreation industry met at the Outdoor Recreation Coalition of America (ORCA) Summit on Outdoor Recreation to discuss issues confronting the industry. One landmark group composed of the leading legal experts created an invaluable reference called *Developing an Allocation of Risk Document* (Outdoor Recreation Coalition of America [ORCA], 1994). This document recognizes that risk is a critical and inherent part of many outdoor recreation activities and suggests that rather than reduce risk and destroy the very element that makes an activity adventurous, programs should inform clients of these inherent risks so they can choose to participate in the activity. The group emphasized that "participants may not recover from providers for injuries that result from any of the inherent risks of the particular recreational activity. In other words, the provider has no duty to protect the participant from those risks, and has no liability for injuries resulting from those inherent risks" (p. 3-4). The group encouraged programs to formulate an allocation of risk document with their own legal council, tailoring the document to their specific needs.

Whether you and your colleagues create an allocation of risk document, waiver form, or another legally binding participant form, the ORCA group recommends several guidelines. Note such measures need to be selected or approved by the legal council supporting your outdoor program, or they could be worthless in court (programs can't simply adopt legal documents from other outdoor providers, make a few changes, and assume the documents will provide a valid defense in court) (Hansen-Stamp & Gregg, 2003). Based on the work of Priest and Dixon (1990) and van der Smissen and Cotton (1995), we offer a helpful checklist of potential—but not required—considerations. Look to see that the form does each of the following:

- Has a title that accurately describes what the form is
- Identifies who is entering into agreement, such as outdoor leader, client, parent
- Is clear and explicit, that is, expressed in "clear and unequivocal terms"
- Conspicuously displays the word "negligence," such as by using bold print or underlining
- Uses a print size easy to read
- Adequately describes activity, clearly answering the question "What will the participants do?"

- Describes location of activity, for example, wilderness, ocean, gymnasium
- States that risk is inherent in activity
- Warns of some risks involved, for example, "Among the risks are . . ."
- States that listed risks are not all-inclusive, for example, "But not limited to . . ."
- Includes "In consideration of participation . . ." in document
- Affirms voluntary nature of participation
- Uses language that is broad enough to cover all programming aspects (i.e., contemplation). Includes phrases such as "(1) in all phases of the activity, (2) while using the equipment, (3) while on the premises, and (4) any and all claims arising from" (van der Smissen and Cotton, 1995)
- Possesses no fraudulent statements
- Conspicuously displays exculpatory language, such as by using bold print in a prominent place
- Covers unique situations, such as lack of quick access to a hospital setting
- Outlines participant representations:
  - Staff has been available to explain risks more fully
  - Client has no interfering medical condition
  - Client can fulfill necessary physical requirements
  - Presence of program staff does not guarantee safety or lessen risks
  - Client possesses necessary medical, disability, dental, and life insurance coverage
- Includes appropriate disclaimers
- Includes covenant not to sue, waiver, release, and indemnification language
- Includes acknowledgment, acceptance, and assumption of risk statements
- Includes severability clause, that is, the rest of document remains enforceable if one part does not
- Includes final acknowledgment by participant, acknowledging he understands it and voluntarily agrees to it
- Is signed, and possibly even initialed, in appropriate places

☐ Requires signature physically close to exculpatory language

☐ Notes that signatures will be legally binding

☐ If client is minor, includes both child and parent or guardian signatures

Follow this procedure when completing the form:

☐ Provide participants with plenty of time to read the form, ensuring that it is in the client's language (e.g., Spanish, English)

☐ Use no coercion

☐ Ensure that your verbal language is consistent with what is written

☐ Read the document aloud to clients

☐ Verbally describe the document

☐ Reinforce the importance of the document. Do not tell clients to not bother reading it.

☐ Ensure forms are completed before programming begins, that is, before a van ride to the canoeing site

Agreement to Participate for Minors

If participants are minors, that is, younger than the adult age of legal consent or age of majority (under 18 or 21 depending on the state), and legally considered children, you must properly inform both children and parents or guardians of the risks. Having both parents sign forms may be required to validate such forms (check with your program's attorney) (Hansen-Stamp & Gregg, 2002a). You can ask parents to waive the right to sue on behalf of their children, but minors cannot sign away the right to sue since contracts are usually not binding for people under the age of consent ("Colorado Supreme Court," 2002).

Minors can, however, sign an agreement to participate with parental permission. As stated earlier, the agreement to participate describes the risks and responsibilities, then asks the children to sign that they comprehend the dangers of participating in the adventure program. Having both children and parents complete forms may have an added advantage. Although parental consent is necessary, especially to medically treat children if they become injured, parents or guardians cannot sign away their children's rights. Children may sue once they reach the adult age of legal consent until the

statute of limitations expires, which may be several years later.

Health Disclosure

While participants are filling out legal forms, you may wish to include some medical paperwork. Use a **health disclosure form** to collect basic information, such as the participant's name, address, home and work phone numbers, gender, birth date, height, weight, age, blood type if known, first aid certification with expiration date, social security or social insurance number, and medical policy type and number. Also collect their emergency contact's name, address, home and work phone numbers, and type of relationship and their doctor's (including dentist's or therapist's) name, address, and phone number.

The form may include questions on health history, asking about names, descriptions, and dates regarding disabilities; conditions; prior injuries; fears; illnesses; cardiac concerns; past surgery (local or general anesthetic); current medications with dosages; allergies to foods, drugs, insects, plants, or animals; the wearing of glasses or contact lenses and dentures; smoking behaviors; swimming ability; and any other areas that might limit participation. This procedure demonstrates a reasonable and prudent attempt to discover any problems that participants might have. While your program cannot be held liable for undisclosed critical information, you should encourage participants to answer truthfully and completely, guaranteeing them confidentiality, that is, that only staff and medical personnel will have access to the information.

AFTER AN ACCIDENT

Obviously, first aid and evacuation to medical treatment are important after any injury or accident. When providing these, qualified leaders have a duty not to worsen the injury by incorrectly responding, for example, by resetting a shoulder dislocation in the field when a hospital is only 1 h away. Avoid talking with the media, referring them to a program spokesperson or administrator, who should know what to say (Ajango, 2000). Be careful not to admit guilt: it is better to say too little than too much, since more will probably be known later about what truly happened. Keep accurate records, filling out accident and evacuation reports, and complete them as soon as possible so you can accurately recall details. Van der

Smissen (1980) highlights five aspects that you should include when completing accident reports: (1) sequence of the activity, for example, when it occurred and what activities preceded the accident, (2) location, such as where the accident occurred, including a diagram and where other people were (leaders and participants), (3) what happened, including what the injured client and other participants were doing, who was involved, and so on, (4) injured participant's role, including what could, should, or might have been done by the injured client to prevent or reduce the accident and cautions and instructions given to the client that she may not have followed, and (5) aid procedures, including proactive, active, and reactive measures conducted to assist clients in preventing injury and reducing the severity of injury (p. 30). Van der Smissen also suggests not placing opinions on the form stating what was believed to be the cause of the accident or that negligence was the cause. You can include oral statements or separate written statements, making recommendations for changes (p. 30).

Some lawyers recommend submitting all such records to them as privileged attorney–client information so that controlling the use of information lies in the hands of the outdoor program and its attorneys and not the newspapers.

After you have dealt with the accident, it is essential that you contact legal counsel and insurance providers. Note that making quick changes to program procedures as a result of the accident may not be in the program's best interest, as this can suggest the program was operating inappropriately during the accident (van der Smissen, 1980). Make appropriate changes—but only after an accident investigation and program safety committee meeting that takes into account all procedures. Avoid doing anything to anger the injured that may trigger a lawsuit, such as billing them for the program. Counsel and support anyone involved in the accident. Consider visiting the injured in the hospital or at home if appropriate.

Communicate with the family of the injured participant. "Well-informed victims and/or their families with access to accurate information (dealing with compassion) are more likely to reach closure and move on with their lives, possibly resolving the dispute without formal litigation, or through some form of alternative dispute resolution (like mediation or arbitration)" (Hansen-Stamp & Gregg, 2002b, p. 4). Connecting with families should be managed in close consultation and agreement with your program attorneys and insurance company.

Going to Court

An injury (death, dismemberment, disability) may result in litigation partly because of the injured person's or the relative's need for fair and just compensation. It may also be due to the overwhelming number of lawyers looking for cases! If a participant decides to sue the adventure program, do not take offense: we live in litigious times. If your program does have the misfortune to be sued, the leaders involved often experience a great deal of personal pain and guilt. Since the opposing lawyers will attempt to demonstrate negligence, they will closely examine and scrutinize the leader's conduct in a very detailed manner. In addition to attorney assistance, leaders can benefit from counseling support as well.

The insurance company or adventure program (if self-insured) may prefer to settle out of court. This action may save time or money and avoid negative publicity. In fact, the matter can be settled out of court at any time during the trial proceedings.

If you do find yourself going to court, the incidents and events that occur will vary depending on the laws of the state, province, region, or country. Here, we offer one possible series of events to informally and briefly overview what could occur. Remember, however, that the actual procedure will vary and you can do very little at this point to change the course of actions: for better or worse, it is in the control of the legal system.

The trial proceedings begin with **pleadings,** during which the plaintiff's lawyer files a complaint outlining a claim and its foundation with the appropriate civil court. Filing the complaint results in a summons being sent to the defendants, notifying them of the claim and requesting a formal response. The defendant's lawyer then files an answer to the complaint, normally denying the allegations and listing defenses to the claim of negligence.

A **discovery period** follows during which several steps take place: depositions, which are testimonies of key witnesses under oath; interrogatories, which are written questions and answers exchanged between parties; inspections of health records, legal forms, damaged equipment, or other objects; and examinations, including medical evaluation of the injured. Immediately before the trial, the two parties may hold a conference to encourage an out-of-court settlement or to shorten the trial by limiting the presentation of witnesses and evidence.

The **trial** determines whether the four factors of negligence (duty of care, determining breach, causation, and injury compensation) existed or not. Both parties' lawyers and the judge interview potential jury members to ascertain their fairness and objectivity.

After opening statements from both sides, **presentation of evidence** begins with the plaintiff, who holds the burden of proof. The plaintiff's lawyer establishes the facts alleged in the earlier complaint by calling witnesses and showing documents or other exhibits of evidence. Witnesses answer questions from the plaintiff's lawyer during direct examination and from the defendant's lawyer during cross-examination. The process is then repeated in reverse for the defendant's response to the allegations. The plaintiff's rebuttal and the defendant's rejoinder follow. After closing statements from both sides, the judge instructs the jury, and the jury retires to consider its verdict.

Once the jury has rendered its verdict, either party may request a judgment notwithstanding, which is an immediate reversal by the judge to a contrary verdict, a new trial if a mistake was made, or a relief from the judgment by leniency of the judge. If these requests are refused, either party may appeal the decision on the basis of procedural error or abuse of discretion to a higher court. This court will not retry the complaint, but will review the trial record for errors or abuses. This appellate court judgment is binding and may overturn, uphold, or modify the lower court decision. In the end, the plaintiff may still win an award for damages.

For another perspective of legal proceedings in the United States, van der Smissen (1980, p. 29) offers a brief but illustrated course of events.

Reducing the Award

One final defense against litigation is contributory negligence or contributory fault. **Contributory negligence** is when a participant fails to use proper care for their own protection and by not doing so contributes to their own injury (van der Smissen, 1990). People who participate in adventure programs know they are engaging in activity designed to be risky. Therefore, they are expected to assume some of the responsibility for those risks, and the amount of assumption will vary with age, that is, less for children and more for adults, and with information provided them, that is, less for the poorly skilled and more for the highly skilled. Thus the importance of clearly and repeatedly informing participants of appropriate rules and warning them about inherent and other risks before beginning any adventure activity. It is also important to have informed participants orally or in writing of expected behaviors. Document what information was presented, how it was presented, and participants' behaviors (van der Smissen, 1998).

Just like leaders, courts will also expect that participants conducted themselves as reasonable and prudent people and that they can be held accountable if their misconduct contributes to an injury. The award from a successful suit can be reduced by proving **comparative negligence.** For example, if the jury found the plaintiff to have assumed 50% of the risks by virtue of being a sensible adult who knew what she was getting into or having equally contributed to her own injury, they would reward only half of the claim (e.g., $500,000 of a $1 million claim). Remember, legal experts suggest avoiding any admission of guilt after an accident and writing down any admission of partial responsibility made by participants after injury. While you may feel a sense of responsibility for an accident, this feeling does not mean that you are legally liable.

Insurance

If all else fails, your program should carry two kinds of insurance: **liability coverage** to pay awards due to negligence and **accident coverage** for medical and disability costs. Liability coverage may be difficult or expensive to obtain, however, performing a high standard of care and following detailed risk-management plans can reduce the difficulty and cost. If insurance is very expensive, programs may pool together to obtain reduced premiums. Check that accident coverage covers the extra costs of emergency evacuation, such as the expense of helicopter airtime. Be aware that all types of coverage usually have a predetermined ceiling, or limit, on the amount of payment. Your program can purchase coverage either for the general program or for one specific event.

Insurance policies are contracts established in writing that precisely describe what is covered and what is not. If an insurance policy contains an **exclusionary phrase** that limits coverage to a list of activities, locations, or clients, then make very sure that the policy list includes all the activities, locations, or clients of your adventure program. Don't assume that any policy provides blanket coverage to all program aspects, as this is rarely

◄ EFFECTIVE OUTDOOR LEADERS ►

► Understand the advantages and disadvantages of being in a profession that deliberately puts people at risk.

► Understand the legal concepts behind liability and negligence.

► Understand the legal concepts behind standard of care and inherent risk.

► Know the importance of participant forms, including what is written as well as what is verbally stated to clients when they are completing the forms.

► Are familiar with the different legal procedures necessary to protect the adventure

program, such as warning and informing, having participants sign waivers or agreements to participate and complete health disclosure forms, employing contributory or comparative negligence defenses, and obtaining accident and liability insurance.

► Know the legal difference between working with clients under the age of majority and adults and how age influences programming.

► Know what to do after an accident and how to write up an accident report.

► Comprehend their roles in a legal trial.

---

the case. If you plan to work with a particular activity, location, or client that is not listed in the general insurance policy, obtain further accident and liability coverage specific to the necessary addition. Remember, an ounce of prevention is worth a pound of cure.

SUMMARY

Liability refers to the amount of legal responsibility or obligation that people or programs have for repairing damages from injuries to participants. This responsibility often involves financial settlements. Negligence may be found by a court of law if the defendant owed a duty of care to the plaintiff, which is accepted as true in adventure programs; if the duty of care was substandard or breached, either by malfeasance, misfeasance, or nonfeasance; if the breach caused injury to the plaintiff; and if the injury can be compensated. Proving one condition to be false can successfully defend liability due to negligence. But reasonable and prudent leaders are expected to operate at or above a standard of care. Courts generally determine standard of care based on expert opinion and publications of common or acceptable practices.

Two obvious preventive measures to liability include appropriate risk-management procedures and protection by legal procedures. Such legal procedures may include warning and informing people of the risks and responsibilities of participation and having them sign a waiver containing a statement of, an assumption for, and a liability release of the risks and responsibilities, perhaps

with an exculpatory clause releasing the program from liability due to any negligence. When using these forms, laws applying to children generally differ from those pertaining to adults. Simultaneous completion of a health disclosure form, which should contain the participant's personal details, medical history, and emergency contact information, ascertains in advance any health problems or concerns participants might have (Hansen-Stamp & Gregg, 2002b).

Five aspects that you should include when completing accident report forms are the sequence of the activity, the location, what happened, the injured participant's role, and aid procedures. Do not place opinions on the form about the cause of the accident or state that negligence was the cause. Include oral statements or separate written statements to recommend program changes.

Do not take offense at litigation, but do protect the feelings of leaders named in a lawsuit. If an out-of-court settlement is not reached, then the claim goes to trial. Pleadings include filing an alleged complaint, which results in a summons, which in turn is answered with a defense. During the discovery period, depositions, interrogatories, inspections, and examinations take place. A pretrial conference attempts to encourage settlement or shorten the trial by limiting evidence presentation. At trial, the judge determines duty of care and a jury determines breach, causation, and injury compensation. The trial proceeds with the opening statements, plaintiff's presentation of evidence (direct examination and cross-examination of witnesses), defendant's response, plaintiff's rebuttal, defendant's rejoinder, and closing statements. After the judge instructs the jury, it retires to consider a verdict. The verdict may be followed by requests for changes or appeals for review by either side. Appellate decisions are final and binding.

Contributory negligence is a defense against a liability award resulting from a verdict. Courts expect participants who know and assume the risks of an adventure program to perform as reasonable and prudent people and to assume some responsibility for their own injuries if they do not. The amount of a negligence award also can be reduced by comparative negligence, which compares the plaintiff's contributions to the accident with the program's accountability, adjusting the award amount proportionately.

Your adventure program should consider two kinds of insurance: liability coverage to pay negligence awards and accident coverage to pay for medical and disability costs. Policy coverage may be limited by defining maximum payments and excluding activities, locations, or client types. Your program should check that its coverage is as complete as necessary.

QUESTIONS TO THINK ABOUT

1. Define liability and negligence.

2. What are the four conditions of negligence? Which one is almost always present? Which one is usually the center of a defense against negligence?

3. In your own words, explain the concept of "reasonable and prudent," and describe what it means to a volunteer outdoor leader with numerous certifications.

4. For outdoor leaders, how do courts determine the standard of care?

5. Differentiate among malfeasance, misfeasance, and nonfeasance. Give examples of each.

6. In order to warn and inform participants, what would you do and say to them in an orientation meeting?

7. What is the difference between a waiver of claims form and an agreement to participate form? When should you use each?

8. What is the difference between a release of liability and an assumption of risks? When should you have participants sign each?

9. Why include an exculpatory clause about negligence?

10. What does inherent risk mean? Why is it so important to an outdoor leader as opposed to a person leading another type of recreational activity?

11. What elements would you include in a waiver?

12. What is the most important legal consideration for including minors in adventure programs?

13. Why ask participants for true and full disclosure of their health?

14. Aside from first aid and evacuation procedures, what should you do and not do in response to an accident?

15. What should you include in an accident report?

16. What is your biggest worry if a claim goes to trial? How will you deal with this concern?

17. Differentiate between contributory and comparative negligence. Give examples of each.

18. Differentiate between liability and accident insurance coverage. Give examples of each.

19. How should exclusionary phrases in an insurance policy concern you?

REFERENCES

Ajango, D. (2000). *Lessons learned: A guide to accident prevention and crisis response*. Anchorage, AK: University of Alaska.

Brown, T.J. (1998). Risk management: Research needs and status report. *Journal of Experiential Education, 21*(2), 71-83.

Camargo, L. (2003). Managing risks and logistics in Latin America. *The Outdoor Networker, 14*(3), 1 & 26-29.

Cloutier, R. (2000). *Legal liability and risk management in adventure tourism*. Kamloops, BC: Bhudak Consultants Ltd.

Colorado Supreme Court voids waivers signed for minors. (2002, June). *The Outdoor Network*. Retrieved July 27, 2004 from the World Wide Web: www.outdoornetwork.com/ton_outdoorhead_archive/2002/06/26/eng-outdoornet-000007/eng-outdoornet-000007_150950_180_479158165399.html.

Dickson, T.J., Chapman, J., & Hurrell, M. (2000). Risk in outdoor activities: The perception, the appeal, the reality. *Australian Journal of Outdoor Education, 4*(2), 10-17.

Dougherty, N.J. (1998). *Outdoor recreation safety.* Champaign, IL: Human Kinetics.

Garvey, D. (1998). Risk management: an international perspective. *Journal of Experiential Education, 21*(2), 71-83.

Hansen-Stamp, C., & Gregg, C.R. (Eds.). (2001). The elusive "reasonable person." *Outdoor Education & Recreation Law Quarterly, 1*(1), 3-15.

Hansen-Stamp, C., & Gregg, C. (Eds.). (2002a). Parents' signatures on release forms: Is one enough? *Outdoor Education and Recreation Law Quarterly, 2*(3), 5.

Hansen-Stamp, C., & Gregg, C.R. (Eds.). (2002b). Medical screening in adventure programming— How far do you go? *Outdoor Education and Recreation Law Quarterly, 2*(1), 3, 15-16.

Hansen-Stamp, C., & Gregg, C. (Eds.). (2003). Is it really worth the paper it is written on? Releases and related agreements part 1: General concepts.

Outdoor Education and Recreation Law Quarterly, 3(3), 4-8.

Outdoor Recreation Coalition of America (ORCA). (1994). *Developing an allocation of risk document.* Boulder, CO: Outdoor Recreation Coalition of America.

Priest, S., & Dixon, T. (1990). *Safety practices in adventure programming.* Boulder, CO: Association for Experiential Education.

van der Smissen, B. (1980). *Legal liability—Adventure activities.* Las Cruces, NM: Educational Resources Information Center (ERIC).

van der Smissen, B. (1990). *Legal liability and risk management for public and private entities.* Cincinnati: Anderson Publishing.

van der Smissen, B. (1998). Legal responsibility for recreational safety. In N.J. Dougherty (Ed.), *Outdoor recreation safety* (pp. 11-24.). Champaign, IL: Human Kinetics.

van der Smissen, B., & Cotton, J.D. (1995). *Everything you always wanted to know about waivers—But were afraid to ask.* Handout presented at the 1995 AAHPERD Convention, Portland, OR.

Instruction in Adventure Programming

Experiential Education

Most adventure programs are founded on the belief that learning, behavior change, personal development, and growth occur through actual experiences. At the heart of this belief are the central principles of experiential learning. The process of experiential learning places clients as close as possible to the experiences for learning. Educators create such situations because they believe that direct experience is more valuable for transmitting knowledge than vicarious forms of learning, such as lectures (Bobilya & Akey, 2002; Campbell, Liebowitz, Mednick, & Rugen, 1998).

Remember, we can informally define **experiential learning** as learning by doing combined with reflection. It is an active rather than passive process, requiring learners to be self-motivated and responsible for learning and instructors to be responsible "to," yet not "for," the learner (King, 1988).

Experiential learning is also based on the belief that change occurs when people are placed outside a position of comfort (e.g., homeostasis, acquiescence) and into a state of dissonance, or a state in which the current situation and desired future differ. In such a state, people are challenged by adapting to reach a new equilibrium while they are supported by leaders and peers. Reaching these self-directed states results in growth and learning. One of the major differences between experiential learning and other educational formats is that experiential learning is not a product of learning, but a learning process that is implemented under appropriate circumstances.

The Association for Experiential Education (AEE) has defined a series of principles that reflect many of these ideals. The AEE encourages professionals to follow these principles, most visibly through the AEE's program accreditation materials, procedures, and process (Williamson & Gass, 1993), ethical guidelines (Association for Experiential Education [AEE], 1992), and practices of experiential education (AEE, 1995; Warren, Sakofs, & Hunt, 1995). These principles include using direct and purposeful experiences that appropriately challenge clients and that have natural consequences. The principles we outline in this chapter are client based, have present and future relevance, require synthesis and reflection, demand personal responsibility, and are actively and inherently engaging.

1. Adventure programs use **direct and purposeful experiences.** All change and growth have experience as their origin, and experiential methodologies place the client as close as possible to that origin. This process can be more valuable for producing and maintaining positive change than other learning methodologies.

2. Adventure programs focus on **appropriately challenging** clients. Experiential practices are based on the belief that change occurs when people are placed outside of positions of comfort and into states of dissonance where there is perceived risk and where they must use their competence to regain equilibrium (see chapter 4). Reaching these self-directed states of equilibrium necessitates change, resulting in the growth clients are attempting to achieve. In order for this positive growth to occur, we strive to place clients in appropriate environments and situations where the level of risk—both real and perceived—motivates clients both to change and to retain change.

3. The activities in these programs are also real and meaningful in that they have **natural**

consequences. Natural consequences are those that occur from the setting, situation, and circumstances of the adventure experience without human intercession. The ramifications of clients' decisions or actions provide realistic, immediate, and, often, individualized feedback. This means that when possible, you should utilize natural consequences to match a client's choices or behaviors, thereby providing the basis for growth. Conversely, artificial consequences occur if a human or human system anticipates or responds to a client's action, causing an artificial consequence to modify the natural consequences.

4. Natural consequences, rather than artificial ones, result in changes that are client based rather than leader determined. **Client-based changes** begin as appropriate for each client and progress at his own pace to an outcome that meets his needs. In this process, clients make personal investments in choosing the type, level, and value of their experiences.

5. Such changes are designed to have **present and future relevance** for the client. Not only are these changes useful in resolving the uncertainty of the adventure experience and attaining a new state of equilibrium, but they will also help the client improve daily life.

6. **Synthesis and reflection** are used as elements of change. Since change from experience is not always an automatic result, synthesis and reflection enhance the internalization of change for the client. This reflection can be achieved in a number of ways, including individual and group discussions, debriefings, solo experiences, journal writing, drawing, or other creative arts. As a professional outdoor leader, you should encourage reflective processes in your clients' learning to deepen the experiential process. Adventure programs without a form of reflection are simply not using experiential methodologies.

7. Clients are compelled to become **personally responsible** in their adventure experiences. The activity itself draws clients into action; they are not forced to participate by you or other leaders. Experiential teaching applies methods and activities that encourage personal involvement and personal responsibility, especially challenge by choice, to give clients power and control over their learning.

8. Clients become **actively engaged** in adventure activities. These experiences inherently require problem solving, curiosity, and inquiry, and they are followed by synthesis and reflection.

Clients can deal with new situations by applying what they have learned in previous situations. Remember, the process is active rather than passive, requiring clients to be self-motivated and responsible for their own learning and growth. Your job is to facilitate this responsibility, respecting each client's particular needs and abilities.

Experience plays a pivotal role in learning. In fact, some authors consider the term "experiential learning" to be a tautology, or a redundancy, (Joplin, 1981) since all learning involves doing, whether you're learning by "doing" a test, book, or lecture. But you, as an outdoor leader with knowledge of how people learn from experiences, can provide more effective learning opportunities through your program's adventure activities.

RATIONALE FOR FOSTERING FUNCTIONAL GROWTH

Given these eight principles, you can see the application of experiential learning in adventure programming. Like experiential learning, clients of adventure programming achieve learning, behavior change, or growth by being supported through challenging activities in a manner that works best for them.

What is it about adventure programming that produces such positive changes? While many methods of conducting adventure experiences are generally accepted, several universal components seem to serve as specific rationale for fostering functional growth (Ewert & Sibthorp, 2000). Gass (1993) has identified seven principles that summarize this rationale, providing a theoretical framework for conducting experiences. These principles include action-centered programming, use of an unfamiliar environment, a climate of change, assessment observations, supportive small-group development processes, a focus on successful functioning, and changes in the leader's role.

Action-Centered Programming

As a forum for change, experiential learning helps clients become actively involved in "doing" their learning rather than just listening to how it is done, which often characterizes didactic, or verbal, learning. In adventure programs, didactic processes, such as lecturing, are augmented or replaced by concrete actions and experiences. Clients are asked to "walk" rather than merely "talk" their behaviors in adventure programming. The interaction of talk and action becomes observable and multidimensional, involving physical and affective areas for learning as well as cognitive ones. The action-oriented nature of adventure programming also increases the nonverbal interaction among clients (Gillis & Bonney, 1986), allowing a more accurate examination of how clients truly interact. Mason (1987) pointed out that in many contexts, nonverbal communication is five times more believable than verbal communication. This supports the validity of nonverbal client interaction, which creates richer sources of learning and leads to beneficial change.

Unfamiliar Environment

When clients enter into adventure programs that focus on change, they may strongly resist change, that is, they may be in homeostasis, or in a state they desire to keep the same. Adventure experiences often reduce such resistance by placing clients in situations that are new and unique, yet supportive. One reason resistance decreases is that clients have few expectations or preconceived notions about what defines success in adventure experiences. They lack the knowledge of what is correct or how they are supposed to act in unfamiliar adventure experiences. When properly implemented, this dynamic creates a risk-free atmosphere, freeing clients to explore new learning opportunities rather than become overwhelmed or incapacitated.

Furthermore, such a dynamic can limit self-destructive behaviors, such as dysfunctional interaction with others, freeing intellectual and emotional energy for adaptation and change. Another benefit is that unfamiliar environments are simplified and straightforward, presenting clear problems for clients to address (Walsh & Golins, 1976). This simplification can limit side issues or external stressors that can complicate many of the everyday concerns confronting clients. The unfamiliar environment also provides a medium that clearly contrasts a client's current reality. As stated by Walsh and Golins, "Contrast is used to see generality, which tends to be overlooked by human beings in a familiar environment or to gain a new perspective on the old, contrasting environment from which the learner comes. The learner's entry into a contrasting environment is the first step towards reorganizing the meaning and direction of his [sic] experience" (p. 4). Clients are able to see elements of learning they

Clients of adventure programming achieve learning, behavior change, or growth by being supported through challenging activities in a manner that works best for them.

may have overlooked in their current situations because adventure experiences are different or unfamiliar. Clients may also learn new pieces of information that will help them learn when they return to more familiar environments.

Climate of Change

While traditional learning environments create positive changes in some cases, at other times these same environments hold little motivation for clients to change. When properly implemented, adventure experiences can introduce conditions that increase client motivation to change, generally through using eustress (Selye, 1974). Eustress, a healthy form of stress, motivates clients to use problem-solving abilities in a functional way, such as through trust, cooperation, and communication, to accomplish tasks in adventure experiences. One of the features associated with eustress is "adaptive dissonance" (Walsh & Golins, 1976), in which clients must adapt their behaviors to resolve a difference between present and future states and to achieve desired equilibrium. By adapting to create desired change, clients are provided with rich sources for learning. Adventure experiences also motivate through clear feedback from consequences arising out of appropriate and inappropriate behaviors. This feedback vividly and accurately represents clients' positive and negative behaviors. A client's interpretation of these behaviors provides both a powerful medium for change and an increased motivation to change.

Assessment Observations

Much of the material used for constructing change is obtained from the actions of clients in adventure experiences. Kimball (1993) relates this construction process to the psychological theory of "projection." Clients project a clear representation of their behavior patterns, personalities, structures, and interpretations on to the adventure activities because of their unfamiliarity and the ambiguity of the situation. As outlined by Kimball, "Wilderness challenges are high in ambiguity. The client must interpret or structure the task demands as well as his/her own response to it. The challenges of the wilderness expedition offer great latitude in response. The greater the latitude and the higher the stress, the more likely the client will 'project' unique and individual personality aspects into the 'test' situation" (p. 153). Careful observation of responses to a broad and deep selection of adventure activities allows accurate identification of "life-long behavior patterns, dysfunctional ways of coping with stress, intellectual processes, conflicts, needs, and emotional responsiveness. When properly observed, recorded, and articulated, these data can be the basis for long term therapeutic goals" (p. 154). These observations become extremely valuable for planning change processes. They are particularly helpful in constructing metaphors, for designing future adventure experiences, and in producing lasting functional change.

Supportive Small-Group Development

Unlike a typical classroom setting, most adventure experiences are conducted in small groups of 8 to 15 people. The small-group setting often serves as a critical factor for behavioral change. Properly orchestrated small-group interactions can exponentially increase a group's ability to accomplish tasks through members' reciprocal interactions or sharing in strengths and weaknesses. Small groups can also provide a rich source of emotional safety and support when members are involved in the products as well as the processes of adventures. For example, as we discussed in chapter 5, conflicts sometimes arise in groups during adventure experiences. By implementing supportive group processes, such as the full-value contract (see page 186) or other group norms that support emotional safety, you can help groups resolve conflict through positive discussions.

Focus on Successful Functioning

Remember, clients often bring problems or even a history of failure with them when they start adventure programs. These problems can heighten defense mechanisms, thereby increasing clients' resistance to change. But in adventure environments, you can give clients opportunities to focus on their abilities instead of on their disabilities. This orientation can diminish initial defenses and lead to healthy changes, especially if you combine this approach with opportunities to successfully complete progressively more difficult and rewarding tasks. Your support helps clients expand their perceived limitations and discover untapped resources or new strengths rather than resist learning. You can also encourage clients' efforts by focusing on the potential for becoming personally empowered by establishing and maintaining functional behaviors.

Changes in the Leader's Role

Adventure activities create several changes in the dynamics between outdoor leaders and clients. One example is changing your role from being a director to a supporter. When you are in a supportive role, you are able to assume a more approachable position with clients. During shared adventure experiences, you have the opportunity to work with clients during their various challenges, rather than be the source of challenges. These dynamics, combined with the informal setting of the adventure experience, can remove many of the barriers limiting interaction that may exist in other more formal educational processes. While still maintaining clear and appropriate boundaries, you can become more approachable, creating richer interactions with clients. All of this can bring greater overall change.

EDUCATIONAL MODELS SUPPORTING ADVENTURE PROGRAMMING

Several worthwhile models have been created that explain the experiential process of adventure programming. These include the Outward Bound process model (Walsh & Golins, 1976), the "hurricane-like" spiral of experiential education (Joplin, 1981), a numeric measurement scale for experientiality (Gibbons & Hopkins, 1980), and several experiential learning cycles (Dewey, 1938; Kolb, 1984; Pfeiffer & Jones, 1980; Priest, 1990).

Outward Bound Process Model

As we outlined in chapter 2, one of the most influential models in the brief history of adventure programming is the Outward Bound process model created by Walsh & Golins (1976). It was one of the first efforts to list and organize the elements of the Outward Bound adventure program into an interactive and replicable process that could be used by other programs. As shown in figure 11.1, the seven elements of the Outward Bound process model are the learner, prescribed physical environment, prescribed social environment, characteristic set of problem-solving tasks, state of adaptive dissonance, mastery, and reorganization of the meaning and direction of the learner's experience. Each of these seven elements is an important feature of adventure programming.

When considering the change process, this model appropriately begins with the learner. Determining the needs, corresponding objectives, and motivation of the learner before starting any program is key to orchestrating a successful experience. While somewhat dated in its rationale (e.g., the authors point to "ways of minimizing the handicaps of the physically disabled so that he can participate in the mastery peculiar to Outward Bound" [p. 3]), the model presents the idea that learners need to be assessed by instructors before the adventure program.

Using the concept of unfamiliarity, the model states that the adventure environment must contrast to the clients' "home" environments with which they are familiar. The difference between these environments allows clients to receive valuable information from two sources: the elements they overlook in their familiar environments and the elements present in the adventure environment that do not exist in their familiar environments.

The adventure program accomplishes this contrast by using **prescribed physical environments** that are generally multisensory, neutral, and straightforward. Most adventure environments are multisensory: they possess a number of features to see, hear, smell, taste, and touch. These environments are also neutral: The rules of the adventure experience are not arbitrarily made by people. Nor do intervening features, like staff intercession, always buffer clients from the adventure experience: they must deal with what the physical environment presents. The physi-

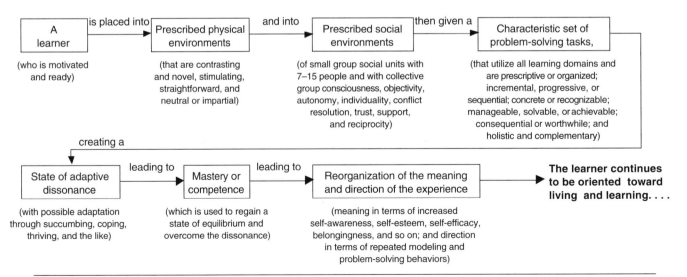

Figure 11.1 The Outward Bound process model (Walsh & Golins, 1976).

cal environments used by adventure programs are straightforward and easily identifiable and contain no outside distractions to divert clients' attention.

One of the critical features of Walsh and Golins' (1976) work is acknowledging the effect that a **prescribed social environment** has on the success of adventure programs. Their model points to the need for creating a particular group dynamic, that is, "an interdependent peer group with anywhere from 7-15 individuals who have a common objective" (p. 5). Four group dynamics that support adventure programming are all related to size. The group needs to be large enough to produce a wealth of differing behaviors, yet small enough so that separate subgroups do not form and diversify the group. The group needs to be large enough that conflict results from differing opinions, yet small enough that the group possesses the ability and resources to resolve any conflicts. The group needs to be large enough to create a collective force with which it may attain certain goals that cannot be attained by individuals, yet small enough that the group can also support each client's individual goals. The group needs to be large enough that a supportive state of reciprocity occurs, which is "an exchange system whereby strengths and weaknesses can be traded off within a group" (p. 6), yet small enough that the group members can contribute their individual strengths, and through such an exchange, utilize the strengths of others in areas in which they themselves may be weak.

The Outward Bound process model identifies a **characteristic set of problem-solving tasks** common to the challenges encountered in adventure experiences. These characteristic tasks contribute to competence, functional change, and other positive benefits experienced by clients. These characteristic tasks are organized, incremental, concrete, manageable, consequential, and holistic. Adventure experiences are most successful when they meet the needs of clients and when they are sequenced progressively, or conducted "incrementally in terms of complexity and consequence" (Walsh & Golins, 1976, p. 7). Thus, clients should begin with easier tasks and gather senses of competency and mastery from accomplishing these tasks and then attempt more difficult tasks with an established base of skills and confidence. Adventure experiences are generally concrete and easy to define in terms of content, that is, the tasks are easily recognizable (if not visually stimulating), and in terms of time, that is, the tasks generally possess a definite

beginning and end. Adventure challenges, while initially appearing insurmountable to many clients, can be managed or accomplished by clients with the resources they possess. In other words, initially these resources and their coordination may be unclear to some clients, but accomplishing the task is based on the clients' abilities to manage resources and personal skills. Adventure experiences are consequential, and the results, positive or negative, generally have an immediate, nonarbitrary, and direct effect on clients. Adventure experiences incorporate learning from a variety of domains, including cognitive, social, emotional, and psychomotor/kinesthetic learning. Combining these learning domains often provides a more holistic perspective for clients on how they can change in productive ways.

Presenting clients with problem-solving tasks in unfamiliar physical and social environments generally creates anxiety in the form of dissonance. This dissonance lies between where the client currently is, which is facing a problem, and where she would like to be, which is solving the problem successfully. Without resolving this dissonance, clients become disempowered, disinterested, or both.

What you must implement are **adaptive dissonance situations.** These are situations in which clients choose to overcome the dissonance by adapting their behaviors to meet their intended objectives. Adapting both instills a sense of mastery or competence as well as gives clients insights into their behaviors that they can transfer to their home environments.

While not outlined in Walsh & Golins' (1976) model, one feature critical to successfully implementing adaptive dissonance and mastery is challenge by choice. As pointed out by Klint (1999) and Kiewa (1994), the freedom to choose directly relates to a client's ability to experience personal growth and attribute such growth to his own efforts rather than "plain, old luck" or manipulation by a facilitator (see chapter 4). Also critical to adaptive dissonance and mastery is the need to individualize these choices to client needs. Clients play the major role in determining adaptive dissonance and mastery by acting on what they see as enriching and worthy of mastery. Some clients will value externally focused challenges and associated mastery, such as the experience of conquering the environment, whereas other clients will value more internally focused challenges and associated mastery, such as the experience of bonding with the environment and thereby overcoming self-imposed limits.

The **mastery** or **competence** produced by successfully resolving the adaptive dissonance presented by a situation motivates behavior change. This idea is related to Bandura's (1977) theory of self-efficacy, which theorizes that mastering tasks, particularly difficult ones, will increase clients' beliefs that they can successfully accomplish other meaningful tasks (see also chapter 4). Key additions to this mastery or competence should also include compassion and service to others (McKenzie, 2003).

While mastery provides the motivation for change, completing problem-solving tasks in unique physical and social environments also informs clients on the **reorganization of the meaning and direction** of change in their lives. The lasting impact of this reorganization is only as strong as a client's ability to transfer change in a manner that is lasting and continuous.

Five-Stage Model of Experiential Education

Joplin (1981) created a five-stage model of experiential education based on her review of existing experiential programs. The five stages of this model are focus, action, support, feedback, and debriefing. The **focus stage** presents the learning task and helps clients concentrate their attention on this task. The **action stage** involves doing the actual task, which is often unfamiliar or stressful to the client. In the **support stage,** the group members or you provide security and caring to assist clients in their efforts. In the **feedback stage,** you inform clients about their efforts and accomplishments to help advance their learning. In the **debriefing stage,** you help clients learn from their experiences through reflective processes that help them organize and integrate what they've learned. Joplin arranged these steps in a progressive and continuous chain of "hurricane-like" spirals (see figure 11.2).

Using her model, Joplin identified eight characteristics associated with experiential processes that apply to adventure programming. These characteristics are that the process is student, not teacher, based; personal, not impersonal; process and product oriented; evaluative for internal and external reasons; holistic in understanding and not simply represented by one way of learning or knowing; organized around experience; perception, not theory, based; and individually, not group, based.

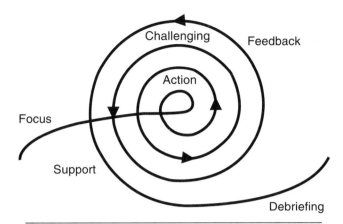

Figure 11.2 One spiral of Joplin's (1981) model of experiential education.

Learning is centered on client needs and interests rather than on your needs and interests. The effective leader individualizes the subject matter to fit the client in terms of both the affective and the cognitive. The process by which a learner accomplishes a learning task is valued as much as the product or completion of the task. The learner evaluates outside individuals, such as school personnel, as well as receives evaluation. In other words, evaluation is done by as well as to the client. Learning can be holistic—cognitive, affective, and psychomotor—as well as be expressed or analyzed in a number of differing, yet possibly interconnected components. Experience serves as the central source for learning: the program is built around experiences, and clients acquire personal knowledge primarily through reflecting on their experiences. Thus, you must emphasize that your clients share, explain, and justify what they've learned from their own perspective more than learn the right answer from theoretical experts. You should encourage clients to judge their accomplishments by what they achieved rather than by how they compared to others as is done in, for example, norm-referenced tests.

Scale of Experientiality

To avoid increasing confusion surrounding the definition and application of experiential education, Gibbons and Hopkins (1980) developed a scale of experientiality that outlines various degrees of experiential programming. Their scale measures the amount of actual experience in the learning situation. Five criteria determine this amount:

1. The degree to which the experience was mediated, that is, the more direct the experience, the more experiential

2. The degree to which the client was involved in the planning and execution of the experience

3. The degree to which the client was responsible for what occurred in the experience

4. The degree to which the client was responsible for mastering the experience relative to the fullest extent possible

5. The degree to which the experience enabled the client to grow in directions that were helpful to him

Using these five criteria, Gibbons and Hopkins identified five increasing modes of experientiality: receptive, analytic (examination), productive, developmental, and psychosocial. With each mode divided into two submodes, a total of 10 submodes represent a continuum of experientiality from least to most experiential: simulated, spectator, exploratory, analytical, generative, challenge, competence, mastery, personal growth, and social growth (Gibbons & Hopkins, 1980, p. 33-34). Each of these modes and submodes has a cumulative effect, with the more experiential modes possessing the elements of the less experiential modes beneath them (see figure 11.3).

In the **receptive mode,** experiences, or representations of them, are presented to learners who remain a passive audience. Learners passively experience slides, pictures, films, or other simulations of reality. In the spectator experience, learners experience the object of the study, but only as observers.

In the **analytic (examination)** mode, learners conduct field studies in which they apply theoretical knowledge and skill in order to examine an event, analyze an aspect of the environment, or solve a practical problem. The exploratory experience exposes learners to interesting sites and encourages them to explore the possibilities of the materials at hand. In the analytical experience, learners study systematically, often applying theory to solve problems in practical situations.

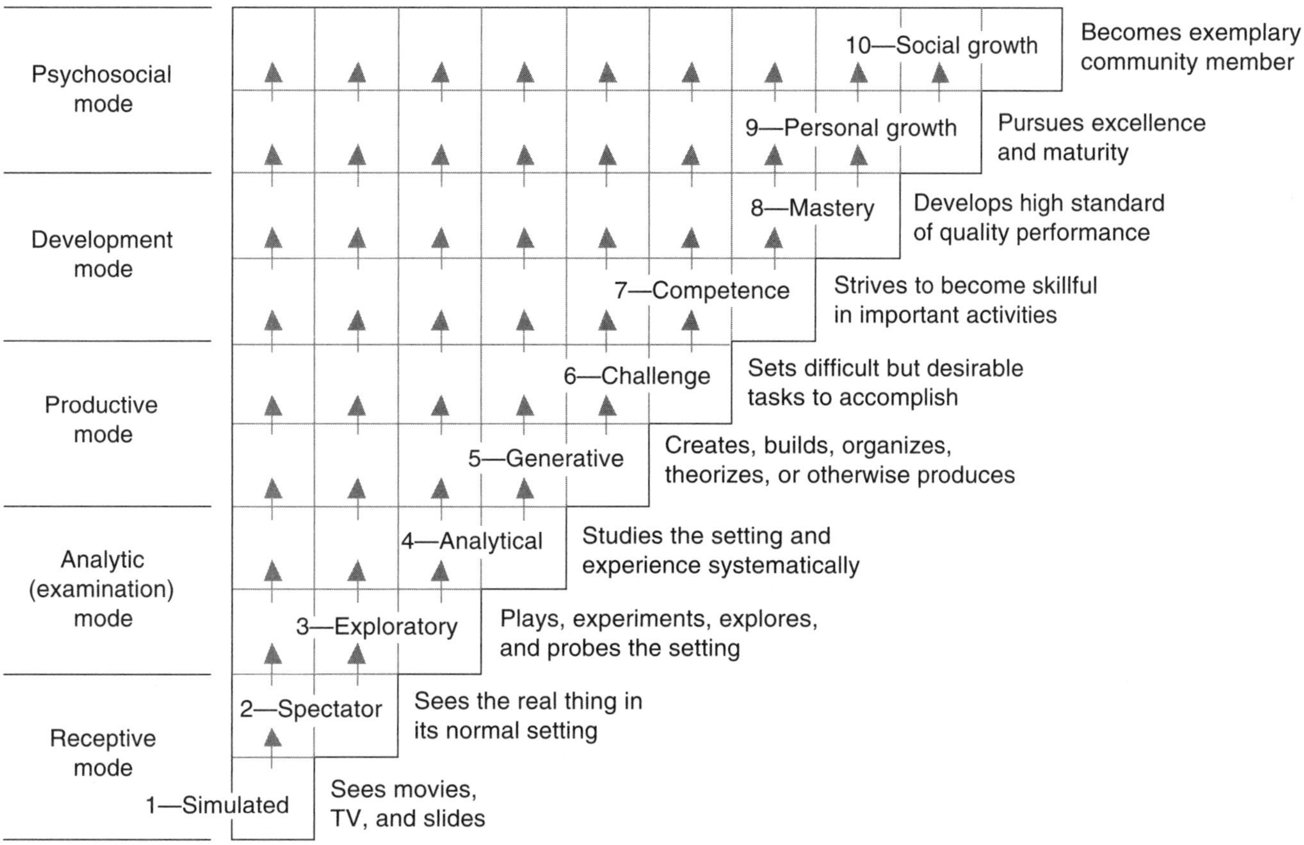

Figure 11.3 Gibbons and Hopkins' (1980) scale of experientiality.

In the **productive mode,** learners generate products, activities, and services that have been assigned by you or that the learners have devised themselves. The generative experience allows people to learn by building, creating, composing, organizing, or otherwise generating products in appropriate settings. Naturally, the challenge experience challenges the learners or allows them to challenge themselves as they struggle to achieve productivity or accomplishment.

In the **developmental mode,** learners pursue excellence in a particular field by designing and implementing long-term programs of study, activity, and practice. The competence experience encourages learners to focus on a particular field, to practice skills, to become absorbed in the activity, and to achieve recognized competence in it. The mastery experience encourages learners to go beyond competence to develop commitment, to set high personal standards in their pursuit of excellence, and to become a master of their chosen area.

In the **psychosocial mode,** learners understand themselves and their relationships with others. They accomplish the tasks presented by their particular stage of maturity and contribute to the lives of others. The personal growth experience enables learners to understand themselves as unique individuals and to effectively and responsibly direct their own activities. The social growth experience enables learners to become more socially competent with people of all ages and to act in more socially responsible ways by using their accomplishments to serve the community.

Process of Experiential Learning

Several authors have examined the cyclical nature of experiential learning. Dewey (1938) was the first of these. He believed that the "formation of purposes is a rather complex, intellectual operation. It involves (1) observation of surrounding conditions, (2) knowledge obtained partly by recollection, and (3) judgment, which puts together what is observed and what is recalled to see what they signify" (p. 69). Figure 11.4 represents Dewey's three-step process.

A number of educators, most notably Kolb (1984), constructed models based on Dewey's process. Kolb interpreted a variation of Kurt Lewin's experiential learning cycle, and combined with Dewey's work, created a four-step recurring model (see figure 11.5). In Kolb's model, "immediate concrete experience is the basis for observation and

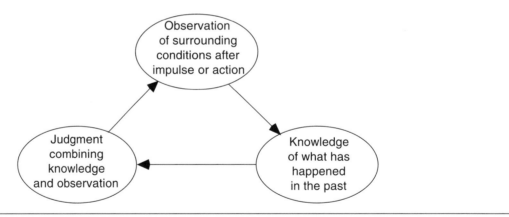

Figure 11.4   Dewey's (1938) process of experiential learning.

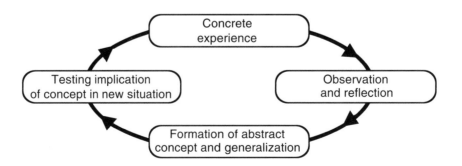

Figure 11.5   Kolb's (1984) interpretation of Lewin's experiential learning cycle.

reflection. These observations are assimilated into a 'theory' from which new implications for action can be deduced. These implications or hypotheses then serve as guides in acting to create new experiences" (p. 21).

Pfeiffer and Jones (1980) outlined their model of the process of experiential learning for group facilitators in five steps (see figure 11.6). Step 1 involves the action of doing or experiencing in order to generate information for analysis in subsequent steps. Step 2 incorporates sharing reactions to and observations from the experience in what the authors termed "publishing," likening this step to computer data input. Step 3 involves systematically examining the experience during processing by discussing the patterns and dynamics that arose from the reactions and observations. We can view the combined publishing and processing steps as an "inductive process: proceeding from observation rather than from a priori 'truth' [as in the deductive process]. Inductive learning means learning through discovery" (p. 3-4). Step four infers principles about the real world by generalizing from the publishing and processing steps. In this step, the learning becomes truly pragmatic by showing its relevance to reality. Step five infers applying new action and planning more effective behavior using the generalized principles. The cycle repeats, which "is meant to indicate that the actual application of the learning is a new experience for the participant, to be examined inductively also" (p. 7).

Experiential Learning and Judgment Paradigm

According to Dewey (1938), judgment plays the pivotal role in the experiential learning process.

He wrote that the "crucial educational problem is that of procuring the postponement of immediate action upon desire until observation and judgment have intervened" (p. 69). Dewey might have paraphrased judgment as an ability to learn how, as well as where, to look before leaping. Priest (1990) explains judgment as a six-step procedure that you undertake when information important to problem solving or decision making is missing, vague, or unknown. In order to continue the problem-solving or decision-making process, you use judgment to substitute reasonable values for the missing, vague, or unknown ones (see also chapter 20).

Specifically, experience-based judgment follows six steps: experience, induce, generalize, deduce, apply, and evaluate (see figure 11.7). First, you collect specific experiences, whether firsthand, observed, or vicarious, and store them in the brain through the senses. Second, you subject these specific experiences to inductive reflection, moving from the specific to the general. Third, you form generalized concepts and store them in memory (either long- or short-term) as a map of connected concepts. When faced with uncertainty, your brain searches these memory maps for relevant concepts. Fourth, you subject the retrieved concepts to deductive reflection, moving from the general back to the specific. Fifth, you apply your judgment (prediction, guess, estimation, or even speculation) to the situation as a substitute for the uncertainty. Sixth, you evaluate the effectiveness of this application. The outcome of your assessment acts as a new experience for the cycle to repeat. In this way, you refine judgment over time, and learning takes place through repeated reflections on experiences. This process can result in a tremendous amount of client growth.

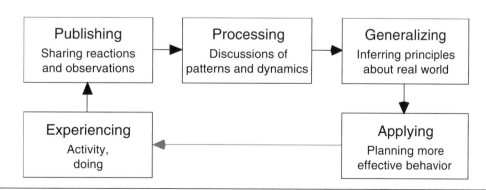

Figure 11.6 Pfeiffer and Jones' (1980) model of experiential learning.

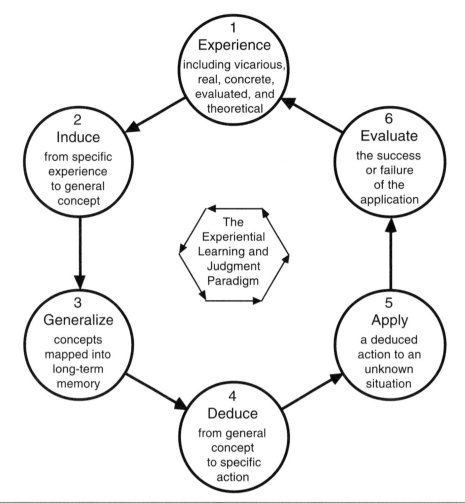

Figure 11.7 Priest's experiential learning and judgment paradigm.

Adapted, by permission, from S. Priest, 1990, "Everything you always wanted to know about judgment, but were afraid to ask," *Journal of Adventure Education and Outdoor Leadership* 7 (3), 5-12.

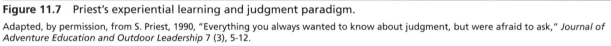

◄ EFFECTIVE OUTDOOR LEADERS ►

► Base adventure programming on sound philosophical principles and educational theories.

► Design adventure programs that contain direct and purposeful experiences, that challenge clients, and that have natural consequences.

► Use program activities that are client based, have present and future relevance, require synthesis and reflection, demand personal responsibility, and actively and inherently engage participants.

► Conduct adventure programming that is action centered and that utilizes unfamiliar environments, a climate of change, assessment observations, supportive small-group development processes, a focus on successful functioning, and changes in the leader's role.

► Measure the quality of learning experiences by criteria such as interaction and continuity, or by the scale of experientiality.

► Consider the role of service to others in adventure programming.

► Understand behavioral, cognitive, and experiential theories of learning to provide the most effective learning opportunities possible.

► Understand the contributions of the elements in the Outward Bound process model to adventure programming.

► Understand how the multiple-step cyclical models of experiential learning apply to adventure programming.

SUMMARY

Adventure programs use direct and purposeful experiences that challenge clients and have natural consequences. Adventure experiences are client based, have present and future relevance, require synthesis and reflection, demand personal responsibility, and actively and inherently engage participants. Adventure programming is action centered and utilizes unfamiliar environments, a climate of change, assessment observations, supportive small-group development processes, a focus on successful functioning, and changes in the leader's role.

The Outward Bound process model describes how change comes from the adventure experience. An adventure places the learner into unique, prescribed physical and social environments, presenting her with a characteristic set of problem-solving tasks. This situation creates a state of adaptive dissonance, leading to increased competence or mastery. This success reorganizes the meaning and direction of the learner's experience and has positive implications for the future.

Joplin's (1981) "hurricane-like" spiral model has five stages: focus, action, support, feedback, and debriefing. From the model, she identified eight characteristics associated with experiential processes and adventure programming. They are: student, not teacher, based; personal not impersonal; process and product oriented; evaluative for internal and external reasons; holistic understanding and component analytical; organized around experience; perception, not theory, based; and individual, not group, based.

We can use a scale of experientiality to measure the amount of actual experience in the learning opportunity. The amount is determined by the mediation, involvement, responsibility, mastery, and potential for growth. Five modes of increasing experientiality are based on these five aspects: receptive, analytic (examination), productive, developmental, and psychosocial. Each mode has two submodes, attaining a continuum of experientiality: simulated, spectator, exploratory, analytical, generative, challenge, competence, mastery, personal growth, and social growth.

Dewey's three-step process explains the cyclical nature of experiential learning: observation, knowledge, and judgment. Kolb uses a four-step cycle that is an interpretation of Lewin's work: concrete experience, observation and reflection, formation, and testing implications. Pfeiffer

and Jones' model has five steps: experiencing, publishing, processing, generalizing, and applying. Priest's experiential learning and judgment paradigm has six steps: experiencing, inducing, generalizing, deducing, applying, and evaluating. In conclusion, all learning is experiential at least to some degree.

QUESTIONS TO THINK ABOUT

1. In your own words, discuss the concepts expressed by the two quotes at the beginning of this chapter from Plato and John Dewey.

2. Explain the concept of direct and purposeful experience.

3. Explain the statement "Instructors are responsible 'to,' and not 'for,' the learner."

4. Take the eight principles advanced by the Association for Experiential Education and apply each to a specific adventure experience.

5. Provide your rationale for how adventure experiences foster the development of functional growth for clients.

6. Explain the concept of "contrast" and how it adds to client growth.

7. State the strengths and weaknesses of the Outward Bound process model.

8. Clarify when you should use information assimilation and when you should use experiential learning in adventure programming.

9. Recall your latest adventure program experience and explain the level you were at on the scale of experientiality.

10. Recall your latest leadership experience and explain the level your clients were at on the scale of experientiality.

11. Choose one of the cyclical models that explain experiential learning and describe how this model might apply to an adventure experience you will lead in the near future.

REFERENCES

Association for Experiential Education (AEE). (1992). *Ethical guidelines for the Therapeutic Adventure Professional Group (TAPG)*. Boulder, CO: Author.

Association for Experiential Education (AEE). (1995). Principles of experiential education practice. In *Association for Experiential Education Directory and Handbook.* Boulder, CO: Author.

Bandura, A. (1977). Social learning theory. *Psychological Review, 84*(2), 191-215.

Bobilya, A.J., & Akey, L.D. (2002). An evaluation of adventure education components in a residential learning community. *Journal of Experiential Education, 25*(2), 296-304.

Campbell, M., Liebowitz, M., Mednick, A., & Rugen, L. (Eds.). (1998). *Guide for planning a learning expedition: Expeditionary learning outward bound.* Dubuque, IA: Kendall/Hunt.

Dewey, J. (1938). *Experience and education.* New York: Collier Books.

Ewert, A., & Sibthorp, J. (2000). Multivariate analysis in experiential education: Exploring the possibilites. *Journal of Experiential Education, 22*(2), 108-117.

Gass, M.A. (Ed.). (1993). *Adventure therapy: Therapeutic applications of adventure programming in mental health settings.* Dubuque, IA: Kendall/ Hunt.

Gibbons, M., & Hopkins, D. (1980). How experiential is your experience-based program? *Journal of Experiential Education, 4*(1), 32-37.

Gillis, H.L., & Bonney, W.C. (1986). Group counseling with couples or families: Adding adventure activities. *Journal for Specialists in Group Work, 11*(4), 213-220.

Grube, G.M.A. (Ed.). (1974). *Plato's republic.* Indianapolis: Hackett.

Joplin, L. (1981). On defining experiential education. *Journal of Experiential Education, 4*(1), 17-20.

Kiewa, J. (1994). Self-control: The key to adventure? In E. Cole, E. Erdman, & E. Rothblum (Eds.), *Wilderness therapy for women: The power of adventure* (pp. 29-42). New York: Harrington Park.

Kimball, R.O. (1993). The wilderness as therapy: The value of using adventure programs in therapeutic assessment. In M.A. Gass (Ed.), *Therapeutic applications of adventure programming in mental health settings* (pp. 153-160). Boulder, CO: Association for Experiential Education.

King, K. (1988). The role of adventure in the experiential learning process. *Journal of Experiential Education, 11*(2), 4-8.

Klint, K.A. (1999). New directions for inquiry into self-concept and adventure experiences. In J.C. Miles & S. Priest (Eds.), *Adventure education* (pp. 163-168). State College, PA: Venture.

Kolb, D.A. (1984). *Experiential learning.* Englewood Cliffs, NJ: Prentice Hall.

McKenzie, M. (2003). Beyond the Outward Bound process. *Journal of Experiential Education, 26*(1), 8-23.

Mason, M. (1987). Wilderness family therapy: Experiential dimensions. *Contemporary Family Therapy, 9*(1-2), 90-105.

Pfeiffer, J.W., & Jones, J.E. (1980). *The 1980 annual handbook for group facilitators.* San Diego: University Associates.

Priest, S. (1990). Everything you always wanted to know about judgment, but were afraid to ask. *Journal of Adventure Education and Outdoor Leadership, 7*(3), 5-12.

Selye, H. (1974). *Stress without distress.* New York: Signet Books.

Walsh, V., & Golins, G. (1976). *The exploration of the Outward Bound process model.* Denver: Colorado Outward Bound School.

Warren, K., Sakofs, M., & Hunt, J.S. (1995). *The theory of experiential education.* Dubuque, IA: Association for Experiential Education.

Williamson, J., & Gass, M. (1993). *Manual of program accreditation for adventure programs.* Boulder, CO: Association for Experiential Education.

Instructional Methods

Education is a lot like learning to swim in a pool that has shallow and deep ends. Some people learn to swim in the shallow end and move to the deep end when they have their basics down. Some people plunge right into the deep end, hoping they learn quickly before drowning. Still others enter the shallow end, wade around with a great deal of trepidation, and never develop the confidence to progress further. In all of these cases, some flounder and a few sink, but the ones who become independent swimmers accomplish this feat because they build on and connect all of the elements of their learning experiences. And although many prefer just to get their feet wet, none are truly educated unless they venture into deeper waters!

Learning has a "shallow" and a "deep" end. Shallow learning involves retaining and understanding theory. But knowing theory is rarely enough. To fully learn, you must pragmatically use knowledge by testing whether a theory works in real situations. This deep learning involves utilizing and creating practice from theory. In this chapter, we discuss instructional models you can use to foster deep learning as well as strategies and skills for successful teaching, including public speaking, teaching tips for effective lessons, and objective and goal setting. You'll be able to directly apply all of the models, skills, and strategies we discuss to adventure programming whether the focus of your program is on recreation, education, development, or therapy.

FIVE DEPTHS OF LEARNING

We can view learning as having five depths, ranging from a shallow, basic end to a deep, complex end. These five progressively deeper levels are memorization, comprehension, application, generalization, and systemization.

1. At the first, or **memorization,** depth, the learner memorizes by repeating factual information and identifying right and wrong answers. For example, a memorizing learner will be able to list the key rules of belaying (anchor, proper steps to belay, communication signals, and so on). The learner can also identify right or wrong ways to belay, such as not keeping the "breaking" hand on the rope at all times.

2. At the **comprehension** depth, the learner is able to explain how processes work and why, when, and where the learning can be used. For the same belaying example, a comprehending learner can describe the step-by-step sequence of hand movements for belaying and detail situations in which belaying may or may not be necessary.

3. At the **application** depth, the learner applies her comprehension by practicing or demonstrating the learning in the specific situation for which it was intended or in which she initially learned it. For the belaying example, an applying learner is able to set up and handle a horizontal belay in the classroom and transpose this to setting up and operating a vertical belay in top-rope rock climbing.

4. At the **generalization** depth, the learner modifies or adapts the learning to suit new and different environments. For example, a generalizing learner is able to vary the technique from belaying on a river crossing to belaying during a rappel to belaying a lead rock climber. Each situation is different, requiring specific modifications.

5. At the final, **systemization,** depth, the learner creates new knowledge from her base of existing knowledge. In the belaying example, the systemizing learner is able to find a new and perhaps better way to belay. Recent changes to using tubular or camming belay devices instead of plate or body belays are examples of systemization at work.

A client's success in reaching a particular depth of learning depends heavily on your instructional methods. In this chapter, we look at the inquiry–discovery approach to learning (Hammerman & Priest, 1989), the learning gradient (Priest & Hammerman, 1990), and the Socratic method of questioning.

Inquiry–Discovery Approach to Learning

The **inquiry–discovery approach to learning** is useful for teaching cognitive concepts. Inquiring and discovering are natural ways to learn, the ways people have always learned on their own without intercession by a leader or instructor. The process begins with a question and the answers follow from rational, logical, and systematic study.

As the name implies, the learning approach has two segments: inquiry and discovery. **Inquiry** involves three parts: questioning, investigating, and analyzing. **Discovery** also involves three parts: interpreting, understanding, and answering. The relationship between the two segments is cyclical: inquiry leads to discovery, and in turn, discovery leads to new inquiry (see figure 12.1).

Let's look more closely at the inquiry process. **Questioning** almost always begins with the postulation of a theory, the recognition of a problem, or the formulation of a hypothesis. **Investigating** uses a method or procedure to secure evidence to support the theory, resolve the problem, or test the hypothesis. In **analyzing,** the learner scrutinizes information for patterns of relationships, similarities, or differences. Once he identifies these patterns, he may move to discovery, considering and discussing them in relation to the initial theory, problem, or hypothesis during the **interpreting** step. Then, in the **understanding** step, he explains whether these connections support the theory, solve the problem, or refute the hypothesis. In this manner, he can explain the original question in the **answering** step, and good answers lead to more good questions.

This sequence is similar to the scientific method with one exception. For the scientific method, the learner formulates a hypothesis or theory and then collects information through questioning to see whether the hypothesis is true or not. In the inquiry–discovery approach to learning, however, you assist this process by adding additional questions to the client questioning. Because of this dialogue, inquiry and discovery are time-consuming. They involve great interaction between teacher and learner. As the teacher, you stimulate learning by posing questions to learners, causing them to think about what they have observed, what is likely to occur next, and the steps to pursue in order to bring about a certain action or solve a particular problem (Hammerman & Priest, 1989; Sakofs et al., 1995). In this way, the inquiry–discovery approach moves learners beyond mere memorization to address the middle depths of learning (analyzing, interpreting).

Learning Gradient

The **learning gradient** combines useful methods to teach psychomotor or physical skills, such as how to paddle, climb, or ski. The gradient is a continuum of four methods: **speaking** (telling), **demonstrating** (showing), **simulating** (doing), and **confirming** (questioning) as shown in figure 12.2. In the speaking method, you tell, or lecture, about

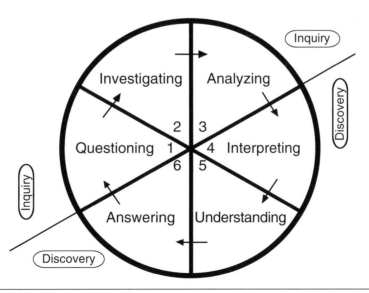

Figure 12.1 The inquiry–discovery approach to learning.

Adapted, by permission, from D. Hammerman and S. Priest, 1989, "The inquiry/discovery approach to learning in adventure," *Journal of Adventure Education and Outdoor Leadership* 6 (2), 29-32.

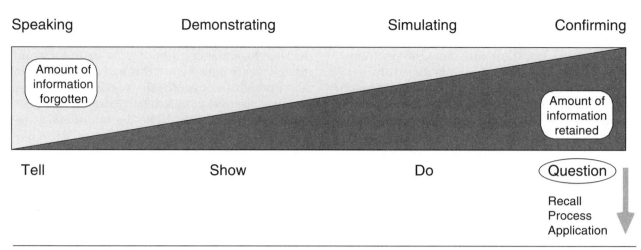

Figure 12.2 The learning gradient.

Adapted, by permission, from S. Priest and D. Hammerman, 1990, "Teaching outdoor adventure skills," *Journal of Adventure Education and Outdoor Leadership* 6 (4), 16-18.

a particular skill. The client simply assimilates the information. For the demonstrating method, you show the particular skill, and the client watches. In the simulating method, the client performs the same skill, and you evaluate the performance. In confirming, the client answers questions posed by you as you test for learning depth. As the learner progresses along the continuum, the amount of information retained increases.

For example, say you are teaching a lesson in knot tying. You begin by telling, progress to showing and doing, and end with questioning. You tell the group information, such as terminology (e.g., standing part, bight) and typology (e.g., knot families, breaking strengths). Once the group has a fundamental understanding of key concepts, you show them how to tie knots one knot at a time, since too much information at once often proves wasteful early in learning. Once the group members have seen the various steps to tying one knot, they practice the same knot. After they have shown their competence at tying that knot, you ask questions about the application, or "dressed," shape of the knot before moving on to the next tying exercise.

Mere "telling is not teaching" (D. Hammerman, W. Hammerman, & E. Hammerman, 1985). Since people forget most of what they hear, clients will not learn to tie knots by being told a large amount of information. Similarly, seeing several knots being tied is usually insufficient for learning, although demonstration will have greater impact than lecturing. Clients must practice knot tying before they can even begin to learn. The old adage, "I hear and I forget, I see and I remember, I do and

I understand" (Confucius), has obvious connections to skills learning. Adding, "You ask me and I know," to this process can further cement what was learned, mirroring the four progressive steps of the learning gradient:

▶ Speaking (telling)—I hear and I forget.

▶ Demonstrating (showing)—I see and I remember.

▶ Simulating (doing)—I do and I understand.

▶ Confirming (questioning)—You ask me and I know.

Socratic Method of Questioning

Both the inquiry–discovery approach and the learning gradient require the correct use of questioning to realize their full teaching–learning potential. Both cases employ the **Socratic method** of questioning. As you probably know, this method is named after the Greek philosopher Socrates, who frequently used questions to elicit thinking from his students.

Questions used for the Socratic method come in three principal forms: recall, process, and application (D. Hammerman, W. Hammerman, & E. Hammerman, 1985). **Recall questions** ask learners to remember principles based on earlier experience. They encompass counting, describing, identifying, matching, naming, observing, remembering, and selecting. Process **questions** ask learners to reason for answers. They involve analyzing, classifying, comparing, contrasting, experimenting, explaining, grouping, implying, inferring, and ordering. **Application questions** ask learners to come up with examples showing that they fully understand a concept by putting it in use. Application questions embrace evaluating, extrapolating, generalizing, hypothesizing, interpolating, judging, predicting, speculating, and theorizing (D. Hammerman, W. Hammerman, & E. Hammerman). These questions help you probe the shallower three depths of learning: memorization, comprehension, and application.

Asking these types of questions in this order (recall first and application last) is the most effective for confirming learning. In the example of knot tying, recall questions could be "What is this part of the rope called? What kind of knot is this?" Process questions might include "How are these two knots similar and different? What is wrong with this knot?" Application questions might include "How could this knot be used? If I add an extra loop to this knot, what does it become?" For each question, students' thinking processes increase in complexity and sophistication as questions range from recall through process to application.

Questions not only confirm learning as in the learning gradient and guide learning as with inquiry and discovery, but they also motivate students to learn. Asking questions for which learners do not have immediate answers makes them more likely to remember the answer than when someone else provides it. Questioning stimulates thinking through adaptive dissonance, thereby increasing retention.

PUBLIC SPEAKING

Public speaking is an essential tool to you as an outdoor leader, but like many people, you may greatly fear it. Still, called on to teach concepts and skills, debrief emotions and feelings, and introduce adventure activities, you must be a capable speaker. So practice to become an effective public speaker. Try these suggestions for public speaking when making presentations, not speeches:

► Be yourself and act naturally. Don't be false or try to copy someone else's style. Allow spontaneity to occur. Don't read the presentation or make a speech. This can be as boring as reading a textbook aloud! Let your enthusiasm shine through. Don't hold back on appropriate feelings, personality aspects, and convictions.

► Before a presentation, try conducting voice warm-up exercises, practicing resonance, articulation, projection, annunciation, and pronunciation. Casually talking with people or singing

alone before speaking can substitute for these exercises. Practice relaxation techniques to reduce your apprehension. Deep breathing, listening to soft music, and positive mental imagery (seeing success) can make a big difference in getting the stomach butterflies to fly in the right formation. Don't dwell on things that could go wrong!

► If possible, arrive early and set up any equipment you need, such as audiovisuals, teaching props, handouts, and the like, and if you use notes, be certain they are accessible and in the correct order—but remember, don't depend on notes! If formal introductions are called for, wait to be introduced; otherwise, introduce yourself or have a friend introduce you. Open with a brief story, personal anecdote, dramatic statement, or rhetorical question that relates to your presentation's topic. Be careful when telling jokes as openers: they rarely relate to the topic and can distract or alienate an audience. By all means use humor, but only if it is appropriate and natural.

► Know the audience and its competence levels (Campbell, Liebowitz, Mednick, & Rugen, 1998). Avoid speaking about topics that are beyond clients' realm of comprehension, and don't talk down to them. Treat an audience with respect. Clients will be reluctant to learn if they perceive you as arrogant or discourteous. Prepare content with the particular audience in mind. Consider their age, education, knowledge, interest, and size when planning. Before any presentation, take the time to meet, talk with, and learn about representative members of the audience, especially in an unknown group.

► Be enthusiastic and prepared. If you aren't interested in the topic, then clients certainly won't be! Organize and rehearse the presentation in a logical order and know the content extremely well; otherwise, expect many mistakes, some disappointed clients, and the occasional mistake of running overtime. Practice speaking to friends who will give you honest feedback. As you refine your presentation, use a tape recorder to double-check the points your friends made.

► During a presentation, move around. When you vary your position, you help focus audience interest and attention. Stand erect; shift eye contact among a variety of people; use effective body language, for example, using hand gestures instead of nervously playing with coins in your pocket; breathe steadily for voice control; and utilize a variety of speaking methods, varying clarity, volume, speed, and pitch.

▶ Speak with authority. Speak clearly, loudly, and slowly to overcome surrounding noises. Be certain the learners who answer questions also speak clearly, loudly, and slowly so all may hear. Speaking too slowly, however, may permit a client's attention to wander, while speaking too fast may prevent clients from assimilating information. Avoid speaking in monotone and running words together. Distinguish similar sounding words by clearly enunciating each syllable. Use voice inflection to vary the pitch of speech and vary volume to highlight important points.

▶ Give plenty of examples and analogies to connect the presentation to real life. Make these examples clear, emphasizing the key concepts. Summarize the key concepts, highlight them by varying speech volume or tone, and repeat them often for significance. Pause occasionally: silence can be an effective tool. Provide an agenda for the presentation by displaying the outline on a flip chart, board, or screen; refer to this outline to let clients know how the presentation is proceeding. Use the "signpost" words, that is, the same indicator words used in the agenda, to convey location within the presentation. Avoid slang words and clichés. Use vivid language that is rich in symbolism, imagery, and metaphor. List important words on an outline, defining or explaining any term clients may not know.

▶ Notice audience reaction to the presentation. Monitor body language and energy levels. If clients appear bored, be prepared to shorten the presentation by dropping a few points. If the presentation content is dry and boring, consider using audiovisuals to spice it up. Since a picture is worth a thousand words, slides, videos, photographs, and even overhead transparencies can improve a presentation and therefore the degree of learning that takes place. Address all responses or comments from the audience by paraphrasing or repeating them for all to hear. Don't ignore this input. Instead, praise or reinforce all contributions, then ask clients questions that elicit deeper comprehension.

▶ While asking questions seems relatively simple on first examination, you can choose to follow one of several procedures. Ask clear, concise, and open-ended questions, that is, ones that cannot be answered with a short response such as yes or no. Pause and allow plenty of time for thinking. If no answers are forthcoming, gently request one from a particular person. Listen carefully to the answer, paraphrase or repeat it for all to hear, and respond to the person who gave the answer. One sure way to reduce the number of answers given by a group is to criticize ideas. Instead, thank each person for her contribution and probe for greater detail. If an answer is incorrect, ask further questions that help the learner discover this fact without letting on that you think he's wrong. While trying to understand clients' opinions, you may sometimes find your own logic in error or may see things from a fresh perspective. Always connect answers to the lesson of the presentation, to reality, or to the next question.

▶ After a presentation, sum up key points and ask clients for their questions (unless clients have been free to interject questions during the presentation). If you don't know an answer, say so, pledge to find out, and then follow up with an answer for that client. Seek feedback (verbal and possibly even written) from clients about the effectiveness of the presentation by asking them for their opinions and by observing their use of the presentation content in future learning situations.

DESIGNING EFFECTIVE LESSONS

While the suggestions for public speaking fit well with presentations, presentations constitute only a small amount of teaching in outdoor leadership. More common by far are teaching lessons in the outdoors. The fundamentals of public speaking still apply to this instruction, yet a number of tips and tricks can improve your outdoor teaching, including those for lesson planning, setting up the teaching environment, getting started, delivering the information, finishing up, and substituting for audiovisual aids.

Lesson Planning

The key to lesson planning is constantly taking the learner's perspective: always ask what the learner might think of the lesson. Although many different ways to plan a lesson exist, they all have aspects in common with the following procedure:

1. List all the skills and concepts that learners need to get from the lesson.
2. Organize these into a logical flow, or sequence, of learning. Such organization is usually, but not always, linear. You can progress from the known to the unknown, from the inductive (which is reasoning

from the particular to the general) to the deductive (which is reasoning from the general to the particular), from the general rule to the example, from the observed to abstract principles, from reality to theory, from whole to piece, from simple to complex, from primitive to sophisticated, and possibly from the reverse of all these.

3. Once you have organized the skills and concepts into the main body of the lesson, add a conclusion that summarizes the lesson. Be sure to include a review of the main points and suggestions of ways to apply the lesson to future learning.

4. After completing the first three steps, add an introduction that outlines what the lesson will be about and that motivates the learner by explaining the usefulness of the lesson. Be sure to include the purpose of the lesson, its context within the grand scheme of the adventure program or course curriculum, and its possible connection to past learning.

Teaching Environment

In setting up the teaching environment, design an environment that builds community, security, and trust (Frank, 2004). Also consider your two likely locations: indoor and outdoor. In both locations, consider the clients' comfort in terms of temperature, for example, by adjusting the thermostat or encouraging clients to add or remove clothing layers; lighting, for example, by adjusting light switches or having clients face away from the sun; and air quality, for example, by adjusting air conditioning or having clients sit away from campfire smoke. Whether teaching in the classroom sitting in chairs or outdoors sitting on the grass under a tree, let the lesson format determine the seating formation. For verbal discussion, form a circle, which permits eye contact for all. For two-way exchange, that is, a lesson with some discussion and some presentation, use a semicircle arrangement. For lecturing, seat the group in rows.

Getting Started

Begin with names and introductions. Avoid the usual "introduce yourself" in favor of a name game or a partner or group introduction. Next, ascertain the clients' expectations. Have clients finish sentences like "I expect this program to . . ." or "This experience will help me . . ." and "The adventure will be good if. . . ." You can have them write down their conclusions, shuffle them, and then have them read by another for anonymity or put on a wall for all to see. These responses often

Effective lessons in the outdoors don't just happen; they involve careful lesson planning, evaluation of the teaching environment, knowing how to get started, delivering the information, and finishing up.

prove useful for setting goals and objectives (see the last section of this chapter). Once clients have shared their expectations with you, you should share your expectations with clients. Detail leader roles and responsibilities in the lesson or program. This is also the time to demonstrate congeniality. At best, authoritative leaders can make clients feel inadequate. At worst, they can make clients feel foolish and humiliated. But as an approachable leader, you can make clients willing to reveal their ignorance about the lesson material and to gamble on asking you for help.

Delivering Information

When delivering information, you can choose to do so in different modes depending on whether you are demonstrating, actually performing the skill, or having clients simulate your demonstrations, copying the movement that you demonstrated. During demonstrations, break skills into their components. For example, the Dufek stroke, used in white-water paddling, is a combination of four different paddle movements: high brace, standing draw stroke, draw stroke to the bow, and power forward stroke. For students to learn such a complex stroke in one fluid motion demands that you teach it in pieces and then show students how to assemble the pieces. Pass demonstration equipment around for everyone to see and touch before you use it. Keep an eye open for clients who practice their simulations early, during the demonstration. This action may indicate that they have absorbed too much information and are trying to retain it by practicing. If so, break the demonstration into smaller parts, reminding clients to watch first and try later on. Always begin with easy skills or concepts and increase the difficulty as the learners gain confidence and competence.

When clients are simulating, be sure everyone has finished practicing before giving the next demonstration. If clients get left behind at this point, you will expend extra energy helping them catch up in the future, especially if they become lost or disinterested. Assign a helper to work with those who need extra practice. Enlist talented or quick learners to partner with a peer who needs assistance. Avoid definite statements like "It's simple!" because clients who don't catch on right away will feel even more inadequate. Disclose the criteria you use to evaluate performance and then adhere to them so that clients clearly know what you expect.

Finishing Up

When finishing up, don't forget to question, confirming learning. Monitor the group for their reactions, and don't let clients sit still for too long. Let them participate for brief times throughout the lesson to ward off boredom in situations in which you are asking clients to assimilate large amounts of information.

Substituting for Audiovisual Aids

Audiovisual aids are useful for breaking monotony, presenting complex data, stimulating discussion, providing examples, and emphasizing key learning points in a classroom lecture. Unfortunately, slides or overhead projectors, black- or whiteboards, video players, and flip charts are rarely practical or accessible in the outdoors. But drawing in the sand or dirt can be almost as effective as high-tech visual aids. Clients may pay greater attention if you use handouts as substitutes for audiovisual aids since then they don't have to continually take notes. Still, the litter and convenience concerns limit the use of handouts in wilderness areas. If you do use handouts, be aware that they may distract clients from presentations, demonstrations, or simulations. Models are another substitute, but their effectiveness can be less than that of high-tech equipment for some clients. For example, you could demonstrate the "ferrying" technique for paddling laterally across river currents by using a stick and string in a gentle stream. This may not be as compelling or convincing as a computer simulation, a movie, or an actual hands-on demonstration. You may use high-tech aids in preparatory classes before the adventure and then reinforce the application of this information on-site.

OBJECTIVE WRITING AND GOAL SETTING

Goals and objectives form the foundation for all lessons taught in adventure programs. Setting goals and objectives is critical to outdoor leaders and is almost as important to clients. You should use goals and objectives to define the direction of the adventure program and to prepare and organize adventure experiences. Clients should use them to plan for after the adventure program as they continue dealing with daily life. In all cases, writing detailed goals and objectives can augment the reasoning processes for both yourself and your clients.

Goals are general intents that stem from the adventure program's purpose. **Objectives** are specific target declarations that clarify and expand each goal. If, for example, the purpose of a program is to reduce juvenile delinquency in a community, then one goal might be to reduce self-destructive behaviors in at-risk youth who are clients. Furthermore, one of several objectives for this particular goal might be to improve the self-concept of youth clients, as measured by their scores on the Tennessee Self-Concept Scale or other assessment tools, through adventure activities conducted over 3 mos. Although you and your clients should write down goals and objectives, consider these goals to be always in flux, never carved in stone. Note that a program could also use goals and objectives to direct leader or client behavior or performance.

We can divide goals into four different kinds: regular work goals, problem-solving goals, innovative goals, and developmental goals. Let's examine these four types for an adventure program working with female survivors of sexual abuse. Note that we have written these goals with the behavior you should target in mind.

▶ **Regular work goals** are those that make up the major portion of your responsibilities to ensure the safe, effective, and efficient delivery of program services.

Example: Empower clients by giving them greater control over the experience.

▶ **Problem-solving goals** give you opportunities to solve major problems and to prevent program quality from suffering by doing so.

Example: Intervene in potential flashback situations that may limit client benefits.

▶ **Innovative goals** proactively improve the delivery of program services.

Example: Anticipate and eliminate barriers to transfer of learning when clients return to society.

▶ **Developmental goals** are intended to improve your performance so that a program can improve services, adjust to changing market conditions, deliver better quality services, and reinvest in staff.

Example: Educate staff on upcoming minor alterations in the boundaries associated with physical contact with clients.

Objectives are extremely detailed, and several may constitute a general goal. In other words, one goal may have multiple objectives. With corporate clients, a normal goal is to develop teamwork. Four resulting objectives for this singular goal could be related to trust, support, cooperation, and communication. For example, on completion of the adventure program, the client will have demonstrated the following:

1. Trust in group members by completing the Trust Fall into others' arms from a tabletop

2. A willingness to accept and offer help as evidenced by sharing at least five ideas during a complex group task without receiving discouraging comments from any group members

3. An ability to work with others without argument under adversity or time deadlines

4. Effective listening skills by speaking one at a time during all debriefing sessions and not making comments unrelated to the discussion

Note that we have written these objectives with the participant's targeted behavior in mind. All four of these interdependent objectives identify elements of conduct, conditions, or criteria (Mager, 1984). Conduct denotes what you expect a client to do, generally using active verbs to portray either a process or a product of performance. Conditions describe the circumstances under which performance takes place. Criteria indicate acceptable performance, generally using some measure of evaluation to determine success. Objectives ideally include all three of these elements. For example, after finishing the module on kayak strokes, the novice client will be able to paddle forward and backward, to skull laterally through an English gate 1 m (3 ft) wide on flatwater (conduct), with no wind (conditions), and without touching the gate with the paddle or craft (criteria).

Another way of writing objectives is to make them SMART: specific, measurable, achievable, realistic, and time bound.

▶ **Specific:** You should precisely state the expected outcome. If you want to be richer, specifically how much money do you need to obtain to easily meet your needs?

▶ **Measurable:** Define the change as an outcome to reach. If you don't know where you

◄ EFFECTIVE OUTDOOR LEADERS ►

▶ Are aware of models on the depth of learning, the inquiry–discovery approach, the learning gradient, and the Socratic method.

▶ Apply these models of learning to teach effectively.

▶ Strive to be capable public speakers and teachers.

▶ Deliver effective lessons both indoors and outdoors.

▶ Set goals and write objectives for learning and performance.

are going, how will you know when you get there?

▶ **Achievable:** Change should be possible. Setting unachievable objectives merely leads to frustration. Do you have the resources necessary for achieving this objective?

▶ **Realistic:** You should base the change in actual circumstances. Is change real or valuable if it takes place during imaginary role-playing?

▶ **Time bound:** You should expect the change to be accomplished by a certain deadline. If you have no time limit for completion, will you have the incentive to finish?

Last, adventure programs are typically evaluated based on goals and objectives. For goal and objective setting to be of any value, the goals and objectives you set must be relevant, concise, and measurable. The more accurate as well as appropriate the goals and objectives set, the greater the true reflection of learning achieved.

SUMMARY

We can describe the depth of learning on a spectrum moving from memorization through comprehension, application, and generalization to systemization. The ability to reach a depth of learning depends on instructional methods, such as the inquiry–discovery approach, the learning gradient, and the Socratic method, as well as on skills and strategies, such as public speaking, effective teaching, and appropriate objective or goal setting.

The inquiry–discovery approach to learning helps teach cognitive concepts and has six parts arranged in a cycle: questioning, investigating, analyzing, interpreting, understanding, and answering. In short, this is the scientific method supplemented with guidance in the form of questions from you, the outdoor leader.

The learning gradient helps teach activity skills and is a continuum of four methods: speaking, demonstrating, simulating, and confirming. In short, you tell the client some fundamental information about the skill, show the skill, have the client practice the skill, and then ask questions about the skill to cement learning.

The Socratic method includes three types of questions: the recall of principles, the process of reasoning, and the application of learning to new situations. When you ask these types of questions in sequence, as opposed to randomly, they guide, confirm, and motivate learning.

Public speaking is a common fear of leaders but an important teaching tool. The keys to public speaking are to relax and be yourself, warm up your voice before speaking, know the audience well, prepare well with its needs in mind, rehearse in advance, vary your style of presentation, speak with clarity and authority, use plenty of examples and relate them with vivid language, monitor the audience's reaction and adjust accordingly, ask open-ended questions, and seek feedback afterward so you can do better next time. Some crucial tips and tricks for teaching in the outdoors are to plan lessons in a logical progression, to provide a comfortable place for learning, to ascertain client expectations in advance, to share leadership expectations, to break complex skills down into component parts, to question to confirm learning, and to substitute for audiovisual aids.

Prepare, organize, and teach your lessons for your adventure program using written program goals and objectives. Then, when planning for future client change and for your program's administrative direction, look at the goals and objectives again. Goals are general intents that stem from the adventure program's purpose. Objectives are specific targets that clarify and expand each goal.

One goal may have several related objectives, and both goals and objectives should remain flexible. Goals come in four types: regular work, problem solving, innovative, and developmental. Objectives should mention conduct, conditions, or criteria. Make them SMART: specific, measurable, achievable, realistic, and time bound.

QUESTIONS TO THINK ABOUT

1. Compare the five depths of learning to the six parts of inquiry–discovery learning.

2. Compare the five depths of learning to the four methods of the learning gradient.

3. Compare the five depths of learning to the three types of questions used in the Socratic method.

4. Recall the last time you spoke in public. Which of our suggestions did you use and not use?

5. Recall the last time you taught a skill or concept. Which of the teaching tips and tricks did you use and not use?

6. Think of the purpose of any adventure program and then set four goals for that program, using one of each of the four types.

7. Write three objectives for each of the four goals you wrote.

8. Contrast conduct, conditions, and criteria with the SMART way to write objectives.

9. Plan an outdoor lesson using either the six parts of the inquiry–discovery approach or the four methods of the learning gradient.

REFERENCES

Campbell, M., Liebowitz, M., Mednick, A., & Rugen, L. (Eds.). (1998). *Guide for planning a learning expedition: Expeditionary learning outward bound.* Dubuque, IA: Kendall/Hunt.

Frank, L.S. (2004). *Journey toward the caring classroom: Using adventure to create community in the classroom and beyond.* Madison, WI: Woods N Barnes.

Hammerman, D.R., Hammerman, W.M., & Hammerman, E.L. (1985). *Teaching in the outdoors* (3rd ed.). Danville, IL: Interstate.

Hammerman, D., & Priest, S. (1989). The inquiry/discovery approach to learning in adventure. *Journal of Adventure Education and Outdoor Leadership, 6*(2), 29-32.

Mager, R.F. (1984). *Preparing instructional objectives.* Belmont, CA: David S. Lake.

Priest, S., & Hammerman, D. (1990). Teaching outdoor adventure skills. *Journal of Adventure Education and Outdoor Leadership, 6*(4), 16-18.

Sakofs, M., Armstrong, G., Proudman, S., Howard, J., and Clark, T. (1995). Developing a teacher development model: A work in progress. *Journal of Experiential Education, 18*(3), 128-132.

CHAPTER

Teaching Models

Teaching is a lot like white-water boating: To be successful the work must be divided up into a series of interconnected choices made before, during, and after the white-water experience. Before each rapid, boaters choose where they intend to go, what they take with them, when they go, and who goes in what order. In the rapids, boaters often choose their speed and route, pause in an eddy, or move upstream to retry a segment of a rapid. After the rapids, boaters make choices about evaluating the success of the passage, discussing how to do it better next time, and preparing for the next set of rapids.

Teaching is much the same: When conducting learning experiences, you have to make choices before, during, and after the experience. In this chapter, we describe in detail a range of teaching styles through which you can slowly shift the control over the learning experience from yourself to your clients. The last area of control you surrender is usually the planning done beforehand, since this area has the greatest power and influence over clients' learning. We have based much of the paradigm used to illustrate this teaching process on the ideas of Mosston and Ashworth (2002) and Priest and Gass (1997).

The model in figure 13.1 shows six teaching styles as well as a seventh shared style. The six styles differ by who, you or your clients, predominantly holds responsibility when making key choices in the preexperience, experience, and postexperience phases of learning.

PHASES OF THE LEARNING EXPERIENCE

Before discussing the teaching styles, let's look at the learning phases and their respective options (see figure 13.2).

Preexperience

The **preexperience phase** concerns the choices made before an adventure experience. We can characterize these choices using the following six questions about teaching:

▶ **Why?** refers to reasons for teaching; possible uses of information, such as practical or theoretical; depth of information, such as memorization, comprehension, application, generalization, and

	Preexperience Before: why, what, how, who, where, and when to teach	Experience During: introduction, pace, direction, resting, redoing	Postexperience After: reflection, evaluation, integration, feedback, follow-up
Dictated	Leader	Leader	Leader
Prescribed	Leader	Leader	Client
Directed	Leader	Client	Leader
Consulted	Leader	Client	Client
Interpreted	Client	Client	Leader
Automated	Client	Client	Client
Shared	Leader and client	Leader and client	Leader and client

Figure 13.1 The seven teaching styles for adventure programming.

	Preexperience	Experience	Postexperience
Why	Teaching reasons Information uses Information depth Client relevance	**Introduction** Briefing and framing **Pace and rhythm** Learning speeds	**Reflection** Gaining meaning Appropriate methods **Evaluation**
What	Subject matter Intended objectives Expected outcomes Required resources Evaluation methods	**Direction** Adjustments **Resting** Teachable moments	Who establishes criteria Procedures used **Integration** Linking learning
How	Methods and styles Feedback and evaluation	**Redoing** Reexperiencing	**Feedback** Verbal or nonverbal Source, delay, or withhold
Who	Clients and groups		
Where	Setting and positioning		**Follow-up** Enhancing transfer
When	Scheduling and sequencing		Alternatives available

Figure 13.2   Decision options for the three phases.

systemization (see chapter 12); and relevance of the information, such as whether it will appropriately meet the clients' needs.

▶ **What?** refers to content or subject matter, such as which topics and in what proportions; intended objectives, that is, what the lesson should achieve; expected outcomes, or what should happen; required resources, such as what equipment you should gather and what other logistics you must deal with; and possible methods of evaluation, that is, how clients' performance might be objectively or subjectively evaluated.

▶ **How?** refers to teaching methods, for example, how to use Socratic questioning or modeling; feedback, such as how to give or receive it; evaluation, including how to establish criteria or procedures; and teaching styles, including how best to communicate information.

▶ **Who?** refers to the clients, who are receptive to learning, and to the group, which you should teach as individuals or in pairs and in small or large units.

▶ **Where?** refers to the setting, including the best location, environment, or weather for teaching, and to positioning, such as where to place yourself in relation to the clients.

▶ **When?** refers to scheduling, such as when to start or finish and take breaks, and to sequencing, such as when to teach each piece of information

in the lesson and when to teach this lesson in the context of all information to be taught.

Experience

The **experience phase** contains all the choices associated with learning during the adventure, such as introduction, pace, direction, resting, and redoing.

▶ **Introduction** refers to briefing clients on the learning experience in a manner that is consistent with the objectives, for example, using isomorphic framing to enhance metaphoric transfer (see chapters 14 and 16).

▶ **Pace** refers to teaching information with a rhythm that matches the diversity of learning speeds.

▶ **Direction** refers to making minor adjustments on the run as to where the learning is going (sometimes referred to as "thinking on your feet!") since learning rarely progresses according to the preexperience plan.

▶ **Resting** refers to stopping for a teachable moment or a breather as well as to terminating the teaching session if it becomes inappropriate, ineffective, or miseducative.

▶ **Redoing** refers to allowing clients to experience the opportunity to learn once again. For example, repeating a rapid is never the same: it is very different each time, facilitating further learning.

Postexperience

The **postexperience phase** includes the choices you make after clients have experienced learning through adventure. These options focus clients' attention on gaining meaning and relevance from the experience through reflection, evaluation, integration, feedback, and follow-up.

▶ To encourage **reflection,** you may select from many methods, such as solo contemplation, group discussion, guided debriefing, and journal writing, to help clients learn the most from any experience (Hoban, 1999; Sugerman, Doherty, Garvey, & Gass, 2000).

▶ You have several decisions to make for **evaluation,** such as who establishes criteria (you or clients) and which procedures you will use. For example, you might help clients compare or contrast their performances against the learning criteria and the intended objectives or expected outcomes.

▶ To facilitate **integration,** you must choose the best way to link the learning in the present experience with past and future experiences (Priest, Gass, & Gillis, 2003).

▶ You can make several selections about **feedback,** including whether to give it, delay it, withhold some part of it, or use verbal or nonverbal channels and including which source to use: yourself, other clients, the individual, or a partner.

▶ For **follow-up,** you must consider the alternatives available for enhancing transfer, such as holding formal or informal meetings or social reunions, action planning, mentoring or coaching new behaviors, involving significant others in feedback sessions, and offering professional support groups for alumni.

RANGE OF TEACHING STYLES

The resulting combinations of leader–client control create six styles of teaching: dictated, prescribed, directed, consulted, interpreted, and automated. First we look at these six styles in more detail, examining a specific example of how you could apply each. Then we tie all six styles together in a single example to demonstrate their similarities and differences. Last, we present the seventh style of shared teaching in which you and your clients share the choices in all three phases of the learning event, and then we give you some modified examples.

Dictated Style

In the **dictated style,** you hold total responsibility for the choices made in all three phases: preexperience, experience, and postexperience. The clients have little or no control in any of these phases. In the preexperience, you determine the why, what, how, who, where, and when of teaching. During the experience, you "command" the briefing, rhythm, adjustments, breaks, start or finish, and repetition. In the postexperience, you determine the choice of reflection, evaluation criteria and procedures, learning integration, feedback, and transfer follow-up. In short, you determine every aspect of the learning experience.

The dictated style may seem constricting or overbearing in a profession that aims to empower its learners, but it has its place in a few learning situations. Consider risk management and the need to do things the right way to avoid injury. In fact, teaching safety skills is the best time to employ a dictated style. For example, while you can teach belaying in many different ways, when consistency is critically important and risk management is of paramount concern, all clients and staff must belay the same way. When you dictate that everyone must belay the same way, you can easily survey a group of belayers and immediately spot individual discrepancies.

Prescribed Style

The **prescribed style** is the same as the dictated style with one exception: The clients control the postexperience phase. But you still retain responsibility for the preexperience and experience phases. During the preexperience, you still answer the why, what, how, who, where, and when questions and dictate all the critical choices during the experience. But in the postexperience phase, you let the clients determine how they will interpret, evaluate, integrate, and use what they have learned.

The prescribed style is particularly effective in teaching skill acquisition and application in specific situations, for example, when teaching how to cave, bike, climb, paddle, or ski in certain conditions. Consider the tandem paddling techniques necessary for turning a canoe. As you probably know, opposite strokes performed at the

If someone has to look into the sun, make sure it is the instructors who do so.

bow and stern can rotate a canoe about its center point. While a number of stroke combinations can perform this task, such as the sweep and reverse sweep, forward and reverse, draw and crossover draw, or push away and pry, only certain combinations work in a specific situation because of its specific conditions, such as water depth, turning space, or water movement. When using this particular style, you prescribe the acceptable technique for the specific condition and then direct the client to execute the technique in the situation. In this way, clients evaluate how certain strokes work in specific conditions and apply this knowledge to future situations. If they fail to execute the proper strokes, they will still learn in the postexperience phase through the natural consequences of their actions. For example, they may get stuck in shallow water by using incorrect strokes. They may even capsize, but since you have set up a controlled instructional setting, outcomes tend be more recoverable and acceptable.

Directed Style

With the **directed style,** you hold responsibility for the preexperience and postexperience phases. The clients control the experience phase. Before the

experience, you still decide the why, what, how, who, where, and when to teach. After the experience, you determine how the clients reflect, who will evaluate, where the learning fits in, whether to employ feedback, and how to follow up. But you allow clients choices during the actual experience, such as how fast to go, which direction to take, when to rest or stop, and what pieces to repeat.

The directed style is very useful when client freedom is important, yet your control over verifying risk management is equally important. Take tying knots as an example. Most knots can be tied in many variations. Some variations can lead to knots that appear correct to the untrained eye, but can fail under certain circumstances. So you should direct clients through tying the many variations and then let them experiment with tying. You should even allow the clients the freedom to try their own variations, choosing the one that works best for them. Then, in the postexperience phase, you perform a final check of each knot's structure so as to confirm its accuracy, giving feedback to the clients on how well they have done. Risk management is critical again, as with the dictated and prescribed styles, but you give clients the freedom to tie the knot any way they choose while you still double-check for appropriateness. When you use the directed style, you give clients both direction and the freedom to make their own choices.

Consulted Style

The **consulted style** is the same as the directed style with one exception: the clients control the postexperience phase as well as the experience itself. You retain responsibility for the preexperience phase only. You plan the experience by selecting critical teaching reasons, contents, objectives, outcomes, methods, styles, locations, positions, and schedules. Once the experience begins, however, you step back and let clients determine how the experience will proceed and how they will interpret their learning.

The consulted style is especially effective when risk management is not critical, and yet consequential learning is very important. One example is when setting up camp. You inform clients of the basic ground rules and then permit them to explore their own preferences for setting up in such aspects as pitching the tent, lighting a stove, and cooking a meal. If the tent is pitched poorly, the stove cannot be lit, or the meal is cooked for too long, then the clients experience feedback in the form of real and natural consequences: the tent collapses in a storm, the meal is cold, or the food gets burned. You do not provide feedback, because the learning environment does this for you. Instead, your role is to carefully plan the preexperience phase, selecting circumstances that are ripe for consequential learning without the risk of injury. As with the directed style, under the consulted style clients are free to experiment within the experience, but the consulted style goes beyond the directed style by giving additional freedom in the postexperience phase and allowing clients to learn from their mistakes.

Interpreted Style

In the **interpreted style,** you hold responsibility only for the postexperience phase. The clients control the preexperience and experience phases. The clients plan and execute the experience, making the best choices about why to learn, what to learn, how to learn, who learns, where to learn, when to learn, which speed to take, whether to stop, and what to repeat. Afterward, you guide their interpretation by making key choices about reflection, integration, evaluation, feedback, and follow-up.

Some leaders may be reluctant to offer this much control to learners. However, if one aim of adventure programming is to empower free-thinking and self-reliant learners, then you must use this style. Nevertheless, you should only decide to use this style (or the automated style) after carefully considering the ramifications and only after properly preparing clients for the responsibility. Major projects, such as expeditions and service learning, are excellent times to use an interpreted style. Clients plan and complete all of the preparations and executions before and during the learning project, while you help them interpret the experience. Like the consulted and directed styles, the interpreted style gives clients control over their experiences. But unlike any of the styles we've discussed so far, the interpreted style also gives clients control over the design of their experiences. Beware, however: you should not surrender this control frivolously, particularly when risk management is a concern.

Automated Style

The **automated style** goes beyond the interpreted style to give the clients control over the postexperience phase as well as the other two phases. Thus, you relinquish responsibility for all three phases and—as hard as it may be—avoid interfering. Clients make all the choices about planning, executing, and interpreting their learning. As the supervising leader, your role is simply to support clients as they implement their choices.

The automated style is appropriate for clients who have mastered the fundamentals of a skill and are in the final stages of applying their learning. An excellent example of this is peer leadership, when several clients, now leadership candidates, organize a trip for others. They may take school children on a nature walk or senior citizens on a bike tour. The leadership candidates take responsibility for the preparation, execution, and evaluation of the trip. Much like planning and implementing their own expeditions under the interpreted style, the automated style both gives them freedom and allows them to interpret the experience for themselves. The key difference is that feedback comes from the peers—not the experienced, supervising leader. Peers evaluate the experience with minimal input from the supervising leader, who observes, often from a distance.

Shared Style

In the foregoing six styles, the responsibility primarily rests with either you or your clients. In reality, however, control in the preexperience,

The Range at Work: Learning Navigation

You may combine all six teaching styles over time in order to change clients from dependent learners under your direct supervision into independent learners under indirect supervision. The following six examples for learning navigation show the gradual shift of responsibility from you to your clients as they become more masterful at learning within each teaching style.

Early in the process, clients identify the position of symbols on a map by grid references. Grid references are six-digit numbers that describe a precise location and so must be recorded correctly in a consistent sequence. Failure to follow the specific sequence can result in an incorrect number representing another location 100 km (62 mi) away! Such errors could be fatal in certain situations, especially if the grid references were being used to identify emergency pickup points. You should teach grid references with a dictated style. Dictate that clients learn and use only one way to establish references. Retain total control over all phases: preexperience, experience, and postexperience.

Later on in the learning sequence, clients begin to take compass bearings on a map and to sight those bearings in the field. Most topographic maps are drawn to true north, but the compass needle points to magnetic north. Due to this phenomenon, clients must learn to account for the angular difference, or declination, between the two northerly directions. Failure to cope with this magnetic declination can distort bearings by a considerable number of degrees. Three methods exist for dealing with declination. First, clients can redraw the true north lines on the map so they line up with magnetic north, accounting for the difference on the map. Second, once clients take a map bearing, they can adjust it for declination by adding or subtracting the angular difference to get the field bearing, accounting for the difference while moving from the map to the field. Addition or subtraction depends on whether the declination is to the east or west of true north: "West is best and east is least." Third, when sighting the field bearing, clients can permit the red tip of the magnetic needle to point to the local declination value instead of true north as indicated on the compass housing, accounting for the difference in the field. What matters is not which method is used, but that the method is correctly used.

Given these factors, you can teach magnetic declination with a prescribed style. Prescribe several accepted ways to deal with declination and then allow clients to use the method they prefer. Take responsibility for all aspects of the preexperience and experience phases, but allow the clients to decide how they will reflect on, interpret, integrate, apply, and follow up this learning in the postexperience.

Once they have mastered the basics of map reading and compass use, clients often practice these skills through orienteering events. One example is score orienteering for which you provide clients with multiple locations marked on a map and give them a specified time limit in which to reach as many locations as possible. Distant locations are worth more points, while closer ones are less valuable. Clients aim to earn as many points as possible by visiting the locations by using the most effective combination of travel routes and times. This is an example of directed teaching. You direct the clients by setting up the experience and controlling their interpretation of it. But you permit the clients to direct the speed and course of their own experiences.

With a reasonable knowledge of navigation, clients are commonly presented with realistic map-reading exercises. In such an exercise, clients may bicycle from place to place, following a road map. Along the bicycle route you have selected, clients choose which way to go and for how far. The route finding includes you as a member of the group, but you are only present in case of a problem. This is an example of consulted teaching in which you consult with the clients when they have difficulty with the exercise or need other assistance. You take responsibility for the preexperience, but the clients govern the speed and course of the experience and take responsibility for its interpretation and application.

In a last step before a solo expedition, clients navigate cross country for several days by compass. They free-form plan the route at all stages, from picking the area to visit to choosing the campsites to selecting the final bearings between campsites. When they travel, they do so

(continued)

The Range at Work: Learning Navigation   *(continued)*

as a group, but without you. You shadow the group from a distance, resisting the temptation to interfere. With an interpreted style of teaching, you help the group interpret what it has learned after the experience but play no deliberate role in planning or running the experience.

On a solo expedition, clients route-find and plan all aspects of a canoe journey without any help from you. You do not attend the expedition, and each client goes alone on her own route. Obviously, clients must be well prepared for this task, because considerable learning and responsibility have been transferred to them. Such an automated style of teaching is possible because you have done a tremendous amount of work beforehand. You can now afford to allow the individuals to go alone and to let them run on automatic! The clients take full responsibility for the preexperience, experience, and postexperience phases. This occurs when clients have moved on to becoming peer outdoor leaders!

experience, and postexperience phases is not absolute. When you or your clients are in control, one entity mostly influences the choices, but the minority still has representation in those decisions. As a result, responsibility, control, and influence vacillate between you and your clients so that the six styles do not have precisely defined boundaries. Styles overlap and interact.

A mix of two or more styles is often appropriate, hence the need for a seventh style, the shared style. In the **shared style,** you and your clients work together in the preexperience, experience, and postexperience phases. You participate jointly in all choices associated with planning, executing, and evaluating the learning event.

The decision to blend two or more styles into a shared style often depends on two factors: risk management and consequences. Recall that the dictated and directed styles afford you great control over setting up and checking experiences in which risk management is a major concern. Remember, too, that the prescribed and consulted styles surrender a great deal of that control to clients when you want them to learn from consequences. The key to selecting styles or creating the best blend of styles lies with balancing your concern for risk management with your desire for clients to learn from real and natural consequences.

You can easily modify any of the six examples we gave for the first six styles into shared teaching by adding either leader or client influence at any phase and by including both at all phases. Consider the two examples of belaying (dictated style) and peer leadership (automated style) from the extreme ends of the range of instructional styles.

Belaying involves a high concern for risk management and may require that all clients belay the same way under a dictated style. But on the rare occasion that risk management is not such a concern, you can relinquish a little control over the learning experience. For example, you can give clients some say in learning other acceptable ways to belay, allowing them to select the method that is most comfortable for them. A shared style is appropriate to permit them this freedom, but only if risk management is not of paramount concern, which may occur later in the program.

In contrast, peer leadership involves a desire for consequential learning in which clients are free to make mistakes. If risk management is ever a greater concern than it was in our example, then you, as the supervising leader, must exert a shared style and greater control over planning, implementing, and evaluating the experience. The clients and you should discuss and negotiate much of the trip content, and you might even attend as a group member rather than shadow and observe from afar. A shared style permits you appropriate control with the automated style, but only if risk management is a major concern.

SELECTING THE MOST APPROPRIATE STYLE

No single best style exists. The most effective style is the one that suits the situation and the preference of the leader and clients. Rarely will you find yourself utilizing only one style. You should be able to select the most appropriate teaching style for the maturity, needs, and best interests of the

◄ *EFFECTIVE OUTDOOR LEADERS* ►

► Understand and recognize the elements of the preexperience, experience, and postexperience phases of any lesson.

► Identify their level of concern for risk management and consequential learning in any experience.

► Select an appropriate style of instruction based both on their concerns and the needs of clients.

► Are able to use all seven teaching styles and move between styles as instructional situations change.

► Gradually transfer responsibility to the clients by shifting teaching style accordingly.

---

clients and for your own interest in risk management and desire for consequential learning. For example, you could easily teach how to set up camp by pitching a tent, lighting a stove, and cooking a meal with a consulted (as in our example) or another style, depending on the balance of concern for risk management and consequences. In some cases (e.g., with extreme weather), it would be dangerous to use a consulted style with inexperienced clients when learning shelter construction. As risk-management concerns increase and consequential-learning concerns decrease, you could accordingly shift your style from directed to prescribed to dictated. Similarly, as risk-management concerns decrease and consequential-learning concerns increase, you could shift your style toward interpreted and automated. When in doubt, compromise and utilize a shared style. This middle ground gives you the flexibility to meet clients' needs and your desires as well as gives a smooth transition to other styles if called for. You should shift responsibility to the learners whenever they are ready to accept more obligations and greater accountability.

SUMMARY

The preexperience, experience, and postexperience phases of an adventure can be controlled by either you or your clients while planning, executing, and evaluating the experience. Various combinations of leader or client control create different styles of instruction. These styles can range from dictated and prescribed through directed and consulted to interpreted and automated. A seventh shared style blends the elements of these six depending on your concern for risk

management or desire for clients to learn from consequences.

QUESTIONS TO THINK ABOUT

1. Share with colleagues examples of the discussed teaching styles that you have experienced. Did these styles work? Why or why not?

2. Select a lesson you wish to teach a group of clients participating in an adventure program. Identify all the elements of the preexperience, experience, and postexperience phases for that lesson.

3. For the same lesson, identify your level of concern for risk management and consequential learning. What is the best teaching style for you to use in this lesson and why?

4. For the same lesson, list the elements of the preexperience, experience, and postexperience phases that you would control and those that you would allow your clients to take responsibility for. Explain why you and your clients should have the primary power to make each of these choices.

5. Describe how you could modify your preferred teaching style for the lesson to become a shared style.

REFERENCES

Hoban, G. (1999). Using a reflective framework for experiential education in teacher education classes. *Journal of Experiential Education, 22*(2), 104-111.

Mosston, M., & Ashworth, S. (2002). *Teaching physical education* (5th ed.). Boston: Allyn & Bacon.

Priest, S., & Gass, M.A. (1997). The range of teaching styles in adventure programming. *Journal of Adventure Education and Outdoor Leadership, 14*(4), 12-14.

Priest, S., Gass, M.A., & Gillis, H.L. (2003). *Essential elements of facilitation.* Seattle: Tarrak Technologies.

Sugerman, D., Doherty, K.L., Garvey, D.E., & Gass, M.A. (2000). *Reflective learning: Theory and practice.* Dubuque, IA: Kendall/Hunt Publishing Company.

PART

IV

Facilitation
in Adventure
Programming

CHAPTER 14

The Process of Facilitation

The day had been long but extremely successful for the group. While kayaking was the adventure activity taught during the day, much of the group's success seemed to stem from its outdoor leader's ability to orchestrate an enriching experience and to enable the members to connect kayaking with each of their futures. The group norms established at the beginning of the day (including challenge by choice and the full-value contract, both explained later in this chapter) served as a constant source of mutual support, creating a strong willingness in each group member to try. The leader's assessment of both group and individual needs seemed to grow stronger as the day progressed, and this was evident in the way the leader guided discussions and solo time, as the group reflected on the experience. While the gains were achieved by the group members, the leader definitely helped to make these gains more attainable and made a difference for everyone.

As the use of adventure experiences for reaching recreational, educational, developmental, or therapeutic goals has grown, so have certain facilitation methods and techniques that increase the likelihood of achieving those goals. In this chapter, we overview these methods; we delve into each particular technique in subsequent chapters.

While experience serves as the source for achieving client objectives in adventure programs, you can employ a variety of facilitation techniques to make attaining these objectives easier. Sometimes referred to by other names, such as processing and debriefing, we can define **facilitation** as "those techniques that are used to augment the qualities of the adventure experience based on an accurate assessment of the client's needs" (Gass, 1993, p. 219). The purposes of facilitation are to enhance the learning experience, to assist clients in finding directions and sources for functional change, and to create changes that are lasting and transferable. Facilitation has been labeled the "cornerstone" of effective adventure learning experiences (Nadler & Luckner, 1992).

WHY FACILITATE ADVENTURE EXPERIENCES?

As a young Outward Bound instructor, Rusty Baillie was quoted as saying, "Let the mountains speak for themselves." He was referring to the innate power and majesty that such environments have to bring about lasting change in people. Clients, however, do not always receive the "message of the mountains," especially if they are first-time adventurers so caught up in the experience that they miss the meaning of the message.

Certainly, without facilitation, people learn, grow, and change, but perhaps not as effectively as with the aid of facilitation. Years down the road, they might recognize the importance of their experiences and may even find a later use for what they had gained, but without facilitation, they may lose years of potential learning, growth, and change. Facilitation offers people a chance to share what they have learned and to recognize that they are supported, or not alone, in their efforts.

People simply don't learn, grow, or change without reflecting on their experiences; evaluating the good and bad; analyzing mistakes, failures, or successes; considering the impact of actions or decisions; anticipating consequences or committing to new behaviors; and understanding how they can use new learning, growth, and change. You can facilitate these gains by escorting and accelerating people through the change process.

IMPORTANCE OF TRANSFER OF LEARNING

Transfer is a key concept in facilitation. It represents the integration of learning from the adventure program into the participant's real life. Adventure programs are typically characterized by small groups led by 1 or 2 leaders. Participants engage in challenging activities that inherently involve risks, forcing them to use personal competence. But clients may or may not be able to successfully apply what they learn in the adventure environment to other environments, such as on the job, within the family, or at school, because these other environments are very different from the adventure program. Still, our hope as adventure program leaders is that clients will transfer and

By appropriately facilitating groups involved with outdoor learning experiences, change can come more rapidly and be longer lasting.

apply the change and growth started in the adventure activity to their real-world situations. We may view transfer as successful if this occurs, making the new learning permanent.

Gass (1985) has identified three types or levels of transfer in adventure programming:

1. **Specific transfer** involves the learning of particular skills, habits, or associations for use in closely related situations. Learning to type (on a typewriter) for the purpose of operating a computer terminal is an example of specific transfer. The skill being learned is used in the same manner to another situation where it was previously learned. Applying knots from sailing to rock climbing is an adventure example of specific transfer, because learning the knots in one situation helps participants when learning knots in another situation, even though the activities are different. **Specific transfer** uses the **same products** of learning from one situation to another learning situation.

2. **Nonspecific transfer** refers to the learning of general principles or behaviors and applying them to a different situation. For example, mastering a new way to solve problems in a classroom situation potentially has use in other settings. In adventure programs, the general principle of trust developed during belaying to protect against physical injury

can translate to trusting one another for support in other types of risk taking, such as sharing secrets, volunteering ideas, or lending money. **Nonspecific transfer** uses the **same processes** of learning from one situation to another learning situation.

3. A third and specialized form of transfer is known as metaphoric transfer. A metaphor is an idea, object, or description used in place of a different idea, object, or description in order to denote comparative similarity between the two. Metaphors can occur quite often in adventure education because the activities can have a strong similarity to actual life experiences.

Metaphoric transfer occurs when parallels exist between two learning environments. For example, an individual rappelling or abseiling, poised on the edge of a cliff, may see the parallel connection between the risk in the activity and real life. In the activity, the risks are the perceived physical risk of descending versus the perceived social risk of "stepping back" from a challenging issue that is preventing an individual's positive growth. In real life, the perceived risk may be not seeking psychiatric counseling versus the perceived financial risk of paying for it with time and money. Another of many metaphors in rappelling or abseiling is gathering internal strength in order to commit to the first step of the descent and gathering sufficient courage to begin other endeavors in life, such as beginning a new job, starting a recovery program, or entering a new social situation. **Metaphoric transfer** uses **similar processes** from one situation to another learning situation.

The key to metaphoric transfer often lies in the strength of the metaphoric connection between the adventure and actual life experience. The stronger are the parallels, the clearer are the connections. And the clearer the connections appear between the two environments, the more likely a person is to carry over the new learning. Therefore, if an individual personally identifies the metaphors linking the adventure experience with daily living, the potential for transfer is enhanced. Your job is to use various facilitation techniques to strengthen such connections, thereby enhancing transfer.

EMPOWERING CLIENTS

To enhance the learning experience, assist clients in finding sources for functional change, and create changes that are lasting and transferable, two policies must be present in adventure programming: challenge by choice and the full-value contract.

Challenge By Choice

Originated by Rohnke (1984), **challenge by choice** empowers clients by proactively informing them that they, not you as the outdoor leader, determine the degree of challenge, risk, and competence with which they will engage in the adventure experience. This policy is more than simply not forcing people to be involved. The purpose of advising clients is not to lead them to withdraw from the experience, but to provide them with opportunities to challenge themselves in the manner they wish, in the amount they would like, and with the type of support they want. In short, clients may select levels of participation, including but not limited to full or partial participation or observation in physical, social, and emotional events. Since, however, nonparticipation makes learning impossible because of the absence of a common experience, you should encourage clients to engage, but at whatever levels they desire.

Schoel, Prouty, and Radcliffe (1988) describe challenge by choice as offering clients

  ▶ a chance to try a potentially difficult or frightening challenge in an atmosphere of support and caring,

  ▶ the opportunity to back off when performance pressures or self-doubt become too strong and to know that an opportunity for a future attempt will always be available,

  ▶ a chance to try difficult tasks and to recognize that the attempt is more significant than performance, and

  ▶ respect for individual ideas and choices (p. 131).

Challenge by choice also extends to participation in debriefings. Clients have the right to pass at any point in a discussion.

Full-Value Contract

We can trace the origins of the **full-value contract** to Medrick's (1979) interpretations of Berne's (1961, 1964, 1972) "contracting" work in transactional analysis. The contract focus was to have participants agree to not discount themselves before beginning an adventure experience. This was done to allay client fears, to validate client reasons for being involved, to reduce client passivity, and to motivate participation. Let's examine one way in which you might introduce this concept of not discounting to participants in the following sample presentation:

> In response to our concern that every participant gets what they came for on our programs, we ask for two commitments. The first is what we call a "no-discount" or "passivity confrontation" contract. We ask you to agree to pay attention to the information that we provide for your safety and satisfaction. We ask you to follow and support these guidelines to the best of your ability and judgment. When you have questions or are in disagreement with any of these, we ask you to make this known and to work with us to take care of your concerns. In addition, we ask each to agree to confront or be confronted if you observe others or are observed discounting information you have about the provisions taken for your safety and satisfaction. (Medrick, 1979, p. 1)

Building on this work and popularizing its use throughout the profession, Project Adventure reframed the "no-discount" concept to highlight the positives of a group focus with the term "full value." Schoel, Prouty, and Radcliffe (1988, p. 95) described the three elements of the full-value contract as agreements to

1. work together as a group toward individual and group goals,
2. adhere to certain risk-management and group behavior guidelines, and
3. give and receive feedback, both positive and negative, and to work toward changing behavior when change is appropriate.

One method of presenting the full-value contract, constructed similarly to Medrick's presentation, is as follows:

> In response to our concern that every participant get what they came for during our programs, we ask each of you to agree to abide by what we call the full-value contract while you are a member of this group. There are two parts to this contract, the first being that you agree to fully value, respect, and consider yourself during all of our activities. This includes your reactions to all physical and emotional issues that may arise. Treat yourself as you want to be treated, and if not receiving the type of support you expect, we encourage you to not wait until the group picks up on this, but to let us know yourself.
>
> The second part of the contract is that you agree to fully value, respect, and consider others during our activities. For example, validating someone's efforts and letting them know that you think they can improve even more is better than calling people names or using put-downs. If you see another group member who may not be valued, agreeing to the full-value contract also means that you will address this rather than thinking, *That's their issue,* or *They can take care of themselves.* Fully valuing yourself and others is a serious undertaking, but a condition that we've found extremely helpful in making sure our experience together is productive and valuable.
>
> Is this contract clear to everyone? If so, we'd like everyone to verbally agree that they are willing to work by these two principles while we are together. Okay?

Taking Care of One Another: The CARES Model

Once you have oriented a group to the activity and structured the task, you are free to discuss the risks and responsibilities of the activity. The CARES model can be used to complement the full-value contract and challenge by choice processes, particularly to stress the importance of acting safely toward self, others, and the environment when facing physical, social, emotional, or intellectual dangers. CARES can be an acronym for

Physical	*Social*	*Emotional*	*Intellectual*
Caution	**C**onsideration	**C**oncern	**C**ommitment
Alertness	**A**dmiration	**A**ppreciation	**A**wareness
Response	**R**ecognition	**R**espect	**R**easoning
Eliminate	**E**ncouragement	**E**mpathy	**E**mpowerment
Safeguard	**S**ynergy	**S**haring	**S**upport

Again, CARES is another way of expressing challenge by choice and the full-value contract. Initially, you might explain CARES guidelines and seek adherence. But if the group creates its own operating principles as it works through activities, then members are more likely to own and follow these guidelines and not to devalue themselves, others, or nature with words or actions. Examples of operating principles include celebrating and valuing diversity in the group, seeking input and ideas from everyone, making all criticism constructive, and protecting the environment. Examples of devaluing include making fun of people, using zingers or put-downs, ignoring belaying or spotting responsibilities, fighting, or littering. A verbal or written contract created by you, your coleaders, and your group can outline acceptable or unacceptable behaviors and their consequences.

During such presentations, you need to watch clients' reactions and, if confusion appears, encourage clients to ask questions. Once everyone understands the contract, ask them to verbally agree to participate under the full-value contract or have them sign a written contract.

FACILITATION GUIDELINES

Beyond challenge by choice and the full-value contract, you need to follow particular guidelines and make certain assumptions in order to create positive conditions for participants to achieve their goals (see "Facilitation Assumptions"). You also need to look for ways to refine your skills as a facilitator (Priest, Gass, & Gillis, 2003). Some of the fundamental rules that you can implement to become a better facilitator include 10 guidelines regarding group position, time, single speaking, nonviolence, participation, responsibility, commitment, role clarity, confidentiality, and other ethical issues (Hammel, 1986; Hovelynck, 2000; Knapp, 1990, 1993; Nadler & Luckner, 1992; Schoel & Maizell, 2002; Schoel, Prouty, & Radcliffe, 1988; Sugerman, Doherty, Garvey, & Gass, 2000).

1. **Group position** is important for effective communication. Group members need to be in a physical configuration that permits them to see the things that are most relevant for the facilitation process, such as eye contact, facial expressions, and body language. You must provide a setting that allows for this observation and is also warm and relaxing to encourage discussion. For example, position clients in a circle where everyone can see each other but stay in shade so no one is blinded by the sun.

2. **Time** is critical. Schedule sufficient time to reflect on the experience. Match the length of debriefing to the maturity, needs, and abilities of the clients. Unless working with children or people who are intellectually challenged, spend equal amounts of time doing and discussing. But some clients may not be able to sit still even this long!

3. **Single speaking** is a sign of group respect. Having one person speak at a time ensures an opportunity for each person to be heard and for everyone to hear what is being said.

4. In keeping with the full-value contract, **nonviolence** is a must; violence is never acceptable in any form, whether physical or emotional.

5. In accordance with challenge by choice, clients have the right to pass on **participation** in activities or discussions, selecting their own ways of getting involved in the experiences.

Facilitation Assumptions

Knapp (1990) identified four assumptions that underlie the facilitation process in adventure experiences.

▶ As an outdoor leader, assume that your **facilitator assistance** will benefit clients' insight and comprehension and that such benefits will further client efforts toward reaching their goals. Moreover, assume that you possess the facilitation skills to assist clients in achieving the functional changes they desire. Also assume that if you don't possess the facilitation skills to assist a client, you will not become involved with him as a leader.

▶ Most adventure experiences are conducted in a **controlled group setting** (see chapter 5). Assume that using a group and its associated influences, such as reciprocity and support, will also assist clients in obtaining their objectives.

▶ Assume that clients' learning or change that takes place in the facilitation process has **application** and relevance to situations the clients encounter outside of the adventure experience and in the real world.

▶ Assume that the stress and adaptive dissonance produced in an adventure experience (see chapters 4 and 11), combined with appropriate facilitation, can provide the necessary elements, stimuli, and **impetus for change.**

These are standard assumptions for almost all adventure programs that are educational, developmental, or therapeutic. If any of these assumptions are invalid, adapt your style or approach to maintain the effectiveness of the facilitation process described in the next section.

6. Let each client know that she is the only one who possesses the **responsibility** for her own behavior.

7. Place group members in situations in which they can **commit** to the entire facilitation process and not in situations that prevent them from being committed, such as in inclement weather or during exhaustion.

8. Facilitating **role clarity** in the group process is important to clients. Proactively establishing your role and the group's responsibilities can alleviate potential confusion, such as clients asking, "Why didn't you let us know we were going in the wrong direction five miles ago?" You need to be clear about what you are there to do and what you're not there to do (see chapter 19).

9. Make sure that clients understand when information can be shared outside the group. Promise **confidentiality** only when it can be maintained, understanding its limitations. For example, situations in which you fall into the role of a mandated reporter and are dictated by law to report certain issues, such as abuse, override confidentiality issues.

10. Beyond confidentiality, many other **ethical issues** exist. Considering how to handle these issues in advance is critical to your preparation. These issues could include but may not be limited to conflict of interests, sexual issues, value differences, client rights, environmental concerns, and individual needs versus group needs. Refer to chapter 23 for further details.

SIX GENERATIONS OF ADVENTURE FACILITATION

Facilitating adventure experiences has evolved through several distinct stages of development with earlier styles fostering the growth of more recent ones (Bacon, 1987; Doughty, 1991; Priest & Gass, 1993). From these stages several different facilitation styles have emerged that are used today. We can categorize these styles, or generations, in order of development and sophistication as follows:

1. Letting the experience speak for itself—learning by doing

2. Speaking for the experience—learning by telling

3. Debriefing the experience—learning through reflection

4. Directly frontloading the experience—direction with reflection

5. Framing the experience—reinforcement with reflection

6. Indirectly frontloading the experience—redirection before reflection

A major philosophical and evolutionary shift in facilitating adventure experiences occurred between the third and fourth generations. The first three generations are used *after* the adventure activity to bring about change. The leaders react to the experience, simply commenting on the group's learning. The last three generations are used *before* and *during* the adventure activity as well as *afterward*. In these latter generations, leaders are proactive, creating unique learning opportunities that enhance later reflection.

Primarily, the philosophical shift between the former and latter generations relates to when change takes place during the facilitating process. The difference lies in the belief that the experience itself (not just reflection) can be a powerful medium for change. Therefore, you can facilitate changes before and during the experience as well as after. Debriefing is used for discovering learning in the first, second, and third generations. It remains a part of the fourth, fifth, and sixth generations, but leaders use it more for reinforcing and redirecting prior learning rather than for actual discovering.

The following are brief explanations of the generations with examples of how you might use each of them with the well-known adventure activity, the Spider's Web (Webster, 1989).

Letting the Experience Speak for Itself

The first-generation experience, **letting the experience speak** for itself, is found in numerous adventure programs in which clients sort out their own personal insights (Doughty, 1991). When properly sequenced and designed, the inherently enriching qualities of adventure activities lead clients into their own insights and discoveries through learning and doing. This approach is fine as long as you're not concerned with achieving identified or prescriptive intra- and interpersonal goals. Clients may have a good time and become proficient at new skills, but they are less likely to learn anything about themselves, how they relate to others, or how to resolve certain issues confronting them in their lives.

Phases of Facilitation

The process of facilitating adventure experiences can be arranged into five phases: diagnosis, design, delivery, debriefing, and departure. In the diagnosis phase, you learn the goals people have for the adventure program. In the design phase, you plan the best experiences to meet those goals. In the delivery phase, you present the experience in an environmentally sensitive and educationally effective manner. In the debriefing phase, you guide a reflective discussion or analysis of the experience to help people get the most out of the adventure program. In the departure phase, you provide follow-up and ongoing support to continue the benefits people obtained from the adventure program.

These five phases can be presented in four sequential approaches: linear, cyclical, nested loops, and spiral as diagrammed in figure 14.1. The linear approach arranges the five phases one after the other in a line. The cyclical approach arranges the five phases into a circle with depar-

ture leading back into diagnosis. The series of nested loops begins with diagnosis followed by three phases repeated in small loops and terminated with departure. The spiral approach repeats all five phases like in a cycle but on a continual and integrated basis, especially the diagnosis and departure phases.

The model you should follow depends on your training as well as on the program. The linear model works best with recreational adventure programs for which the purpose is to have fun, learn a new skill, or be entertained. For example, you diagnose the goal as learning white-water paddling skills. So you plan, execute, and evaluate a kayaking trip. Afterward, you provide a list of resources to help people practice and improve their new skills. The phases proceed in a straight-forward manner.

The nested-loops model works best with educational adventure programs for which the purpose is to understand new concepts, enrich

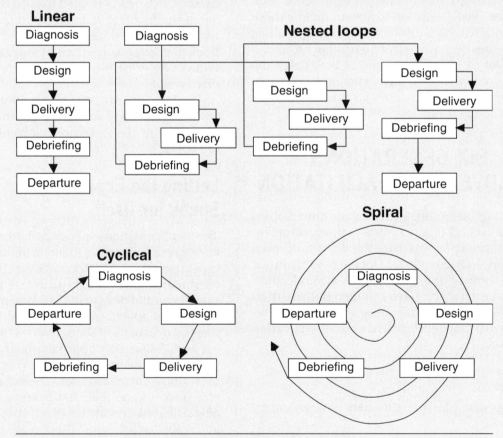

Figure 14.1 Four models of the five-phase facilitation process.

knowledge of old concepts, or generate an awareness of the need for change. For example, you diagnose the goal as learning about risk taking and fear. So you plan and supervise a sequence of increasingly difficult rock climbs. You design, deliver, and debrief each climb, paying attention to risk taking and fear. At the end of the day, you discuss with the clients their strategies for applying what they have learned about risk taking and fear to their home, school, or work lives.

The cyclical model works best with developmental adventure programs for which the purpose is to improve functional behavior or train new and different behaviors. For example, you diagnose that the group goal is to enhance teamwork. So you plan and present a problem exercise that requires teamwork for its solution. After the exercise, you direct a discussion of what was learned and how this knowledge might be useful in the future. But during the exercise, you note that the group has poor communication. So you use this information when diagnosing the next cycle of designing, delivering, and debriefing a communication exercise. In this second exercise, you note a lack of trust among group members and so the cycle repeats once again, the third time focusing on trust. In all cycles, later phases feed information into early phases in the next cycle.

The spiral model works best with therapeutic adventure programs for which the purpose is to reduce dysfunctional behavior or condition positive behaviors. For example, you diagnose that the group goal is to manage drug addiction. Addiction, however, is such a complex and personal behavior that you rarely will have the total diagnostic picture or developmental answers for each individual. Therefore, diagnosis and departure must be ongoing during the entire therapeutic experience. As you design, deliver, and debrief a series of activities, new information arises and helps you refine your diagnosis and departure strategies. As these phases change, so do the designing, delivering, and debriefing approaches to subsequent activities. The relationships among all five phases are merged, integrated, and reciprocal. The CHANGES model, which we discuss in chapter 17, is an example of a related and integrated spiral approach to diagnosis.

Often the design, delivery, and debriefing phases can form a small repeated cycle within one of the programming models we've already discussed. Shown in figure 14.2, this small repeated cycle can be particularly useful for group initiatives as well as other adventure activities (Priest, 1989). The diagram is based on the optical illusion of an "Eternal Staircase" designed by the Penroses in 1958 and popularized by Escher in

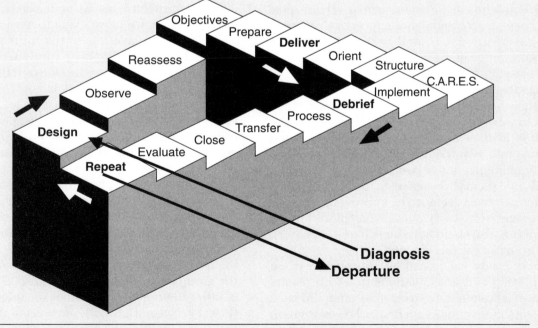

Figure 14.2 Design, deliver, debrief, and repeat the steps of facilitation.

(continued)

Phases of Facilitation   *(continued)*

his infinity artwork of the 1960s. "Eternal" suggests a cyclical sequence that repeats as necessary. "Staircase" indicates steps that may be skipped or taken in any reasonable order, allowing you to customize your presentations as desired. For example, information obtained during the delivery or debriefing phase can feed back into the diagnosis or design phase and help you refine your original diagnosis via the observation or assessment steps of the cycle.

Although the four facilitation models fit the four types of adventure programming, with practice, you can easily mix and match approaches to suit the situation. But until you have plenty of background knowledge, facilitation expertise, and practice, you should stick to the simpler models. In reality, the linear model is the easiest to apply, while the spiral model is the most difficult and the cyclical and nested-loops models represent intermediate variations of these extremes. Whatever the model, the content of each of the five phases remains relatively constant.

In letting the experience speak for itself, you do not add any insights regarding the Spider's Web exercise when the experience finishes. If you make any comments, they might pertain to how much fun the experience was and encourage the group to try the next event: "That was great! Good job! Now let's try something new and different."

Speaking on Behalf of the Experience

To enhance programming efforts, several programs have implemented the second-generation approach of **speaking on behalf of the experience.** You (often in the role of an expert) interpret the experience for the clients, informing them what they have learned and how they should apply their new knowledge in the future.

In speaking for the experience, you provide the group members with feedback about their behaviors after the activity: what they did well, what they need to work on, and what they learned from the exercise. Statements might include "You've learned to cooperate by working together and succeeding. Your communication is poor, everyone is talking, and no one seems to be listening to anyone's ideas. The level of trust seems to be improving, since no one appeared to worry about being picked up by the others. You could have benefited from having a coordinator for this activity!"

Learning by telling can be appropriate when role-playing and in simulations in which results are predictable and reproducible time and time again. In the adventure experience, however, group members bring unique behavioral histories to bear on the way they act under stress. The results of these experiences seem to be more unpredict-able and unique. Due to this uncertainty, client learning is generally varied and personal. Telling individuals what they received from the Spider's Web experience can invalidate and alienate them, possibly disconnecting you and hampering future learning opportunities.

Debriefing the Experience

One solution to the problems arising from telling is the "learning through reflection" style that enables clients to discover learning after the experience. As clients state issues or personal commitments to change, they are more likely to follow through if they own such issues. By your asking instead of telling, clients are more likely to assume ownership. This idea gave rise to the third-generation approach of **debriefing the experience,** popularized in North America as the Outward Bound Plus model (Bacon, 1987). You ask clients to reflect on each adventure activity, discussing learning that you believe took place. If an experience is to have true meaning for clients or if they are going to make use of new learning, they should have a vested interest in the experience and bear responsibility for their actions or for how they functioned during the experience. In this model, clients learn under the guidance of a questioning leader, who helps the group members to discover their own learning. Although numerous methods of debriefing exist, the most common approach in North America is the group discussion. Some successful examples of other debriefing approaches include funneling (Priest & Naismith, 1993), portions of the Adventure Wave (Schoel, Prouty, & Radcliffe, 1988), and other methods based on cognitive hierarchies (Quinsland & Van Ginkel, 1984; Hammel, 1986).

In debriefing the Spider's Web experience, you facilitate a group discussion concerning the details, analysis, and evaluation of the group's behavior following activity completion. Questions might include "What happened? What was the impact of this? How did that make you feel? What did you learn from this? What aspects of this activity were metaphors of your life? What will you do differently next time?"

Directly Frontloading the Experience

Since reflection is typically accomplished after the experience, a number of leaders have concluded that directing the clients before the experience may also be beneficial. This kind of thinking led to the fourth-generation approach of **directly frontloading the experience.** Frontloading means highlighting, or loading, the learning before, or in front of, the experience. In most adventure activities, you brief clients before the experience by explaining how the activity should work and describing tasks, rules, or risk management, and then you debrief them afterwards by guiding reflective discussions. In the fourth generation, however, you hold a frontloading session right before the adventure as an extra "prebriefing" during which you emphasize several key points:

1. **Revisit:** what behaviors or performances were promised and learned from the last activity

2. **Objectives:** what are the aims of this activity and what can be learned or gained from it

3. **Motivations:** why experiencing this activity might be important and how it relates to life

4. **Function:** which behaviors will bring success and how to optimize them

5. **Dysfunction:** which behaviors will hinder success and how to overcome them

When frontloading, you focus clients on certain learning outcomes that you have ascertained as valuable. By loading the learning up front, debriefing simply becomes "direction with reflection," reemphasizing the learning rather than reacting to events as in earlier generations.

In frontloading the experience, you introduce the Spider's Web with the same logistical briefing as usual: group members should be passed through the opening in the web without touching the strands. Contact with a strand wakes the spider, who bites you, causing you to start over. A repeated contact sends your whole group back to the beginning. In addition to this briefing, you add a series of questions to focus the learning before the activity: "What do you think this exercise might teach you? Why is learning this important? How might what you learn help you in the future? Do you recall from past exercises what each of you wanted to work on in situations like this?" Since this prebriefing covers many of the topics you usually cover in debriefing, you can concentrate the concluding discussion on changes.

Isomorphically Framing the Experience

A fifth generation of facilitation involves **isomorphically framing the experience** and is still a rare approach in adventure programming. Recall that metaphors are the analogous connections clients make between the adventure experience and their real lives. Isomorphs are the parallel structures you add to the adventure experience to encourage clients to make certain metaphoric connections (Gass, 1991; Gass & Priest, 1993). For example, if you use the word "marriage" to describe a canoe, you may be creating an isomorph that links the skills of tandem paddling to the dynamics of living with a partner. Strong linkages, that is, those that are meaningful and relevant, increase client motivation and usually enhance transfer of learning. If you can "frame," or introduce, an activity with several isomorphs, mirroring reality for the clients, then any changes they express in the adventure experience may match the changes desired for daily living. Successful framing results in effective transfer since the dynamics and processes of the two experiences are not that different. As with the frontloading style, you need to lead only a little debriefing afterward. Thus, debriefing becomes reinforcement in reflection since clients discuss the similarities and immediately see the connections for themselves. Clients think that if a strategy works here, it can work in real life, too.

So in isomorphic framing, you address the prebriefing in terms of the similarities between the adventure and corresponding life experiences of the client. For example, with a group working in a company warehouse, the Spider's Web activity might be transformed into a distribution network (the web) through which goods and services (team members) are passed from the warehouse (one side) to the customers' many outlets (other side). Passage takes place along unique routings (openings), and contact with the network (brushing up against a strand) damages the goods and services, which means they need to be returned to the warehouse.

If damaged goods and services are purposely passed on to the customer, then the customer will refuse all shipments and return them to the warehouse to be fixed and shipped again! If this briefing mirrors the workplace and current reality of the company warehouse, then the debriefing need only focus on reinforcing the needs of the organization that were met during the activity and on those needs that weren't achieved due to particular shortcomings.

One critical feature of framing adventure experiences is that the basis for constructing appropriate frames lies within what the client, and not the facilitator, brings to the experience. Too often this form of facilitation has failed when facilitators have presented their own "favorite frame" of an adventure experience that makes sense to their reality and has little isomorphic connection to the clients' reality. Mack (1996) termed these isomorphs "imposed metaphors" and called for using "derived metaphors" from clients. As we see in chapter 16, frames are derived from what clients bring to the adventure experience and are created by the client and the facilitator on the basis of what the clients need.

Indirectly Frontloading the Experience

The rarest generation of facilitation involves **indirectly frontloading the experience.** Effective leaders generally use this style only as a last resort: when all other approaches have failed, when it is in the clients' best interests, and when addressing continuing problematic issues. This approach may help when the harder a client tries to eliminate an unwanted issue, the more it occurs, or when the more a client tries to attain a desired result, the more elusive this result becomes. Indirect frontloading can take several paradoxical forms: double binding (e.g., "win–win" frames), symptom prescription, symptom displacement, illusion of alternatives, and proactive reframing (Waltzlawick, 1978). See chapter 16 for more information on this type of facilitation.

ADVENTURE PROGRAMS AND FACILITATION STYLES

Because of the unique goals of each type of adventure program, certain styles of facilitation are more commonly used with certain types of programs (Priest, Gass, & Gillis, 2003; Ringer, 1999):

▶ In **recreational** adventure programs, in which having fun, learning a new skill, and being entertained are the purpose, the first and second generations tend to be the most appropriate facilitation approaches.

▶ In **educational** adventure programs, in which understanding new concepts, enriching old concepts, and generating an awareness of the need for change are the purpose, the third generation is most commonly used.

◀ EFFECTIVE OUTDOOR LEADERS ▶

▶ Implement challenge by choice and the full-value contract in their adventure programs.

▶ Are able to apply the 10 facilitation guidelines.

▶ Comprehend the four facilitation assumptions.

▶ Know the different types of transfer, understanding when to use each type in an adventure program.

▶ Correctly apply the six generations of facilitation techniques to the four types of adventure programs.

▶ Determine the best facilitation process to use in each particular adventure program.

▶ Are capable of hypothesizing client's needs and goals from interviewing multiple sources.

▶ Are capable of observing behaviors, assessing needs, setting objectives, and preparing activities to meet the objectives.

▶ Are capable of facilitating groups in areas of briefing group objectives, structuring for individual objectives, discussing risks and responsibilities (CARES guidelines), and implementing activities as a referee and counselor.

▶ Are capable of guiding reflection by processing, transferring, closing, and evaluating the learning.

▶ Are capable of establishing support, planning for action, and following up.

- In **developmental** adventure programs, in which improving functional behavior and training new and different behaviors are the purpose, third, fourth, and fifth generations fit best.
- In **therapeutic** adventure programs, in which reducing dysfunctional behavior and conditioning clients to use positive behaviors are the purpose, the fifth and sixth generations are most effective.

You have a responsibility to your adventure program, which provides a service, and to your clients, who consume that service, to be clear as to the level of facilitation you can and should provide. For example, the reputation and credibility of the profession suffer when a client requests therapy with the intent of getting specific prescriptive change, the program provides education with a more general focus, and the leader offers recreation with little or no facilitation! Thus, you must consider the types of programs you can offer, which generations are appropriate for your programs, and how the generations will affect clients.

SUMMARY

Facilitation is the collection of techniques you use to optimize the learning and change which come from an adventure experience. Challenge by choice and the full-value contract are two policies at the center of good facilitation. Challenge by choice puts the client, not you, in control of selecting how and when to participate in activities or discussions. The no-discount concept or full-value contract suggests operating principles governing how people should treat themselves and others. There are 10 facilitation guidelines concerned with group position, time, single speaking, nonviolence, participation, responsibility, commitment, role clarity, confidentiality, and other ethical issues. Four facilitation assumptions include facilitator assistance, controlled group setting, application, and impetus for change.

Transfer of learning is successful when changes in the adventure program are retained in clients' daily lives. Transfer can be specific when particular skills are applied to similar situations and nonspecific when general principles are applied to different situations. Metaphoric transfer refers to a special type of transfer that occurs when several elements of the adventure program appear—in the minds of the clients—similar to their everyday lives. Clients begin to think that if they can change in an activity that is very similar to their home, school, or work situation, then perhaps they can

change in real life. A more metaphoric connection yields a greater transfer.

Facilitation techniques in adventure programs have evolved through six generations. The first generation involves no debriefing at all. The second two generations are normally used in the debriefing phase, and change takes place after the activity. The fourth, fifth, and sixth generations are usually most effective when applied to the design or delivery phases, and change takes place before or during the activity, although reflective debriefing still plays an important role.

The first generation, letting the experience speak for itself, involves no debriefing. In the second generation, speaking on behalf of the experience, you tell the group what they learned. In the third generation, debriefing the experience, you guide reflection about the experience, typically by asking carefully sequenced questions. In the fourth generation, directly frontloading the experience, you emphasize key learning points before the experience. In the fifth generation, isomorphically framing the experience, you introduce the activity with isomorphs (prescriptive metaphors) to make it uniquely meaningful and relevant to the client. In the sixth generation, indirectly frontloading the experience, you use paradox to create change in extremely difficult situations. These six generations suit particular types of adventure programs, such as recreational, educational, developmental, or therapeutic. You have a responsibility to know which generation of facilitation you can or should perform and what influence your chosen techniques will have on clients' needs and on program types.

The process of facilitating adventure experiences involves arranging five phases: diagnosis, design, delivery, debriefing, and departure. In the diagnostic phase, you assess clients' needs, determining program goals by interviewing as many sources as possible to create, confirm, or reject initial hypotheses about the group and its members. In the design phase, you observe the group and its members, reassess your original hypotheses, set your objectives, and prepare the best activity to meet those objectives. In the delivery phase, you orient the group to the task by briefing group objectives, structure the activity in order to meet individual objectives, discuss the risks and responsibilities of the activity by sharing CARES guidelines, and implement the activity paying attention to those guidelines, all while playing the roles of referee and counselor. In the debriefing phase, you guide the group through reflecting about the experience by processing what was learned, which involves looking backward, by transferring this new learning, which involves looking forward, by closing the activity with feedback, and, finally, by evaluating whether or not the experience met the objectives. In the departure phase, you establish support for the group and its members, planning practical strategies and follow-up. These five phases can be presented in linear, cyclical, or spiral models, or in a series of nested loops. Each model suits a particular type of adventure program: linear for recreation, nested loops for education, cyclical for development, and spiral for therapy.

QUESTIONS TO THINK ABOUT

1. Differentiate among the three types of transfer. From your own learning, give examples of each type in action.

2. Explain the rationales behind challenge by choice and the full-value contract.

3. Contrast the 10 facilitation guidelines with the four facilitation assumptions.

4. Differentiate among the six styles of the facilitation process. Using outdoor activities you know, give examples of each phase in action.

5. Differentiate between the two different uses of the word "process" in this chapter.

REFERENCES

Bacon, S.B. (1987). *The evolution of the Outward Bound process.* Greenwich, CT: Outward Bound USA. (ERIC Document Reproduction Service No. ED 295 780).

Berne, E. (1961). *Transactional analysis in psychotherapy.* New York: Grove Press.

Berne, E. (1964). *Games people play.* New York: Grove Press.

Berne, E. (1972). *What do you say after you say hello?* New York: Grove Press.

Doughty, S. (1991). Three generations of development training. *Journal of Adventure Education and Outdoor Leadership, 7*(4), 7-9.

Gass, M.A. (1985). Programming the transfer of learning in adventure education. *Journal of Experiential Education, 8*(3), 18-24.

Gass, M.A. (1991). Enhancing metaphoric transfer in adventure therapy programs. *Journal of Experiential Education, 14*(2), 6-13.

Gass, M.A. (Ed.). (1993). *Adventure therapy: Therapeutic applications of adventure programming in therapeutic settings.* Dubuque, IA: Kendall/Hunt.

Gass, M.A., & Priest, S. (1993). Using metaphors and isomorphs to enhance the transfer of adventure learning. *Journal of Adventure Education and Outdoor Leadership, 10*(4), 18-23.

Hammel, H. (1986). How to design a debriefing session. *Journal of Experiential Education, 9*(3), 20-25.

Hovelynck, J. (2000). Recognizing and exploring action theories: A reflection-in-action approach to facilitating experiential learning. *Journal of Adventure Education and Outdoor Learning, 1*(1), 7-20.

Knapp, C. (1990). Processing experiences. In J.C. Miles & S. Priest (Eds.), *Adventure education* (pp. 189-198). State College, PA: Venture.

Knapp, C. (1993). Processing experiences. In M.A. Gass (Ed.), *Adventure therapy: Therapeutic applications of adventure programming in therapeutic settings.* (pp. 239-244). Dubuque, IA: Kendall/Hunt.

Mack, H. (1996). Inside work, outdoors: Women, metaphor, and meaning. In K. Warren (Ed.), *Women's voices in experiential education* (pp. 24-31). Dubuque, IA: Kendall/Hunt.

Medrick, R. (1979). *Confronting passive behavior through outdoor experience: A TA approach to experiential learning.* Denver: Outdoor Leadership Training Seminars.

Nadler, R., & Luckner, J. (1992). *Processing the adventure experience: Theory and practice.* Dubuque, IA: Kendall/Hunt.

Priest, S. (1989). A model of group initiative facilitation training: GIFT. *The Outdoor Communicator, 20*(1), 8-13.

Priest, S., & Gass, M.A. (1993). Five generations of facilitated learning from adventure experiences. *Journal of Adventure Education and Outdoor Leadership, 10*(3), 23-25.

Priest, S., Gass, M.A., & Gillis, H.L. (2003). *Essential elements of facilitation.* Seattle: Tarrak Technologies.

Priest, S., & Naismith, M. (1993). A model for debriefing experiences. *Journal of Adventure Education and Outdoor Leadership, 10*(3), 20-22.

Quinsland, L.K., & Van Ginkel, A. (1984). How to process experience. *Journal of Experiential Education, 7*(2), 8-13.

Ringer, M. (1999). Two vital aspects in the facilitation of groups: Connections and containment. *Australian Journal of Outdoor Education, 4*(1), 5-11.

Rohnke, K. (1984). *Silver bullets.* Hamilton, MA: Project Adventure.

Schoel, J., & Maizell, R.S. (2002). *Exploring islands of healing: New perspectives on adventure-based counseling.* Beverly, MA: Project Adventure.

Schoel, J., Prouty, D., & Radcliffe, P. (1988). *Islands of healing: A guide to adventure-based counseling.* Dubuque, IA: Kendall/Hunt.

Sugerman, D., Doherty, K.L., Garvey, D.E., & Gass, M.A. (2000). *Reflective learning: Theory and practice.* Dubuque, IA: Kendall/Hunt Publishing Company.

Waltzlawick, P. (1978). *The language of change.* New York: Norton.

Webster, S. (1989). *Ropes course safety manual: An instructor's guide to initiatives, and low and high elements.* Dubuque, IA: Kendall/Hunt.

CHAPTER

15

Basic Facilitation Techniques

During a challenge course, two groups moved on to their next low element, the Spider's Web. With the groups facing the web, each outdoor leader overviewed the rules and safety procedures and asked if there were any questions. After clarifying these points, the leaders gave each group 25 min to complete the task.

After the first group completed the experience, the leader led a lengthy discussion concerning the details, analysis, and evaluation of the group's behavior during the activity. The leader asked, "What happened? What was the impact of this? How did that make you feel? What did you learn from this? What aspects of this activity were metaphors of your life? What will you do differently next time?"

For the second group, the outdoor leader asked questions to focus the learning *before* the activity: "What do you think this exercise might teach you? Why is learning this important? How might your learning help you in the future? Do you recall from past exercises what each of you wanted to work on in situations like this?" After the experience, the outdoor leader led a brief discussion summarizing the answers the group discovered during the activity.

The two scenarios may appear similar, but are quite different. The first is an example of debriefing the experience: asking the questions afterward. The second is an example of frontloading the experience: asking the questions beforehand. With debriefing, clients change after the debriefing and in the next activity. With frontloading, clients change in the present activity. You should, however, reserve frontloading for those few times when learning needs to be primed. In this chapter, we examine some of the basic approaches to facilitation, including discussion and nonverbal techniques, debriefing, and the more recently developed frontloading.

DISCUSSION TECHNIQUES

Discussion is an unstructured form of debriefing that permits clients to analyze past experience and to transfer learning from their adventures to their future lives. By verbalizing reactions to an adventure, clients reinforce their perceptions and see the situation from fresh perspectives. Furthermore, knowing that a discussion follows the activities, many clients will be more attentive to what goes on during an experience and will exhibit a heightened awareness of outcomes related to relationship dynamics, task products, group processes, and so on. To accomplish these outcomes, you must guide the discussion, using facilitation tips and tricks to make the content and format valuable to clients. These same tips and tricks equally apply to the third, fourth, fifth, and sixth generations of facilitation covered in the next two chapters, such as funneling, frontloading, and framing.

Remember, to begin a discussion, you should typically arrange clients in a circle. This allows them to more easily hear what everyone says and to see one another. Clients should be comfortable and ideally should all stand or all sit to allow eye contact. You should also be part of the circle so you can guide discussion, read body language for signs of discomfort, and make eye contact (but not enough to dominate or threaten). If the sun is shining, you should face the sun, keeping it out of the clients' eyes.

Client investment in the group and willingness to change stem from a safe and supportive atmosphere. Such an atmosphere is characterized by mutual trust, respect, equality, flexibility, freedom, empathy, acceptance, and anonymity. Physiological needs for food, water, shade, and shelter are met. Psychological safety is protected through fully valuing the self and others and through challenge by choice. With a supportive atmosphere, clients are able to take risks by experimenting with new thoughts, feelings, and behaviors. They take personal responsibility for their own learning, and change comes more easily than when the atmosphere is competitive, harmful, fixed, controlled, or critical.

To create a supportive atmosphere, you must establish and expect clients to follow certain ground rules. Furthermore, you must help the group evolve its own operating principles. These may include, but are not necessarily limited to, speaking for oneself; single speaking; listening and talking in the here and now instead of dwelling on the past; respecting self, others, and the environment; giving everyone the right to pass and not respond; welcoming all points of view; agreeing or disagreeing with the idea, not the person; avoiding put-downs; and maintaining confidentiality.

You should never facilitate beyond your ability. If a client discloses a psychiatric concern, don't open that can of worms unless qualified in psychiatry; instead, refer the individual to professional counseling. You should research the client group in advance and assess its needs and objectives for the adventure.

Before the discussion, you should explain the difference between a product and process, adding that discussions will center on group dynamics although clients may be tempted to talk about task outcomes. In addition, explain the concepts of transfer and metaphors. Remind clients to search for metaphors throughout the program.

The ensuing discussion should progress from positive topics to negative issues, then end on a positive note. Ask open-ended questions (see "Sample Questions for Funneling and Frontloading" on pages 208-211) of the entire group and speak loudly so everyone can hear. Speak clearly and concisely by avoiding complex wording. After asking one question, provide plenty of time for

clients to think about the question, answers, and how they will respond within the group. Listen to clients answer and then correctly paraphrase their responses in order to confirm and clarify the intent for others. Acknowledge and validate all responses with a thank-you or a nonverbal signal, such as a nod of your head.

You must also act as a gatekeeper for discussion by giving everyone a chance to contribute. While recognizing that silence can be a form of contribution, you should be attentive to clients who are always quiet or speakers who are too dominant, run off on tangents, and talk forever.

Invite quiet clients to contribute by asking them by name, seemingly at random, without putting them on the spot. Make gentle eye contact, lean forward, and smile invitingly. Provide a legitimate way out if the person chooses not to share by shifting your eyes to other clients and backing off.

Listen to overbearing speakers for a useful statement. Once you hear one, ask, "What do others think of this point?" Ask the speaker to reemphasize the point if necessary, but clearly move on to others.

Arranging clients in a circle is often the first step of the discussion process.

Redirect tangential speakers back to the topic of discussion without sounding critical or angry. You can ask them to relate their comments to the theme or you can note a time limitation, indicating the need to return to the main issue. Support the speakers' ideas, but put them on hold and return to them later. Avoid confronting the individual, thereby inhibiting future valuable comments from others.

Interrupt lengthy speakers politely. Excuse yourself and explain your reasons for stopping them. If repeated interruptions become necessary and seem ineffective, you can introduce the burning-match constraint. Each client is given the same number of matches and may only speak as long as one match keeps burning.

Another technique is fishbowling, which splits the group in two with one half surrounding the other. The outer circle observes the inner circle's discussion and notes the frequency with which people speak and what they say or do. The outer circle reports their findings to the inner circle, and then clients change places. Tossing a ball of string, with the tail unraveling from speaker to speaker, also enables group members to identify a pattern of dominant and recessive talkers among them.

You may also have clients pass a talking stick or other inanimate object in one direction around the circle. Only the person with the stick may talk. This procedure can give quieter group members a chance to speak and may be less intrusive than picking on the silent ones by name.

Sometimes private conversations within the discussion can interfere with client learning, and so you may need to deal with them. Calling attention to this potential problem before beginning the dis-

Discussion Dos and Don'ts

Several dos and don'ts apply to the when and where of facilitating discussions.

Do:

- Take discussions seriously and schedule plenty of time for them. But if energy levels fall, end the discussion early.

- Discuss often and immediately after each experience. If this is not possible, have a brief discussion afterward and save a lengthy discussion for later.

- With most populations, spend as much time on the discussion as was spent doing the activity. If on a multiday experience, hold periodic discussions throughout each day.

- Discuss in the activity location unless noise from running water or blowing wind interferes with hearing. The location permits clients to more readily visualize what took place and where and how it happened.

- Pick a special place, such as a rock by a lake or the darkness of a forest, or a regular time, such as campfires or meals, for holding discussions during residential programs. This way, clients will know to concentrate on discussing at the chosen time or place.

- Encourage clients to ask their own questions that fit the theme. This permits self-discovery, freeing you from some of the responsibility for client learning.

- Remain alert for client metaphors and incorporate them into the discussion using client language. For example, if a client says, "I feel like a volcano," you might ask, "What kinds of eruptions have you experienced lately?"

- Welcome client contributions with a relaxed posture, open facial expression, and verbal appreciation. Observe body and verbal language and respectfully communicate in return with the same movements and words.

Don't:

- Lead clients by suggesting words or finishing their sentences. Ask questions instead of offering answers.

- Compare clients with other groups that have gone before or judge their actions as good or bad.

- Give false feedback. Instead, avoid giving insincere praise or unwarranted criticism.

- Assume you know what is best for clients, forcing them to change.

- Accept only one answer as correct, since this creates a situation reminiscent of the reward and punishment mentality of institutionalized schooling. If you accept only one answer, soon you will receive only one, because clients will fear being wrong.

cussion may provide a nonthreatening, proactive way to deal with this problem. When they occur, figure out why. One person may be clarifying a discussion point for another. Or the discussion may be so boring that two people are making small talk on the side. If the reason is appropriate, you can ask the two to share their thoughts with the whole group or you can break into small groups to encourage side discussions before returning to the big group. If the reason is inappropriate, you can comment on the distraction being counterproductive or you can even terminate the discussion and go to the next activity.

Occasionally, clients can get stuck in a rut during an activity. They may have promised change in the last discussion, but can't seem to get it together in this activity, or they may have just fallen apart as a team, straying dangerously off the task. At times like these, you can call a time-out or freeze the action and then follow with a single, well-chosen comment. This careful intervention and brief interjection can get the clients out of the rut, putting the group back on track to positive change.

When clients fail a task, they frequently concentrate on how they could fix the product of their actions, that is, what physical things they could have done better. Instead, you should focus the discussion on the process of their actions: the human relationships and group dynamics used to solve the problem. But if clients continually return to the task during the discussion, let them talk about this hang-up until they are satisfied enough with their product to be willing to talk about the process.

Balance the discussion. You shouldn't always examine mistakes, setbacks, failures, and other weaknesses, but should generally balance such negativity by also discussing strengths, such as success and achievement. Too many negatives can prolong agonies and lead to "paralysis by analysis," in which some clients become reluctant to discuss anything, freezing up in fear of constantly examining their shortcomings.

ALTERNATIVE REFLECTIONS AND NONVERBAL METHODS

Most of the tips and tricks we have discussed apply to verbal reflection. Certainly, verbal reflection is the most common form of debriefing conducted in North America. Not all clients are masterful at expressing their feelings through words, however, and a few may not even speak

English or be cognitively mature enough to benefit. Therefore, alternative ways of reflecting may prove more beneficial and less intimidating than verbal reflection. You should consider nonverbal methods of reflection, such as art, drama, music, dance, poetry, writing, storytelling, photography, presentations, or even repeating the same activity (Greenaway, 1993; Priest, Gass, & Gillis, 2003). These methods should fit the age and culture of the clients. Be aware, however, that these methods can become routine, so use them in moderation, alternating methods often.

Art can take many forms: cartooning, making collages, drawing, graphing, painting, sculpting, or mapping. Cartoon balloons can convey true feelings. Clients can cut up old outdoor magazines to make collages that interpret their experiences. They can draw posters to represent their thoughts. They can graph their energy levels over time to infer shifting morale and motivations. They can paint murals to share their ideas. They can sculpt clay to illustrate emotions.

Realistic art is often the most difficult to create in a limited time and is usually the least useful for generating discussion since it is too close to what actually transpired. Abstract and symbolic art provide the greatest opportunities for making metaphoric connections. For example, a trip down a river can be a journey metaphor for completing projects in daily life. By drawing on plastic over the trip map, adding key points during the journey, clients can link key points of the project by using a second plastic sheet or by overlaying the first plastic sheet on the project time line. Once linked in either manner, metaphoric connections become conspicuous (Ringer, 1999).

Drama enables clients to act out what happened during the experience, what should have happened but didn't, and what they expect will happen next time. Drama can be accomplished through fantasy skits, modeling group members as if they are clay, or through reenacting the activity. Clients can perform in silence or by talking.

Clients can sing songs or play instruments. Music also proves useful in solo reflection. Expressive dance or creative movement can enhance the music. Poetry can take the form of cinquains, couplets, haiku, or limericks. Writing can be analytical, as in a newspaper article or quantitative and qualitative questionnaires, or be creative, as in a journal and short stories. Fantasy storytelling by leaders and clients can effectively impart metaphoric messages through quotes, morals, fantasies, legends, parables, or fables.

Photography, slides, video, or still snapshots from instant film can be useful when reviewing an experience. As you replay videotapes or audiotapes with an occasional pause for discussion, people can remark on what they were feeling or thinking at the time. You can display slides and pictures on the wall for clients to comment on.

Presentations are formal showings from the adventure. Clients can write a report on the trip, share photo albums with their families, give a slide show to the next group of incoming clients, or demonstrate new skills to the general public during an open house. In doing so, clients reexamine the experience from the viewpoint of an outsider. They must find a way to explain their personal and significant life-changing adventures to people who haven't yet experienced one for themselves.

Repeating the same activity a second time without debriefing the first time or frontloading can provide people with an opportunity to reflect alone and then improve what may not have worked well the first time. They may increase the product of their efforts, but they will more often enhance the process. In addition, you can have group members exchange roles. They may act differently in someone else's shoes.

To summarize, sometimes verbal debriefings may be limiting or inappropriate for producing functional change. Verbal debriefings may center on complicated and dynamic interactions, requiring you to deal with extremely complex issues. Less complex, speech-dependent, group-oriented, and rigid alternatives can be more effective than verbal debriefings (Smith, 1986). Moreover, alternatives may require less complex facilitation skills and therefore may be easier for leaders with less experience. Some clients may find expressing their thoughts with speech incredibly difficult, provoking anxiety, withdrawal, defensiveness, or frustration. Alternative methods are often less threatening. Traditional debriefing procedures rely heavily on group processes, and some clients are reluctant to interact and share in group settings. Many alternative techniques are oriented more toward the person; thus, individual clients may find them more meaningful and relevant. Alternatives may also provide a more beneficial structure than verbal debriefings for some clients, who then increase their involvement. Alternatives may be easier to schedule than debriefings that require the entire group's time, so you can implement them on an as-needed basis. Alternatives may make the logistics of facilitation more flexible.

DEBRIEFING THE EXPERIENCE

As stated in chapter 14, as the popularity of adventure programs grew in North America during the 1960s, more teachers, counselors, therapists, and other human service professionals became involved in conducting experiences. Many of these individuals imported techniques from their professions to heighten the experience. One import was using debriefing techniques to discuss the experience afterward. While debriefing sometimes met with resistance from proponents of the "let the experience speak for itself" model, it changed the very foundation of adventure programming.

The initial thought behind debriefing was that if clients discussed issues and stated personal commitments to change based on what they accomplished in their adventure experiences, they would own such issues and be more likely to follow through. The term "debriefing" was used because of the technique's similarity in structure (but not in content) to military debriefings that were familiar to early Outward Bound instructors with backgrounds in military service.

As a facilitator, your role in debriefing is usually to guide clients through reflective processes so they discover their own learning. You should not proclaim judgments about what you think; rather, you should guide clients in their learning by asking effective questions. In this way, you encourage clients to share their personal observations and own their behaviors or the consequences of their actions. Two successful examples of questioning are funneling (Priest & Naismith, 1993) and cognitive hierarchies (Quinsland & Van Ginkel, 1984; Hammel, 1986; Schoel & Maizell, 2002; Schoel, Prouty, & Radcliffe, 1988).

Funneling

One type of debriefing that is successfully used by a number of adventure programs is the **funneling approach.** In this process, you guide the group through a series of steps that funnel client attention from the experience toward making beneficial changes in their lives. These steps expand the classic three questions from Gestalt therapy: "What? So what? Now what?" (Borton, 1970).

Figure 15.1 illustrates the debriefing funnel. During the funnel process, you pour experiences through a series of six "filters," or types of questions, that "distill" learning changes through client reflection and answering. Each question filters out unwanted parts of the experience, narrowing

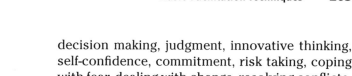

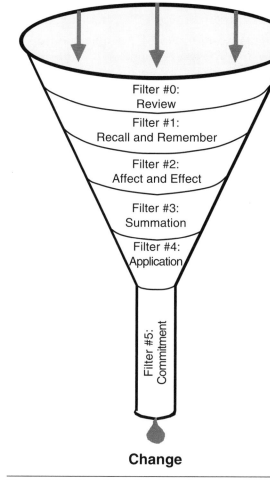

Experiences

Filter #0:
Review

Filter #1:
Recall and Remember

Filter #2:
Affect and Effect

Filter #3:
Summation

Filter #4:
Application

Filter #5:
Commitment

Change

Figure 15.1 The debriefing funnel.

clients' concentration toward discussing wanted changes. The six filters are review, recall and remember, affect and effect, summation, application, and commitment.

Before the funneling can take place, you must thoroughly and correctly understand client needs. Without this knowledge, you can easily misdirect clients, no matter your good intentions. Obtain this information by observing the group members during the experience and keeping mental or written notes on what they say, how they behave, with whom they interact, and what incidents occur during the experience. Your toughest choice may be sorting out which issues and topics to debrief! Identifying specific learning objectives in advance that are based on your assessment of client needs can help you make this decision (see chapter 17). Examples of debriefing topics for most adventure experiences include trust, cooperation, communication, teamwork, planning, problem solving,

decision making, judgment, innovative thinking, self-confidence, commitment, risk taking, coping with fear, dealing with change, resolving conflicts, leadership, gender inequity, group split, and emotional disclosure. Of course, you can't focus on every topic every time! But if you and your group miss an issue, it generally resurfaces in the next adventure activity or its debriefing.

The review question (filter 0) focuses the group on the topic or issue of interest based on client needs, your program objectives, and any incidents that took place in the activity. During this initial review, you can ask the group members to replay the experience in their minds or to describe it aloud in order to refresh everyone's memories. In this way, you get the group to concentrate on a single topic to the exclusion of everything else that happened during the experience. If the topic of concern is obvious from the experience outcome, then this filter may not be necessary (hence filter 0). Once the group agrees to center further discussion on this one topic, you can progress to the next level.

The recall-and-remember question (filter 1) gets clients to identify an incident relating to the topic that took place during the experience. If you bring up the incident, the group may deny it or perhaps feel confronted. Therefore, you should ask a question that gets the group to bring up the issue, giving it ownership and control over the situation. If a group is reluctant to speak about a topic or issue, you still have a few choices. Pushing a confrontation will likely be the least productive, so you should leave the denied topic and start a funnel of questions about another issue or design the next activity to more obviously highlight the point you'd like to make. We discuss dealing with denial further in chapter 16.

The affect-and-effect question (filter 2) addresses emotions and causes. Once clients bring up and buy into a specific incident related to an issue, you can ask other questions to ascertain the impact of that occurrence. These questions examine how each individual felt and how the group was influenced by the event. The answers permit a group to recognize positive or negative impacts of its behaviors and to separate personal impacts from group impacts. At this level, discussion is about sharing feelings and noting concerns. Once again, you must get partial acceptance from the group about the validity of these questions before moving on to the next type of question.

The summation question (filter 3) highlights new learning. Once you have ascertained the

The Reluctant Group

North Americans are generally more comfortable than others when it comes to speaking aloud, talking about themselves, or discussing in a group. Nevertheless, public speaking scares most people. You can always expect to encounter people who are uncomfortable discussing issues because they are afraid of failing, people who prefer to avoid negativity, or people who deny their problems, or to encounter a group reluctant to discuss issues in general. At these times, you can modify your approach to increase a client's willingness to enter into a discussion. Some of these modifications include nonverbal responses, closed questions, trigger questions, written responses, partnerships, trios, gift giving, reporting, and rounds.

You can encourage clients to nonverbally respond to simple statements you make to generate discussion. They can signal a thumbs-up or thumbs-down or raise a number of fingers to express agreement on a scale from 0 to 10. They can also form a line according to who contributed or listened from most to least. Or they can be targeted by positioning themselves near or far from an imaginary bull's-eye to represent whether they believe certain statements are right on or miss the mark.

You can ask the occasional closed question, but these should not make up the whole discussion. Clients, responding with either a yes or no, can get used to speaking with short, easy answers before you ask probing questions. After warming up with closed questions, you can ask trigger questions to evoke controversy, motivating people to dissent and speak their minds. For example, ask, "What is the role of competition in teamwork?" This question assumes competition has a role in teamwork, and some clients may disagree with this assumption.

Have clients write their responses before responding aloud. They can respond to your questions or statements, or they can finish sentences you start. By writing their ideas first, clients can collect their thoughts, reducing their chances of making mistakes while speaking. This approach ensures that quieter and more reluctant clients have as much time to respond as more eager clients.

Another way to allow clients to prepare for discussion is to give them a little solo time beforehand. Clients can go off on their own to contemplate the topics of the upcoming discussion. Music, natural sounds, or silence can enhance introspection. Encourage controlled breathing, meditation, or relaxation to "center" clients before asking them to contemplate your questions.

You can also divide clients into partners who discuss the topics in advance. Their mutual reinforcement of one another's ideas and comments can strengthen their resolve to speak out. Making partners into trios can introduce interviewing with an observer. While two discuss the topics, the third observes, reporting after the partners finish. In both these procedures, people may speak for themselves or can paraphrase and report their partner's responses. These approaches help because speaking on behalf of others is normally less stressful than talking for oneself.

You can build speaking practice into the discussion through gift giving and reporting. Clients can present physical gifts found outside or made from art supplies or inexpensive materials or nonphysical gifts of words or mimed actions to give one another feedback. Making gifts, whether physical or nonphysical, encourages clients who are more comfortable with or talented at nonverbal communication to participate more fully in verbal communication by bridging the gap between nonverbal and verbal. To use reporting, you can select people to perform the roles of interaction observer or quality inspector. They observe process or product issues and then report their findings to the group. Both gift giving and reporting encourage clients to speak out.

In rounds, clients take turns reviewing the activity. When one person forgets an occurrence or loses track of the order, the next person can chime in and so on around the circle. Clients identify points from the experience that were positive or negative, good or bad, easy or difficult, and funny or interesting. Clients need only identify these points and need not discuss them in any depth to begin with. In the ensuing discussions, you can probe only the positive topics until clients loosen up to the point that you feel you can move on to any negative topics that need attention. Last, you can go first and disclose something very personal, then ask clients to follow the precedent you set.

impact of the event, you ask clients to summarize what they have learned about the issue. So far, they have identified an occurrence and discussed its influence on their task performance and group dynamics. Now they talk about what they have distilled from all of this. When several clients' summaries of learning are in accord with their objectives, you can move to the next filter.

Once clients have identified new learning, you must help them apply it to real-life situations, thereby reinforcing learning and helping solidify its transference. The application question (filter 4) helps establish such linkages. Ask clients to make connections in the form of metaphors, or analogies, between the adventure and reality. When a number of clients concur that the metaphoric links are accurate and understand how the experience is like real life, you can ask the final type of question.

The commitment question (filter 5) looks toward change. Once clients have noted the usefulness of the new learning and how they might apply it in their daily lives, ask them to make a pledge and plan for action. You should press for answers in the form of an "I" statement and get the group to support members who commit to doing things differently as a result of their guided reflection on the experience.

Too much to remember? Before debriefing, you may want to write a list of questions that you will likely ask clients. This list should focus on the original objectives for the experience and on some predictable topics that may arise. But if unexpected issues surface, you should remain flexible, tailoring your questions to address them. To help you prepare debriefings, we have listed some sample questions in figure 15.2 based on the funnel model.

Remember, for funneling you identify a topic for discussion (review); ask for examples of its occurrence (recall and remember); ask about its impact on the clients, group, or task (affect and effect); ask what clients learned from this impact (summation); ask how the learning pertains to real life (application); and ask what people pledge to change (commitment). For example, groups often communicate poorly in the early stages of an adventure program. Clients may all speak at once, rarely listening to one another. Next is a sample "funnel" you might follow to get the group to improve its communication.

To begin, you might ask, "Can we talk about communication?" Unless someone objects, you can then ask the group to review their communication in the past activity and rate their performance by asking, "What rating would you give yourselves for communication on a scale from 0 (low) to 10 (high)?" If the average rating is low, you could add, "Are you interested in improving your communication?" If the average rating is high, you could ask, "Are you interested in making your communication a 10 or better?" Either question readies the group for identifying where communication broke down and a question such as "Can you give me an example of communication that could be enhanced?" Specify your questions if clients can't recall or remember the instance you wish to focus on: "Can you relate an instance in which listening

---

Review

Let's talk about (issue or topic). Can you review the last activity for me? On a five-point scale, hold up the number of fingers that indicates your level of performance, with five being excellent.

Recall and Remember

Do you remember an example of excellent (or poor) (issue or topic)? Can you recall a particular time when (issue or topic) was good (or bad)?

Affect and Effect

What affect (emotion) did you experience? How did this make you feel? How did this emotion affect the group? What influence did it have on the task?

Summation

How does the moral of this story go? What did you learn from all of this? Can you sum up what you have gained from our discussions (reflections)?

Application

Do you see a connection between this learning and your life back at school? Can you apply this on the job? Do you see any parallels to your family?

Commitment

What will you do differently next time? Begin with the words, "I will. . . ." How can you commit to change? Who will help support you in upholding this pledge?

Figure 15.2 Funnel guide questions.

was not done well?" Next, you can ask about affect or effect: "How did that affect the group morale? How did you personally feel about that? How did that resolve the task?" You can follow these questions with others about summation and application: "What have you learned from this? Does this ever happen back home?" Finally, you can seek commitment: "What will you do differently in the next activity? How are you going to change when you return home?"

Some groups may be reluctant to answer questions and to talk about things it did poorly. You can overcome reluctance by running funnels on positive topics, asking about things the group did well. Once members are comfortable talking about themselves and their actions, you can address negative issues or areas for improvement. Again, once you have completed the debriefing, composed of positive and negative funnels on several topics, you may often offer a new experience that gives the group a chance to put its pledges into practice.

In the debriefing after this new experience, revisit a funnel on communication to see if client strategies worked. This funnel might contain a few key questions such as "On a 10-point scale, how was communication this time? Give me an example of where it was improved. What caused this improvement? What were the results of the improvement? What did you learn from these results? How can you use this learning at home? How will things be different in the future?" Note that this abbreviated sequence of questions leaves room for you to probe for deeper answers with more complex questions or to confirm answers by paraphrasing client responses.

Debriefing experiences requires that you remain flexible in your questioning. You must use your best judgment in "customizing" questions. For this reason, "cookbook" approaches to debriefing rarely obtain 100% success; you will have to modify any approach. Once you are comfortable with this debriefing model, we encourage you to adapt it to suit your own style and your clients' needs. Furthermore, we encourage you to remember not to be bound by a single view of debriefing as the only way to guide reflection.

Cognitive Hierarchy

Another type of debriefing that has been successfully used by a number of adventure programs is based on Bloom's (1956) taxonomy of cognitive objectives. As with funneling, you lead the group through a series of questions that stem from the adventure experience and are designed to foster positive changes in clients' lives. The sequence of questions mirrors Bloom's six levels of cognitive thought: knowledge, comprehension, application, analysis, synthesis, and evaluation (Quinsland & Van Ginkel, 1984).

Following this model, you ask questions that progressively develop the cognitive knowledge about the adventure experience. Through this development, clients organize information at more concrete levels, that is, the knowledge, comprehension, and application levels, so they can answer debriefing questions at more abstract levels, that is, the analysis, synthesis, and evaluation levels. The questions you ask at the abstract level, particularly evaluation questions, focus on producing the positive and transferable changes clients will use in the future. Table 15.1 (Hammel, 1986) illustrates the levels of cognitive thought, debriefing functions, and corresponding sample questions that fit this hierarchy.

Knowledge operates at a memory level and involves remembering information by recognition or recall. Comprehension operates at an understanding level and involves interpreting or explaining information in a descriptive or literal manner. Application operates at a usage level and involves using information correctly. Analysis operates at a relationship level and involves breaking information down into component parts and detecting relationships among parts. Synthesis operates at a creative level and involves putting pieces of information together to form a whole in new and innovative ways. Evaluation operates at an opinion level and involves judging the value of ideas, solutions, and events (Gass & Gillis, 1995).

For example, a group of clients on the ropes course might be learning about cooperation. A knowledge question might be "Step by step, what happened between you and your belayer?" Clients typically respond with examples of how they worked in partnership. You follow with a comprehension question: "What exemplified cooperative behavior between you and your belayer?" Clients talk about the seriousness of trust or support. You ask an application question: "What were you doing to make cooperation so successful?" Clients answer with examples of listening better to their partner's needs. Then you ask an analysis question: "When do you think you cooperated best?" Clients identify a specific highlight for them in cooperating with their belay partner. You continue with a synthesis question: "How does this

Table 15.1 Cognitive Hierarchy

Cognitive thought	Debriefing function	Corresponding questions
CONCRETE LEVELS		
Knowledge (memory)	Review and describe events, feelings, thoughts, and problems.	What did you do when . . . ?
Comprehension (understanding)		What happened when . . . ?
Application (usage)		How did you feel when . . . ?
		What did your group do when . . . ?
ABSTRACT LEVELS		
Analysis (relationship)	Make comparisons.	What was the highlight for you?
Synthesis (creation)	Relate to daily life.	What was the most challenging?
Evaluation (opinion)	Propose solutions.	Does this remind you of anything?
	Examine values.	What have you learned today that may help you in the future?
		What have you learned about yourself?

From Hammel, 1986.

highlight compare with your regular way of working with others in daily life?" Clients discuss the similarities and differences, to which you add an evaluation question: "How do you think you will work together in the future?" Clients talk about changes they will make and strategies for transferring their learning.

An obvious weakness of this model, as with most verbal debriefings, is that expressing emotional experiences in words and thinking about feelings in cognitive terms is difficult for most people, especially children. So you may wish to debrief with metaphoric stories or other alternatives.

FRONTLOADING THE EXPERIENCE

Recall that **frontloading** constitutes the fourth generation of facilitated learning in adventure education (Priest & Gass, 1993; Priest, Gass, & Gillis, 2003). "Front" indicates that the facilitation takes place up front, or before the experience. "Loading" refers to the fact that the learning is loaded together, or emphasized, in combination beforehand. In summary, frontloading means punctuating the key learning points in advance of the adventure experience rather than reviewing or debriefing any learning after.

Direct frontloading typically addresses one or more of the following five functions: revisiting,

objectives, motivation, function, and dysfunction. The excitement of adventure activities can help a group focus intensely on completing a task, distracting it from the changes it's there to accomplish. The revisiting question reminds group members of the behaviors they pledged to perform after the last activity. Just before the new activity begins and after you have explained the task, you can pose a single question: "One more thing: What were the commitments that the group made last time?" This brief question brings the previous answers to the "do things differently next time" question to the front of clients' minds so that clients are more likely to act on their revisited affirmations during the activity.

Besides a revisiting question, you can ask four other types of frontloading questions in combination or alone. Objective questions ask about the aims of the activity and what can be learned or gained from the experience. Motivation questions ask why experiencing the activity may be important and how learning relates to daily life. Function questions ask what behaviors will help bring about success and how the group may optimize them. Dysfunction questions ask what behaviors will hinder success and how the group can avoid or overcome them. These five areas of frontloading are very similar to those of the filters of the funneling model; the difference is that you ask frontloading questions before instead of after the experience.

The five areas can be illustrated with The Wall initiative. This activity includes a 12 to 14 ft (3-4 m) structure with a ledge on the back side. The group is challenged to pass its members up the front side and over the top. One difficult aspect of getting over the wall is getting the first person up. Generally, the crux of the problem is getting the final person over the wall with no one remaining below to lift him. In a typical briefing before the activity, you introduce the problem by mentioning the group goal of getting everyone over the wall; task constraints, such as not holding onto the edges or not using props other than the available resources; safety rules, including no more than two people on the ledge at a time and no holding people upside down; safety procedures, such as

removing jewelry and spotting at all times; and the time limit, such as 30 min including planning. Many programs then give clients the right to pass and be challenged by choice; some programs employ helmets and harnesses to prevent head injury or torn clothing; and a few programs include handicaps such as blindfolds or muting. During the briefing, you could also add the frontloading questions outlined in figure 15.3.

Frontloading can take place either before or after the logistical briefing. You may even occasionally include frontloading within the briefing. But we caution you about too much frontloading. The average person can juggle 5 to 9 thoughts in the mind at once. A typical adventure activity briefing has a half dozen or so important points

---

Revisiting (commitments)

Our last event this morning concluded with some personal pledges about what we were going to do differently this afternoon and when we depart from this program. Would each of you care to share those commitments with the group one more time before we start?

Objectives (learning summation)

What do you think the group will get out of doing this activity? What do you think this exercise is designed to teach?

Motivation (application to reality)

Where might this learning be useful in your regular lives?

Function (positive actions)

What will the group need to do in order to succeed? What strategies does the group have for making sure it does these things?

Dysfunction (negative actions)

What things has this group done in the past that may get in the way? What can the group do to ensure these don't occur?

Figure 15.3 Frontloading functions and corresponding questions.

Sample Questions for Funneling and Frontloading

Knapp (1990) identified a series of questions associated with common adventure program topics that may prove useful for formulating funnels or frontloads. These topics include communication, feelings, prejudice, listening, leadership, followership, decision making, cooperation, diversity, trust, and closure. Use these questions as models for developing your own funnels and frontloads, making them your own so you can ask them in a natural manner tailored to specific client needs. Remember that you can't cover every topic in one discussion. Instead, pick one topic that may

lead to another and stop discussion before clients become tired or restless.

Communication

1. Can anyone give an example of when you thought you communicated effectively?
2. How did you know that what you communicated was understood?
3. Who didn't understand someone's attempt to communicate?
4. What went wrong in the communication attempt?

5. What could the communicator do differently next time to give a clearer message?

6. What could the message receiver do differently next time to understand the message?

7. How many different ways were used by the group to communicate messages?

8. Which ways were the most effective? Why?

9. Did you learn something about communication that will be helpful later? If so, what?

Feelings

1. Can you name a feeling you had at any point in completing the activity?

2. Where in your body did you feel it most?

3. What personal beliefs were responsible for generating that feeling?

4. What was the main thought behind the feeling?

5. Is that feeling a common one in your life?

6. Did you express that feeling to others? If not, what did you do with the feeling?

7. Do you usually express feelings or suppress them?

8. Would you like to feel differently in a similar situation?

9. If so, how would you like to feel?

10. What beliefs would you need to have in order to feel differently in a similar situation?

11. Could you believe them?

12. How do you feel about the conflict that may result from expressing certain feelings?

13. How do you imagine others felt toward you at various times during the activity?

14. Were these feelings expressed?

15. What types of feelings are easiest to express? Most difficult?

16. Do you find it difficult to be aware of certain feelings at times? If so, which ones?

17. Are some feelings not appropriate to express to the group at times? If so, which ones?

18. What feelings were expressed nonverbally in the group?

19. Did expressing appropriate feelings help or hinder completing the initiative?

Evaluating others

1. Is it difficult for you to avoid judging others? Explain.

2. Can you think of examples when you judged others in the group today?

3. When you didn't judge others?

4. What were some advantages you gained by not judging others?

5. What were some advantages others gained when you didn't judge them?

6. How did judging and not judging others affect the completion of the activity?

7. Were some behaviors of others easy not to judge and other behaviors difficult?

8. Would deferring judgment be of some value in other situations? Explain.

9. Can you think of any disadvantages of not judging others in this situation?

Listening

1. Who made suggestions for completing the activity?

2. Were all of these suggestions heard? Explain.

3. Which suggestions were acted on?

4. Why were the other suggestions ignored?

5. How did it feel to be heard when you made a suggestion?

6. What interfered with your ability to listen to others?

7. How can you overcome this interference?

8. Did you prevent yourself from listening well? How?

9. Did you listen in the same way today as you generally do?

10. If not, what was different about today?

Leadership

1. Who assumed leadership roles during the activity?

2. What were the behaviors that showed leadership?

(continued)

3. Can everyone agree that these behaviors are traits of leaders?

4. How did the group respond to these leadership behaviors?

5. Who followed the leader even if you weren't sure that the idea would work? Why?

6. Did the leadership role shift to other people during the activity?

7. Who thought they were taking the leadership role? How did you do it?

8. Was it difficult to assume a leadership role with this group?

9. Why didn't some of you take a leadership role with this group?

10. Is it easier to take leadership in other situations or with other group members? Explain.

11. Did anyone try to lead the group, but felt you were unsuccessful?

12. What were some possible reasons for this? How did it feel to be disregarded?

Followership

1. Who assumed a follower role at times throughout the activity? How did it feel?

2. How did it feel to follow different leaders?

3. Do you consider yourself a good follower?

4. Was this an important role in the group today? Explain.

5. How does refusal to follow affect the leadership role?

6. What are the traits of a good follower?

7. How can you improve your ability to follow in the future?

Decision making

1. How were group decisions made during the activity?

2. Were you satisfied with the ways decisions were made? Explain.

3. Did the group arrive at any decisions through group consensus?

4. Were decisions made by one or several individuals?

5. Did everyone in the group express an opinion when given a choice? If not, why not?

6. What is the best way for this group to make decisions? Explain.

7. Do you respond in similar ways in other groups?

8. What did you like about how the group made decisions? What didn't you like?

Cooperation

1. Can you think of specific examples of group cooperation? Explain.

2. How did it feel to cooperate?

3. Do you cooperate in most things you do?

4. How did you learn to cooperate?

5. What are the rewards of cooperating?

6. Are there any problems associated with cooperation?

7. How did cooperative behavior lead to successfully completing the activity?

8. How can you cooperate in other areas of your life?

9. Did you think anyone was blocking the group's efforts to cooperate? Explain.

Diversity

1. How are you different from some of the others in the group?

2. How do these differences strengthen the group as a whole?

3. When do differences in people in a group keep a group from reaching certain objectives?

4. What would this group be like if there were very few differences in people?

5. How would you feel if this were so?

6. In what cases did being different help or hinder group members from reaching objectives?

7. How are you like some of the others in the group?

8. Were these common traits helpful to the group's approach to the task? Explain.

9. Did these common traits hinder the group's approach to the task? Explain.

10. Do you think you have other things in common with some of the group members?

11. How did this setting help you discover how you are similar to others?

Trust

1. Can you give examples of when you trusted someone in the group? Explain.

2. Is it easier to trust some people and not others? Explain.

3. Can you think of examples when trusting someone would not have been a good idea?

4. How do you increase your level of trust for someone?

5. On a scale of 1 to 10, rate how much trust you have in the group as a whole.

6. Can you explain your rating?

7. How does the amount of fear you feel affect your trust of others?

8. What did you do today that deserves the trust of others?

Closure

1. What did you learn about yourself?

2. What did you learn about others?

3. How do you feel about yourself and others?

4. What new questions do you have about yourself and others?

5. What did you do today of which you are particularly proud?

6. What skill are you working to improve?

7. Was your behavior today typical of the way you usually act in groups? Explain.

8. How can you use what you learned in other life situations?

9. What beliefs about yourself and others were reinforced today?

10. Would you do anything differently if you were starting the activity again with this group?

11. What would you like to say to the group members?

◄ EFFECTIVE OUTDOOR LEADERS ►

► Are competent at facilitating verbal debriefing.

► Know how to handle groups that are reluctant to enter into verbal debriefing.

► Are able to debrief experiences using reflective alternatives to verbal debriefing.

► Are able to debrief experiences according to both the funneling and cognitive hierarchy models.

► Are able to frontload experiences by all five direct methods, using the technique in moderation.

clients must retain for safety and accuracy. Adding more than 2 or 3 extra points by frontloading can overload clients, possibly causing them to forget the key points you're teaching. Even so, when used in moderation, frontloading can be an effective teaching tool.

SUMMARY

Basic facilitation involves discussion and alternative methods. Discussion is unstructured debriefing that allows analysis, sharing, and reinforcement of learning and change. Arranged in a circle and talking in a supportive atmosphere created by accepted ground rules and operating principles, the group discusses its experience as you guide it with open-ended questions. You listen to its answers and then ask probing questions. By managing overbearing, tangential, and lengthy speakers and by using discussion tips and tricks, you ensure input from all clients. Work with reluctant groups by encouraging nonverbal responses, asking closed and trigger questions, requiring written responses and reporting, and arranging for solo time, partnerships, trios, gift giving, and rounds. Since verbal debriefings disadvantage some clients, provide for reflection through alternative methods such as art, drama, music, dance, poetry, writing, storytelling, photography, presentation, and repeating the same activity.

To verbally debrief an activity, ask questions after the experience. To frontload, ask the questions beforehand. These reflection techniques were developed in North American adventure programs in the 1960s and 1970s, respectively. Debriefing can take any number of nonverbal forms, but is most commonly a verbal experience guided by you. You ask questions so that the clients discover their own learning. If you make statements for them, clients might feel confronted and deny learning. Funneling and cognitive hierarchy are two models for verbal debriefing.

Funneling includes six types of questions that successively filter the experience, narrowing the clients' focus onto change. The six filters are review, recall-and-remember, affect-and-effect, summation, application, and commitment questions. You follow this sequence of questions to focus on a predetermined learning objective, a topic that warrants discussion, or an issue that arises during the experience.

Debriefing by cognitive hierarchy is based on Bloom's taxonomy of learning, which includes six levels: knowledge, comprehension, application, analysis, synthesis, and evaluation. You ask questions at the lower, concrete levels (knowledge, comprehension, and application) to help clients organize the learning, and then you progress to the higher, abstract levels (analysis, synthesis, and evaluation) to help clients transfer the learning.

Frontloading stacks the learning before the activity by using prebriefing instead of debriefing. You ask questions similar to debriefing questions, but you ask clients to anticipate the future rather than respond to the past. Direct frontloading has five forms: revisiting, objectives, motivation, function, and dysfunction. Too much frontloading can overload clients; you must use the technique only occasionally and only when emphasizing key points ahead of time is required or helpful.

QUESTIONS TO THINK ABOUT

1. Prepare a funnel by writing six filter questions in sequence to use with an individual client (rather than a whole group) who has just experienced an adventure activity of your choice.

2. Ask a peer to role-play for that individual and ask her the questions. Modify your questions as needed based on her answers as you progress through the funnel.

3. Repeat the first two questions using the cognitive hierarchy model.

4. Compare and contrast the funnel and cognitive hierarchy models. Which one do you prefer? Why? Are there times with certain groups when one model might work better than the other?

5. Prepare five questions using the frontloading model and practice asking them of a peer.

REFERENCES

Bloom, B.S. (1956). *Taxonomy of educational objectives.* London: Longman Group.

Borton, T. (1970). *Reach, touch, and teach.* New York: McGraw-Hill.

Gass, M.A., & Gillis, H.L. (1995). Focusing on the "solution" rather then the "problem": Empowering client change in adventure experiences. *Journal of Experiential Education, 18*(2), 63-69.

Greenaway, R. (1993). *Playback: A guide to reviewing activities.* Edinburgh, Scotland: Callander Printers, The Duke of Edinburgh's Award, and Endeavour Scotland.

Hammel, H. (1986). How to design a debriefing session. *Journal of Experiential Education, 9*(3), 20-25.

Knapp, C. (1990). Processing experiences. In J.C. Miles & S. Priest (Eds.), *Adventure education* (pp. 189-198). State College, PA: Venture.

Priest, S., & Gass, M.A. (1993). Five generations of facilitated learning from adventure education. *Journal of Adventure Education and Outdoor Leadership, 11*(1), 18-24.

Priest, S., Gass, M.A., & Gillis, H.L. (2003). *Essential elements of facilitation.* Seattle: Tarrak Technologies.

Priest, S., & Naismith, M. (1993). The debriefing funnel. *Journal of Adventure Education and Outdoor Leadership, 10*(3), 20-22.

Quinsland, L.K., & Van Ginkel, A. (1984). How to process experience. *Journal of Experiential Education, 7*(2), 8-13.

Ringer, M. (1999). Two vital aspects in the facilitation of groups: Connections and containment. *Australian Journal of Outdoor Education, 4*(1), 5-11.

Schoel, J., & Maizell, R.S. (2002). *Exploring islands of healing: New perspectives on adventure-based counseling.* Beverly, MA: Project Adventure.

Schoel, J., Prouty, D., & Radcliffe, P. (1988). *Islands of healing: A guide to adventure-based counseling.* Dubuque, IA: Kendall/Hunt.

Smith, T.E. (1986). Alternative methodologies for processing the adventure experience. *The Bradford Papers Annual, 1,* 29-38.

CHAPTER 16

Advanced Facilitation Techniques

TRUST FALL

Probably lots of you think that this exercise has something to do with trusting others, or with knowing that people will support you if you let them. And that's a fine meaning to get out of this activity. But our purpose in choosing this exercise is actually pretty different; we picked it because we feel there is an even more important lesson here. And that lesson concerns letting go of an old lifestyle. Let me tell you a bit more about what I mean.

Each of you will be getting up here and holding on to this tree before falling backwards. Before you fall, I'm going to ask you to close your eyes and imagine that the tree is that part of your personality—that piece of you—most responsible for your drinking and drugging. I don't want you to think of this as a tree anymore; I want you to think of it as the most powerful factor responsible for your

using. And I want you to hug it like you love it—like it's all you've got.

Because after you hold on to it for awhile, for 30 seconds, I'm going to ask you to let go—to give up and let go of whatever it is that keeps you drinking and drugging. You'll just lie back and fall towards these people.

And don't be surprised if you feel a little nervous. All alcoholics/addicts have at least some love for their old lifestyle, no matter how much they really want to change it. And there's always some degree of hesitation towards committing to a drug-free life. 'Cause you don't know what it is like. So I'd be surprised if you didn't feel some kind of nervousness about falling.

—Bacon, 1991, p. 11-12

ROPES COURSE

I'm sure that many of you have heard descriptions of this next activity: the high ropes course. As you can see, it's a big jungle gym in the trees. But it's a jungle gym that tends to have a large impact on clients; many participants talk more about this than anything else in the program. They tend to talk about how scary it was.

From our point of view, the ropes course isn't included to practice courage or risk taking or anything like that. I mean, what good would that be? Does it really help your sobriety to be able to walk a narrow log between two trees? Does the fact that you can do that mean you won't take a drink? No, it doesn't!

But we think the ropes course does have something to do with sobriety. At some point on this ropes course, we expect that you'll feel some degree of challenge, risk, and maybe even fear. And we want you to feel that not because we want you to experience those things for their own sake—but for another reason. When we see that you are in the midst of a serious challenge, we're going to do a rather strange thing.

Before telling you exactly what that strange thing is, I need to diverge for a moment. Research has shown that many alcoholics return to drinking because they can't resist temptation. You know, like the temptation of having a friend or acquaintance invite you out for "just one," or whatever. So we've designed this particular ropes course activity with this temptation problem in mind.

I know you are all used to depending on staff for support for your sobriety and you have probably also gotten used to the idea that the Outward Bound instructors are on your side; but today, because we think it'll help your sobriety, we're going to reverse that. Out there in the real world, you're going to be tempted and when that happens, you're going to be all alone. It may be your best friend pushing alcohol on you just when you really want a drink.

So to help you with that situation, we've decided that we're going to let you have a little pre-temptation training. Just when it gets real hard on the ropes course and you're really tempted to quit, we—that is, the [Outward Bound] instructors—are going to try and talk you into quitting. That's right, instead of offering support or help we're going to try and get you to come down. You might hear us say, "Hey, you've done enough." Or, "It's OK to come down; this doesn't really have to do with sobriety." Or, "You've already done as much as can be expected of you, given your fear of heights. Why don't you just come down now?"

What I'm saying is, you can't trust us on this one. Or maybe I'm saying that you need to trust your own ability to know what's right and do it no matter what others tell you. We want you to know that in reality, we all really hope that you'll complete the element. And I can tell you that right now in a very clear manner. It would please us all if every one of you had a total success. But we won't be acting like that in a few minutes. During the course, from time to time, you'll see and hear us trying our best to tempt you or your friends. You'll see us trying to talk you off of the ropes course. Of course, most of the time we'll just be helping out, just like we usually do, but when the crunch is on, you may notice that we've shifted into another perspective.

Do all of you understand this? Do you know why we may be encouraging people to quit or take the easy way out?

—Bacon, 1991, p. 9-10

As outlined in chapter 14, facilitation styles in adventure programs have evolved through a generational process. Primarily influenced by the work of Milton Erickson and investigators of his work, Bacon (1983) published *The Conscious Use of Metaphor in Outward Bound.* In his book, Bacon paid specific attention to using metaphors in facilitation processes in adventure programming. By focusing on metaphors as a cornerstone for creating future relevance from adventure experiences, the paradigm of facilitating adventure experiences evolved to include the fifth and sixth generations. Most of the examples in this chapter apply to corporate and therapeutic situations, since most of the applications for the latter generations have been associated with these populations.

Bacon and Kimball (1989) identified three ways in which adventure programming uses metaphors: spontaneous, analogous, and structured. With **spontaneous metaphoric transfer,** learners spontaneously discover important and relevant connections between the adventure experience and their lives without assistance from you, the outdoor leader. Spontaneous metaphoric transfer is often found in the first generation of letting the experience speak for itself.

With **analogous metaphoric transfer,** you employ discussions and other debriefing techniques, such as verbal therapy and social learning, to help clients understand the importance and relevance of what they learned in retrospective, or "after the fact." Often, you carefully choose and ask questions after adventure experiences are completed. Typically, you can use analogous metaphoric transference in the second, third, and fourth generations: speaking on behalf of, debriefing, and directly frontloading the experience.

With **structured metaphoric transfer,** you purposefully frame adventure experiences before client participation, often through a briefing that strengthens the metaphoric message. You do this to increase the probability of the spontaneous discovery or analogous recognition of metaphors during the debriefing session. But you can also use structured metaphoric transference in the fifth and

The trust fall can serve as an experience for structured metaphoric transfer.

sixth generations: isomorphically framing and indirectly frontloading the experience. In this chapter, we look at these two methods of facilitation.

ISOMORPHICALLY FRAMING THE EXPERIENCE

Of all of the critical features of utilizing metaphors in adventure experiences, probably most important is **isomorphism,** which literally means "equivalent structures." Highlighted by a number of professionals in the field (Bacon, 1983, 1987; Gass, 1985, 1991, 1993; Mack, 1996; Nadler & Luckner, 1992) as well as outside (de Shazer, 1982; Minuchin, 1981; Zeig, 1994), isomorphism explains how metaphors create current relevance as well as future importance for clients in adventure experiences. Once again, an isomorph is an idea, object, or description that is identical in form or structure—but not necessarily composition or function—to another idea, object, or description. Consider the isomorphs in the two introductory vignettes. In the Trust Fall, the tree represented a personality component responsible for substance abuse and served as an isomorphic relationship for the client. On the ropes course, several isomorphs existed: the ropes course represented the challenges of life; the leaders' unusual behavior represented temptation; quitting and coming down represented succumbing to enticement and relapsing; and completing the course despite temptation represented maintaining sobriety in the face of seduction. When metaphors isomorphically connect to the client's goals, they offer powerful vehicles for producing functional change. Thus, isomorphism is central to the success of the fifth or sixth generation of facilitation.

Mack (1996) criticized Bacon's example of the Trust Fall quoted previously, labeling it "imposed" and representative of many of the expectations imposed on women in a patriarchal society. She is correct when such a framework makes little sense to a client's reality, that is, has little isomorphic connection to the particular client's issues. Her work reminds us that isomorphic frames must be derived from what clients bring to the adventure experience and then cocreated by the client and the facilitator on the basis of what the client needs. Such "cocreation" is necessary for functional change to occur, unless the metaphoric transfer occurs spontaneously (Hovelynck, 1998, 1999).

As introduced in chapter 14, the fifth generation of facilitation involves framing an experience so that it mirrors the client's issue. This framing includes how you structure the activity as well as a facilitated introduction. Framing that mirrors the issue differs from the framing that some sources have described as briefing or orienting a group (see Schoel, Prouty, & Radcliffe, 1988, p. 90-92). **Isomorphic framing** matches a client's needs, mindset, and objectives with an adventure experience in such a way that successfully completing the adventure experience mirrors successfully resolving the client's issue. This framing is done before

the adventure experience to produce behavior change within the context of the experience (Schoel & Maizell, 2002). This contrasts to creating analogies with reflective techniques after the experience as done in discussion or debriefing.

To better understand isomorphic framing, look at the first introductory vignette in which clients with issues of substance abuse are involved in a Trust Fall. As stated in this isomorphic frame, the leader is not using this activity to address trust. Rather, the leader is focusing client attention on how the experience relates to letting go of an old addictive lifestyle by isomorphically relating the tree to this client's addictive personality. Framing this tree as something to let go of creates other isomorphs in the client's mind. These isomorphs also connect certain features of the adventure experience with client issues, thereby strengthening the overall metaphor and enhancing transfer. Some additional examples of the isomorphic connections in this Trust Fall scenario include hugging the tree as a desperate hanging on to an addictive lifestyle; giving up and letting go of the tree as committing to giving up and letting go of forces sustaining addiction; nervousness in the adventure as anxiety or hesitation to commit to a drug-free lifestyle; fear of the unknown involved with falling backward as the terror of not knowing what it's like to enter into a drug-free lifestyle; and being caught by the group as being supported by others while maintaining sobriety.

Isomorphic frameworks need to be relevant to the clients and the structure of their issues. Illustrations like the vignettes provide wonderful examples of what introductory metaphoric frameworks may look like. But unless the framework makes sense, is relevant, and is "owned" by the client through the use of isomorphic structures, its utility for the client will be lessened or even worthless. As identified by Gass (1993), the "most difficult tasks in creating metaphoric (isomorphic framing) transfer in adventure programs generally lie in (1) constructing therapeutic metaphors that are isomorphic to client needs, (2) framing experiences in such a manner that they can be interpreted and integrated into clients' perspectives, and (3) using appropriate debriefing techniques after the experience to reinforce change" (p. 249).

Developing Isomorphic Frames

How do you create **isomorphic frameworks** that are relevant to client issues? Gass (1991) outlined a process for creating overall metaphors by establishing multiple isomorphic connections. The seven steps in this process are assess, identify, and rank client goals; select the metaphoric adventure experience; identify successful resolution to the therapeutic issue; strengthen the isomorphic framework; review client motivation; conduct the experience with revisions; and debrief.

1. A thorough needs assessment is the first step to **assess, identify, and rank client goals.** Before you can develop isomorphic frameworks, you must understand clients and their particular needs. To best understand your clients, you should list—and then rank in order of importance if possible—the attributes, needs, and objectives of the client group. These attributes, needs, and objectives are typically the central features for creating the isomorphic framework of the adventure experience.

2. Next, you need to **select a metaphoric adventure experience** that already possesses a strong isomorphic relationship to meeting client needs. Experienced outdoor leaders often do this by second nature, since they know which structures of adventure activities match particular client needs. You may find selection made easier by listing the attributes of an adventure activity, including goals, rules, equipment, facilities, settings, typical outcomes, and successful problem resolution and comparing and contrasting them with the group's needs and goals. It's your job to ensure that the adventure experience mirrors each client's objectives with matching attributes that can become an isomorphic link when you help the client make the connection. Note that these experiences are cocreated with input from clients based on their needs and input from you based on your knowledge of how certain adventure experiences naturally create opportunities for client growth in particular areas.

3. Once you have created these isomorphic connections, you must **identify successful resolutions to the therapeutic issue.** Do this by hypothesizing how a positive resolution in the adventure activity will correspond to a similar result in real life. Moreover, consider how a failure, setback, or negative outcome may mirror an inability to overcome dysfunctional behaviors. In other words, if the group succeeds in its efforts, then the behaviors it uses to succeed in the adventure should mirror resolutions for its identified needs. On the other hand, if the usual dysfunctional behaviors persist, they should bring about failure in the activ-

ity that results in natural consequences, such as getting wet, falling to dangle on a rope, traveling extra distance, setting up camp in the dark, losing credits accumulated during the program, or eating delayed meals.

4. Once you have developed these initial isomorphic structures and resolutions, you must **strengthen the isomorphic framework.** Concentrate on adapting the metaphor and enhancing its presentation through symbolic language. The activity may benefit from a new isomorphic title. For example, the Trust Fall becomes "Letting Go of Old Lifestyles." You must examine each connection for how it might fit into the context of the metaphor as well as for how you should present each isomorph. It may be necessary to change the rules, facilities, props, or equipment to strengthen the framework. When you are satisfied with the framework, combine all the isomorphic links and alterations into a rich and descriptive introductory frame and meaningfully present it in the client's jargon. Using familiar language enhances symbolic meaning for clients as well as brings identity and relevance to the client's adventure. The experience ceases to be an activity and becomes an analogous exercise in the client's reality. The isomorphic frame, coupled with symbolism, creates a powerful metaphor that fosters clients' associations between the concepts and complexity of the experience and real life.

5. Before presenting the frame and conducting the activity, however, you need to **review client motivation** by double-checking that the metaphor will compel clients (i.e., with appropriate issues and language) without overwhelming them with anxiety or detail. In addition, you must make sure that the isomorphs creating the metaphor possess the appropriate content, whether positive or negative, and that you have correctly linked the adventure and daily life situations.

6. Next, **conduct the experience with revisions.** Begin by introducing the isomorphic framework and associated safety guidelines. As the clients listen to the framework, you may need to adjust in order to highlight the isomorphic connections. Clients may recognize links that you missed but can now emphasize. Occasionally, clients may miss or purposefully discount the metaphor by negatively interpreting the framework, requiring you to reframe their interpretations in a new perspective. For example, clients who state that the Trust Fall activity has nothing to do with letting go of dysfunctional lifestyles may be failing to

perceive the metaphor or choosing to obstruct the process. To help them see the connection more clearly, you might ask the group members to discuss what links they see within the activity. A peer explanation often contains more appropriate symbols, permitting the unaware clients to grasp the metaphor or unmotivated ones to alter their obstructive behavior.

7. After the experience, reinforce positive changes, reframe negative changes, and guide the integration of functional changes into the client's lifestyle through a **debriefing.** As with debriefing most isomorphically framed adventure activities, you can concentrate more on applying the learning or on committing to change than on events and impacts. Other topics such as "what happened" or "what this meant" were already obvious to clients within the initial frame. When conducted with metaphoric framing, debriefings tend to focus on "change by doing" as clients prove they can function in situations that are similar to their daily lives and recognize that repeating their newly learned behaviors in their real-world setting will result in reaching their goals.

Isomorphic Example

Gass (1991) described the creation of a metaphor with several isomorphic connections for a substance-abuse group. The listing and ranking of client needs and attributes resulted in three main needs:

1. The ability to ask for help
2. The ability to set appropriate boundaries around issues of recovery to maintain abstinence
3. The elimination of dysfunctional behaviors that undermine the ability [of others] to maintain abstinence [and] placing the needs of others ahead of the [personal] need to stay sober (p. 8)

Group attributes were that some members were currently addicted; others were inpatients in a recovery program, many of whom were having difficulty letting go of their abusive patterns and holding on to abstinence; and some were involved with the initial steps of a 12-step recovery process.

The Maze activity was selected to meet these needs because it possessed a strong metaphoric relationship to the needs. The following attributes of the Maze were important for creating isomorphic links: the Maze is built from a length of rope strung between trees at about waist height to create a random enclosure. One small opening is created between two trees. While blindfolded, clients are placed inside the Maze and challenged to find their way out by locating the opening without getting lost. Rules prevent crawling under or jumping over the rope, letting go of the rope, and removing blindfolds. When individuals successfully exit the Maze, they may reenter to assist others, but must remain blindfolded.

The outdoor leaders who designed this activity determined that a successful resolution would be if each client asked for help, choosing to place personal abstinence above others' needs. These behaviors were meant to mirror the initial steps to recovery. The outdoor leaders considered a negative outcome to be rescuing others, which indicated placing the needs of others above personal sobriety. This behavior was seen as a parallel to the insidious and distracting nature of the clients' addictions.

The outdoor leaders matched many client and activity attributes, forming potential isomorphic links. The rope represented a pathway to recovery; the enclosure, the addiction process; and the opening, reaching sobriety. Blindfolds mirrored the limitations of addiction, symbolizing how the disease prevents clients from helping themselves and getting a true perspective on reality. Maintaining contact with the rope represented staying committed to the recovery process, while reentering the Maze represented placing the needs of others above maintaining sobriety. The designers ignored some attributes to ensure the design did not become too complicated and altered other attributes to make them more isomorphic, strengthening the metaphor.

Then the designers modified the Maze to make it mirror their clients' reality. They changed the title to "Path to Recovery" in order to emphasize the clients' current reality. They sealed up the small opening physically and planned to create an isomorphic exit when clients asked for help from the outdoor leaders. The leaders also made minor rule changes, including having all clients put on their blindfolds before the briefing. After double-checking for structure clarity and reviewing client motivation, one outdoor leader introduced the activity:

> The next activity is called the "Path to Recovery." It's called that because a number of the obstacles you'll encounter

are very similar to obstacles many of you are currently encountering in your addictions. Our addictions often blind us on our path to a substance-free lifestyle, and we often fail because we don't remember to live by principles that will allow us to free ourselves from abusive substances. After my description of this activity, we will place you on the [path] to recovery by putting your hand on a rope. This rope leads you along a path of indeterminable length. Along your journey to recovery, you will meet a variety of other people going in different directions. Some of these people will be in a great hurry, showing a lot of confidence. Others will be tentative, moving cautiously. Some will seem to know the right direction, whereas others will seem lost. Don't let go of the rope, because if you do you will lose the path. . . . The goal of your journey is to reach one of the exits to abstinence. There are several exits in this maze, and as you reach one of these exits, I'll be there to ask you an important choice. The choices will be (1) stepping out of the maze. If you make this decision, I'll ask you to remove your blindfold and sit quietly in the abstinence area until this initiative is over; or (2) you may choose to go back into the maze to help others. If you choose to go back into the maze, you run the risk that this particular exit may be shut when you return, forcing you to find another exit. If at any time during this activity you would like to receive help, all you need to do is ask for it and guidance will be provided. Otherwise we would like everyone not to speak throughout this initiative until it is completed. (Gass, 1991, p. 8; Gass & Priest, 1993, p. 22)

As the activity progressed, the exits remained closed until each client asked for help. In that instance, the leaders informed the client that asking for help had created a pathway from addiction to an area of abstinence. Next, clients were faced with a decision critical to maintaining abstinence: stepping out of the Maze of addiction and removing their blindfolds or returning to the Maze blindfolded and possibly losing the exit to abstinence.

In the course of this adventure experience, two clients became frustrated with the activity and ripped off their blindfolds, each stating, "I'm not going to play this game any more!" After checking what each client meant by his remark, the outdoor leader embraced a critical opportunity to revise the framing to highlight the initial isomorphs and address the different needs of each client.

For one individual, the outdoor leader reframed this display of frustration as a breakthrough. The outdoor leader reframed the frustration as a celebration, stating, "I'm struck by the way you recognized the futility in playing the 'game of addiction,' and I think this is wonderful! It's obvious to me that you are prepared to take positive action and not remain endlessly trapped in the maze of the addictive process." This response reframes a negative interpretation of failure in a positive light: success was achieved by a different method. Note that the leader was aware of the fit or correctness of the intervention by observing its meaning for this particular client.

The other individual's behavior indicated an inability to accept personal responsibility for recovery. On the basis of this perception, the outdoor leader commented on the client's unwillingness to admit powerlessness and take the first step toward recovery. The outdoor leader reframed the situation by expressing this recognition to be valuable. This second response, while somewhat challenging for a client to hear, led to a stronger personal resolve to commit to a substance-free lifestyle.

For this activity, the therapeutic objectives focused on asking for help, making healthy choices for a functional recovery process, and avoiding behaviors that could undermine the recovery process or the ability of others to maintain abstinence. The first two objectives encompassed positive recovery behaviors, while the last one addressed avoiding a negative or dysfunctional one. The outdoor leaders' debriefing focused on these three objectives, but also dealt with other issues, including how asking for help assisted people, how an important decision was made at exits, what failing to hold on to the rope represented, what abstainers felt while observing others lost in the maze of addiction, what struggling to get out was like, and what behavior was necessary in order to stay on the straight path. Given the power of the metaphor in this activity, clients discussed their experiences in light of trying to reach or maintain sobriety. They elaborated on their choices, indicating that the activity was meaningful and realistic to them. More importantly, several demonstrated the two positive behaviors of asking for help, particularly when feeling lost or "blinded" by their addictions, and of making positive choices to leave their addictions behind. Furthermore, others did not succumb to the temptation of relapse and avoided the risk of becoming permanently lost in the maze of addiction.

Bacon (1987) clarified the differences between framing and other forms of facilitation: "The difference between the approaches is that [usually clients] do not realize the metaphoric nature of the event until the post-activity debriefing [when using earlier styles]. Conversely, [fifth] generation [clients] perceive the metaphoric qualities of the experience as they pass through it; their post-activity discussion focuses on how they reacted to the metaphor, not on how they reacted to the literal experience" (p. 12-13). The strength of framing lies in the metaphoric briefing, rich in isomorphs, which enables clients to focus on the issues at hand. Resolving the adventure experience parallels resolving real-life issues so that the experience creates lasting changes.

Drawbacks to Isomorphic Framing

While the isomorphic framing approach to facilitating adventure experiences has obvious benefits for client groups with prescriptive needs and is a powerful way to address these needs, it does have at least six drawbacks. If you choose to operate in the fifth generation, you ought to be aware of the following shortcomings:

1. Isomorphic framing is far more complex than the previous four facilitation styles. In addition to all the other tasks associated with facilitation, such as diagnosis, design, delivery, debriefing, direction, safety, and ethics, the structuring and framing give you even more responsibility when conducting the experience. This complexity can limit the use of this technique to those facilitators with advanced training and abilities. At the very minimum, it demands a strong sensitivity to a client's needs, an ability to cocreate meaningful experiences with clients, and a deep understanding of how adventure experiences can successfully resolve client issues.

2. To produce change through framing, you must be more prescriptive in your techniques. This often requires assessing a client's needs to a greater breadth and depth as well as understanding what change will mean to the client's life if it occurs. Without this information, this approach can be destructive and changes can be short-lived.

3. The efficacy of framing depends on a client's ability to see parallel structures. Metaphors and isomorphs are confusing to the uninitiated. Confusion can easily lead to dismissal, creating dissension among the group members and therefore inhibiting learning. You must be able to match framing to the capabilities of the group and in some cases teach clients to think metaphorically.

4. Presenting isomorphic frameworks requires an ability to balance your introduction with the client's reality. Knowing each client's language and other symbols is important, but you cannot underestimate the importance of properly comprehending each client's context and related background issues. Truly effective framing requires more than merely placing labels or images from the client's environment on to adventure activities.

5. No two members of a group are alike, so you must account for individual differences when working with groups. Creating frames that are open enough for each client to internalize personal perspectives will lead to greater individual change. Presenting closed or restrictive frames may hinder group development.

6. By narrowing the focus of a frame to a predetermined metaphoric message, you are dictating what will be learned in the activity. Even if you are on target with the frame, by prescribing the way the experience will be interpreted, other metaphors may not be available for the group. Since the power of transfer is closely linked to metaphoric connections, losing other meaningful metaphors may inhibit overall transfer for some clients.

INDIRECTLY FRONTLOADING THE EXPERIENCE

As you know, the fifth generation of facilitation involves directly framing an adventure experience so that it mirrors the client's goals and needs for the activity. You and the client work in a deliberate and expected way toward reaching a specific objective, and generally speaking, the more you coconstruct efforts to attain the client's objective, the greater the success of the experience.

For a number of reasons, a small percentage of the time such direct efforts fail. Failure often happens with groups or individuals labeled "dysfunctional," such as clients with therapeutic issues who resist change or corporations with a long history of failure at eliminating unwanted behaviors. Either the more you and the client try to eliminate unwanted behaviors, the more the unwanted behaviors occur, or the more you and the client try to attain a desired result, the more elusive the result becomes (Waltzlawick, 1978). In such cases, helping clients may not lie in working harder to facilitate, but in working easier at facilitating differently. Consider Bacon's (1987, adapted by Gass, 1993) facilitation dilemma in working with delinquent adolescents during a backpacking experience:

> When [a leader] asks an adolescent to put on his pack and hike, this request potentially places the adolescent in a dilemma. If he complies with the [leader's] suggestion, he is obeying an adult order. Not only does the delinquent have many experiences that have taught him that following an adult's advice often leads to problems, he also has typical teenage developmental needs to defy adults in order to sustain his newly formed sense of individuation. In addition, he belongs to a peer culture where he gains status by resisting adult directives. If the delinquent complies with the request, he will feel as if he is betraying his individuality, losing status, and trusting problematic advice. However, if he defies the request, he will reap the [leader's] displeasure and is likely to become the recipient of a variety of negative consequences. In addition, he may lose the benefits of the Outward Bound course. The adolescent is in a lose-lose situation. Given the way he sees the world, he has no choices that lead to unambiguous success and satisfaction. He has succeeded at transforming a helpful, direct suggestion—put on your pack and participate in this program—into a non-therapeutic double bind. It is no wonder that such adolescents are marked by hostility, distrust, depression, labile affect, and other negative emotions and behaviors; their world view and the typical responses of others to that world view frequently double bind them into lose-lose situations. (Gass, 1993, p. 261)

As Bacon illustrates, the adolescent is placed in a **negative double bind** when given a direct request. Such situations are inadvertently structured by well-meaning leaders, and then adolescents believe that whichever action they choose will produce a negative outcome. In addressing

such behaviors, the answer for you may lie in being less direct. Support the adolescent's attempts at being functional by providing a situation in which both options lead to beneficial results. You must create a win–win situation: a positive double bind.

Say that in this same situation, several clients have demonstrated consistently resistant behaviors, such as not putting on their packs after repeated requests from leaders. Bacon offers an alternative approach to facilitating these behaviors:

> At Outward Bound, especially after things start going well and people are getting more motivated, the pace of the course sometimes gets faster; the group hikes farther and more quickly, climbs more, and so on. This increase in pace tends to make folks nervous because some students start wondering if they are going to be able to keep up; they start worrying that they might be the ones who will mess up and slow the group down. In some groups, students solve this concern by having one or two students be the regular "screw-ups." These are the people who always get up late, or complain, or hike slowly, or forget something. On the surface, it may seem like these people are messing up badly, but actually they do a lot for the rest of the group. First of all, it reassures the other students to know that they aren't the worst group member—the screw-up has being in last place all locked up. In addition, the screw-up usually distracts everyone from their own problems; there's nothing like finding a scapegoat to blame for everything when you're feeling blue. At this point, the leader stops and asks a few questions about scapegoating to ensure that the clients understand these points. Following this brief discussion, the leader continues by pointing out that although the screw-up helps everybody else, he also tends to lose out pretty seriously. Most of the time, people are mad at him. So, while this group may choose to have a scapegoat to gain the benefits, maybe the only fair thing to do is to be willing to share the screw-up role around equally—kind of like [chores are] shared. Everyone could take a turn. The [leader] wonders [aloud]: who would volunteer to be the first screw-up? (Bacon, in Gass, 1993, p. 262)

Such a statement is certainly not direct. What empathetic, caring, concerned outdoor leader would ask clients already burdened by a "dysfunctional" label to purposefully "screw up"? By looking at the intention behind the outdoor leader's comments, however, an indirect yet truly empathetic method of assisting clients emerges. Let's see what Bacon has to say:

> [After delivering such a request] the group can follow [such] directions—an atypical act—and cooperate by having a member function as the scapegoat, or it can defy the [leader] and refuse to allow any group member to assume that role. It is most probable that the [clients] will unite against the [leader] and his "crazy" request and refuse to allow anyone to volunteer to be the scapegoat. Even if someone does volunteer, their misbehaviors will be pseudo misbehaviors, not the real thing. The group is in a win-win situation; any choice it makes leads to success. If a [client] does begin to act out genuinely, the [leaders] can comment that someone has decided to volunteer to help the group by being the scapegoat after all. This reference brings some humor into a typically tense, confrontive situation and provides an easy way for the acting out [client] to apologize without losing much face. He can agree that, yes, he was just doing a bit of spontaneous volunteering. Finally, if the situation continues to escalate, the group can be asked to view the misbehavior from a different context. They can be questioned about whether they really need this [client] to help them in this way. The [clients] will probably respond in the negative and proceed to confront the misbehaving [client] about his unsolicited assistance and inappropriate behaviors. One of the significant benefits of using therapeutic double binds is that they are unusual and unexpected; it is unlikely that a person who has chronically maladaptive personality strategies has ever encountered this type of intervention. As mentioned above, such people do have sophisticated ways of resisting typical change strategies, but they are usually defenseless against the paradoxical qualities of the double bind because they simply have never encoun-

tered it before. After all, how often is an adolescent asked to [voluntarily] act out? (Gass, 1993, p. 263)

Approaches like this indirectly work in the client's best interests. Directly confronting client behavior often produces great resistance, and in a sense, makes it more difficult for the client to achieve her objective from the adventure experience. Indirect efforts, while much more difficult to implement than all of the techniques in other generations, may produce the best results for clients. Notice in this last example and in the ropes course vignette given earlier, the leader's behavior is unusual and unexpected: a behavioral paradox. Paradoxical behavior is common in indirect frontloading.

You can find other examples of indirect frontloading, such as symptom displacements, illusion of alternatives, and proactive reframing, in other sources (see Waltzlawick, 1978). We caution you, however, that these other techniques require greater psychotherapy training than the previously discussed five generational approaches. You should especially consider the ethical use of indirect approaches. Don't use them as power tactics or trickery, but with empathy and the client's best interests in mind. The ethical concept of nonmaleficence, which means "above all else, do no harm to the client," is probably most true and appropriate for indirect approaches (see chapter 23). Indirect frontloading works best when done truthfully. Contrived indirect frontloading can often backfire on you, leading to client mistrust.

Let's look at another situation involving double binds as well as a related technique called symptom prescriptions as a further example of indirect frontloading.

Double Binds

> *In order for you to become a better leader, we are assigning you as leader in this next activity.*

As we have seen in the example of backpacking with delinquent adolescents, one indirect intervention you can implement when direct frontloading fails is a **double bind.** Because it is so valuable, yet difficult to apply, this advanced technique deserves further discussion.

But what is a bind? A bind prevents or restrains a person from natural or customary behaviors.

When you place a client in a dilemma, or a situation that demands opposing behaviors, you "bind" him to a certain behavior. Remember, a bind may be positive (win–win) or negative (lose–lose) as it obligates a person to act in a new or unusual manner.

In another example of a positive double bind, a corporate group is working on the Spider's Web. This particular group has experienced an ongoing problem with gender equity, that is, the men dominate. Furthermore, the group is in denial of this fact: some members are unaware of it, while others refuse to acknowledge it.

Let's look more closely to further illustrate the ease with which frontloading may turn into a negative or positive double bind. Say that during the frontloading brief, a well-meaning male leader innocently comments that the women need to be more empowered and spontaneous in their group roles. While unintentional, this statement creates a negative double bind: a lose–lose situation. If the women ignore the statement, they lose because they fail to achieve empowerment or spontaneity, remaining submissive or powerless within the group structure. If they take charge of the Spider's Web in response to the outdoor leader's comment, they also lose because any perception of empowerment or spontaneity will be false. How can they be truly empowered or spontaneous if told to be so, particularly by a male? In other words, they have not earned the empowerment, because the "spontaneity" was generated and preplanned. With these remarks, the outdoor leader has lost a learning opportunity and negatively bound these clients into continuing their dysfunctional behaviors. This lose–lose double bind is similar to the negative double bind stated at the beginning of this section: how can a person be a leader when they are assigned the leadership role?

The example, however, focuses on creating a positive double bind for clients. The outdoor leader offers this alternative frontload:

Most . . . groups who attempt the Spider's Web tend to do it in a particular way. At the beginning, they mill around a bit with lots of people offering their suggestions. After some time a couple of dominant males tend to start the group off. They get a few men to the other side of the web and then throw the women through like sacks of potatoes and often with embarrassing remarks about female anatomy

disguised as humour. Then the same group of dominant males decides how to do the hardest part [of the task] which is getting the last few people through. Afterwards, during the discussion of the exercise, everyone agrees that the leadership was more-or-less sexist and there are various emotional reactions to that. There are other ways to do the Spider's Web. (Gass & Dobkin, 1991)

Stated this way, the frontloaded double bind is positive, creating a win–win situation. If the group members perform the task in a sexist manner, they win because their true behaviors will become painfully obvious, and the awareness or denial of the sexist behavior will be heightened for the debriefing. If they perform in a nonsexist and equitable manner, they also win since they have clearly demonstrated that they can act differently and may continue to do so in the future. One way brings dysfunction to the forefront of discussion while the other breaks old habits and leads to new learning. With this frontloading technique, the outdoor leader has positively bound the resistant clients, bringing them to a unique turning point.

Another example of a double bind occurs in the second introductory vignette, in which the group of alcoholics deals with temptation. Coming down from the ropes course represents a relapse, or a return to substance abuse. Offered in an appropriate atmosphere, this framework enhances a client's motivation to complete the course and usually results in success: people accomplish preset goals despite temptation not to. The fear of succumbing to temptation mirrors fears associated with heights or lack of strength. Representing another "win" opportunity, if someone does descend, the group may argue that temptation won out. If a supportive atmosphere exists for debriefing, the postactivity discussion provides a powerful opportunity for clients to talk about how they will deal with temptation once they leave treatment.

Remember that all indirect techniques must be (1) offered with true sincerity and (2) presented with the clients' best interests in mind. To use them to negatively manipulate clients, as in some sort of power struggle, or without regarding the clients' needs, will lead to intervention failure, will lose the trust and rapport that you may have developed with your clients, and is contrary to the ethical guidelines of an adventure professional.

Paradoxical Symptom Prescriptions

> *Please, don't tell me anything
> that you don't want me to know
> until you're ready to talk about it.*

A **paradox** is a piece of information that seems to contradict common sense or oppose the generally accepted opinion. It may appear quite absurd, but in reality may be quite true. At one time or another, you may encounter clients inhibited by certain dysfunctional behaviors with which direct techniques fail. At these times, remember that you may address the issue more indirectly to empower the client to change. We've examined double binds; now let's investigate another indirect approach, paradoxical symptom prescriptions, in which you prescribe the very issue that seems to keep the client from success.

One example of this technique is with clients who are anxious about participating in adventure activities. In some cases, their worries about upcoming activities, such as ropes courses, expeditions, or skits, continually "freeze" them with indecision and inaction. This paralysis can prevent them from learning. You might be tempted to assist by inspiring, supporting, reasoning, or confronting anxious clients by sharing stories of success by others, offering verbal comfort and reassurance, listing all the good that will come from the experience, or by stating that worrying won't make a difference.

Unfortunately for some anxious clients, these direct responses may not work. Such clients often decide that they are different from others so success won't come to them, that they are less worthy or able, that they don't need the benefits, or that worrying makes them feel good. The more you press such clients with direct responses, the more the clients argue and resist. By resisting, the clients are actually receiving attention and partial acceptance in the form of reassurance from you, which makes them feel good. The more this occurs, the more inadequate they feel, negating the benefits of the adventure experience. As Bacon (1993) explains, "They are capable of becoming more helpless regardless of the amount, quality, and type of help offered. Everything leads them to assert their inadequacy: inspiration makes them feel weak, support causes them to claim they are not worth all the fuss that is being made over them, and confrontation generates tears plus an implicit or explicit counterattack accusing the confronter

of a deficit in empathy" (p. 264). Their behavior is a paradox.

In such cases, you must recognize that anxiety is an involuntary emotion beyond human control, one that cannot be prevented by sheer willpower. To counteract the dysfunctional paradox that keeps such clients from achieving the gains they want, you need to prescribe the actual symptom of anxiety. To do this, you encourage clients to experience anxiety at least once a day before the upcoming activity that has them so worried. You suggest that they contemplate their apprehensions, since fear is an important guard, preventing injury in outdoor pursuits. By consciously concentrating on their fears for a set period each day, they may be able to avoid danger when the activity arrives. The connection between anxiety and danger avoidance is important because it reframes a negative occurrence in a positive light: it gives usefulness and meaning to something the clients are troubled by.

In this manner, clients find that experiencing true anxiety is extremely difficult for many and impossible for some. Bacon (1993) elaborates, "Since, by definition, anxiety is something which arises without solicitation—something that is neither invited nor welcomed—the consciously created anxiety generated through this assignment is not 'real' anxiety" (p. 265). In short, the clients will either experience pseudoanxiety from their daily contemplations or they will decide that your suggestion seems stupid and will resist the suggestion to the point of excluding their previous worries. In this manner, the paradox appears contradictory, but in reality, it's both a valid way to address dangers and an effective way to help clients deal with their anxieties.

Through paradoxical suggestions, you encourage clients to view things from a perspective that contradicts their usual reality. Either they will abandon the old reality in favor of a new one in which they no longer perceive anxiety, or they will retain the old, but abandon the behavior that stemmed from it in favor of new behavior—pseudoanxiety instead of a genuine attack. The contradictory content of the paradox encourages clients to redefine their perspectives of their problems, thereby enabling them to find new solutions.

Direct approaches to facilitating growth in adventure experiences work 90 to 95% of the time. During the other 5 to 10% of the time, when certain client behaviors and goals make these approaches ineffective and lead clients toward becoming even more "stuck" in their self-defeating and limiting behaviors, explore indirect techniques to change unproductive dynamics.

Indirect approaches, such as double binds and paradoxical symptom prescriptions, work because they are unusual and unexpected. It's likely that dysfunctional individuals have never encountered these techniques before. As a result, when faced with a paradox or double bind, the clients' normal strategies to resist change fail, and clients become obligated to make breakthroughs as they resolve the discrepancies of the dilemma they find themselves in. The outcome can be especially therapeutic for resistant clients.

Again, paradox and double binding are extremely sophisticated frontloading techniques that demand great care. They are beyond most outdoor leaders, especially those not properly trained in psychotherapy, and you should not use them without appropriate experience. We encourage you to practice the five points of direct frontloading (mentioned in chapters 14 and 15) and to reserve paradox and double binding until you have proper training and practice under qualified supervision. Nevertheless, you can benefit from fully understanding these techniques, especially if you cofacilitate with a psychotherapist or other trained professional who uses these approaches.

SUMMARY

Metaphors can serve as a key foundation of transferring change from adventure to daily life. The three types of metaphoric transfer and their corresponding generations of facilitation are spontaneous (first), analogous (second, third, or fourth), and structured (fifth or sixth). Fifth-generation facilitation uses metaphors composed of multiple isomorphs to frame or introduce an experience so that it is meaningful and relevant

to client needs. An isomorph, in which both life experiences have the same form or structure, represents a specific link between the adventure experience and daily life experience. Combining several isomorphs can create a general metaphor that matches client issues. Using isomorphic framing before the adventure means that successfully completing the experience mirrors successfully resolving client issues.

You can create an effective isomorphic framework by following seven steps. Before an experience, you should assess, identify, and rank client goals; select metaphoric adventures; identify successful resolution to the issue; and strengthen the isomorphic framework. During and after an experience, you should review client motivation; conduct the experience with revisions; and debrief. Using fifth-generation techniques has some drawbacks. These include greater complexity; the prescriptive nature; the need to rely on parallel structures, balance with client reality, and account for personal differences; and the potential loss of spontaneous metaphors.

On those rare occasions when all direct facilitation fails by increasing client resistance, you may need to use indirect methods. Two of many methods of indirect frontloading are the double bind and the paradoxical symptom prescription. A double bind channels behavior by giving the client two choices. When both choices are lose–lose, the double bind is negative. Negative binds are unintentional, but unfortunately common in some situations in which outdoor leaders are controlling clients. When both choices are win–win, the double bind is positive. A positive bind is difficult to create, but works because it is unusual and unexpected. It lowers a client's resistance to change.

A paradox seemingly contradicts the expected, but for good reason. To create one, you act in a way that clients are not used to. Symptom prescription refers to demanding the behavior that prevents clients from changing. It allows clients to see things from a fresh perspective that refutes their understanding of the situation. They redefine their interpretations and may find new ways of behaving.

You should use indirect frontloading with great caution and only for the right reasons. Never use these advanced techniques without psychotherapy training or without first practicing under supervision. Never try to gain power over or trick a group. Use these sophisticated techniques only with empathy and the group's best interests in mind. Always desire not to harm clients and to be truthful. While accumulating experience as an outdoor leader, stick to the five methods of direct frontloading we discussed in chapter 15.

QUESTIONS TO THINK ABOUT

1. From your own experience in outdoor activities, give an example of a powerful metaphor.

2. Remember a learning situation that was a metaphor of reality and describe what new strategy you transferred and how you did it.

3. Describe three ways that you might use metaphors in adventure programming. Outline which types of metaphors are found in which generations of facilitation.

4. Define "isomorphism." Why is isomorphism so critical in the use of metaphors in adventure experiences?

5. List the seven steps to developing isomorphic frameworks. Using these steps, design an isomorphic framework for a specific population.

6. Give four examples of adventure experiences that embody a strong, preexisting metaphoric relationship to cooperation. Give another four examples of adventure experiences that embody a strong, preexisting metaphoric relationship to decision making.

7. Outline the benefits and drawbacks of using isomorphic framing.

8. Explain when you might implement indirect frontloading.

9. List the ethical guidelines you should use when considering indirect frontloading.

10. Differentiate between positive and negative double binds. Explain how the statement "In order for you to become a better leader, we are assigning you as leader in this next activity" is a positive or negative double bind.

11. Define "paradoxical symptom prescriptions." Explain how the statement "Please don't tell me anything that you don't want me to know until you're ready to talk about it" is a paradoxical symptom prescription.

REFERENCES

Bacon, S.B. (1983). *The conscious use of metaphor in Outward Bound.* Greenwich, CT: Outward Bound USA.

Bacon, S.B. (1987). *The evolution of the Outward Bound process.* Greenwich, CT: Outward Bound USA. (ERIC Document Reproduction Service No. ED 295 780).

Bacon, S.B. (1991). Using the ropes course to help alcoholics resist temptation. In M.A. Gass and C.H. Dobkin (Eds.), *Book of metaphors: Volume I* (pp. 9-12). Available from editors at University of New Hampshire, Durham, NH.

Bacon, S.B. (1993). Paradox and double binds in adventure-based education. In M.A. Gass (Ed.), *Adventure therapy: Therapeutic applications of adventure programming in mental health settings* (pp. 259-282). Boulder, CO: Association for Experiential Education.

Bacon, S.B., & Kimball, R.O. (1989). The wilderness challenge model. In R.D. Lyman (Ed.), *Residential and inpatient treatment of children and adolescents* (pp. 115-144). New York: Plenum Press.

de Shazer, S. (1982). *Patterns of brief family therapy.* New York: Guilford Press.

Gass, M.A. (1985). Programming the transfer of learning in adventure education. *Journal of Experiential Education, 8*(3), 18-24.

Gass, M.A. (1991). Enhancing metaphoric transfer in adventure therapy programs. *Journal of Experiential Education, 14*(2), 6-13.

Gass, M.A. (1993). *Adventure therapy: Therapeutic applications of adventure programming in mental health settings.* Boulder, CO: Association for Experiential Education.

Gass, M.A., & Dobkin, C.D. (1991). *Book of metaphors: A descriptive presentation of metaphors for adventure activities.* Durham, NH: University of New Hampshire.

Gass, M.A., & Priest, S. (1993). Using metaphors and isomorphs to enhance the transfer of learning in adventure education. *Journal of Adventure Education, 10*(4), 18-24.

Hovelynck, J. (1998). Facilitating experiential learning as a process of metaphor development. *Journal of Experiential Education, 21*(1), 6-13.

Hovelynck, J. (1999). At the boundaries of our images: The changing of task-related metaphors. *Horizons, 3,* 16-17.

Mack, H. (1996). Inside work, outdoors: Women, metaphor, and meaning. In K. Warren (Ed.), *Women's voices in experiential education* (pp. 24-31). Dubuque, IA: Kendall/Hunt.

Minuchin, S. (1981). *Family therapy techniques.* Cambridge, MA: Harvard University Press.

Nadler, R., & Luckner, J. (1992). *Processing the adventure experience.* Dubuque, IA: Kendall/Hunt.

Schoel, J., & Maizell, R.S. (2002). *Exploring islands of healing: New perspectives on adventure-based counseling.* Beverly, MA: Project Adventure.

Schoel, J., Prouty, D., & Radcliffe, P. (1988). *Islands of healing: A guide to adventure-based counseling.* Hamilton, MA: Project Adventure.

Waltzlawick, P. (1978). *The language of change.* New York: Norton.

Zeig, J. (Ed.). (1994). *Ericksonian methods: The essence of the story.* New York: Brunner/Mazel.

Facilitation Roles

It was a sunny yet breezy morning as the group completed its final approach to the rock climbing site. Some members of the group were eager to begin, while others were a bit nervous about the upcoming experience and various issues associated with the day's activity. Both coleaders knew the clients' purposes for rock climbing: to assist them in meeting their particular goals, for gains toward these goals to be integrated into their daily lives, and for those gains to have a lasting and meaningful influence for them. As the leaders finished setting up the climbs, they gathered the group in a circle to implement various facilitation processes designed for the clients. Later that same afternoon, the group was back in a circle with some members arguing over what had just occurred, blaming one another for mistakes that were made. Other group members had stopped listening and several others were retreating from the group's circle. Both leaders began to use facilitating strategies that emphasized the group's strengths as well as addressed this issue in the context of the clients' goals.

The instructor's role is one of facilitation, that is, making interventions as needed to stimulate and encourage the development of positive relationships among group members. By means of creating and structuring diverse opportunities for interaction, the instructor seeks to move a newly formed social unit from disarray to collective unity. Due to the nature of this objective, facilitation is not at all an easy task. It places constant demands on the instructor to be at once aware of himself [or herself], observant of the group, sensitive to changing needs, and resourceful in directing the process along educative paths. A degree of maturity as well as many helping skills are required to effectively guide people in such an intense program setting.

—*Kalisch, 1979, p. 83-84*

What are your facilitation responsibilities and how can you provide these vital services to clients? Though a number of roles exist, let's focus on seven:

A = Assess needs.

B = Be neutral.

C = Construct change processes.

D = Deal with resistance.

E = Exceptions produce solutions.

F = Feedback aids learning.

G = Good listening elicits useful questions.

ASSESS NEEDS

Effective facilitation depends on a thorough needs assessment or diagnosis (see the facilitation process in chapter 14). Remember, you must constantly examine and determine what clients need from an adventure program (Priest, Gass, & Gillis, 2000). Find what clients need through **assessment.** Assessment is an ongoing procedure through which you acquire and evaluate information in order to help clients attain their objectives. Using assessment advances the idea of client-based programming. Adventure programs that believe one type of experience fits all individuals will fail to reach the true potential of an experience. Proper assessment, however, provides you with the knowledge and ability to customize programs to meet the unique needs of a particular client group. In this section, we examine two methods of assessing client needs in adventure programming and their interaction: the CHANGES and GRABBS models.

CHANGES

The **CHANGES model** (Gass & Gillis, 1995a) is organized into seven interactive steps and focuses on acquiring information for developing functional client change (see figure 17.1). These seven steps, which make up the acronym CHANGES, are context, hypotheses, action, novelty, generating, evaluation, and solutions. One way to view these seven steps is in a time sequence. For the most part, the first pair of steps is accomplished before the adventure experience, the next three occur during the adventure, and the final pair takes place after the experience.

In preparing for a therapeutic program, you must identify the **context** of an adventure experience and the client group. This includes gathering all that you know about the general client popula-

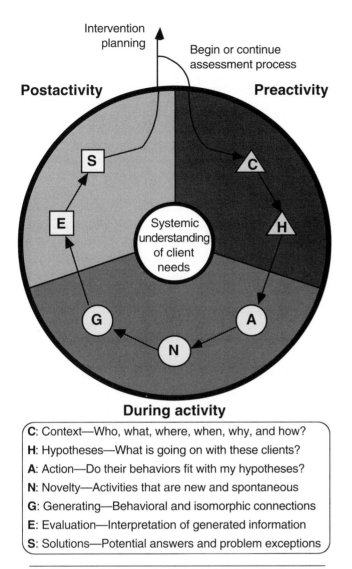

Intervention planning

Begin or continue assessment process

Postactivity   **Preactivity**

S   C

E   H

Systemic understanding of client needs

G   A

N

During activity

C: Context—Who, what, where, when, why, and how?

H: Hypotheses—What is going on with these clients?

A: Action—Do their behaviors fit with my hypotheses?

N: Novelty—Activities that are new and spontaneous

G: Generating—Behavioral and isomorphic connections

E: Evaluation—Interpretation of generated information

S: Solutions—Potential answers and problem exceptions

Figure 17.1 The CHANGES model (Gass & Gillis, 1995a).

tion, the specific client group, the adventure setting, any therapeutic issues, available resources, program purpose, and scheduling. You must draw on your judgment (see chapter 20) from previous experiences with similar clients in similar places for similar reasons.

Questions that provide contextual information include "Why has the client or client group entered into the adventure therapy experience? How long will they be involved? What are their stated goals as a group and as individuals? How does your level of training and competence with adventure activities and various client groups match up? How well do your goals, competencies, and past experiences match those needed and desired by the client group? Should you hold the sessions

inside or outside? What equipment is available for the adventure experiences? How will the weather and physical surroundings determine which activities you can use?"

From this context of past experiences, you should establish initial working **hypotheses** about group and client behavioral patterns by tracking what happens and in what order. Specifically, create these hypotheses from information collected from intake interviews, pencil and paper tests, and simple games conducted early in a program. Then supplement these working hypotheses with your knowledge of typical and unusual client behaviors and with informal sources, such as intuitively analyzing how the group members feel about engaging in an activity, their physical abilities, comments about where they are emotionally and socially, and what they expect will happen (Sugerman, 2001). Once these are established, verify your working hypotheses by observing client behavior in the adventure experience.

Client responses to experiences with **action** will either confirm or contradict your hypotheses. By comparing observed behaviors with hypothesized ones, you can obtain additional information to further assess client needs and to reconstruct, reinforce, revise, or reject your hypotheses accordingly. Using adventure experiences in this manner adds to the validity and richness of assessment as well as provides additional context for developing possible interventions.

Activities that have **novelty** and are unfamiliar cause clients to struggle with the spontaneity of an experience. They don't know how they are expected to behave socially. The need to act quickly prevents them from hiding behind a false self and forces them to show their true behaviors. By seeing if these behaviors match your hypotheses, you can confirm or adapt your hypotheses.

The intent of **generating** information about clients is to determine how and why client behaviors make sense to them. You may generate information regarding client values and belief systems, patterns of behavior, levels of intimacy, boundaries, roles, alliances, power, communication, feedback, language, and "walking their talk." Then use such information as a resource for diagnosing client needs, planning objectives and procedures, and evaluating treatment. By validating hypotheses in previous steps, you reach a more accurate understanding of clients' belief systems and behavior. Another rich source of confirming your understanding of client behavior is to track behavior patterns, or examine what behavior happens in what sequence, during an adventure experience. The purpose of generating is the very motive for assessment: piecing together hypotheses validated by actual experience to obtain the true stories of clients' behaviors. Finally, and most importantly, you must interpret the information you have gathered to get a clear picture of the clients' issues, one that will lead to evaluation and solutions.

Thus, you must **evaluate** which hypotheses client behaviors support or refute. You must integrate and interpret knowledge gathered in the previous steps to diagnose processes and symptoms, identify client motivation, and determine possible interventions.

In conjunction with evaluation and with the aid of clients, you must then identify and construct potential **solutions** to client issues. Create solutions by examining exceptions to client problems, or those times when client issues aren't present and client behaviors are functional. Finally, determine what strategies or solutions will resolve the issues.

GRABBS

The **GRABBS model** (Schoel & Maizell, 2002; Schoel, Prouty, & Radcliffe, 1988) also provides a useful way to conduct ongoing client assessment. As with the CHANGES model, apply the GRABBS model to acquire and evaluate client information in order to help clients reach their objectives. GRABBS stands for Goals, Readiness, Affect, Behaviors, Bodies, and Stage. Ask questions such as "What are the **goals** of the experience—those of the group, of its individual members, and of yourself? What is the state of the group's **readiness?** Are members physically and psychologically safe for the activity? What is the level of feeling, or **affect,** among group members? What **behaviors** have clients shown toward the experience, each other, and you? Are group members treating each other's **bodies** respectfully? What **stage** of development is the group in: forming, norming, storming, performing, or adjourning? Where is experience set and where will group members return to when the experience is completed?"

Combining the Models

While you can use each model independently, Gass and Gillis (1995a) have pointed out that you may use both models together to achieve a beneficial,

interactive effect. The GRABBS model can work within the context of the first five steps of the CHANGES model. You can use GRABBS as a scanning device to search for and monitor the status of the six interests within CHANGES. The models' interaction and the unique information each model contributes to assessment help make the overall process more effective.

BE NEUTRAL

You will work best when you align yourself with a variety of belief systems, realities, or client interpretations and not as well when you align your perspective with only one opinion, especially your own. Maintaining **neutrality** without being distant to clients will make you more mobile in your facilitation processes. In other words, you'll be able to take on a variety of positions concerning a topic without taking sides. You cannot afford to become sided or fixed on a single path toward change.

One way to maintain neutrality and achieve mobility is to remember and act on the maxim: "As a facilitator, I am responsible 'to' you, but not 'for' you" (adapted from King, 1988) (see chapter 11). This attitude places clients in charge of what they gain from an experience and you in a flexible role that allows you to avoid getting caught up in the clients' issues. In this way, clients are free to direct their own facilitated experiences.

Ironically, you can remain neutral if you know what issues you cannot remain neutral about. These issues are sometimes referred to as **nonnegotiable values:** issues that are fixed for you as a leader. For example, several clients may begin to make sexist comments. For many leaders, depreciating others because of gender is not acceptable, especially under a full-value contract. This behavior is clearly nonnegotiable, and you should proactively address it. If you inventory your nonnegotiable values before working with clients, you'll quickly know if you can remain neutral when problems arise. Moreover, you will be more prepared to deal with value-laden issues, which, we must warn you, constantly arise in adventure programming.

CONSTRUCT CHANGE PROCESSES

One of your primary roles as an outdoor leader is to provide mechanisms that can help clients create the functional changes they seek. Conducted within the context of adventure programming, these mechanisms are often problem-focused or solution-focused facilitation approaches (Gass & Gillis, 1995b). As their names imply, the two approaches differ depending on where you center your attention and on client awareness: is the focus on the problem or the solution?

When you apply a **problem-focused facilitation approach,** you attend to what is not working, fixing what is out of order, that is, the dysfunctional action. Using this approach, you should know as much as possible about the problem so you can help the client correct the behavior. The more you understand the problem, the more helpful you can be in solving it. Therefore, as a problem-focused leader, ask questions such as "Why did the problem happen and what causes it?"

When you use a **solution-focused facilitation approach,** you take another tack by identifying what is working, that is, the functional action, and holding it up as a model for change and integrating the positive behavior into the client's reality. Using this approach, you should know as much as possible about exceptions to the problem. The more you identify and understand these exceptions, the more help you'll be to the client. Therefore, as a solution-focused leader, ask questions such as "When doesn't the problem happen and what takes place when the problem is absent?" With this approach you gain a more concrete perception of the problem, but only in light of how it pertains to possible solutions. This approach also emphasizes what clients are doing already that is useful, and this knowledge directs them to highlight, access, and build on their strengths.

You need to evaluate each approach and then select the one that makes the most sense for your particular clients at a particular time. But are you wondering how you'll apply these approaches in real life? Let's look at examples of each approach for activities conducted before, during, and after an adventure experience.

As you know, frontloading takes place before an adventure experience (see chapters 14, 15, and 16). Direct and indirect frontloading provide some of the most influential facilitation techniques you can use to help clients construct functional change. With these techniques, you allow clients to seek positive behaviors, often by asking them to consider possible growth in advance of an adventure experience.

As a problem-focused leader, you might frontload clients' attention on issues that have been somewhat problematic in the past. These type of "problem saturated" frontloading questions may include how problems will hinder success, how the group will deal with these problems if they arise, and how the group will work together to overcome the problems. In this approach, clients center their attention on resolving these issues during the experience.

As a solution-focused leader, you might frontload the activity by asking the group to identify behaviors that might help success, how it can optimize these successful behaviors, and when it feels successful behaviors are most likely to happen during the adventure experience. You could also challenge each client to do something different in order to make other group members feel better about the group's ability to work together toward its objectives, or you could encourage members to "have their antenna up" so as to figure out what the others did to support them (Kiser, Piercy, & Lipchik, 1993, p. 236).

In an adventure experience, you could use a **stop-action,** or **freeze,** to take advantage of a teachable or therapeutic moment. With this technique, you stop the action in order to analyze and learn from what is going on at that moment. For example, in the middle of an adventure experience, communication among group members can break down with everyone talking at once and no one listening. At an opportune moment, you or any client can call a time-out to discuss why things are going poorly. The group stops the experience as soon as possible after the call and discusses the issue until it feels ready to continue the action.

As a problem-focused leader, you might focus clients' attention on identifying, analyzing, and fixing the problematic elements that caused the group to have poor communication. The intent of this discussion would be to help clients improve communication skills through better understanding how and why the dysfunction occurred.

As a solution-focused leader, you might ask the group to identify, analyze, and discuss times during the adventure experience when communication was good. If the group responds that no such times occurred, then you should ask clients to consider what good communication might look like—as a hypothetical exception. To turn clients toward such solutions, you should also ask them to highlight and concentrate on what they would do if they were communicating better, what they would do differently if they were communicating at their best, or how they would know if they were communicating well.

Scaling is a technique used to self rate performance following the adventure experience. For example, you could ask group members to evaluate how they cooperated in an experience on a scale from 0 to 10, either by stating the score aloud, holding up fingers, or writing it down. Zero represents a total lack of cooperation and 10 represents complete cooperation. Clients can use scaling to quantifiably evaluate the experience or to launch into a discussion of their performances. Let's assume this group rates its efforts with a mean of 5, which represents average cooperation.

As a problem-focused leader, you should center clients' attention on identifying, investigating, and eliminating those negative elements that prevented them from obtaining a higher mean score for cooperation. Then have the group focus on completing its next adventure experience by reducing these negative elements.

As a solution-focused leader, you should ask the group to consider the positive elements that made the score a 5 and kept the score from being lower. This encourages the group to focus on building these positive elements in order to increase the score. You could also ask the group about the small things it will be doing differently when it obtains a higher score for cooperation in the future.

DEAL WITH RESISTANCE

People don't resist change, they resist being changed! Clients can sometimes feel forced to grow, and so they often resist. Applying further external motivation may simply cause greater internal resistance. Blocking (inhibiting the resistance) might prove fruitful some times, but it often fails to address the underlying reasons of why resistance occurs.

You can deal with resistance using clarifying and reframing. Both methods require you to view resistance as the clients educating you on how to best help them. Thus, you must learn to see resistance not as client opposition, but as encouragement for you to understand their needs and issues (de Shazer, 1984). Don't block, disperse, diffuse, or deflect resistance: use it to better serve the clients.

In the **clarifying** method, you explain to the group that you are genuinely confused by what is happening and respectfully ask the group to help you understand. In answering your honest and honorable inquiry, clients offer their own interpretations and expectations for the situation.

In an open and honest manner, you are merely relating those parts of the experience which are truly confusing you. By responding to this lack of clarity, clients become clearer about these same issues. Not surprisingly, clarifying fails miserably when it sounds fraudulent or sarcastic. Consider this sincere use of clarifying:

> Y'know, I've probably done over a hundred Spider's Webs before in my life as a professional, and I must admit that I've never seen anyone (any group) really act in this way. I don't know if it's just me or the day, but I can't get over how incredibly different this Spider's Web is. Usually groups come and (here, the leader discusses typical behaviors for the activity), but I just don't see this happening with this group. Did I give the wrong directions? Did I forget to tell you something at the beginning?

In the **reframing** method, you put forth new ways of looking at a situation. By offering new perspectives or alternative reasons for resistance, you attempt to see how opposition to change can benefit clients. For example, you ask yourself, "What function does resistance serve? Why do clients see it as useful?" Proposing new interpretations or helping clients construct their own can redirect resistance, possibly enhancing efforts to change. You can reframe both the content and context of an experience.

With **content reframing,** you encourage clients to look for a new and more positive meaning of a behavior within the adventure. For example, a client comes off a climb after having spent 60 min attempting the final crux. The client is very dejected because of an inability to succeed. In reframing, you may point out that a more valid thing to learn from the experience is the client's ability to persist and how this may be of much more value for him than actually completing the climb.

With **contextual reframing,** you encourage the client to look for a new and more positive meaning of the behavior by applying an action to a different and more relevant circumstance. Using the same climbing example, you should downplay the shortcomings of the actual climbing by pointing out that the client could learn several lessons from the experience, such as when to stop when faced with a task he can't complete, what he needs to do in the future to complete a task, and what his strengths and weaknesses are when really pushed to the limit. Then, you could say, "We learn from our mistakes," helping the client apply the lessons to real life.

EXCEPTIONS PRODUCE SOLUTIONS

The answers to client questions and the solutions to their problems can often be found in the **exceptions** to their issues (de Shazer, 1985; Walter & Peller, 1992). This is the case when you ask clients, "When the problem is not happening, what is happening instead?"

For example, if one issue for a group is lack of trust, you could focus on an exception to this lack, or a time when clients were trusting well. If clients claim never to have been able to trust one another, you can ask about speculative exceptions, or an imagined time of trusting. You should ask, "When this problem is not present, what are things like? What would happen if the group was more trusting? What would you be doing differently if you trusted more? How would you know if you trusted more?"

Questions about exceptions to client issues positively focus clients' minds on solutions and not on problems. In answering these questions, clients highlight for themselves—as well as you—what they should do differently. This gives them ideas for acting differently in the future.

Another way to find solutions is to foster expectations for success by posing the **miracle** question (de Shazer, 1985). Ask clients to respond to a question that focuses on what success would look like before the program even starts. Two miracle questions might go as follows:

> Say at the end of this course, you're driving home with another participant. She turns to you and asks, "What did you think of that experience?" What will have had to happen in this program for you to truly respond, "That was incredibly valuable! It could not have gone any better!"?

> Imagine yourself after this course. You're home discussing your experience with a friend or family member. How would you complete this sentence: "That was the best (or worst) and most (or least) valuable program I've ever experienced, because I . . ."?

Responses to miracle questions indicate client's definitions and impressions of success, which in turn inform you what clients are looking for and hoping to gain from the program. These needs and desires can form the basis of upcoming learning and change.

Since clients often arrive at adventure programs apprehensive about what will happen, dreading embarrassment, or afraid of getting hurt, you can allay these concerns by implanting positive prospects at the program's outset. Responses gathered early in a program can form the foundation for goal setting and may shed light on the values clients hold in high regard or the concerns they have for the future. Sharing anonymous answers aloud or posting written answers focuses clients on understanding one another and on successfully working for solutions rather than on failure caused by dwelling on problems.

FEEDBACK AIDS LEARNING

A critical feature of facilitation is providing for **appropriate feedback** to clients from themselves, other clients, and you. Upcraft (1982, p. 80) defined feedback as the "exchange of verbal and non-verbal responses among group members based on commonly observed behavior" and identified eight characteristics associated with providing feedback between a sender and receiver (Upcraft, 1982, p. 81-83; Nadler & Luckner, 1992, p. 34):

1. Appropriate feedback is **descriptive** rather than evaluative. To give descriptive feedback, the sender offers observations of the event. Evaluative feedback assesses the value of what a receiver has done. Describing a behavior, rather than a personal reaction to it, allows recipients to use feedback in a manner that works best for them. Moreover, avoiding evaluative language reduces recipient defensiveness.

2. Appropriate feedback is **specific** rather than general. Learning what specifically caused a behavior lessens the possibility of misinterpretation. For example, being told an idea is stupid probably is not as valuable as being told, "When we came to this point in the trail, I didn't understand why you decided to . . ."

3. Appropriate feedback is **well-intended.** You must keep in mind the purpose of feedback: to produce positive changes in an individual or to make the group more functional. When the motivations for presenting feedback shift to destructive intentions, such as to make another person feel bad or to feel powerful at the expense of another,

you should look closely at why they shifted. In examining such motivations, take into account the needs of the recipient as well as the sender. Failure to meet both their needs can lessen the value and future integration of the feedback.

4. Appropriate feedback is **directed toward** change; it is something the receiver can act on. Constructive feedback about shortcomings the receiver has no control over can only increase frustration. For such issues, search for other solutions or better uses for such behaviors. For example, you might say, "To me, it seems as if you don't have the background in this area. Do you agree? Would it work better if you were put in another role?"

5. Appropriate feedback is **solicited** rather than imposed. Feedback is most useful when clients seek it, rather than when it is thrust on them. Asking if the person would like to receive feedback on performance as well as the manner of and forum for reception (when, where, how, who) produces more constructive results.

6. Appropriate feedback is **well-timed.** Feedback immediately following experiences reduces confusion that can develop over time. But in some situations immediate feedback is not possible or appropriate due to logistical constraints or the person's readiness to hear it.

7. Appropriate feedback is **checked out with the sender.** While giving feedback, check with the recipient periodically to increase the likelihood that the message and intentions you're sending are being received. Have the recipient repeat those portions of the feedback she finds most valuable as a "reliability check" for the sender.

8. Appropriate feedback is **checked out with the group.** When appropriate and possible, invite other clients to provide a sounding board for the feedback. They can give information on the reliability of the feedback and possibly offer other interpretations of what took place. Adding consistency or variation to feedback can increase its richness and aid its reception. Be careful, however, to monitor group dynamics in order to ensure negative consequences, such as the recipient's feeling ganged up on or the introduction of inappropriate side issues, don't result.

Feedback brings learning and change. To this end, you should **implant circular feedback loops** in the group. This means getting members to observe one another, either covertly or overtly, and to report back, either privately or publicly,

Facilitators should avoid lecturing to their groups.

◄ *EFFECTIVE OUTDOOR LEADERS* ►

- ► Understand assessment processes involved in adventure experiences and know how to implement assessment information in order to best assist clients.
- ► Remain neutral and mobile in regard to client issues.
- ► Are able to construct change processes from either a problem- or solution-focused perspective.

- ► Deal with resistance through the clarifying or reframing methods.
- ► Are able to help clients look for exceptions to their issues.
- ► Provide appropriate feedback and elicit it from clients.
- ► Are good listeners, staying alert for active verbs.

their observations. Relationships in groups are recursive, that is, one person's actions positively or negatively influence the behaviors of others and the group's performance, and they are reciprocal, that is, the reverse is also true, and the group's performance influences the individual's performance. Therefore, encouraging and monitoring these recursive and reciprocal interactions can further develop most groups. Introducing declared feedback loops places clients on alert for their behaviors, possibly making them more likely to experiment with changing negative ones.

GOOD LISTENING ELICITS USEFUL QUESTIONS

Good listening skills are fundamental to facilitation. If you don't hear or understand the answers to your questions, facilitating change by questioning is extremely difficult and possibly a waste of time. You must develop good listening skills, so let's look at a few key ways to do so (see also chapter 19).

Maintain eye contact with the speaker. Signal verbal and nonverbal attentiveness by saying, "uh-huh" or "yeah" and by nodding your head. Don't initially express agreement or disagreement. Instead, simply indicate that you understood the message. Wait through pauses to encourage the speaker to resume talking. Don't rush to fill silences: be patient. Don't take the focus of the conversation away from the speaker by publicly disagreeing or by changing the subject. Use open-ended questions to encourage the speaker to elaborate. Summarize or restate the speaker's remarks from time to time to show you comprehend the ideas. Respond to the feelings that may lie behind the speaker's words. Show understanding of or

empathy for how the speaker feels. Use a gentle tone of voice that expresses caring rather than judging. Last, seek feedback from other leaders about how to improve your listening skills.

Listen for action words. Active verbs depict a process rather than a product or the individual. Participants can describe themselves and their issues in active terms, and by doing so, can become partially accountable for what is happening; yet separate themselves from their problems rather than see themselves as the "problem." For example, instead of being depressed, clients can be depressing. Using active terms can help them identify issues and their sources, as well as having participants see themselves separate from the "problem." Once again, listen for actions that the client states as unchangeable as well as for things that sound changeable. You need to know the difference and have the wisdom to act accordingly.

SUMMARY

The seven facilitation roles are: assess needs, be neutral, construct change processes, deal with resistance, exceptions produce solutions, feedback aids learning, and good listening elicits useful questions.

The CHANGES model is one way to assess client needs by using actual adventure activities as the measure rather than by using the more traditional intake interviews, observations, or psychological diagnostic instruments (Kimball, 1993). When you facilitate adventure experiences correctly, the information they generate can help you assess client behaviors and in many cases can provide an ongoing information source richer than one-time, traditional procedures. Another advantage of CHANGES is that it is a continual feedback loop in which adventure activities are both sources for assessment and interventions for change: a truly reciprocal process.

GRABBS stands for goals, readiness, affect, behaviors, bodies, and stage. Using this model, you ask questions about these topics in order to check client status throughout the assessment process. The CHANGES and GRABBS models can work together to each contribute unique information for assessing client needs.

You need to be neutral and remain mobile enough to adopt a variety of positions in response to client issues. You can accomplish this by determining for yourself which issues are flexible and which are nonnegotiable.

You can construct change from either a problem-focused or solution-focused facilitation approach. In the former, you and clients concentrate on solving the problem of dysfunctional behavior or changing negative actions. In the latter, you both concentrate on finding exceptions to the problem and emphasizing the times when behavior is functional, thereby reinforcing and enhancing positive behavior.

Resistance is the clients' way of telling you how to better help them. When you cannot deal with resistance by employing extra motivation or by blocking opposition, clarifying and reframing often prove fruitful. These methods cause clients to examine their issues from a fresh perspective, which may bring new change. Clarifying is the truthful and conscientious way to highlight your confusion. Reframing helps clients examine the source of resistance by investigating it within the content or context of the experience.

Exceptions to client issues often hold the answers to their questions and the solutions to their problems. Frequently, you can encourage clients to identify exceptions to issues, or times during which the problem isn't present. When clients look for exceptions, they often find explanations for previously unexplained behaviors.

Appropriate feedback is descriptive, specific, well-intended, directed toward change, solicited, well-timed, checked out with the sender, and checked out with the group. Implanting multiple opportunities to give and receive feedback in a group enables clients to learn and grow.

If you don't hear or understand client answers, you may find methods for facilitating change by asking questions for clarification. Among many suggestions for attending to communication is listening for action words or verbs ending with "-ing." As mentioned earlier in this chapter, these expressions can help you point out the sources of client issues.

QUESTIONS TO THINK ABOUT

1. Use the CHANGES model with a group and evaluate its effectiveness.

2. Explain how you would use the GRABBS model.

3. Identify your nonnegotiable values that you will not be able to remain neutral about.

4. Decide whether your approach to facilitation is problem- or solution-focused and explain how the two differ.

5. Differentiate between the clarifying and reframing methods of dealing with resistance.

6. What is the difference between content and context reframing? Give an example of each.

7. Describe how exceptions to problems can lead to solutions. Give an example.

8. Design a miracle question for your next group (actual or imagined).

9. Practice giving appropriate feedback to someone in a realistic situation. Ask that person or an observer to give you appropriate feedback on your performance.

10. Listen to a person in a realistic situation and practice attending to them. Ask a third person acting as an observer to give you feedback on how effective your listening skills are.

11. Listen to another person speak about an experience. Identify all the action words and active verbs she uses.

12. Explain how facilitation makes learning and change easier for clients.

REFERENCES

de Shazer, S. (1984). The death of resistance. *Family Process, 23,* 11-21.

de Shazer, S. (1985). *Keys to solution in brief therapy.* New York: Guilford Press.

Gass, M.A., & Gillis, H.L. (1995a). CHANGES: An assessment model using adventure experiences. *Journal of Experiential Education, 18*(1), 34-40.

Gass, M.A., & Gillis, H.L. (1995b). Constructing solutions in adventure therapy. *Journal of Experiential Education, 18*(2), 63-69.

Kalisch, K. (1979). *The role of the instructor in the Outward Bound educational process.* Three Lakes, WI: Honey Rock Camp.

Kimball, R.O. (1993). The wilderness as therapy: The value of using adventure programs in therapeutic assessment. In M.A. Gass (Ed.), *Adventure therapy: Therapeutic applications of adventure programming* (pp. 153-160). Dubuque, IA: Kendall/Hunt.

King, K. (1988). The role of adventure in the experiential learning process. *Journal of Experiential Education, 11*(2), 4-8.

Kiser, D.J., Piercy, F.P., & Lipchik, E. (1993). The integration of emotion in solution-focused therapy. *Journal of Marital and Family Therapy, 19*(3), 235-244.

Nadler, R., & Luckner, J. (1992). *Processing the adventure experience: Theory and practice.* Dubuque, IA: Kendall/Hunt.

Priest, S., Gass, M.A., & Gillis, H.L. (2000). *Essential elements of facilitation.* Seattle: Tarrak Technologies.

Schoel, J., & Maizell, R.S. (2002). *Exploring islands of healing: New perspectives on adventure-based counseling.* Beverly, MA: Project Adventure.

Schoel, J., Prouty, D., & Radcliffe, P. (1988). *Islands of healing: A guide to adventure-based counseling.* Dubuque, IA: Kendall/Hunt.

Sugerman, D. (2001). Inclusive outdoor education: Facilitating groups that include people with disabilities. *Journal of Experiential Education, 24*(3), 166-172.

Upcraft, M.L. (1982). *Learning to be a resident assistant.* San Francisco: Jossey-Bass.

Walter, J., & Peller, J. (1992). *Becoming solution-focused in brief therapy.* New York: Brunner/Mazel.

PART

V

Metaskills for Outdoor Leaders

CHAPTER

18

Flexible Leadership Style

A novice leader has marched a group of expert climbers up a long trail to an alpine meadow to establish a base camp for a week of climbing in California. The weather is clear, spirits are high, and plenty of low-impact campsites are available. Nevertheless, the novice leader tells the group members where they must put their tents. Arguments ensue, many of the climbers revolt, and eventually the entire group mutinies and selects a new leader. The old leader isn't sure how things got so out of hand!

An expert leader has allowed a group of novice paddlers to find its way back to camp after a full day of sea kayaking among a maze of islands off the coast of British Columbia. In fact, this schoolteacher has relaxed during most of the afternoon as the students have done much of the work to successfully find their way back. Still an hour from camp, at the end of an open crossing, the group spots a stranger waving frantically on the beach. The teacher simply paddles on by and asks the students to take care of the situation! The group investigates and finds that the man is injured. The paddlers are unsure of what to do and so fall into arguing; one tired student begins to cry. The teacher returns an hour later and is surprised to see things much the same as when the group first arrived!

In the two scenarios, both leaders made the same mistake. They simply failed to shift their styles to suit the conditions they encountered. Instead, they implemented the same style they had used throughout the day and probably used frequently when leading other trips. In each case, the leaders could have been far more effective had they expressed a more appropriate style for each situation. In this chapter, we discuss how and when to adapt, or "flex," leadership styles by presenting a model to guide you when making these critical choices.

LEADERSHIP STYLES

Leadership styles are the ways in which you express your influence. We can categorize styles in many different ways. For example, as a leader, you can be seen as telling, selling, testing, consulting, joining, and delegating in your efforts to influence (Tannenbaum & Schmidt, 1973). Such styles are often portrayed as a range of approaches characterized by how much authority you exercise and how free group members are to contribute to the situation (D. Grube, Phipps, & A. Grube, 2002; Warner, 2004).

When using the telling style, you make the decision and demand action from the group members. When selling, you make the decision and convince the group members of its merit. When testing, you present the decision, but invite group members to modify it. When consulting, you present the problem and seek input in the decision. In joining, you outline the entire problem and let the group formulate the entire decision. In delegating, you let the group members outline the problem for themselves and come to their own decision.

We can group these styles into three sets of pairs to define three outdoor leadership styles that form a continuum of decision-making power: **autocratic** (telling or selling), **democratic** (testing or consulting), and **abdicratic** (joining or delegating). (See chapter 5 for how the three styles relate to group development.) The autocratic style is characterized by an authoritarian approach in which you hold complete power over decision making and dictate the needed response. The democratic style involves shared decision making, with you and the group working together to solve problems. The abdicratic style is an outgrowth of the laissez-faire, or "leaving to do," approach (Lewin, Lippitt, & White, 1938), in which you abdicate all decision-making power to the group and agree to abide by their resolutions. True dictatorial, or all-leader power, and laissez-faire, or all-group power, have limited application in outdoor leadership settings, since negotiated involvement by both parties is often a necessary part of adventure experiences, and effective leadership involves influence from both parties as well. Figure 18.1 summarizes the three outdoor leadership styles along a continuum of actions leaders can take.

LEADERSHIP ORIENTATION

Historically, researchers have identified two dimensions that determine a leader's orientation to leadership: task and relationship (Stogdill &

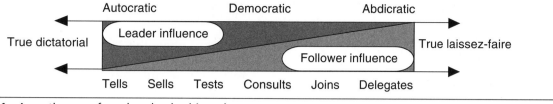

Figure 18.1 A continuum of outdoor leadership styles.

Leadership Power

Groups will not follow a leader they perceive as powerless or not influential. But no matter what your level of leadership experience, you possess some bases of power from which you can influence others. Leadership power has been categorized as coming from at least five sources: referent, legitimate, expert, reward, and coercive (French & Raven, 1960; Raven & Rubin, 1976).

▶ **Referent power** is the least obvious source, but is the most voluntarily accepted of the five. When as a leader, you are admired, identified with, or valued by group members, they are more likely to agree with you, support your opinions, and follow you. We can say you have referent power if the group members gauge or mirror their personal actions by your actions.

▶ **Legitimate power** refers to the authority given you when you are appointed by a controlling agency or elected by group members. The more prominent or recognized the appointment or election, the greater is the legitimized power. Most group members will follow you if you have been given the moral right or legal responsibility to make certain decisions on their behalf.

▶ **Expert power** is achieved through perceived competence. The more knowledge, skill, and experience you appear to have, the more likely group members will respect your expertise and the more likely they are to follow you. Often this power is founded on your expertise in one situation and is unlikely to generalize to other situations.

▶ **Reward power** is achieved by giving a reward for effort. As a rewarding leader, you influence group members by offering positive incentives, such as fewer chores or recognition for a job well done. This ploy only works if the group members value the rewards. It fails if group members do not like the incentives.

▶ **Coercive power** involves the threat of punishment and usually follows the failure of reward power to influence people. As a coercive leader, you influence group members by threatening them with negative incentives such as decreased responsibility or carrying more weight on a trip. Ethically, this power has no part in outdoor situations, since forcing people to act ignores challenge by choice and can potentially destroy the adventure experience or create barriers to learning.

Coons, 1957; Blake & Mouton, 1978; Hersey & Blanchard, 1982). As mentioned in chapter 5, the leadership style that you express, especially in difficult times, will depend on your orientation to the dimensions of tasks and relationships. We can think of the orientation to these two dimensions as the levels of concern that you have for getting the job done, or achieving the goal (task), and for looking after group interactions, or maintaining a positive atmosphere among the followers (rela-

tionship). Figure 18.2 shows these two orientations in a matrix.

These leadership orientations help determine the most appropriate style for you to express. If you want to get to the top of a peak at all costs, you may express an autocratic style to push people upward. Or as a laid-back leader, you may float down a river on a lazy day, engaging people in conversation and expressing an abdicratic style. In general, task-oriented leaders tend toward autocracy and relationship-oriented leaders tend toward abdicracy. But without the capability or willingness to flex your leadership style away from your preference, you will fail to be fully effective.

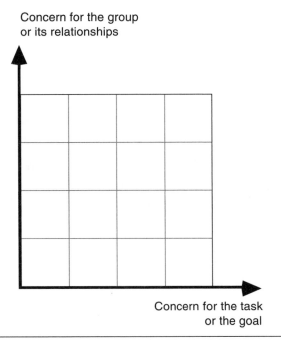

Figure 18.2 A matrix of outdoor leadership orientations.

CONDITIONAL FAVORABILITY

The most influential orientation for you as an outdoor leader, however, is not task or relationship, but the favorability of conditions in which you find yourself (Priest & Dixon, 1991). Conditional favorability for outdoor leadership is a mix of five factors (Fiedler, 1967; Benson, 1986; Ford, 1987):

1. **Environmental dangers:** weather, perils, hazards, and objective and subjective risks
2. **Individual competence:** experience, confidence, skill, attitude, behavior, and knowledge
3. **Group unity:** morale, maturity, cooperation, communication, trust, responsibility, and interest
4. **Leader proficiency:** credibility, judgment, stress, fatigue, and perceived capability
5. **Decision consequences:** clarity of the problem, sufficient solution time, available resources, expected ramifications, and degree of uncertainty or challenge

Figure 18.3 summarizes the favorability of conditions expressed as a continuum from low to high.

CONDITIONAL FAVORABILITY

Low	Medium	High
Bad weather Many perils and hazards Mostly subjective risks not easily controlled	Environmental dangers	Good weather Few perils and hazards Mostly objective risks under human control
Disintegrated and divided Distrustful and competitive Immature and irresponsible	Group	Cohesive and unified Trusting and cooperative Mature and responsible
Novice members Incompetent, unskilled, unable Unsure, inexperienced, unknowledgeable	Individuals	Expert members Competent, skilled, able Confident, experienced, knowledgeable
Deficient and incapable Lacks power base for credibility Poor judgment, stressed out, fatigued	Leader	Proficient and capable Holds strong power base for credibility Sound judgment, in control, fit
Problem cloudy and uncertain Insufficient time and resources available Challenge high with unacceptable outcomes	Consequences of the decision	Problem clear and defined Sufficient time and resources available Challenge low with acceptable outcomes

Figure 18.3 A spectrum of conditional favorability.

CONDITIONAL OUTDOOR LEADERSHIP THEORY MODEL

Combining the information on leadership styles, leadership orientations, and conditional favorability creates the **conditional outdoor leadership theory** (COLT; Priest & Chase, 1989). Figure 18.4 illustrates this theory. Note that the orientations, or the concern for tasks and the concern for relationships, are represented by the x- and y-axes, respectively, and that conditional favorability is represented by the z-axis. With this graphic framework in place, the three outdoor leadership styles can be spread across the matrices created at high, medium, and low favorability.

Conditions of **medium favorability** highlight the typical outdoor settings in which the dangers are acceptable, the leader is proficient, the individuals are reasonably responsible, the group gets along fairly well, and the consequences of decisions are mostly recoverable. Under moderately favorable conditions, if your orientation is toward relationships, you may express an abdicratic style, and if your orientation is toward tasks, you may express an autocratic style. If your orientation is balanced between both tasks and relationships, you may express a democratic style. The style depends on the "pull" of the respective concerns. A greater pull by one concern as well as your preferred orientation will cause you to favor one style over another.

Conditions of **high favorability** exemplify a more desirable outdoor setting in which the dangers are minimal, the leader is most proficient, the individuals are very competent, the group gets along extremely well, and the consequences of decisions are minor. Under highly favorable conditions, like many leaders, you may shift toward a relationship orientation, allowing an abdicratic style to prevail. Given a strong enough orientation toward the task, however, a democratic style or perhaps even an autocratic style can be appropriate. When things are good, like many leaders, you may pay more attention to the group and therefore transfer decision-making responsibility. Hence, if you find yourself in this situation, you will likely employ an abdicratic style, delegating power to the group.

Conditions of **low favorability** hallmark the less desirable outdoor setting in which the dangers are extreme, the leader is deficient, the individuals are incompetent, the group gets along poorly, and the consequences of decisions are major. Under unfavorable conditions, like many leaders, you may shift toward a task orientation, favoring an autocratic style. But given a strong enough orientation toward relationships, a democratic style or perhaps even an abdicratic style can be appropriate. Still, when things are bad, you will probably pay stricter attention to the task and therefore retain decision-making responsibility. Hence, if you find yourself in this situation, you will likely employ an autocratic style to authoritatively vest power in yourself.

APPLYING THE COLT MODEL

Let's look at a real-life example by applying the COLT model to a backpacking adventure. You are responsible for teaching route finding to five participants on the first day of a three-day trip near timberline during the summer in the Rocky Mountains.

At the trailhead, you inform the group members that they are in charge of reading their maps, using their compasses, and finding their way to the campsite. You have chosen an overall abdicratic style because conditions are high in favorability. The participants are skilled in navigation, their spirits are high, you are a master orienteer, well within the proficiency requirements for this activity, the weather is clear with no apparent danger, and the consequences of the backpackers getting lost are minor since they have plenty of daylight and all their overnight gear. Furthermore, at this time, your concern lies with relationships. You are giving group members a chance to learn for themselves as they work together as a team. Therefore, an abdicratic style is appropriate, leaving the group to learn from its own minor mistakes. If your attention shifts more toward the task and somewhat away from relationships, you would probably flex toward a more democratic or autocratic style.

As time goes on, conditions deteriorate, and such a flex does indeed become necessary! It's several hours later, and group members are experiencing some confusion at a trail junction. The group has stopped discussing possible solutions and is now arguing over which path to choose: the left or the right. The members all have strong opinions as to which direction to take, and tempers flare because they are tired and hungry. Confusion erodes group morale. To further depress the conditions, you are frustrated, concerned with the lack of teamwork displayed by the group. The weather

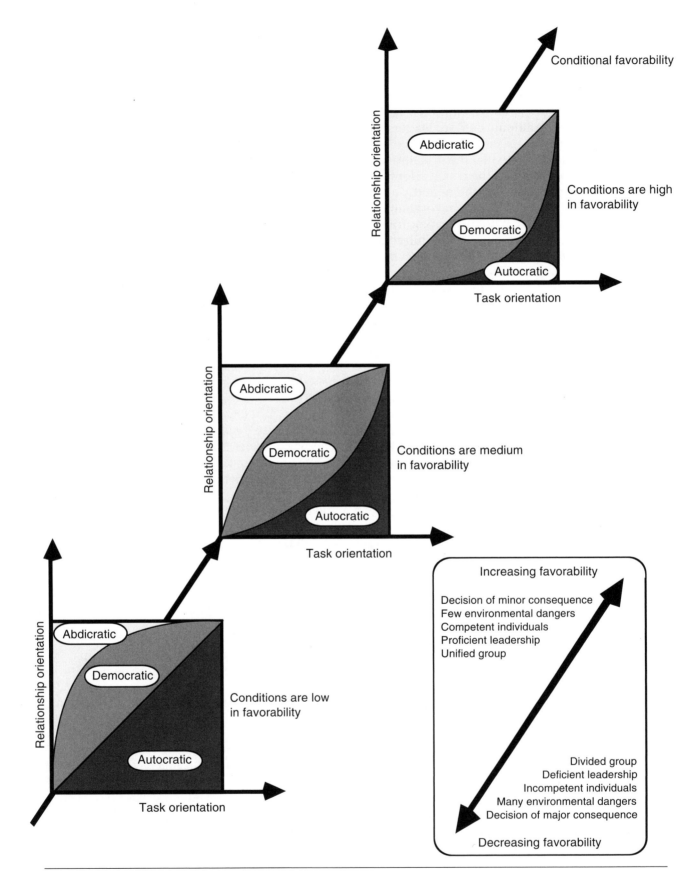

Figure 18.4 The conditional outdoor leadership theory (COLT).

Appropriate choices of leadership style and flexibility can create critical differences in adventure experiences.

is changing dramatically for the worse: snow begins to fall as a few group members express a desire to hurry up and decide, because they are getting cold. You choose to enter into the decision-making process with a democratic style. The final decision rests with both the group and you, but you attempt to influence the group toward picking the correct path. In addition, under such conditions, which we can now label as medium favorability, you are prepared to flex autocratically if the concern of hypothermia arises or abdicratically if the group is ready to work toward the correct decision on its own. In the former case, you are concerned about the task of keeping everyone safe from cold exposure, and in the latter case, you are concerned with rebuilding positive relationships in a dysfunctional group.

Let's say you remain flexible as conditions worsen. Now late in the day and at a much higher elevation, snow is falling steadily, the ground is slippery, and the group has lost sight of any trail it was following. The fog is rolling in, the map indicates intermittent cliff bands in the area, and a poor decision might mean an accident. Individuals are fed, but tired. None are too cold yet, but one person is feeling ill from the altitude. The group members are frustrated with what they perceive to be a failed exercise. At this point, your immediate concern is getting the group to a safe campsite before members become hypothermic or get lost in the fog. You move to an autocratic style because conditions are definitely low in favorability. But if your attention focuses more on the opportunity for group members to get along or less on getting to camp because the group becomes a team or several camping options unexpectedly arise, you could flex toward a democratic or even abdicratic style.

By maintaining flexibility and by expressing the correct leadership style for each circumstance, you will effectively influence the group, helping it to achieve its goals, which are to maintain its relationships and to deal with the variety of conditions it encounters. Using an inappropriate style at any time in this scenario could have been devastating. Imagine the risks for group members in similarly unfavorable conditions if you were to express an abdicratic style, leaving the decisions entirely up to them! Also imagine the same group at the start of the trip if you were to apply an autocratic style,

◄ *EFFECTIVE OUTDOOR LEADERS* ►

► Understand the connections among influence, power, and style.

► Are capable of expressing all three outdoor leadership styles and are aware of their concern for task, relationship, and conditional favorability.

► Flex style to match concerns accordingly and switch style in concert with changing circumstances and conditions.

marching it up the trail in favorable conditions. In the former example, the incorrect style could have resulted in an accident. In the latter instance, the incorrect style would likely have discouraged and frustrated several group members, inhibiting their goals. Thus, your choice of style can make all the difference in an adventure experience. Temper your choice at any given moment with careful consideration for task, relationship, and conditional favorability. Above all, remain flexible in that choice.

SUMMARY

Leadership is a process of influence based on power. Power in outdoor leadership circles comes in five different types: referent, legitimate, expert, rewarding, and coercive. Power refers to control over decision making, and who has the control—the appointed leader or other group members—determines who is being most influential and taking a leadership role.

The three dimensions of the conditional outdoor leadership theory (COLT) are graphically represented by three axes. The horizontal axis (x) is task orientation, or the degree to which you are concerned about achieving the goal or getting the job done. The vertical axis (y) is relationship orientation, or the degree to which you are concerned about interactions within the group and the group's ability to work together. The diagonal axis (z) is conditional favorability, or the degree to which the conditions associated with the task and group relationships are favorable. These are the conditions under which you and your group must function to make decisions. They are derived from five factors: environmental dangers, individual competence, group unity, leader proficiency, and decision consequences.

You may employ a spectrum of leadership styles ranging from autocratic through democratic to abdicratic. The style you choose depends on how concerned you are about task, relationship, and condition favorability at that moment in time. Autocratic styles are wise when you have a high concern for task and a low concern for relationships and are working under unfavorable conditions. Democratic styles are appropriate when your concerns for task and relationship are balanced and you are working under medium favorability. Choose an abdicratic style when you have a low concern for tasks, a high concern for relationships, and are working under favorable conditions. We encourage you to analyze your style in relation to these three variables and flex to suit the particular circumstances.

QUESTIONS TO THINK ABOUT

1. Relate the following words to one another in a single sentence: leadership style, power, and influence.

2. Differentiate among the five types of power.

3. Compare and contrast the three outdoor leadership styles.

4. Discuss the effect that a leader's concerns for task orientation, relationship orientation, and conditional favorability has on expressed leadership style.

5. List the five factors that contribute to condition favorability. Provide three examples of each factor that clearly explain what each indicates.

6. Describe two personal experiences in which you have used appropriate and inappropriate leadership styles. Analyze both experiences with the COLT model to explain why one style was effective and the other was not.

REFERENCES

Benson, L. (1986). *Changing your leadership style because of risk*. Unpublished manuscript.

Blake, R.R., & Mouton, J.S. (1978). *The new managerial grid*. Houston, TX: Gulf Publishing.

Fiedler, F.E. (1967). *A theory of leadership effectiveness*. New York: McGraw-Hill.

Ford, P.M. (1987). The responsible outdoor leader. *Journal of Outdoor Education, 22,* 4-13.

French, J.R.P., Jr., & Raven, B. (1960). The bases of social power. In D. Cartwright & A. Zander (Eds.), *Group dynamics* (2nd ed., pp. 259-269). Evanston, IL: Row Peterson.

Grube, D.P., Phipps, M.L., & Grube, A.J. (2002). Practicing leader decision-making through a systematic journal technique: A single case analysis. *Journal of Experiential Education, 25*(2), 220-230.

Hersey, P., & Blanchard, K. (1982). *Management of organizational behavior: Utilizing human resources* (4th ed.). Englewood Cliffs, NJ: Prentice Hall.

Lewin, K., Lippitt, R., & White, R.K. (1938). An experimental approach to the study of autocracy and democracy. *Sociometry, 1,* 292.

Priest, S., & Chase, R. (1989). The conditional theory of outdoor leadership: An exercise in flexibility. *Journal of Adventure Education and Outdoor Leadership, 6*(2), 10-17.

Priest, S., & Dixon, T. (1991). Toward a new theory of outdoor leadership. *Leisure Studies, 10*(2), 163-170.

Raven, B.H., & Rubin, J.E. (1976). *Social psychology: People in groups*. New York: John Wiley & Sons.

Stogdill, R.M., & Coons, A.E. (1957). *Leadership behavior: Its description and measurement*. Columbus, OH: Ohio State University Press.

Tannenbaum, R., & Schmidt, W.H. (1973). How to choose a leadership pattern. *Harvard Business Review, 51*(3), 162-175, 178-180.

Warner, W. (2004). Changing instructor roles: Directing, teaching, coaching, & mentoring. In J. Gookin & S. Leach (Eds.), *The NOLS leadership educator notebook: A toolbox for leadership educators* (p. 101). Lander, WY: National Outdoor Leadership School.

CHAPTER 19

Effective Communication

Ten novices and their two leaders were on a long weekend backpacking trip, the purpose of which was to teach the basic skills of backpacking experientially. During the first day, the leaders used effective communication to convince their group of what route to follow, where to camp, and what to cook for dinner. Acting as instructors, the leaders taught basic backpacking concepts, attitudes, and behaviors through communicating how to light a stove, respect the natural environment, and act socially in the wilderness. That first evening, the group gathered to debrief the day's events. In this discussion, members shared their perceptions and reflections by communicating what they had learned from their first-day experiences.

On the last day, the two leaders decided to split their group so that one subgroup could take a more challenging cross-country route; the other subgroup would follow the usual trail. The leader of the trail subgroup assumed the cross-country subgroup was headed straight for the parking area, but the cross-country leader was certain they had agreed to rejoin at another junction on the trail. As a result of this miscommunication, the two leaders were stuck waiting for one another in different locations. As nightfall fast approached and group members worried about getting home to family and being late for work the next day, the two leaders began hasty search procedures to find the "lost" subgroups. Hours later they met in the dark halfway between the parking area and trail junction. It was after midnight when everyone finally arrived home. Most people were tired, and the two leaders swore they wouldn't work together again!

The need for effective communication permeates virtually all facets of adventure programming, yet communication is one of the metaskills often overlooked in leadership development (Swiderski, 1987). Communication serves as a catalyst for participant growth by providing a medium for reflection on experience, making it an essential tool for the effective facilitation of learning (Cox, 1984).

Effective communication also helps establish leadership through persuasion and influence, enhances socialization by strengthening intrapersonal and interpersonal relationships, and empowers teaching by improving dissemination of information. Without effective communication, your potential for establishing these crucial processes is severely diminished. Indeed, miscommunication can undermine everything you work to achieve through adventure programming.

COMMUNICATION DEFINED

We can define **communication** as information exchange directed at conveying meaning and understanding between two or more people. **Effective communication** occurs when people receiving the information alter their performances or beliefs on the basis of what the senders meant to convey. In short, communication involves sending a **message** along a **pathway** so that it is received the way it was intended and is effective when behavioral change results. Behavioral change may be as simple as disagreeing with the sender or as complex as overcoming a major problem, such as an addiction to an illegal substance.

A pathway of communication may contain up to three different **channels:** audio, visual, and tactile. The message may hold information in the form of ideas, actions, emotions, or a composite of all three. Typically, we convey **ideas** verbally on an audio channel; hence the receiver needs to listen carefully to the sender. We generally convey **actions** nonverbally on either the visual or tactile channels; hence the receiver needs to carefully watch or otherwise be in contact with the sender. **Emotions** may be conveyed both verbally and nonverbally; hence the receiver needs to look and listen at the same time. Truly effective communication requires both sender and receiver to practice active listening and observation.

One-Way Communication

In order to better understand information exchange, consider a simple linear sequence along which a message is passed in one direction (see figure 19.1). The subsequent addition of feedback makes the model two-way, or fully transactional (Chase & Priest, 1990). But first, let's examine one-way communication.

One-way communication can be a nine-stage process:

1. The sender **generates** the concepts, feelings, or behaviors to be communicated. This is accomplished when the sender thinks about the concepts, feelings, and behaviors.

2. The sender converts thoughts into an **encoded** message. In this message, cognitive concepts become verbal ideas, internal feelings are expressed as external emotions, and visualized behaviors are put into physical actions.

3. The sender establishes a link, or **connection,** between himself and the receiver using eye contact (visual), physical touch (tactile), or personal names (verbal). Failure to link before communicating usually means that the receiver has a difficult time receiving the message.

4. The sender **sends** the encoded message of ideas, emotions, and actions to the receiver.

5. The message is **transmitted** along a combination of the audio, visual, and tactile channels of the communication pathway.

6. The receiver **receives** the message from the sender.

7. The receiver **decodes** the verbalized ideas, externalized emotions, and physical actions. Verbal ideas become cognitive concepts again, external emotions convert to internal feelings, and physical actions are visualized as intended behaviors.

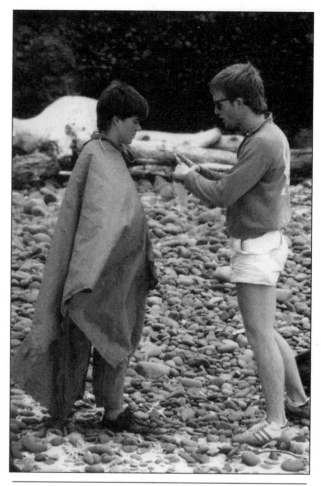

Messages are communicated by actions as well as words.

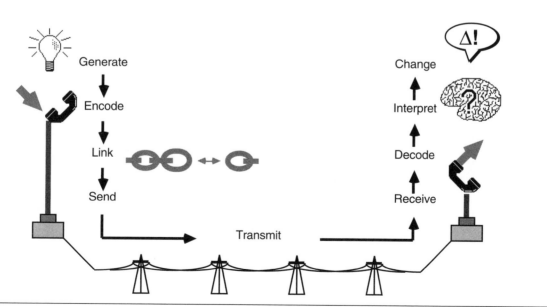

Figure 19.1 A one-way model of communication.

8. The receiver **interprets** the intent of these concepts, feelings, and behaviors.

9. Based on her perceptions of the communicated message, the receiver positively or negatively responds to the message through **changed** performance or beliefs.

For example, say you want a client to stop littering. Communication can be as direct and deliberate as touching the client on a shoulder, making eye contact, and using a first name followed by a verbal request not to litter. Communication can also be as indirect and subtle as saying nothing, but picking up the litter in front of the client so that no one else notices. Your approach depends on many factors, not the least of which is the client's receptivity to change.

Noise

Noise can interfere with communication and may be classified as semantic, internal, or external. Figure 19.2 illustrates several examples of each noise classification as well as the location of interference.

Semantic noise impacts the encoding or decoding stages and results from how words are used and defined. Technical jargon prevents understanding, and a language difference brings misunderstanding. For example, if you use words unfamiliar to clients, you may severely limit the effectiveness of your teaching. Jargon beyond the conceptual understanding of clients may reduce their motivation. Consider slang terms specific to a particular outdoor pursuit, like "dyno" and "pro" in rock climbing. You need to explain these terms to uninitiated clients; otherwise they may feel left out or spoken down to, and you may possibly turn them off to the learning experience. The same word or expression may have a different meaning in a field outside the adventure profession, like "being certified" in outdoor leadership and "being committed" in psychiatric hospitals. Clients may interpret the word or expression in the context of their own cultures or experiences, which may lead to an unfortunate misunderstanding that may inhibit their learning. But you can reduce these misunderstandings and increase learning by simply explaining any unusual terms you use during an adventure experience.

Internal noise influences the generating, interpreting, or changing stages. This interference is commonly the reason for client resistance. Internal noise refers to interference within the minds of the sender and receiver. Mental blocks prevent people from generating ideas, actions, or emotions. Much like a writer's block, senders sometimes can't think of what to say, feel, or do in certain situations. A kind of mental "short circuit" occurs, and they don't say what they mean or they say what they don't mean! Moreover, personal values temper the interpretation of messages as receivers filter them

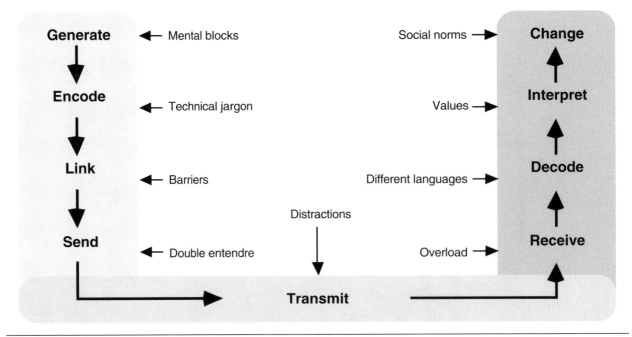

Figure 19.2 Locations of semantic, external, and internal noise interference.

through their moral systems, determining what the messages mean in relation to personal beliefs and ethical opinions. Receivers may totally ignore the message when it opposes their values or may blindly accept the message when it happens to be similar to their values. Furthermore, social and environmental norms may occasionally prevent people from changing in response to a communicated message.

The following are two examples of internal noise in the same experience. Say when working with a group of at-risk youth from two rival gangs, one participant begins to experience a series of breakthrough realizations and positive changes through adventure activities. As this participant's behavior becomes more functional, for example, as she starts cooperating with adults, assisting rival gang members in the group, and asking how she can change her life when she returns to reality, the "noise" these changes make directly conflicts with her past belief system, that is, the generating stage. As she offers assistance to rival gang members, they begin to wonder, "Is this person for real?" The rival gang members then develop internal noise in their interpretation stage of communication. They may think, *This rival gang member appears sincere in helping me and wanting to be my friend. Is this truly sincere behavior or is she setting me up like last time so she can take advantage of me?*

As we saw in these two examples, when existing environments are not conducive to change, change becomes extremely difficult because of internal noise. Clients may remain resistant to change, inhibiting your success in facilitating change until the true messages can speak or be heard more loudly than the internal noise. This may require the client to alter her personal belief system and view of social structure.

External noise influences the linking, sending, receiving, or transmission stage and refers to interference outside the minds of the sender and receiver. Barriers prevent links from being established. For example, in white-water paddling, the roar of a rapid can prevent audio contact. In climbing, the distance between climbers can prevent tactile contact. In skiing, a snow blizzard can prevent visual contact. In all three cases, communication cannot even begin without an established link.

Another communication involves the double entendre, which occurs when a message is sent with mixed meanings or when information on one channel does not agree with information on another channel, like shaking the head "no" while

saying "yes." This disagreement confuses receivers since they interpret two independent messages with opposing meanings as one communication.

Overload is caused by a rapid influx of information. The human brain can convey information through the mouth about 10 times faster than the human ear can accept and transfer it back to the brain. When a sender speaks too fast, the receiver commonly suffers from information overload, and a state of overarousal ensues. Distractions can divert the attention of both sender and receiver during the transmission of a message, possibly disrupting the flow of information or breaking the communication link entirely. When people face a choice between attending to the communicated message and becoming diverted by a distraction, they usually base the decision on whether the message or distraction is more stimulating.

Several factors aid this process of selective perception: intensity, size or proximity, contrast, repetition, motion, and novelty. Stimuli that are extremely intense, for example, louder, brighter, tastier, smellier, or weirder to touch, tend to get people's attention more effectively than less intense stimuli. Larger and proximal (closer) stimuli are more readily attended to by people than smaller objects located farther away. People also pay attention to stimuli that stand out from the immediate surroundings because of contrasting shade or color. Repeated stimuli are likely to get attention—a key reason for repeating important points when communicating. Moving stimuli are more readily attended to than stationary ones. Finally, people pay attention to stimuli that are novel or new in order to do away with the routine or the familiar and maintain a comfortable level of arousal.

These forms of noise may negatively impact communication. **Feedback** can provide one method of defense against ineffective communication.

Feedback and Two-Way Communication

Knowing that some of your message may be lost when noise is present, you can employ feedback techniques to improve your communication. By encouraging clients to give and gather feedback, you can double-check that the receiver's interpretation accurately matches the generation by you, the sender. **Transactional feedback** comes in three forms: paraphrasing, impression checking, and behavior description (see figure 19.3).

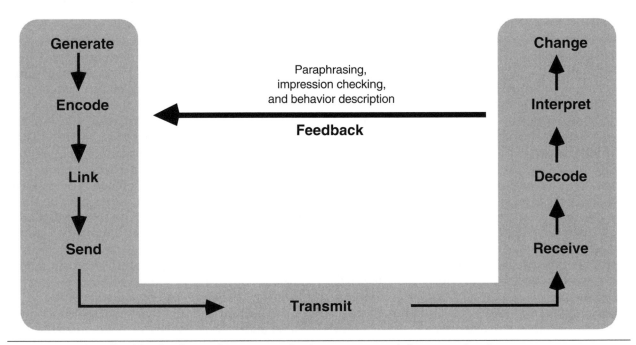

Figure 19.3   The role of feedback in making communication two-way, or fully transactional.

Paraphrase to confirm concepts and determine if the receiver correctly understood the sender's ideas. Paraphrasing is more than merely repeating a statement word for word: it is thoroughly reiterating the statement using different words. Use examples and opposites to help make paraphrasing more effective.

Check impressions to double-check feelings and determine if the receiver has correctly understood the sender's emotions. Read nonverbal clues, or body language, and then describe the perceptions and impressions of the underlying affective state.

Describe behavior to substantiate the observed actions and behaviors of a sender. The receiver descriptively reports observations without evaluating or accusing and without the influence of personal biases toward the sender.

Feedback is most effective when it is dynamic, noncoercive, considerate, descriptive, accurate, and recent (Jung, Howard, Emory, & Pino, 1971). First, make feedback dynamic, that is, about something the person can change. For example, discussing voice stuttering as a barrier to communication is both inappropriate and ineffective. Second, don't coerce or allow anyone else to coerce the person to change. Telling even the least stubborn individual that he must do something will meet with opposition. Third, give and make sure others give feedback in a considerate manner, staying aware of the possible ramifications and consequences of

change (Doran, 2004). In other words, you should consider what will happen if this person takes the advice. Fourth, make the feedback descriptive by reporting observations without inference or implication. For example, gently mention the number of interruptions but not an apparent lack of politeness. Fifth, be accurate. Avoid using value-laden or biased statements: don't judge or prejudge others. Sixth, maintain recency. Give feedback immediately so that it directly relates to the present. Don't discuss water under the bridge!

Finally, feedback is more likely to be heard and accepted if it is delivered as "two apples and an onion." The apples represent positive feedback of a complimentary nature: it tastes good and people enjoy getting it. The onion represents the negative feedback of a critical nature: it doesn't taste so good, but is still edible. For example, when constructively critiquing a person's teaching presentation, mention the good parts first, add the bad bits that need work, and end with a positive comment. Although difficult to achieve in all critiques, this approach proves reliable because two apples tend to soften the impact of an onion and because it permits the receiver to digest all the feedback and act on it later. To continue the analogy, feedback must be digestible; otherwise the receiver may regurgitate the onion and the two apples as well. You can increase the digestibility by clarifying with examples and metaphors.

IMPROVING COMMUNICATION

The responsibility of improving communication lies in your being perceived as a trustworthy and credible sender, your becoming an active listener and observant receiver, and your ability to establish appropriate rapport with your participants (Raiola, 2003). Indeed, being a trustworthy and credible sender goes a long way toward effectively communicating a message. Johnson (1986) cites several factors that affect sender trustworthiness and credibility:

- Validity of the sender as a knowledgeable information source with expertise
- Openness of the sender in relation to motives, in other words, the sender has no hidden agendas
- Enthusiasm and friendliness of the sender toward other people, especially the receiver
- Majority opinion about placing trust and confidence in the sender

The hallmarks of an active listener and observer include watching the sender carefully for any decipherable body language, giving and gathering feedback to determine that the message received was indeed the message sent, and taking the time to absorb every piece of information and process it within the context of the communication, even if a silent pause is necessary. While actively listening and observing may take much time and effort, your rewards will be great, and you will reduce the potential for costly miscommunications.

You may further improve your listening and observational skills by getting a sense of sympathy or empathy for the sender by imagining what the situation must feel like in the sender's shoes or how things must look from the sender's perspective. Other improvements you might use include gaining an awareness of your personal biases that block active listening and observing skills, attending to communications among other people to identify good and bad examples of active listening and observing skills, doing away with bad listening and observing habits by showing genuine interest and courtesy toward the sender, and practicing giving and receiving feedback (Doran, 2004; Johnson, 1986).

Poor listeners and observers can be identified by their frequent use of automatic conversation extenders, such as "okay," "all right," "uh-huh," "oh, yeah," and "yep," combined with a tendency to interrupt, jump on key points without considering context, and ignore body language. They hurry the sender by finishing sentences, avoid eye contact or physical touch, and fail to provide the sender with feedback. Instead of listening to and observing the sender, these people are simply formulating their own response.

Take, for example, the following situation. In discussing which route to take to reach a summit, one group is presenting its idea. Say that another student, Mike, has formulated his own idea about how to reach the summit that he believes is obviously better. During the group's presentation, Mike tacitly responds by a few "okays," "all rights," "uh-huhs," "oh, yeahs," and "yeps" to give the social appearance that he is truly listening. But Mike is also looking at his map, considering how he can sway the

◄ EFFECTIVE OUTDOOR LEADERS ►

- Clearly state ownership of messages by speaking for themselves, rather than for others, and by using first-person language such as "I" statements.
- Encode messages specifically by thinking carefully before phrasing concepts.
- Finish one message before starting another, avoiding sending multiple or mixed messages.
- Suit the message to the receiver by avoiding technical jargon and by speaking the same language.

- Repeat messages by restating key points.
- Send messages on more than one channel, equalizing verbal and nonverbal messages by making sure statements and body language agree.
- Disclose personal emotions and actions by using figures of speech, metaphors, and plenty of examples.
- Ask for feedback often, providing, in turn, appropriate feedback.

group to his way of thinking, and not listening to and observing the senders. Effective listening requires that verbal as well as nonverbal focuses match.

SUMMARY

Communication is a key metaskill that you, as an outdoor leader, should hone. Effective communication is an information exchange between two or more people that results in behavioral change. A sender transmits a message containing information in the form of ideas, actions, and emotions along audio, visual, and tactile pathways.

One-way communication is a nine-stage process: generating, encoding, linking, sending, transmitting, receiving, decoding, interpreting, and changing. Two-way, or transactional, communication uses feedback to reduce the impact of noise, whether semantic, internal, or external, that can interfere with each of the nine stages and to confirm that the message received was the same message sent. Feedback in the form of paraphrasing, checking impressions, and describing behavior should be dynamic, noncoercive, considerate, descriptive, accurate, and recent. Being perceived as a trustworthy and credible sender and becoming an active listener and observant receiver are the keys to improving communication.

QUESTIONS TO THINK ABOUT

1. Recall a time when you effectively communicated critically important information to someone. Describe this process using the nine steps in the one-way model of communication.

2. Recall a time when noise interfered with your attempts at communication. Describe the interference in terms of the types of noise and discuss in terms of the one-way model of communication.

3. Recall a time when you miscommunicated with someone. Describe how you might have used feedback in the two-way model of communication to prevent the error. Detail how you should have done this using the six criteria of effective feedback.

4. As an outdoor leader, what can you do to become a more effective communicator?

REFERENCES

Chase, R., & Priest, S. (1990). Effective communication for the reflective leader. *Journal of Adventure Education and Outdoor Leadership, 7*(1), 7-12.

Cox, M. (1984). Leadership training and development. *Peak Viewing, 19,* 6-12.

Doran, M. (2004). Communication skills. In J. Gookin & S. Leach (Eds.), *The NOLS leadership educator notebook: A toolbox for leadership educators* (pp. 33-34). Lander, WY: National Outdoor Leadership School.

Johnson, D. (1986). *Reaching out: Interpersonal effectiveness and self-actualization.* Englewood Cliffs, NJ: Prentice Hall.

Jung, C., Howard, R., Emory, R., & Pino, R. (1971). *Interpersonal communications: Participant material.* Portland, OR: Northwest Regional Education Laboratory.

Raiola, E. (2003). Communication and problem-solving in extended field-based outdoor adventure education courses. *Journal of Experiential Education, 26*(1), 50-54.

Swiderski, M. (1987). Soft and conceptual skills: The often overlooked components of outdoor leadership. *Bradford Papers Annual, 2,* 29-36.

Experience-Based Judgment

In estimating the time of arrival at a distant camp, two leaders base their predictions on past experience and reasoning. From a previous mastery of map reading, they know the direct distance by map scale, the elevation change according to contours, and the expected vegetation or terrain they'll encounter from the colors and symbols on the map.

But they also know from experience that maps are not always correct. Each leader can recall past incidents in which a map failed to show changes in a trail system, incorrectly interpreted the lay of the land from data gathered by aerial photographs, or was simply out of date regarding recent logging and mining operations. Nevertheless, they need to determine the time it may take their group to reach the camp.

They base their first estimate on the past experience of backpacking on similar trails with groups of this size, age range, competence, and fitness.

They expect a pace of about 5 km/h (3 mi/h) on the flats. They refine this estimate because the trail may change elevation frequently and travel through dense forest, so they figure on 3 km/h (2 mi/h), since this is the lower end of what they feel the group is capable of doing. Last, one leader recalls a recent experience in which a group member became exhausted on the previous trip and is concerned that this may happen again. The leaders finally decide to allow 4 h to travel the estimated 10 km (6 mi) to camp.

On the way, they encounter unexpected deviations from the map and are not moving as fast as they had expected as group members become tired. They reassess their calculations and update the estimated time of arrival every hour or so. As they gain new experience from their earlier estimation errors, their subsequent predictions become more accurate.

Remember, adventures are defined by an uncertain outcome. The uncertainty is created because important information is missing, vague, or unknown. Consider these examples:

1. Uncertain fragility of a rock climbing hold
2. Absence of key knowledge on the avalanche stability of a snow slope
3. Vague obstacles downstream on a new river during high water
4. Unknown reactions to risk by group members

In all these situations in which you need information you cannot easily obtain, problem solving or decision making becomes difficult or even stalls temporarily until this critical information becomes available. To solve the problem or make the decision in such cases, use the indispensable tool of judgment for estimating the uncertainty, substituting for the missing, guessing about the vague, and predicting in place of the unknown. With this "newly created" information, you can continue with the problem-solving or decision-making process (Priest, 1988).

But you only need to use your judgment when uncertainty is present. Interestingly enough, this is all the time in adventures! Since you operate under uncertain circumstances most of the time, you cannot possibly anticipate when a problem or decision may come along. Furthermore, adventure

program administrators cannot prepare standard responses to all situations, because each situation is unique in its uncertainty. To be an effective outdoor leader, your forte must lie in your ability to effectively solve many problems and frequently make accurate decisions in these uncommon situations. Such effectiveness and accuracy depend on sound judgment (Petzoldt, 1984, p. 42).

THE JUDGMENT CYCLE

We can view judgment as a cycle of three reflective processes: inductive, deductive, and evaluative. Let's look at each closely.

Inductive reflection creates general concepts from specific experiences. For example, show children specific pictures of various birds and fish, and they will form general concepts about fish and birds. The more pictures they see and the more information they are told, the more accurate their concepts become.

Deductive reflection makes specific predictions based on general concepts. For example, show the same children a picture of a penguin, asking them to identify it as a bird or a fish, and they will make a prediction based on what they believe to be the truth about penguins.

We use **evaluative reflection** to analyze the accuracy of the prediction, and then we use this analysis as a new specific experience to help us define the general concept or refine the base of experience. For example, if the children's prediction is incorrect (fish), then the children need to identify why they were wrong (swims in water) and use that evaluation to modify their concepts of birds and fish accordingly. Similarly, if the prediction is correct (bird), then they need to identify why they were right (has a beak and feathers) and use this fact to reinforce what they already know about birds and fish.

Consider the judgment cycle diagrammed in figure 20.1 and the outdoor leadership example of backcountry navigation.

As you know, backcountry navigation involves a great deal of uncertainty, giving us the perfect example to explain how the reflection cycle develops sound judgment in outdoor leaders. Consider all the information you receive when first learning navigation: how to read a map, how to use a compass, and how to orienteer off the trail. These specific experiences are input to the brain for processing by inductive reflection. The result is numerous general concepts stored in your memory for future use, including interpreting contour lines, adjusting for magnetic declination, and purposefully aiming off.

When faced with navigating from a ridgetop down to a camp by a river, you can retrieve these general concepts from memory and output them to deductively reflect and create a specific course of action. Perhaps you will walk along the ridge to a low saddle, following the contours, drop down into

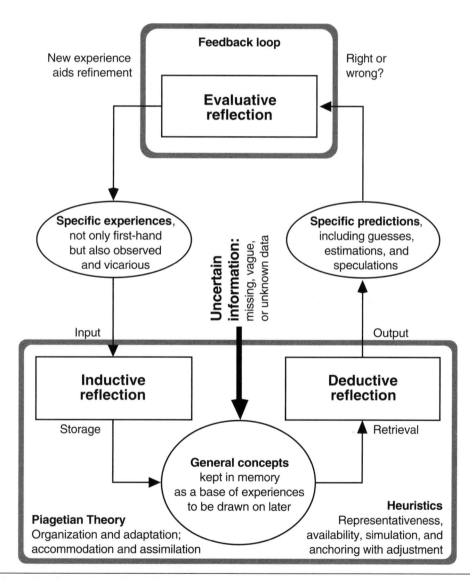

Figure 20.1   The cycle of experience-based judgment.

Adapted, by permission, from S. Priest, 1990, "Everything you always wanted to know about judgment, but were afraid to ask," *Journal of Adventure Education and Outdoor Leadership* 7 (3), 5-12.

Learning navigation involves many skills such as how to read a map, how to read a compass, and how to orienteer. The uncertainty associated with backcountry navigation can be a perfect example to explain how the judgment cycle works.

the woods on a magnetic-adjusted bearing, and head for a point deliberately upstream of the camp by aiming off, only to follow the river downstream afterward. After arriving at camp, you can evaluate the relative success of the exercise and reflect on how you may have done things differently.

But suppose you did not reach the river at the correct place and walked downstream to arrive at a lake instead of the camp. Analyzing this error may show you that your contour interpretations, bearing adjustments, aiming off, or all three may have caused the error. By reflecting on the outcome of this experience and using this new information, you can enhance any general concepts held in your memory so that you navigate better next time.

Thus, you benefit from gathering a breadth and depth of experience from as many sources as possible, not only firsthand experience but also vicarious experience gained through observation and discussion. While gathering experience is important, experience alone does not guarantee that you will have sound judgment. Certainly, experience without reflection cannot result in learning.

Inductive reflection creates a base of intensive and extensive experiences. You hold this base in long-term memory as a complex map of general concepts. The map contains facts, confirmed through repeated judgment cycles; beliefs, partially supported by experience; and hypotheses, as yet untested, arranged together by many common connections, such as the same topic, similar outcomes, and so on. When uncertainty is present and information is missing, vague, or unknown, you access the memory map of general concepts, retrieving those facts, beliefs, and hypotheses you deem to be most relevant to the circumstances. Then you subject these to deductive reflection, composing specific predictions to fill in for the uncertainties. Finally, you should hone your judgment skills and broaden your base of experience by evaluating and analyzing the effectiveness and accuracy of your predictions.

ROLE OF PIAGETIAN THEORY

The input, induction, and storage of experiences are guided by the theories of Piaget. Piaget studied the cognitive development of children and asserted that development took place in phases and at distinct ages. Although many modern researchers dispute Piaget's sequencing and precise age partitioning, most accept his original equilibrium theories of organization, adaptation, assimilation, and accommodation. These four theories form the basis of current research on logical and moral reasoning and are useful for understanding judgment.

Piaget believed that human functions are organized and adapted. **Organization** refers to the fact that these functions are arranged into distinct and coherent systems. For example, we tend to follow an organized system of reasoning and handle information in a sequential manner. This sequencing influences the way information is organized or mapped into memory as well as the way bits of information are arranged on a memory map and connected to other bits of information and to other memory maps.

We also have an exact scheme for every unit of learning. As children grow, they develop many more schemes and become increasingly complex in their organization of these schemes. **Adaptation** refers to the fact that these schemes, or systems, would not function properly had they not evolved to meet the needs of a changing environment. For example, the human reasoning system can learn to think by different and new methods, such as logically or creatively. We can weigh multiple options while decision making, or we can apply a nonevaluative form of brainstorming to problem solving. Simply put, if we couldn't adapt by finding new ways to learn or think, our inability to function would likely lead to our ultimate demise as a species.

The two complementary processes by which humans adapt schemes are assimilating and accommodating. **Assimilation** refers to fitting new and similar information into an existing scheme. **Accommodation** refers to modifying an existing scheme to incorporate new but different information. For example, consider clients learning to route-find in difficult terrain without a map or compass. The clients are inducing general concepts from specific experiences. This induction may be as simple as "Sidestepping on inclined embankments prevents slipping," or as complex as "Because of the slope of the land and underlying geological strata, the trail will always be found on the summit side of creeks." These two general concepts arose from repeated specific experiences. Every time the clients employed sidestepping, they no longer slipped. When the trail was found near a creek, it was always on the summit side with a particular slope and strata present.

But then clients note exceptions to these rules. Someone learns that digging the boot heels into the slope also prevents slipping, and someone else discovers the trail on the valley side of the creek at least once with the usual slope and strata present. The use of boot heels represents new and similar information requiring assimilation into the slipping-prevention scheme. The unusual trail discovery appears to be an exception that requires

the group to accommodate new but different information into a revised trail-location scheme. In both instances, the clients assimilate or adapt their schemes, updating their induced general concepts. Then, they keep these new schemes in their memories as bases of experience to be drawn on later.

This example illustrates how evaluative reflection can be valuable to you as an outdoor leader. By analyzing the belief that a trail will be found on the summit side of all creeks, you may reject the reasons of slope and strata and perhaps replace them with other reasons, such as soil moisture, or may confirm and retain your original reasons by finding some exception to explain the unexpected occurrence, such as a single instance of an exposed cliff bank.

ROLE OF HEURISTICS

Recall that deduction and output are guided by **heuristics,** which are simple principles or rules of thumb. Kahneman, Slovic, and Tversky (1982) outlined several heuristics that influence judgment: representativeness, availability, simulation, and anchoring with adjustment. These heuristics reduce the complexity of making a judgment by identifying similarities, recent information, and starting points relative to your memory maps of general concepts and to your base of past experience.

Representativeness

Representativeness is the extent to which information from a past situation represents or matches information needed for the current situation. When you make judgments, you search your memory map for instances that are identical or at least similar to your present predicament. Consider a white-water paddling trip during high runoff. You and your coleaders compare and assess each piece of information retrieved from memory as to how well it represents the actual river you are on. Past river trips of similar difficulty on rivers during high runoff are likely to be the memory maps you use most heavily for deductively reflecting about what to expect on this river. Obviously, everyone benefits from having had sufficient intensive experiences, conducted under stressful conditions, and extensive experiences, encompassing a variety of situations, environments, and clients, to accurately generate a diverse variety of memory maps.

Availability

Availability is the ease with which you can bring specific information to mind. In making a judgment, you are more likely to be swayed by information that is recently available or that has had a lasting impact than by information you heard a long time ago or that had little bearing on your life. For example, your perception of avalanche probability is likely to be influenced by media reports of avalanche fatalities of well-known skiers or by recent reports of good weather from the local ski resort. But you may not assign accurate importance to such influences. For example, recent negative information may lead to an overperception of avalanche probabilities, while recent positive information may lead to an underperception. This is where simulation can guide your judgment.

Simulation

Simulation refers to the ability to imagine or construct scenarios from retrieved information. Consider the risks involved in expeditioning. These risks are often determined by "imagining contingencies with which the expedition is not equipped to cope. If many such difficulties are vividly portrayed, the expedition can be made to appear exceedingly dangerous, although the ease with which disasters are imagined need not reflect their actual likelihood. Conversely, the risk involved in an undertaking may be grossly underestimated if some possible dangers are either difficult to conceive of, or simply do not come to mind" (Kahneman, Slovic, & Tversky, 1982, p. 13). The degree to which simulation is possible depends on your access to information in memory maps and your ability to combine, compare, and contrast that information. Lack of information or experience can compromise the availability–simulation heuristic and in turn lead to poor judgment.

Anchoring With Adjustment

Anchoring with adjustment is the weighing of information's importance in relation to the time the information was obtained and the interpretation of late information in light of early or already obtained information. First impressions are an excellent example of this heuristic. In estimating a person's expectations of and reaction to an adventure, you are likely to put a lot of faith in your first observation of the individual and then temper your opinion with further observations.

If the individual initially appears confident, you will likely continue to see the person in that light regardless of subsequent deviations, unless the departures are blatant. This type of anchoring is desirable because it defines a reference point from which to judge and refine judgments. Always be cautious, of course, since jeopardy may lie in the first impression being false.

DEVELOPING JUDGMENT

Sound judgment is a lot like memory capacity. It cannot be taught, but it can be developed and improved to an optimal level for any outdoor leader (Clement, 2004). Everyone has an absolute level of judgmental capacity, just as we have maximum memory capacities. However, in contrast to judgment, most people develop their maximum memory capacities in their early years, with a few pushing their limits later on in life. The trick to developing judgment lies not in regurgitating facts memorized for tests, but in reasoning. Unfortunately, instead of asking people to think for themselves and reason through the reflective processes in the judgment cycle, most educational institutions ask people to commit information to memory and reproduce it verbatim on paper for a test! This is a prime example of the fact that while society is rich in information, individuals are poor in experience. As an outdoor leader, you must break out of this trap and concentrate on processing information rather than on memorizing it. You must discard memorization in favor of three-way reflection: induction, deduction, and, especially, evaluation.

All too often, outdoor leaders forget to evaluate successful resolutions and instead analyze only those actions that failed. While analyzing failure aids learning, not evaluating success can lose an equal opportunity forever. Furthermore, the belief that people learn best from their mistakes is frequently touted as the rationale for allowing clients or leadership candidates to make plenty of errors. But this rationale concerns us because it is founded on the obvious ease of figuring out what went wrong versus the difficulty of determining why something worked so well. No matter what happens, spend plenty of time reflecting on negative and positive outcomes alike. You can learn just as much from either.

Strive to optimize your capacity for making good judgments. Try these suggestions to help hone your judgment:

◄ *EFFECTIVE OUTDOOR LEADERS* ►

► Understand the cycle of judgment and use it to follow their reasoning as they develop their judgment.

► Seek a variety of experiences that are both intensive and extensive and inductively reflect on these experiences.

► Practice making predictions (initially under appropriate supervision) by deductively

reflecting on their bases of experience (Garrett, 2002).

► Evaluate the outcomes of their predictions, examining both the successes and failures associated with their judgment.

► Review and discuss their own judgments with others, thereby improving their future judgment.

► Listen to the rules and the exceptions to those rules.

► Gather as much information as possible from lectures, historical case studies, and the horror stories of other leaders.

► Observe other leaders and how they use judgment.

► Develop a questioning attitude and inquire about the predictions others make.

► Recall personal near misses and share them openly with others.

► Consider the analyses of personal mistakes made by others.

► React, either verbally or in writing, to uncertain situations posed by other leaders.

► Keep a logbook of experiences and a judgment journal, reflecting on those experiences.

► Get experience at every opportunity: never turn down any reasonable chance to lead.

► Take a group of peers on an expedition and ask for their honest feedback.

► Undertake practical internships with several programs, always asking someone to observe you and give advice.

► Become an apprentice to an expert leader and have this mentor guide you and pass on responsibility in a gradual manner.

Above all, evaluate and thoroughly reflect on every experience.

SUMMARY

A common thought is that good judgment comes from experience—usually experience that was the result of poor judgment. In other words, you can learn from your mistakes and from everything you ever experience. But simply getting experience will not ensure that you learn what you need to know to make sound judgments. Judgment and learning are more than experience alone: each requires reflection (Gookin, 2004).

Judgment is an experience-based application of the human brain's reasoning in a cycle of three reflections. The input data are a collection of specific experiences, which are firsthand, observed, or vicarious. Inductive reflection on these experiences creates a map of connected general concepts, which you store in your memory as a base of experience from which to draw on later. When the information you need for problem solving or decision making is uncertain, missing, vague, or unknown, you search your memory maps for relevant general concepts. Then you recall these concepts and those connected with them for deductive reflection. The final output occurs when you make an estimation, substitution, guess, or prediction. Last, you evaluate whether the prediction was accurate or effective, providing new data for future cycled reflection.

Deduction and output are often guided by heuristics, or simple principles or rules of thumb. Heuristics that influence judgment are representativeness, availability, simulation, and anchoring with adjustment. Representativeness is the extent to which information from a past situation represents or matches information you need for the current situation. Availability is the ease with which you can bring specific information to mind. Simulation refers to imagining or constructing scenarios from retrieved information. Anchoring with adjustment refers to weighing the importance of information in relation to the time you obtained the information and the interpretation of late information in light of early or already obtained information.

Sound judgment is a lot like memory capacity. It cannot be taught, but it can be developed and improved for any outdoor leader. Listen to the rules and the exceptions to those rules, gather as much information as possible from other leaders, observe other leaders and how they use judgment, develop a questioning attitude, share personal experiences with others and consider their analyses, keep and reflect on a logbook of experiences and a judgment journal, gain more experience and learn from it, get honest feedback from peers and supervisors, undertake practical internships with several programs and ask for observation and advice, and become an apprentice to an expert leader and have this mentor guide you and gradually pass on responsibility. Above all, evaluate and thoroughly reflect on every leadership experience.

QUESTIONS TO THINK ABOUT

1. Differentiate among the three types of reflection. Give examples of applying each type in an outdoor leadership setting.
2. Discuss the differences among Piaget's equilibrium theories.
3. Describe the roles that various heuristics play in deductive reasoning.
4. Identify key components of the judgment cycle in the introductory vignette.
5. Outline the steps you are taking to develop your judgment as an outdoor leader.

REFERENCES

Clement, K. (2004). Can judgement be learned? *Outdoor Network, 15*(1), 1, 33-37.

Garrett, J. (2002). Instructor and guide judgement: Are you training your staff effectively? *Outdoor Network, 36*(13), 1-4.

Gookin, J. (2004). *Defining and developing judgment.* In J. Gookin & S. Leach (Eds.), *The NOLS leadership educator notebook: A toolbox for leadership educators* (pp. 37-38). Lander, WY: National Outdoor Leadership School.

Kahneman, D., Slovic, P., & Tversky, A. (1982). *Judgment under uncertainty: Heuristics and biases.* New York: Cambridge University Press.

Petzoldt, P. (1984). *The new wilderness handbook.* New York: Norton.

Priest, S. (1988). The role of judgment, decision making, and problem solving for outdoor leaders. *Journal of Experiential Education, 11*(3), 19-26.

Problem Solving

The leader had a problem to solve: what would be the best way to portage a heavy load of two packs and a canoe on a long, rocky trail around a class V rapid in Big Canyon in the most appropriate amount of time? His solution was to prop the canoe at an angle against a tree and put the first pack on his front with the straps over his back and the second pack on in the usual fashion. Last, with both packs on, he stepped underneath the canoe and stood up with the canoe supported on the packs so that the canoe's weight, plus the weight of both packs, transferred to his body through the packs' suspension systems.

This solution worked really well until he became tired and wanted to rest. While trying to reverse the "dressing" process, he knelt down and propped the canoe at an angle against a large rock. While standing up from beneath the canoe, he caught one pack on the canoe. The canoe slipped from the rock onto the leader. As he struggled under the weight of two heavy packs to avoid getting hit by the canoe, he stumbled off the trail, rolled down a hill, and struck his head on a small rock. When the next group member found him, he was unconscious and bleeding heavily.

The assistant leader provided first aid and then put a group member in charge of monitoring the unconscious leader's vital signs. The group still had one day to paddle before it could get out of the steep-walled Big Canyon to a helicopter landing site. The assistant leader sent two of the strongest paddlers ahead to get help sent to the helicopter landing site, and now she had a problem to solve: what would be the best way to evacuate this victim by water?

Sometimes the solution to a little problem can create bigger problems. Although the leader's solution to the initial problem was appropriate, his solution to the subsequent problem of needing to rest was not.

Problem solving is finding answers to both simple and complex questions. In its purest mathematical form, problem solving is determining what needs to be done to one side of an equation to make it equal the other side. You find the value of missing variables and calculate the operations on either side to make them equate.

When faced with a problem, such as being lost with your group, you must figure out what to do with the situation to make it "equal" the way you would like things to turn out (Raiola, 2003). You can achieve this outcome by substituting for missing information with judgment. How? By using experience to guess trails, predict directions, and estimate distances and then combining these judgments with available information, such as what you can see on the map and in the field, and by acting on your ideas to reach a successful end result, in this case, correctly finding your way.

Problem solving closely relates to **decision making** and judgment. Decision making is choosing between options: should we do this or that? When problem solving, decision making is useful in deciding what the problem is, the one side of the equation; picking the desired outcome, the other side; choosing possible solutions; and selecting the most probable one (see chapter 22). Remember, **judgment** is logical reasoning used to reflect on past experience and substitute for missing information (see chapter 20). In problem solving and decision making, judgment is useful to restart the processes when they temporarily stall due to the uncertainty of information (Priest, 1988).

MULTIPHASE PROBLEM SOLVING

The flowchart in figure 21.1 diagrams a **multiphase model for solving problems.** The three phases are assessment, analytical, and creative. The analytical phase is scientific and segmented into several steps. It fits the rational, left side of the brain. The creative phase is holistic and is an artistic synergy perspective (it possesses a comprehensive, systemic, and interactive nature) of many techniques. It appeals to the brain's right hemisphere. Like most people, you may prefer one phase for solving problems, yet you may benefit from mixing both.

In the **assessment phase,** you question the problem's reality. If at any given moment you don't recognize a problem, then we encourage you to stay alert for problems. If you do recognize a problem, then you are obliged to enter into the analytical phase of the model.

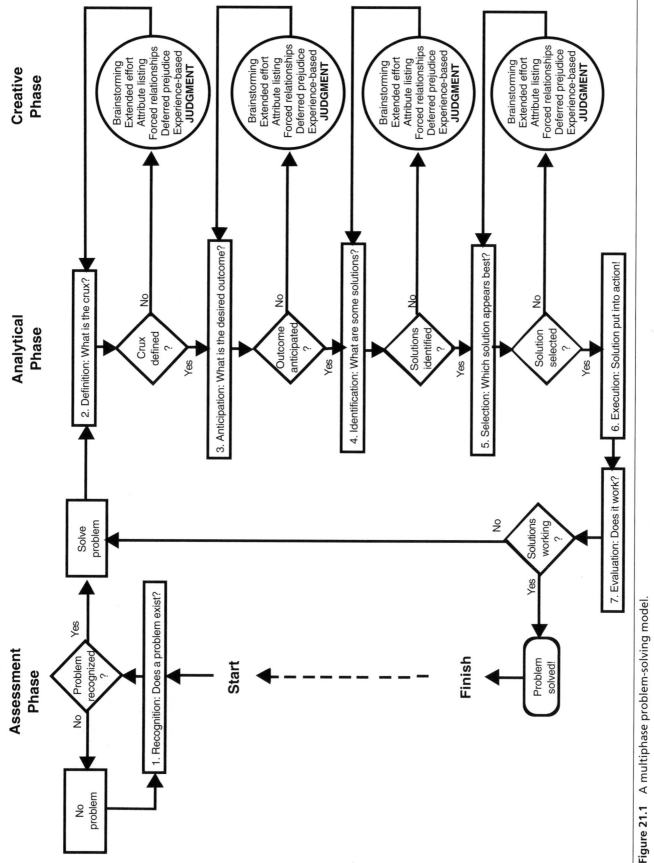

Figure 21.1 A multiphase problem-solving model.

Adapted, by permission, from S. Priest, 1988, "The role of judgment, decision making, and problem solving for outdoor leaders," *Journal of Experiential Education* 11(3), 19-26.

In the **analytical phase,** you define the crux of the problem, anticipate the outcome to be used in later evaluation, identify several possible solutions, select the most probable one, and put it into action.

If you have trouble answering "yes" to any questions of the analytical procedures seen in the next section, you generally use the **creative phase.** Creative techniques include brainstorming, extended effort, attribute listing, forced relationships, deferred prejudice, and experience-based judgment. Sound judgment can also play a role in the analytical phase and in decision making.

Once you have executed a solution, you have the final responsibility of evaluating whether the solution works. If not, you must repeat the cycle.

Analytical Procedures

The analytical phase consists of five steps represented by questions: definition, anticipation, identification, selection, and execution. If you can answer a question affirmatively, then you proceed to the next step. If you answer any question negatively, then you should use creative techniques to generate a more positive and informed response.

The initial question emphasizes **defining the crux** of the problem, or the part that is going to be the most difficult to overcome. Most problems are composed of several little problems. The trick is figuring out which one to focus on first. The next question **anticipates a desired outcome** to success. Then you can assess the outcome as criteria for evaluating the solution when you use it at a later time. Once the problem and end result are clearer, you **identify solutions** to the problem. Listing the known facts and uncertain information can help you identify possible options. Near the end of the analytical phase, you **select the probable solution** and execute it.

You make decisions at every step of the analytical phase by diverging and converging a range of options. We look at decision making as a separate metaskill in chapter 22.

Creative Techniques

The creative phase becomes necessary when answers to questions in the analytical phase are negative or when problem solving stalls. These six creative techniques may prove useful:

1. **Brainstorming** is openly expressing any idea that comes to mind without fear of criticism by other group members. By creating a receptive atmosphere, people are free to share suggestions, no matter how unusual or weird, without anyone else putting them down. The uninhibited sharing of ideas can spark creative new ideas in others. During brainstorming, the generation of ideas usually starts slow, reaches peak production, and then tapers off.

2. **Extended effort** refers to encouraging group members not to give up too quickly. By waiting through any pauses or dry spells, groups usually find that ideas generated later in the process prove to be the most creative and, occasionally, the most useful.

3. **Attribute listing** involves inventorying the characteristics of any idea or piece of the problem. Listing attributes, such as abilities, limitations, strengths, weaknesses, or required resources, helps to draw connections and formulate relationships among the ideas generated. People may possibly combine these characteristics to generate new ideas.

4. **Forced relationships** relate to comparing and contrasting ideas with an eye for creating new ideas by altering old ones. Often it is a forced substitution, combination, adaptation, modification, enlargement, reduction, reversal, or rearrangement that leads to these new ideas.

5. **Deferred prejudice** requires that people remain open to generating new ideas instead of settling on the first one that sounds good to them. By providing ample time and freedom from bias, you provide opportunities to enlarge the pool of generated ideas. You can make better choices from a larger number of ideas.

6. **Judgment,** as we discussed in chapter 20, is necessary when delaying the process due to lack of information, which might compound the problem. In other words, you must balance the need to generate creative ideas with the time restrictions dictated by the problem.

SOLVING PROBLEMS USING THE MULTIPHASE MODEL

Because adventure experiences are situationally, individually, and chronologically specific due to changing risks, competence, time variables, and the like, so is problem solving. You should recognize that no two problems are exactly alike—at least one variable will always differ—which suggests the need to avoid becoming complacent about possible solutions. Remember the portaging accident in which the leader incorrectly reversed the dressing solution to solve the undressing problem without considering that getting out from under the canoe would differ from getting under it? The problem changed in a small way that made an incredible difference.

The complexity of problems can range from simple, for which you know all variables, to complex, for which you must deal with several unknown variables. Since adventures are full of uncertainty, you will rarely come across a problem for which you have all the information; most will miss some piece to the puzzle. Solving a simple problem for which the variables appear known is a relatively straightforward process when applying a short form of the multiphase model, that is, when using only the analytical phase. Solving a complex problem with several unknowns is much more difficult, requiring you to apply sound judgment to substitute for missing information. This requires a long form of the multiphase model that includes creative techniques. Of course, you need to know the kind of problem you are solving to correctly apply the model.

You can use the model, combining analytical procedures and creative techniques, in its long and short forms. Figure 21.2 lists a few criteria for determining what form to apply to a problem. You should consider which of these criteria is most important to your preferred choice of form. To help you see what we mean, we demonstrate the short and long forms of the model shortly. For some problems, elements of one model may be necessary to assist the other. For example, you may need to use creative techniques at any step

in the short model if an answer proves elusive. Thus you might end up using both forms. So be flexible!

Short Form for Simple Problems

The short form of the model is appropriate when answers to the analytical phase come easily and positively: you simply proceed through the sequence. Although judgment does not play a formal role in this process, you cannot abandon judgment at any time while solving a problem.

The dressing problem on the Big Canyon canoe trip is a good example of the short form in action. The leader recognized a simple problem: he had to portage a canoe and two packs from the takeout across the rocky trail to the put-in. The left-hand side of the equation was complete: a collection of equipment was in an unfavorable place.

The leader defined the problem as finding a way to carry all the equipment from the takeout to the put-in without wasting time. If he had defined the problem differently, perhaps including a concern for carrying the equipment in a way that would permit easy resting, his injury might not have occurred. Instead, this leader chose time as the important criterion for evaluating success.

The leader anticipated the desired outcome to be the canoe and two packs located at the end of the rocky trail. The right-hand, or final, side of the equation was complete: the collection of equipment needed to be in a favorable place. The leader now had to move the equipment in order to equate the two sides, and as the crux suggests, he believed his real problem was finding a way to do so without wasting time.

If . . .
crux is known,
problem is simple,
desired outcome is clear,
key information is available,
consequences are expected,
range of options is complete,
time to consider is limited,
decision is *not* life-threatening,
group resources are sufficient, or
success is predictable,
. . . use the short form!

If . . .
crux is unknown,
problem is complex,
desired outcome is vague,
key information is missing,
consequences are unexpected,
range of options is incomplete,
time to consider is ample,
decision is life-threatening,
group resources are lacking, or
success is uncertain,
. . . use the long form!

Figure 21.2 When to use the short and long forms of the multiphase problem-solving model.

The leader had at least six possible solutions from which to choose:

1. Carrying the two packs and the canoe separately, thus making a total of five trips (three outgoing and two return). This first solution had the advantage of not carrying heavy loads, but had the disadvantage of covering five times the distance in triple the time of one portage.

2. Initially carrying one pack in order to become familiar with the trail and then returning for the canoe and remaining pack together, thus making three trips (two outgoing and one return). This second solution had the advantage of one heavy load and one light one, but had the disadvantage of covering three times the distance in double the portage time.

3. Initially carrying the canoe and a pack together in order to carry the difficult load before becoming tired and then returning for the last pack, thus making three trips (two outgoing and one return). Like the second, this third solution had the advantage of one heavy load and one light, but had the disadvantage of covering three times the distance in double the portage time.

4. Carrying the two packs together first and the canoe second, thus making three trips (two outgoing and one return). This fourth solution had the advantage of equal loads, but still had the disadvantage of covering three times the distance in double the portage time.

5. Carrying the canoe first and then returning for both packs together, thus making three trips (two outgoing and one return). Like the fourth, this fifth solution had the advantage of equal loads, but still had the disadvantage of covering three times the distance in double the portage time.

6. Carrying all the equipment in one trip. This sixth solution had the advantage of covering the distance once in the time of a single portage, but had the disadvantage of an extremely heavy load, which may take longer to carry due to rest breaks.

While selecting the best solution, two new alternatives arose. The seventh and eighth solutions came out of the first solution when the leader recognized he could carry the packs and canoe separately, yet in different orders (canoe, then pack A, then pack B; pack A, then canoe, then pack B; or pack B, then pack A, then canoe). In the mind of the leader, the advantages and disadvantages did not change with the order of portage, so he decided to ignore these newly evolved options and stick with considering the single option of carrying the items independently.

After considering the alternatives, he might have determined that the second and third solutions were close to identical, as were the fourth and fifth ones, since these two pairs had similar advantages and disadvantages. By collapsing these pairs, the leader narrowed the choice of solutions to four: carry the equipment one piece at a time (five trips in triple time), carry the packs together and the canoe by itself (three trips in double time), carry one pack alone and the other pack with the canoe (three trips in double time), or carry all the equipment together (one trip in single time).

Since the leader held time as an important criterion in solving this problem, he preferred the sixth solution of taking everything at once, because it afforded the least number of trips and the least time consumed. Had the leader defined the problem in terms of safety, light loads, or a balance of weight and time, he might have put a different solution into action.

Before executing the solution of carrying everything in one trip, the leader considered a contingency plan that helped reinforce the chosen solution. If he got tired during the portage, he could rest, and if the load was too much for him to carry all at once, he could drop everything and reconsider one of the other solutions. Reconsidering was possible only with the solution he had chosen. Exercising any other solution would have limited the number of solutions that he could consider after starting to portage because it would have meant that the equipment was separated on the portage trail.

In this scenario, an accident intervened and evaluation was limited strictly to the execution. Until the accident, the leader believed the solution was working and did not need modification. If the leader had completed the solution, he could have compared the arrival of the equipment at the trail's end with the desired outcome. He would have determined that the two sides of the equation were equal and that the problem was solved.

Naturally, this entire problem-solving process took place in less time than we can describe it, but maybe if the leader had slowed down and thought things through, the outcome might have been better! But not necessarily, as the short form fits simple problems—if you take the time to define the most important problem, which in this case was safety, not time.

Long Form for Complex Problems

Use the long form when answers in the analytical phase are negative or do not come easily. You will benefit from including several creative techniques to get a positive response or at least to be certain you have exhausted all opportunities to find an answer. Of course, judgment also plays a large role in this form of the problem-solving model.

The evacuation problem facing the assistant leader on the Big Canyon canoe trip is a good example of the long form in action. Let's join the group members now on the trail and see how they solve the problem. In the first step, the assistant leader has to define the crux. To her the crux is not immediately obvious, but after some discussion with the group members, they determine that the crux will be transporting the unconscious leader inside a canoe so that he is secure but will not drown if the canoe capsizes.

In the second step, they define the desired outcome, which is more obvious. They agree that a successful resolution will be transporting the leader to the helicopter landing site without further jeopardizing anyone. Safe transportation requires that they portage all major rapids, they all adequately rest when needed, and they find an acceptable method of transporting the injured leader by canoe that does not violate the first two provisions.

In the third step, identifying possible solutions may prove difficult for the leader and her group, since no quick and easy answers are available. The group begins brainstorming, facilitated and recorded by the assistant leader. Avoiding establishing boundaries, group members present some wild and crazy ideas about how to transport the leader. The assistant leader fosters the generation of ideas by preventing members from assessing the ideas when presented, by encouraging members to think harder when the stream of ideas dwindles, and by deferring their prejudices to keep them from jumping on the first good idea that comes up. Once all the ideas are out, the assistant leader helps the group list the attributes of each idea and then guides the group through combining these attributes to create new ideas through forced relationships. The creative phase generates well over 100 ideas and, after carefully considering each one, the assistant leader retains nine. Note that some built on others and that a few resulted from combining others.

Idea one suggested that the unconscious leader be lashed into a canoe with a lightweight person

Canoeing in Canyon country.

in the bow to monitor his vital signs and the strongest paddler in the stern to propel the canoe. Idea two suggested a pair of strong paddlers for extra speed during the evacuation, but no extra person to monitor vital signs due to insufficient room in the canoe. Idea three suggested rafting two canoes side by side with three paddlers in the two canoes and plenty of room left over for the leader and an attendant, but with increased canoe drag and decreased maneuverability. Idea four suggested testing any rigging before going ahead with the arrangements. Idea five suggested using the frame from a backpack to build a partial stretcher to carry the leader and to tie the stretcher across the canoe thwarts. Idea six suggested removing the central thwart to lay the stretcher on the canoe floor, thereby improving the craft's stability. Idea seven suggested the leader not be tied into the stretcher nor the stretcher be tied to the canoe. Idea eight suggested putting two personal flotation devices (PFDs) on the injured leader. Idea nine suggested attaching an extra PFD to the leader's head in order to keep it above water in the unlikely event of capsizing.

At the conclusion of this step, three solutions seemed possible (although many more could have been generated and reduced by the divergence and convergence process we will explain in chapter 22). All three solutions had the unconscious leader wearing two PFDs, with a third acting as a headrest. Solution A had the unconscious leader tied on a backpack-frame stretcher lashed across the canoe thwarts with one attendant and one paddler on board. Solution B also had the leader lying on the canoe floor without a central thwart or any lashing and with two paddlers but no attendant on board—the stern paddler would monitor vital signs. Solution C had the leader tied to a stretcher lashed across the thwarts of two canoes with three paddlers and an attendant on board.

In the fourth step, selecting the best solution from these three possibilities is a matter of eliminating one possible solution at a time by applying key criteria. In this case, the assistant leader applies the safety criteria of craft stability and speed. She recommends that solution A be dropped after testing craft stability and finding that the canoe became top-heavy and capsized easily with a volunteer on the stretcher while solutions B and C passed this test. She then eliminates solution C after a speed test determines that the raft design was slow and clumsy to propel, even with the attendant working part-time as a fourth paddler. Solution B passes the speed test.

The assistant leader subjects the remaining "best" solution to all of the important criteria to double-check for its probability of success. The assistant leader checks solution B against other criteria such as the victim's safety, victim's comfort, group safety, group comfort, and ease of monitoring vital signs. It passes all tests except two: victim's comfort and monitoring vital signs. After regaining consciousness, the leader complains that the bottom of the canoe is a very cold place to lie for an extended period. The stern paddler finds dividing attention between paddling, steering, and monitoring an extremely difficult task. Therefore, they modify solution B before putting it into action. Two extra sleeping pads are inserted

between the leader and the canoe for added insulation. A second canoe is paddled in close and parallel so as to keep a continual watch over the injured leader.

At this point, you may be feeling anxious about the time this decision-making process is taking, considering the leader's injury and lack of consciousness. But remember, it was rushing to make a decision that got the leader into trouble in the first place! Far more time will be lost if the assistant leader acts in haste as well, setting the group up for another accident. So while a group member monitors the injured leader's vital signs, let's see how our story ends.

In the fifth step, executing the solution involves clearly communicating group members' roles. We cannot emphasize enough that effective communication (chapter 19) is a critical metaskill for outdoor leaders. Before the evacuation, the assistant leader consults the map and guidebook, only to remark about the several major rapids that they will need to portage. During the evacuation, she assigns roles to the group members and places the finishing touches on the canoe and PFDs. As the evacuation proceeds, the assistant leader carefully watches the group and the injured leader, remaining alert for new problems that might crop up.

Along the way her judgment proves useful when important information turns out to be vague, missing, unknown, or otherwise uncertain. For example, she uses her judgment about people to assign an appropriate attendant for the injured leader. She uses her judgment about canoe travel at night to select a stretch of river that could be safely completed in darkness, thus permitting a very early morning start to the daylong evacuation. She uses her judgment and experience with previous rapids to extrapolate what subsequent rapids might be like, allowing her to choose which ones to portage and which ones to save time on by paddling—if she correctly predicts the rapids that are washed out by the present river levels and flow rates.

In the sixth step, evaluating the executed solution completes the circuit. In this case, the group emerges from Big Canyon and arrives successfully at the landing site, where a helicopter is waiting to fly the injured leader to the hospital. The problem is solved!

Common Breakdowns

As you might expect, the problem-solving process is prone to breakdowns. Common sources of breakdowns include stress, haste, misinformation, miscommunication, and perceived boundaries.

Stress is a primary factor influencing the breakdown of problem solving. Information may bombard you at a rate that exceeds your capacity to make wise choices. At such stressful times, rushed decisions or unsound judgments may interfere with problem solving. In contrast, in situations in which opportunities are eustressful, or pleasant, such as the perfect challenge, you are more likely to enhance your actions and perform at your best because you are optimally aroused (see chapter 4). But in situations in which opportunities are distressful, or unpleasant, such as working against adversity, you are more likely to feel rushed, and your performance may drop off correspondingly because you are overaroused.

Often emergency situations are limited by time constraints, which can rush you to respond. But remember, haste makes waste. You may miss a good possible solution in the identification step or may jump on the first likely crux that comes to mind in the definition step. When time is short, be sure you don't avoid looking for alternatives, blindly adhere to your original plan, or regress to following established procedures. Also, don't fall into the trap of changing your plans no matter what the cost, searching endlessly for alternatives until time runs out. Neither scenario is desirable, so when given insufficient time, to be an effective outdoor leader you must balance time consumption with idea generation. Take the time to seek diversity in resources and information by considering everyone's ideas. Avoid premature decisions or searching to exhaustion for that one "perfect" solution.

In the selection step, you must select a probable solution from a collection of possible ones by comparing strengths and weaknesses, testing against important criteria, and analyzing consequences. If your information for comparing, testing, or analyzing is flawed, your selection may fail to solve the problem. Thus, misinformation can break down the process. Use your judgment to reinforce and recheck information and to reduce errors in selection. Don't let your judgment be colored by exaggerating, procrastinating, or avoiding responsibility under pressure or by attempting to maintain self-respect, become accepted by peers, profit personally, or allow others to benefit. As an effective outdoor leader, you should remain as neutral as possible while solving problems.

During the execution step, ineffective outdoor leaders may miscommunicate a selected solution to their groups. When it is put into action, the solution may fail because some members were unclear or unaware of their own roles or the roles of others. Miscommunication can also interfere with information, perhaps leading to misinformation. Don't let this happen to you! Work on effective communication at all times so that when the crunch is on, you'll be ready.

Breakdowns in the creative phase often result from perceived boundaries. Thinking creatively requires you to suspend your perceptions of limited resources or capabilities, even if in reality they are truly limited. If you believe an idea won't work, it probably won't! Remaining boundless in mind and spirit directly contradicts the premise of the analytical phase in which you must set parameters at all steps in order to evaluate success. Because of this, resolving the paradox between thinking analytically "in boxes" and creatively "outside the boxes" is one of the toughest tasks in multiphase problem solving. The only answer to this quandary is to practice in actual situations, gaining intensive and extensive experience in solving actual problems under the guidance of an established mentor.

◄ EFFECTIVE OUTDOOR LEADERS ►

- ► Understand the relationships among problem solving, decision making, and experience-based judgment.
- ► Recognize problems and know when to use the short or long forms of the multiphase model to solve them.
- ► Are able to follow and utilize the five steps in the analytical phase of problem solving.
- ► Are able to name and apply the six techniques in the creative phase of problem solving.
- ► Are aware of the ways in which the problem-solving process commonly breaks down and do all that they can to prevent such breakdowns.

The mentor's role is to guide you as you develop sound judgment, decision making, and analytical and creative problem solving.

SUMMARY

Problem solving is finding answers to questions by applying an appropriate strategy to a specific situation to make it turn out the way you desire. This process includes deciding about the nature of the problem, using judgment to speculate on the value of unknowns, and combining predictions with known information to create effective solutions. Decision making is choosing between options at central steps embedded within the problem-solving process. Judgment is reasoning logically from past experience and substituting for information that is missing, vague, unknown, or uncertain. All three skills are closely related but distinctive.

Multiphase problem solving has three phases: assessment, analytic, and creative. The assessment phase involves recognizing and evaluating whether a problem exists before or after the solving process. The analytical phase contains five steps (definition, anticipation, identification, selection, and execution) you should usually follow in sequence to solve a problem. The creative phase includes six techniques (brainstorming, extended effort, attribute listing, forced relationships, deferred prejudice, and experience-based judgment); creativity proves useful when decision making stalls at one of the analytical steps. Combining the phases helps you be more effective in your problem solving than you might be using just one approach.

Problem complexity ranges from simple problems for which everything appears known to complex ones for which you must deal with several unknowns. Apply the short form of the multiphase model when solving simple problems and the long form when solving complex ones. Remember, you must grasp the complexity of the problem accurately so you can apply the correct form.

Stress, haste, misinformation, miscommunication, and perceived boundaries can obstruct the problem-solving process. With practice and sound judgment, you can overcome these potential breakdowns and be a more effective outdoor leader.

QUESTIONS TO THINK ABOUT

1. Use the short form of the multiphase model to solve a simple problem and then describe how well the model worked or didn't work for you.

2. Use the long form of the model to solve a complex problem and then describe how well the model worked or didn't work for you.

3. Identify examples of common problem-solving breakdowns you have experienced in outdoor situations. Explain how they were overcome.

REFERENCES

Priest, S. (1988). The role of judgment, decision making, and problem solving for outdoor leaders. *Journal of Experiential Education, 11*(3), 19-26.

Raiola, E. (2003). Communication and problem-solving in extended field-based outdoor adventure education courses. *Journal of Experiential Education, 26*(1), 50-54.

Decision Making

The avalanche that had buried a student was small in comparison to some of those the head leader had seen in ten years of ski patrol experience. Nonetheless, there was absolutely no sign of the student anywhere. Four hours earlier, the head leader's group of three novices had left the remaining 12 students of the skiing class with two other leaders. The two subgroups (4 and 14, respectively) were making their way to a common meeting place by different routes. With four hours of daylight left, the head leader's group of four was about two hours from the road head when the avalanche struck. The head leader began recalling the events immediately leading up to the accident.

The group of four had been traveling on the ridge top and was descending a leeward slope to reach and follow the valley floor below. The leader had "pit tested" the snow slope's substructure and determined it to be stable. Although they were above treeline, no old slide paths or running cracks had been noticed. Before descending, they had taken all the necessary precautions. Each had removed their straps on skis, poles, and packs to prevent these items from dragging them under in the event of an avalanche. All had zipped up their layers of clothing, and put their hats and mittens on to keep themselves warm. Each had placed covering handkerchiefs across their mouths and nostrils to prevent possible snow inhalation. So as not to expose more than one person to danger at any time, they moved across individually and planned to rest only at points of relative security. The leader had

gone first, planning a careful path from safety point to safety point. Given the beginning nature of the ski touring class, no one had been issued avalanche cords or radio beacons (these were rare and expensive years ago when this accident happened).

Whump! The small slab avalanche had suddenly let loose under the student's feet and thundered down the slope past the leader. The other two skiers saw the student discard a pack and attempt to swim "ferrystyle" to one side of the avalanche, but powerfully it turned the student over and over again, progressing downhill forcibly. Once the snow had settled there was nothing but pristine silence. From a distance the other skiers could not discern the fate of their friend. From their viewpoints, no one could see any visual clues that might lead them closer to the buried skier. They could only hope that as the avalanche had slowed, the student had made a last ditch effort to gain the surface or at least make an air pocket in front of his face.

The leader surveyed the slope for further danger and then assembled the remaining two students above the debris area at the last spot they had clearly seen the student. After briefly pondering the problem, the leader explained that speed and accuracy were of the utmost importance: the longer the student remained buried the lesser the chances of recovering the student alive! The leader realized the obvious problem was to how best to find the student ALIVE and thus faced making a series of very difficult decisions.

—Priest, 1988, p. 1

Decision making is choosing the most probable option from a collection of possible ones (Clement, 2004; Galloway, 2002; Gookin, 2004). The process involves **diverging,** or building a range of several options, and then **converging,** or narrowing that range to select the best option. Making decisions is necessary at several steps of the problem-solving process (D. Grube, Phipps, & A. Grube, 2002; Mitten, 2002). Recall from chapter 21 that the analytical phase of the multiphase problem-solving model contains four central steps: definition (What is the crux?), anticipation (What is the desired outcome?), identification (What are some possible solutions?), and selection (What solution appears best?). These steps require you to pick the best crux, best outcome, best possible

solutions, and best probable solution from a wide range of options.

DIVERGENCE

The wider the range of options generated through **divergence,** the better. As you know, the creative phase of the multiphase model contains several techniques that effectively diverge options: brainstorming, or expressing ideas without evaluation or criticism; extended effort, or carrying the expression of ideas through pauses; attribute listing, or inventorying problems and solutions; forced relationships, or combining, comparing, and contrasting new ideas; and deferred prejudice, or refraining from jumping on the first good idea.

In the avalanche example, the leader identified at least seven options. Two options involve outside help: first, seek a professional search-and-rescue (SAR) team (120 min to roadhead plus 60 min to phone plus 60 min return with SAR team plus 30 min for dogs to find student equals 270 min total), or second, meet up with the other subgroup to gain their assistance (120 min to find the other subgroup plus 180 min to return to accident site plus 45 min to carefully search with new and enlarged group equals 345 min total). The third through fifth options involve the small subgroup and its resources. Third, perform a hasty search with the two remaining students (5 min); fourth, perform a coarse-probe search, for example, move forward 70 cm (28 in.), probe once 2 m (6.6 ft) deep with ski poles (30 min); and fifth, perform a fine-probe search, for example, move 30 cm (12 in.) forward, probe three times 2 m (6.6 ft) deep (120 min). Still other options exist. Sixth, wait for help to find them once they become overdue (several days), or seventh, split the subgroup further, send one student for help while the leader and other student search (unpredictable time limits). Given ample time to apply divergence methods—not very possible in an avalanche situation—a group could easily enlarge the list of options.

CONVERGENCE

Convergence is generally the most difficult part of decision making. You must discriminate the best option from many options. Five methods exist to narrow the field: gathering, weeding out, organizing, weighting, and choosing.

Gathering

Gathering involves collecting all pertinent information supporting or refuting the merit of a particular option and categorizing that information under three headings: facts, or what you know as true; assumptions, or what you judge to be true; and constraints, or possible barriers to success.

Here are three facts that you could gather in the avalanche scenario. Hasty searches find victims 30% of the time. Rescue dogs have a success rate of 90%, but due to the long time required to summon them to an accident scene, the find is rarely a live one. Finally, the half-life for remaining alive after being caught in an avalanche is about 30 min. This

In environments where avalanches occur, the leader must make the best decision based on all of the options available.

means that if a victim survives the initial impact of an avalanche and is buried alive, after 30 min the probability of the victim still being alive is half what it was at the time of the avalanche; after 60 min this probability decreases to one-quarter, and it decreases again to one-eighth after 90 min.

Here are four assumptions that you might make in this avalanche scenario. Using sound judgment based on extensive and intensive experience in ski patrol, the leader estimated the chance of the student being killed by the impact of this avalanche as 36%. If a dog search were employed as a last resort, several hours after the accident, the student's chances of being alive would be very slim, maybe 1%. Since they would be probing with ski poles and the two remaining students had limited practice with this technique, the leader expected that the buried student would not be "hit" by a probe if buried deeper than 5 ft (1.5 m). Given that the avalanche debris area was small and not too deep, the leader estimated the chances of locating the student at 40% for a coarse-probe search and 80% for a fine-probe search.

Here are five constraints that you might consider in this avalanche scenario: time of day, weather, group dynamics, group members' experience, and available resources. Time is clearly of the essence since prolonged burial may lead to suffocation, but also because nightfall is a few hours away and the leader has a duty to care for the other two students. A storm is expected within 24 h, and fresh snow could increase the danger of further avalanches and could camouflage this accident site. The leader in our scenario also considered several group dynamics, including arguments, fears, loyalties, and desires as well as how the dynamics might influence the situation. The leader had already factored into the last pair of assumptions the limitations of having inexperienced students and only ski poles for probing. Furthermore, the leader considered other related concerns, including how inexperience might cause students to react in a crisis and the availability of other survival resources, such as food, water, oxygen, shelter, and warmth.

Weeding Out

Weeding out involves removing those options that are clearly inappropriate. Often a field of seven or more options is too much for most leaders to truly consider. Reducing this number to 3 or 4 options becomes more manageable. Reduce the options you are considering using the plausibility of the information you have gathered. For example, evaluate the cost of exercising the option, the consequences of putting that option into action, and so on.

In the avalanche example, the leader immediately dismissed the second, sixth, and seventh options. The second option of meeting up with the other subgroup to gain their assistance would take 345 min, and finding the buried student may still not have been possible; getting a SAR team—an option with less time and higher chance of success—was clearly a better option than the second one based on these two variables alone, especially since the leader might meet the other subgroup on the way out as a bonus. Either way, darkness would fall before help of any kind could return. The sixth option of waiting for help to find the group a few days later would certainly result in not finding the student alive. The seventh option of splitting the subgroup and sending one student for help while the leader and other student searched would put the single student at risk due to ongoing avalanche danger and to the unfamiliar route: the remaining

group members should stick together regardless of the decision.

A word of caution: don't be tempted to automatically weed out ideas during the divergent process because doing so can inhibit the generation of subsequent ideas. Weeding out is a useful step for shortening the decision-making process under certain limiting conditions, such as time, weather, and so on. When time is ample and you are competent at juggling alternatives, you can consider all options, consequences, and other information.

Organizing

Organizing involves ranking the 3 or 4 remaining options, arranging them in a decision tree. The decision tree is a simple drawing that details your possible choices and the probable chance events that might occur in the course of a solution. You can draw each decision and chance event as branching forks on the tree that divide into separate paths on the basis of choices made. The advantage of a decision tree is that it pairs all options to create choices between two options at a time rather than all options at once. The fewer options to choose from, the easier and more efficient choosing becomes. Ordering enables you to examine any situation from its component decisions, making the overall situation more manageable.

With the avalanche example, the leader arranged the options into two categories: go for help or search without help. The leader further ordered the "search without help" options from quickest to slowest: a hasty search to a slow, fine probe. In this instance, the decision tree contained three choices: go for help or hasty search without help, then go for help or coarse-probe search without help, and then go for help or fine-probe search without help. But you also have to consider the flexibility, alternatives, and contingencies for each decision so that you don't get locked into a dangerous, irreversible direction. In this case, you could also stop searching at any time and seek outside help, and if searching was futile, then getting help would be the final option.

Figure 22.1 summarizes the decision tree for the avalanche vignette with three decision forks (black squares) and a dozen chance-event forks (white circles). Chance-event forks represent the various probabilities of success and failure for each of the options as determined during the information gathering.

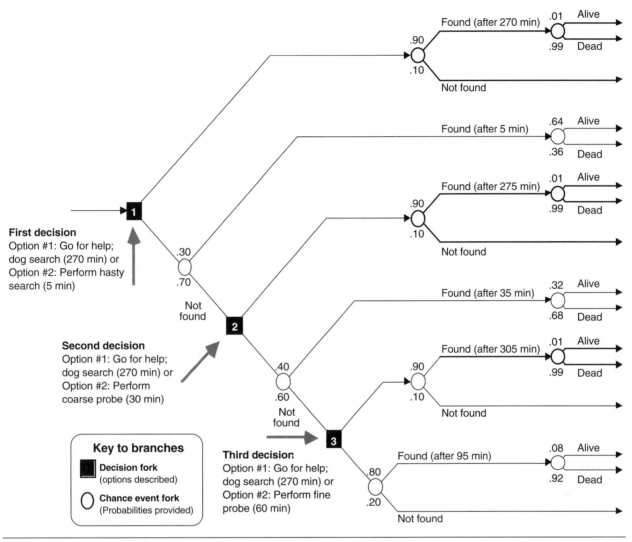

Figure 22.1 Decision tree for the avalanche example.

Adapted, by permission, from S. Priest, 1988, "AVALANCHE! Decision analysis: one way to solve problems," *Journal of Adventure Education and Outdoor Leadership* 5(3), 14-16.

Look at figure 22.1 and picture yourself as the leader in this scenario. The first decision has two options: go for help and return with a dog search team or perform a hasty search. If you elect the former option, then the search team will take over and you will have no further decisions to make. If you elect the latter option, then the student will be either found or not found. If he is not found by hasty search, the need for a second decision arises.

The second decision also has two options: go for help and return with a dog search team or perform a coarse-probe search. If you elect the former option, then again the search team will take over. If you elect the latter option, then the student will be either found or not found. If you

do not find him by coarse probing, then the need for a third decision arises.

Like the others, the third decision has two options: go for help and return with a dog search team or perform a fine-probe search. If you elect the former option, then the search team will take over. If you elect the latter option, then the student will be either found or not found. If you do not locate him by fine probing, you should seek professional assistance as nightfall fast approaches.

Weighting

Weighting involves considering the positive, neutral, and negative aspects of each option at each decision point in the decision tree. For the avalanche example, this means including the probabilities of finding the student by each search method and the probabilities that the student will be alive given the time that has elapsed when the student is finally found.

Going for help and returning with a dog search team has a 90% chance of finding the student and a 10% chance of not finding him. The hasty search has a 30% chance of finding the student and a 70% chance of not finding him. The coarse-probe search has a 40% chance of finding the student and a 60% chance of not finding him. The fine-probe search has an 80% chance of finding the student and a 20% chance of not finding him.

Since the half-life for remaining alive after being caught in an avalanche is about 30 min and the estimated chance of the student being killed by impact was 36%, you can calculate the probability of a live find for each option from the cumulative duration of the searches. After an immediate hasty search, the student has a 64% chance of being alive (100 – 36). After a coarse-probe search, the student has a 32% chance of being alive (since 30 min have passed, the probability of success has been cut in half [64 ÷ 2 = 32]). After a fine-probe search, the student has only an 8% chance of being alive because another two 30 min periods have expired, cutting the probability in half twice more (32 ÷ 2 = 16; 16 ÷ 2 = 8). Due to the length of time needed to secure a dog search, the student has less than a 1% chance of being alive after 270 or more min.

Choosing

Choosing involves selecting a path through the decision tree by picking the preferred option at each decision point. The preferred option is the one with the best overall probability of success. When several factors are at play, overall probability is the product of all probabilities. For the avalanche example, this means multiplying the probability of finding the student by the probability of a live find.

In the first choice, going for help and returning with a dog search team has an overall success probability of 0.9%, based on a 90% chance of finding the student and a less than 1% chance of finding him alive (90 × 0.01 = 0.9). The hasty search has an overall success probability of 19.2%, based on a 30% chance of finding the student and a 64% chance of finding him alive (30 × 0.64 = 19.2). The better first decision clearly is to perform a hasty search. In the second choice, getting help still has an overall success probability of 0.9% while

the coarse-probe search has an overall success probability of 12.8%, based on a 40% chance of finding the student and a 32% chance of finding him alive (40 × 0.32 = 12.8). Clearly, the better second decision is to perform a coarse-probe search. In the third choice, going for help still has an overall success probability of 0.9% while the fine-probe search has an overall success probability of 6.4%, based on an 80% chance of finding the student and an 8% chance of finding him alive (80 × 0.08 = 6.4). Clearly, the better third decision is to perform a fine-probe search. Although getting help is the last resort and is never the first preference due to poor probability that the victim will be found alive, these values could change given closer proximity to a professional SAR team. The lengthy response times make success unlikely for this scenario, but, remember, every decision-making situation is unique.

Overwhelmed with numbers in the weighting and choosing phases? In this example, we have used a **quantitative** method of weighting that is difficult for leaders who are not mathematically inclined or who are unable to juggle and balance several numbers in their heads. We look at a **qualitative** method of weighting in the next section.

QUALITATIVE MODIFICATIONS

You can't break every decision down into quantifiable probabilities. In fact, you will be able to deal with the majority of decisions by effectively considering the qualities of the information you gather for any option. Picture yourself as a bicycle trip leader with a choice of six different routes to take between campsites as mapped in figure 22.2. Driving to the next campsite or staying put are two other options available to you. The problem facing you is how to best balance existing risks with biking pleasure.

By interpreting the map and using judgment, you should gather the facts and assumptions of the six routes. Route 1 (15 mi, 24 km) is a straight line along a major divided highway with a very high volume of traffic, no shoulder, and gentle grades. Route 2 (50 mi, 80 km) follows and crosses a creek on a scenic winding route on hard-packed paths along old railway grades. Route 3 (30 mi, 48 km) has light traffic on a hilly, gravel back road, part of which follows a flat railway cut with a section of road missing, and you think walking the bikes along the side of the tracks might be possible there. Route 4 (20 mi, 32 km) follows minor highways with heavy traffic and parallels

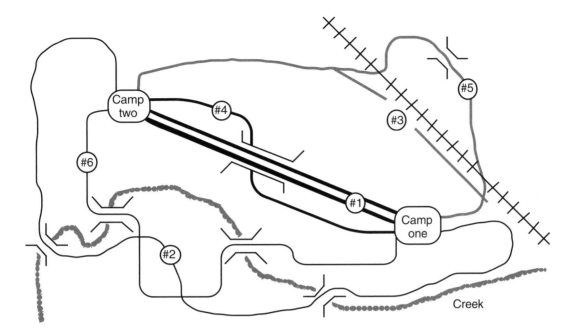

Qualities	Route #1	Route #2	Route #3	Route #4	Route #5	Route #6
Dangers	No shoulder	Bridges	Walk by rail	Underpass	Rail crossings	Bridges
Concerns	Straight	Winding	Missing bit	Straight	Steep hill	Straight
Road type	Highway	Bike path	Back road	Highway	Back road	Farm road
Traffic	Extreme	None	Light	Heavy	Light	Moderate
Terrain	Gentle grade	Flat	Hilly and flat	Gentle grade	Mtn. pass	Flat
Surface	Paved	Hard-packed	Gravel	Paved	Dirt	Paved
Distance	15 miles	50 miles	30 miles	20 miles	35 miles	40 miles
Key points of interest	None	Scenic	None	None	Nice views	Scenic

Figure 22.2 Tabulated summary of the six bike routes.

the major highway and cuts underneath it at one point. Route 5 (35 mi, 56 km) duplicates 3, except that it crosses the railway instead of following it and climbs over a steep mountain pass with nice views on dirt back roads. Route 6 (40 mi, 64 km) rambles along paved farm roads with moderate traffic, crossing the same scenic creek as 2, but by a less direct route of straight segments and right-angled turns. Remember, you also could just drive to the next campsite or hang around the same campsite all day.

Because you are seeking a balance of risk management and enjoyment, you should probably drop the two options of driving to the campsite or staying put for the day during weeding out. Certainly, driving or hanging around doesn't let anyone enjoy bicycling. Once you have weeded out the superfluous options, the six routes remain. This is a large number to subject to the next step,

but you could reduce it by applying some additional criteria, such as avoiding vehicle fumes or hills and seeking paved surfaces or scenery.

Organizing the six routes into a qualitative comparative table, as done in figure 22.2, replaces the quantitative decision tree. The figure is a simple way to compare and contrast the pros and cons of the available options. For the six options, we list qualities worth considering in order of importance and then show sample responses.

Qualities are typically organized around the three themes of positive, such as alternatives, benefits, contingencies, and points of interest; neutral, such as costs, distances, terrain, road type, and surface; and negative, such as traffic and other dangers, concerns, and possible consequences. You don't have to include all themes in such a comparative table, but to be the most effective, you should consider all the available information and evaluation criteria. For example, alternatives and contingencies are often overlooked variables to any consequences that might result if you select an option and put it into action. You should take into account any contingency plan that might make an option more desirable and prepare an alternative plan in case the option you select falls short of expectations.

When following a qualitative approach to weighting the content of these tables, you may prefer to avoid numerical quantities. While the mathematical leader might correctly state that negatives are half the concern, positives a third, and neutrals the remaining sixth (or a similar weighting), this approach is not qualitative. Instead, you may mentally cross out the entries that are equivalent options, recognizing that entries higher on the list carry more weight in the decision.

For example, you can view entire options and entries between options or within the same option as "six of one and half a dozen of another." Exposure to extreme traffic for 15 mi without a shoulder on route 1 may be equivalent to 20 mi (32 km) of exposure to heavy traffic with an underpass to negotiate on route 4. In another light, the bridge crossings on routes 2 and 4 may equal the railway walk on route 3. For route 5, the extra energy expended for the hill climb may be worth the nice views.

For the purpose of choosing, identifying equal entries removes many of the more moderate qualities. Those few extremes that remain may allow the best option to stand out. Thus, once you have accounted for equivalencies, the reduced entries permit you to more effectively choose the option that has the strongest chance of success.

APPLICATION TO PROBLEM SOLVING

Whether you use a quantitative or qualitative approach, the same five divergent steps and five convergent steps can be an effective method for decision making. Figure 22.3 summarizes the divergent and convergent processes of making decisions.

Returning to the multiphase problem-solving model of chapter 21, divergence and convergence fit in at the definition, anticipation, identification, and selection steps. Remember, the problem-solving sequence can stall due to a lack of necessary information, including the crux, desired outcome, possible solutions, and best solution. When this happens, the creative techniques, which are also

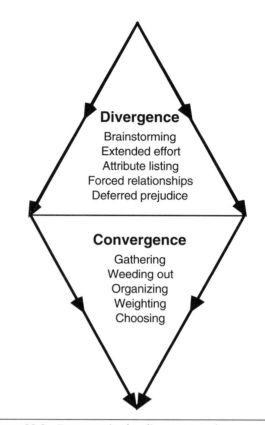

Figure 22.3 Ten steps in the divergent and convergent decision-making processes.

part of divergence, help to come up with a crux, desired outcome, list of possible solutions, or best solution, and allow problem solving to continue.

The difference in using creative techniques to restart problem solving or to generate ideas for the building in decision making lies in whether you are simply trying to find one option or choosing from a range of several options. Sometimes when all the information is present, only creative techniques are necessary to confirm that the one crux or desired outcome is the right one since no others are apparent. At other times when uncertainty is present, which is common in all adventures, you should use creative techniques to generate as many options as possible. In this instance, narrowing down these options to provide the desired outcome is necessary: the full decision-making process is appropriate.

DECISION MAKING AND LEADERSHIP STYLES

Recall from chapter 18, "Flexible Leadership Style," and chapter 5, "Group Development and Dynamics," that decision-making power can reside solely

◄ EFFECTIVE OUTDOOR LEADERS ►

- ► Know when to apply creative techniques and know how much to use them in a divergent process before beginning a convergent process.

- ► Are able to gather and categorize information as fact, assumption, or constraint.

- ► Know the maximum number of options they are capable of managing in a decision-making situation and weed out clearly inappropriate options in order to reduce that number to the maximum limit.

- ► Are able to organize the remaining options by either quantitative or qualitative approaches and know how to construct a decision tree or a comparative table, depending on their preferred approach.

- ► Are able to weight options using the relevant information they have gathered.

- ► Are able to choose the option with the greatest chance of success for resolving the situation.

- ► Develop reasonable alternative and contingency plans and consider these alternatives and contingencies when choosing the best option.

- ► Determine who should be included in the decision-making process and clearly communicate that determination using the appropriate leadership style (autocratic, democratic, or abdicratic) for the situation.

with you the leader (autocratic) or with the group (abdicratic), or can be shared between you and your group (democratic). Likewise, the divergent and convergent process can be used solely by you, your group, or a combination of both. Remember that some situations, such as emergencies, demand that you alone make the decision, while other decisions, such as what to have for dinner, can be the group's responsibility. The fewer people involved in deciding, the better, because many varied opinions are difficult to resolve. Sometimes the group members are going to want involvement, especially in decisions where much is at stake or where they believe they have expertise to share. You must make clear to everyone who is part of the process, who is not, and why you have made these decisions to include or exclude group members.

SUMMARY

Decision making is choosing the most probable option from a collection of possible ones. The process involves diverging, or building, a range of several options and then converging, or narrowing, that range to select the best option. The divergent process of decision making utilizes the same creative techniques found in multiphase problem solving: brainstorming, extended effort, attribute listing, forced relationships, and deferred prejudice. Such creativity should lead to many more ideas in decision making than in problem solv-

ing. The convergent process of decision making uses five methods to narrow the field of options: gathering, weeding out, organizing, weighting, and choosing.

Gathering involves collecting all pertinent information that supports or refutes the merit of a particular option. Weeding out involves removing those options that are clearly inappropriate based on how plausible you evaluate them to be. Organizing involves ordering the 3 or 4 remaining options and arranging them into a decision tree for the quantitative approach or into a comparative table for the qualitative approach. Weighting involves considering the positive, neutral, and negative aspects of each option. Choosing involves selecting the preferred option with the best chance of success on the basis of having the most positives and the least negatives.

QUESTIONS TO THINK ABOUT

1. You are leading a hiking trip with a dozen 11- and 12-year-old students and one other coleader. You stop at a trail junction to count heads and realize one student is missing. List all of the important pieces of information. Using this information and the divergence and convergence model, decide what you would do as a leader.

2. Make another decision using the divergence and convergence model and then discuss

which aspects of the model worked well and which ones didn't.

3. Now make two similar decisions using the quantitative and qualitative approaches (one for each decision) and compare and contrast the strengths and weaknesses of each approach.

REFERENCES

Clement, K. (2004). Can judgement be learned? *Outdoor Network, 15*(1), 1, 33-37.

Galloway, S. (2002). Theoretical cognitive differences in expert and novice outdoor leader decision making: Implications for training and development. *Journal of Adventure Education and Outdoor Learning, 2*(1), 19-28.

Gookin, J. (2004). *Judgment and decision-making.* In J. Gookin & S. Leach (Eds.), *The NOLS leadership educator notebook: A toolbox for leadership educators* (pp. 37-38). Lander, WY: National Outdoor Leadership School.

Grube, D.P., Phipps, M.L., & Grube, A.J. (2002). Practicing leader decision-making through a systematic journal technique: A single case analysis. *Journal of Experiential Education, 25*(2), 220-230.

Mitten, D. (2002). An analysis of outdoor leaders' ethics guiding decisions. *Proceedings from The Coalition for Education in the Outdoors 6th Biennial Research Symposium.*

Priest, S. (1988). AVALANCHE! Decision analysis: One way to solve problems. *Journal of Adventure Education and Outdoor Leadership, 5*(3), 14-16.

Professional Ethics

A group of students on a wilderness-based experiential education course were having a hard time learning the fundamentals of emergency first aid. They were not taking the lessons seriously and wanted to go climbing instead, claiming that first aid was not very important or [was] boring to learn. The instructor of the group had the assistant instructor sneak into the woods where she feigned a severe accident. Cosmetic devices were used to give the injury the look of an actual accident. Hearing her screams, the students ran over and were confronted by a scene of trauma that shocked many group members and impelled them into action. Several minutes later, the group realized that the accident was staged. The instructors debriefed the group on the importance of first aid and several group members expressed their appreciation of the feigned accident. One member of the group was extremely angry that she had been deceived by the instructors.

—Hunt, 1990, pp. 53-54

Sue was an experienced and capable wilderness-based experiential educator. She was 28 years old and unmarried. During one of her courses, she had a student named Al, who was 30 years old, single, and interested in the possibility of pursuing an outdoor career. As the course went on, Sue and Al began to have long talks together when time permitted. The course was going exceptionally well and Sue and Al began to anticipate their time together alone. It became clear to both of them that there was a romantic attraction. Being mature adults, Sue and Al sat down one evening and discussed their emerging feelings for one another. They decided that they better be very careful about the emerging romance, but they also felt they could handle sexual expressions of their feelings during those rare moments when they were alone.

—Hunt, 1990, p. 79

Hearing from a corporate friend in California on the positive value of adventure experiences for building teamwork in organizations, the ABC Corporation (located in Boston) contacted a service provider in California (called California Adventure Training, Inc.) to provide training for them. After going over several logistical details, the California Adventure Training contacted several of the listed facilities close to Boston to ask if they could use their ropes course for part of a five-day training. One of these facilities was Boston Adventures, Inc., which happened to be located near the ABC Corporation. In fact, several of the human resource professionals from the ABC Corporation had heard of the locally based Boston Adventures, Inc. program and contacted them a few days later to find out what corporate adventure training actually entailed, how the ABC Corporation could maximize working with the California Adventure Training, Inc. program, and how good California Adventure Training, Inc. was at providing such services. In speaking with the Corporation, Boston Adventures, Inc. stated they could provide better services for the ABC Corporation and actively pursued the contract. They did not inform California Adventure Training, Inc. that they were stating this information to the ABC Corporation or that they were now negotiating for the contract that California Adventure Training, Inc. had contacted them for in order to use their ropes course. Given this information, the ABC Corporation contacted California Adventure Training, Inc. to let them know that they were no longer interested in using them for these training services and would be signing a contract with a more locally based service provider, who they had been told knows their needs better.

—Gass & Wurdinger, 1993, p. 43

In most disciplines, certain professional actions are more appropriate than others. When these actions pertain to moral decisions and conduct, they are usually identified as ethical issues. **Ethical decision making** involves determining which behaviors in such issues are morally right. As we have seen in the three scenarios opening this chapter, issues of ethical concern arise from a conflict or disagreement over what is the best course of action to follow. Such conflicts raise ethical questions, such as "Is it appropriate for a leader to deceive clients in order to enhance learning, or is it inappropriate to use such means to have the clients take learning seriously? Is sexual intimacy between a leader and client appropriate under certain conditions, or is it inappropriate since it could interfere with group learning? Is 'attracting' a customer away from a competitor good business practice, or could it produce professional dynamics that limit the growth of the industry?" While these questions touch only a few of the potential ethical situations and their dynamics, they illustrate some of the reasons why ethical decision making should concern you as an outdoor leader.

PRINCIPLE AND VIRTUE ETHICS

How does a professional determine ethical conduct, particularly when ethical considerations conflict? While several writers have evolved models for ethical decision making in outdoor leadership (Hunt, 1990; Johnson & Fredrickson, 2000; Mitten, 1994, 2002; Warren, Sakofs, & Hunt, 1995), we can group most approaches to ethical decision making into one of two approaches: **principle ethics** and **virtue ethics.**

Principle ethics are guided by a proactively determined set of impartial rules that are often determined by a governing professional organization or by the current professional standards of behavior if no such guidelines exist. Outdoor leaders following principle ethics examine their actions and choices, looking to answer "What shall I do?" and "Is this situation unethical?" (Jordan & Meara, 1990, p. 108). Principle ethics are also based on the belief that the issues being examined are somewhat similar in context and can be connected to other situations.

Virtue ethicists, however, believe that you must examine the particular factors and influences of each act, asserting that correct behavior is defined for each specific situation and that you cannot link to any decisions made in other situations. Virtue ethics are guided by the particular virtues associated with being a moral outdoor leader rather than the principles of being ethical. Specifically, virtue ethics are concerned with professional character traits, focusing on "Who shall I be?" and "Am I doing the best for my client?" (Jordan & Meara, 1990, p. 108).

The strengths of each approach are the very weaknesses of the other. Principle ethics are independent of the situation. Professional behavior, ethical for a general situation, becomes the rule for all specific situations. Say, for example, that you notice a group has made a navigational error and is heading the wrong way into a fragile ecosystem (Hunt, 1990). Should you tell the clients that they have made a mistake, or should you let them find

A professional should consider both principle and virtue ethics when leading.

that out for themselves? At least three principles are at play here: client learning, client comfort, and environmental protection. Ask yourself, "Will clients learn the lesson by being told or should they experience the consequences? How far do they have to travel off the route to learn? Will they damage the place they are headed into?" In deciding whether to inform clients of their error, you should order all principles by importance and simply make an ethical decision on the basis of the guiding order. For a principle ethicist, this order would remain the same in every similar situation.

In contrast, virtue ethics are dependent on the situation. Professional behavior is contextual or subjective and may vary from one set of circumstances to another. For the navigational example, several virtues are at play: honesty, caring, and sensitivity. As a virtue ethicist, you should ask yourself, "What would an honest person do about informing the clients? What would a caring person do about allowing them to travel out of their way? What would a sensitive person do to protect nature?" Instead of deciding what to do, you are concerned with the type of person to be and the greatest benefit for the client and environment. Therefore, for a virtue ethicist, this decision may differ from or agree with that of the principle ethicist, but it will also be different in any other slightly different dilemma.

While principle ethics ask you to look outside the situation to maintain objectivity in determining ethical behavior, virtue ethics ask you to step inside the dilemma to better ascertain what your professional actions mean. Several authors (e.g., Gass & Wurdinger, 1993) have suggested that using principle or virtue ethics should not be an "either–or" decision: You need to consider both. One model in which you may use either or both is an adaptation of Kitchener's (1984) model of ethical decision making.

KITCHENER'S MODEL OF ETHICAL DECISION MAKING

Kitchener's model consists of multiple steps followed in a process of ethical reasoning that examines issues in a progressive sequence. If you can't make a well-founded ethical decision at one step, you advance to the next one, which is usually more general and abstract in its approach to the issue. Specifically, the five steps of this ethical decision-making model are intuition, option listing, ethical rules, ethical principles, and ethical theory.

Intuition

Ethical responses in the **intuition** level come from prereflective or "gut" reactions to the question "What feels right?" The ethical beliefs associated with these decisions are so established the answer is obtained through "ordinary moral sense." There is little need to even consider that the decision exists since the ordinary moral sense process is predetermined, usually by your "individual experience, ethical knowledge, and level of ethical development" (Zygmond & Boorhem, 1989, p. 271). For example, almost all outdoor leaders would intuitively claim that damaging the environment in a survival situation is acceptable. In order to save lives, they would gladly light signal fires with green wood or build stretchers by cutting down trees.

Option Listing

When you are unable to resolve ethical decisions at the intuition level, **option listing** and evaluating

these options, their outcomes, and their potential ramifications need to occur. This step serves as a foundation for ethical decision making in whichever of the three remaining steps you use. You could list these two options for the example: damage a fragile environment and increase group safety or protect the environment and run the outside chance of someone becoming seriously injured.

Ethical Rules

Ethical rules are externally established codes of conduct, like the guidelines created by the psychological, medical, and legal professions. The guidelines most like ethical rules in adventure programming are those published by the Therapeutic Adventure Professional Group (Association for Experiential Education [AEE], 1992; Gass, 1993) and the ethical criteria established in the *Manual of Program Accreditation Standards for Adventure Programs* published by the Association for Experiential Education (Williamson & Gass, 1993). Professions establish rules to maintain a certain level of ethical behavior, and the creation of ethical rules is generally considered a developmental benchmark in the quest for professionalism. One example of an ethical rule is that adventure programs discriminating on the basis of gender, race, or sexual orientation cannot become accredited by the AEE, and accredited programs found to discriminate in this manner lose their accreditation status.

Ethical Principles

Ethical principles are "enduring beliefs about specific modes of conduct or end-states of existence that, when acted upon, protect the interests and welfare of all of the people involved" (Zygmond & Boorhem, 1989, p. 273). More general than ethical rules, the five principles Kitchener (1984) identified as the most critical for members in the helping professions are autonomy, nonmaleficence, beneficence, fidelity, and justice. **Autonomy** means that individuals have the right to freedom of action and choice as long as their behavior does not infringe on the rights of others. **Nonmaleficence** means that, above all else, no harm is done to people. **Beneficence** means that the focus of an outdoor leader's actions is to contribute to the health and welfare of others. **Fidelity** means to be faithful, keep promises, and to be loyal and respectful of people's rights. **Justice** means individuals are treated as equals and implies a concept of fairness. For example, Rohnke's axiom of challenge by choice (see chapter 14), in which people are not coerced to participate in an adventure, illustrates all five of these ethical principles.

Ethical Theories

When intuitive thought, ethical codes, and ethical principles fail to resolve ethical issues, implement **ethical theories.** These theories help you determine which factors are relevant to the situation and should take precedence. Two principles used in this process are balancing and universalizability. With **balancing,** you compare options to pick the one that brings the least avoidable harm to all parties involved. Balancing is similar to the consequential theory of ethics, which suggests that an action is ethically correct only if it produces the greatest happiness for the greatest number (Mill, 1975). With **universalizability,** you institute and generalize the same ethical actions across similar situations (e.g., if it is ethical to act one way in a situation, then act that way in similar situations). Universalizability is similar to the nonconsequentialist theory of ethics based on the categorical imperative that states that actions should only be taken when they can be fairly and broadly applied as a universal law to all similar cases (Kant, 1964). For the survival and environment example, you should balance the two options against the measure of a human life versus other considerations such as the needs of the environment. In some cases, the cost in money and risk to rescuers in a highly inaccessible environment might dictate not sponsoring government efforts to save human life as in rescue-free wilderness or areas for which the government assumes no responsibility for rescuing people from designated wilderness (McAvoy, 1990). If the option to not rescue was chosen, perhaps because not entering the wilderness with a search team might save more lives in the long run, then this option should be universally applied in all such wilderness areas.

Applying Kitchener's Model

Recall that if you are unable to resolve a situation by determining professional or appropriate action at one level, you should move to the next. But in the Kitchener model, one step is not better than another, only more appropriate for providing professional guidance in an ethical decision. One advantage of this model is that it creates conditions under which you may continually

evolve at all levels of your ethical development. Remember, the more experience you gain making ethical decisions, the more likely your decisions will become intuitive decisions. In other words, as you become more experienced in making ethical decisions, it is more likely that you will be able to resolve dilemmas at this lowest level, using your intuition. Hence, you should practice resolving ethical dilemmas. To give you some more vicarious experience, let's examine the Kitchener model and the third scenario involving adventure organizations competing for corporate customers.

The first step in the model is to examine the practice of attracting customers away from other organizations as an intuitive ethical decision. Using your professional experience and the belief that ethical behavior is important, you should ask yourself if it makes ordinary moral sense to follow such behavior or if such behavior is unethical in all cases. You may determine that this behavior could lead to a wide variety of negative implications for individual programs as well as for the field and so choose not to follow this practice. Or you may determine that this practice is ethically acceptable because the program attracted customers away on the basis of safety standards or actual competence, since Boston Adventures actually did know ABC Corporation's business better than California Adventure Training. If, however, you determine that this issue is not easily resolved due to conflicting ideas, elements, principles, or virtues, then you must move to the next level of the model and list possible options of behavior and the consequences of such behavior.

In the second step, you list your possible options and the strengths and weaknesses of each. Four options are possible for the scenario. In this case, we can call them **prohibitive,** prohibiting stealing since it is unethical; **open market,** allowing competition since it is ethical; **objective conditional,** attracting customers under certain conditions; and **subjective discretional,** attracting customers at your own discretion. If you believe in the absoluteness of the first two options, then they are easy choices made at an intuitive level. In the prohibitive option, stealing is wrong at all times and would not be ethically permissible under any circumstances. In the open-market option, competition is right in all cases and would be ethically expected under any circumstances. The remaining two options are full of conflict, leading to an ethical dilemma. You need to more closely examine these options along with their respective strengths and weaknesses.

The objective-conditional option includes establishing a proactive and objective set of standards that outlines when providers cannot attract customers away from other providers. Some of these set conditions might be possession of a current contract or in negotiation to contract and a waiting period of a few months after the end of an initial contact. At these times, other providers could not approach the customers of these contracted providers. A series of clearly identified conditions in place before a competitive situation arises seeks to prevent some problems. This option does have its strengths. It establishes objective conditions for you to follow while eliminating potential negative exploitation of professional interaction. It provides some freedom of choice among customers wishing to switch providers. It fosters the belief that outdoor leaders and adventure programs may freely interact to provide quality programs without fear of losing customers. It proactively identifies the rules of professional interaction as well as of competition for customers. It encourages a climate of professional collaboration with the advance knowledge that losing customers will not result. This option has several weaknesses as well. It does not remove the possibility that stealing customers could occur after the objective conditions were met. It limits the customers' freedom to choose another service provider.

The subjective-discretional option recognizes that there are times when attracting customers away from other businesses would be unethical and inappropriate. But it would be up to individual outdoor leaders to use their own belief systems to determine when this would or wouldn't be appropriate. The strengths of this position are that it establishes subjective conditions for you to follow, trying to eliminate potential negative exploitation, and it provides for greater autonomy for providers and customers, given that the rights of others are not infringed on. The weaknesses of the position are that it does not remove the possibility that negative exploitation could occur after the subjective condition is met (e.g., beliefs by outdoor leaders that customers were stolen) and it does not promote the positive development of professional collaboration without fear of losing customers.

Once you outline the strengths and weaknesses of various positions, you should look to the third, fourth, and fifth steps for guidance in deciding between options. In the third step, you should examine the ethical rules of the profession. (A code of conduct for outdoor leaders is described in the next section of this chapter.) If you see the central issue to be one of competence in which the California program truly did not possess the competence to conduct the program, but the Boston program did, then you can make your choice based on this ethical rule. If, however, competence is not at the heart of the issue, this step is of little use to you, and you should look at the next one.

In the fourth step, you should evaluate the major advantages and disadvantages of both options, comparing them to the ethical principles of autonomy, nonmaleficence, beneficence, fidelity, and justice. The objective-conditional option (OC) establishes an impartial set of rules regarding contracts and waiting periods that block other providers from attracting customers away. The subjective-discretional option (SD) recognizes that the choice of attracting customers should be made by you and based on the situation and your personal values.

Autonomy seems to be lower for both providers and customers in the OC option, because their rights to choose and freedom to interact outside the contract are restricted by rules. Autonomy is higher for both providers and customers in the SD option, because each is free to choose in a way that does not significantly infringe on the rights of other providers.

Nonmaleficence appears to be higher for providers and moderate for customers in the OC option, because providers are protected by the rules while customers could be harmed by being unable to change their minds if stuck with a poor program. Nonmaleficence is lower for providers and moderate for customers in the SD option, because providers are open to attack from other providers while customers could be harmed by the possible lack of program quality.

Beneficence in the OC option seems to be moderate for providers, depending on whether they gain or lose customers, because collaboration can occur and may bring increased quality or decreased motivation to improve. It is lower for customers, because they lose the chance to benefit from an open selection process that encourages the best program to come to the forefront. Beneficence in the SD option is moderate for providers, again depending on whether they lose or gain customers, because competition can bring increased quality and decreased sharing of information. It is higher for customers, because they benefit from a wide variety of providers and quality programs to choose from.

Fidelity appears to be higher for providers and customers in the OC option, because customers remain faithful to providers, keep written promises, and respect a collaborative environment. Fidelity is lower for providers and customers in the SD option, because customers switch providers, break verbal contracts, and respect only the programs' rights to compete.

Justice seems to be moderate for providers and customers in both options. In the OC option, everyone has equal knowledge of the operating rules in advance and has a fair chance to trust one another in collaboration. In the SD option, everyone has fair access to discussing contracts with one another as they operate in a competitive market with equal opportunity.

In this case, if you believe that one of these two options takes the highest ethical stance for addressing the issue of attracting customers, then you could follow it, completing the ethical decision-making process. But if you were unable to determine the ethical decision based on these principles, you should advance to the final step of the ethical theories of balancing and universalizability.

Balancing considers both options and chooses the stance that produces the greatest benefit for the greatest number of people. In the OC option, everyone including the customer would be indirectly inconvenienced by rules, and the only direct benefit would go to the program with a contract. In the SD option, the only one inconvenienced would be the program who loses a customer to another provider; all others, including the customer, would benefit. Therefore, the SD option seems to be the clear preference for balancing.

Remember, universalizability refers to how well the option applies to all similar cases. The OC option is the clear preference for universal generalizability: its rules suit any situation. The SD option has no universalizability because each situation is decided on its own merits. Since each theory favors each option, in this final step you will have to decide which of these two theories you hold in higher regard.

In following such a model, principle and virtue ethicists would focus on different features. Principle ethicists would strive to remain objective and impartial in following the model, focusing on what you should do to follow the most ethical practice. Virtue ethicists, however, would examine the particular factors and influences of this particular action, attempting to interpret the intentions of Boston Adventures to better ascertain the reasons for their actions.

We encourage you to use both the principle and virtue approaches when possible to achieve a well-balanced view of any ethical decision. While at certain times these approaches conflict with one another, a combined objective–subjective approach will give you a balanced perspective.

ETHICAL GUIDELINES FOR OUTDOOR LEADERS

Probably one of the brightest developments in ethical decision making for outdoor leadership was the formulation of ethical guidelines by the Association of Experiential Education's Therapeutic Adventure Professional Group (AEE, 1992). You can find these guidelines in the ethics section of the program accreditation standards identified in the *Manual of Program Accreditation Standards for Adventure Programs* (Williamson & Gass, 1993). These guidelines were created with the support of the American Psychological Association (APA), the American Alliance of Marriage and Family Therapists (AAMFT), Council on Outdoor Education for the American Alliance of Health, Physical Education & Dance (COE/AAHPERD), Council of Accreditation of Services for Families and Children (CASFC), and the Worldwide Outfitters and Guides Association (WOGA). While these guidelines were not established as an ethical code or as rules professionals must follow or be censured from practice, they do show that the field of outdoor leadership is on record for supporting certain practices. Specifically, the seven guidelines relate to competence, integrity, responsibility, respect, concern, recognition, and objectivity. Although developed for therapists, we paraphrase these seven guidelines for your review.

While these seven guidelines represent a critical and invaluable step in advancing the outdoor leadership profession, following such guidelines does not release you from the need to apply ethical judgment. As you should not blindly follow safety protocols for a technical skill without considering the changing elements of an outdoor setting, you should not forgo the need to constantly examine your behavior in professional endeavors.

Indeed, ethical standards have limitations. Ethical guidelines may conflict within certain cultures, requiring you to adapt them in such instances. Or you may find yourself in a situation in which a conflict exists among legal, organizational, and ethical guidelines. Conflict between ethical guidelines and their interpretation will likely arise and lead to dilemmas for you to resolve. No matter what your course of action, the *summum bonum* (do no harm) ethic you as a professional follow should be guided by empathy for the client. With this in mind, let's look closely at the seven guidelines.

Competence

Professionals conduct experiences with **competence.** As an outdoor leader, promote and conduct activities within your level. Provide services within the boundaries of your education, training, supervision, experience, and practice. Take reasonable steps to ensure the competence of your work. Avoid situations in which personal problems or conflicts will impair your performance or judgment. Stay abreast of current information in the field. Participate in ongoing professional efforts to maintain your knowledge, practice, and skills.

Integrity

Professionals conduct experiences with **integrity.** Conduct activities with honesty, fairness, and respect toward both clients and peers. Avoid false, misleading, or deceptive statements when describing or reporting qualifications, services, products, or fees. Be aware of how your personal belief system, values, needs, and limitations affect clients.

Responsibility

Professionals conduct experiences with **responsibility.** Uphold the ethical principles of your work. Be clear with clients as to what everyone's roles and obligations are. Accept responsibility for your behavior and decisions. Adapt methods to the needs of different populations. Ensure that you possess an adequate basis for professional judgments. Do not offer services when the constraints of limited contact will not benefit client needs (e.g., promising a single-day adventure experience will resolve a deep issue for a therapeutic or corporate population). Continue services only so long as it is reasonably clear that clients will benefit. Conduct experiences in a manner that minimally impacts or only temporarily damages the environment.

Respect

Professionals conduct experiences with **respect** for the rights and dignity of clients. Respect the fundamental rights, dignity, and worth of all people. Respect clients' rights to privacy, confidentiality, and self-determination within the limits of the law. Be sensitive to cultural and individual differences, including those due to age, gender, race, ethnicity, national origin, religion, sexual orientation, disability, and socioeconomic status. Do not engage in sexual or other harassment or exploitation of clients. Respect clients' rights to make decisions as well as help clients understand the consequences of their choices. Inform clients about the services and their rights, risks, and responsibilities. Offer an opportunity to discuss the results, interpretations, and conclusions of the adventure experience with clients. Respect clients' rights to refuse consent to services and activities. Obtain informed consent from clients and, when appropriate, their parents or guardians before beginning services. Accurately represent your competence, training, education, and experience relevant to the program you are delivering.

Concern

Professionals conduct experiences with **concern** for the well-being of clients. Be sensitive to client needs and well-being. Provide for the physical needs of clients, including necessary water, nutrition, clothing, shelter, rest, or other essentials. Monitor the use of emotional and physical risk in adventure experiences. Assist in obtaining other services if the program cannot for appropriate reasons provide the professional help clients may need. Plan experiences with the clients' best interests in mind both during and after the program. Respect clients' rights to decide which confidential material can be made public, except under extreme conditions as required by law to prevent a clear and immediate danger to a person or persons.

Recognition

Professionals conduct experiences with **recognition** for their social responsibility. Be aware of your responsibilities to community and society. Encourage the development of standards and policies that serve your clients' interests as well as those of the public. Respect the property of others.

Objectivity

Professionals conduct experiences with **objectivity** by avoiding dual relationships with clients that impair professional judgment. Do not exploit or mislead clients or other leaders during and after professional relationships. Relationships include, but are not limited to, business, close personal, family, sexual, and otherwise inappropriate physical.

◄ EFFECTIVE OUTDOOR LEADERS ►

► Above all else, do no harm to the client.

► Understand that no governing body, other than the AEE program accreditation, holds outdoor professionals to a standard of ethical conduct.

► Make sure that facilitation efforts are done with the clients' best interests in mind.

► Ensure that the focus of the interventions is to serve the clients, not the leader.

► Are certain that a purpose and reason exist for using a particular technique.

► Know when to use intuitive and rationale approaches for ethical decision making (e.g., listing as in Kitchener's model).

► Are willing to stand up in front of other colleagues and say that they made a particular professional decision and state why.

► Understand the guidelines put forth by the AEE for ethical behavior and implement them when appropriate.

► Remind themselves that the experience possesses the resources to be more powerful than their best efforts.

► When in doubt, do no harm!

SUMMARY

Ethical decision making is usually based on principle or virtue ethics. Principle ethics are independent of the ethical situation and are guided by a proactively determined set of impartial principles focused on actions and choices. Virtue ethics are dependent on the uniqueness of every situation and are guided by desired virtues and character traits.

Kitchener's model of ethical decision making is composed of five steps: intuition, option listing, ethical rules, ethical principles, and ethical theory. The intuitive first level is a gut reaction to what feels morally correct. The second step lists options and their strengths and weaknesses that serve as considerations for the next three steps. Ethical rules are codes of conduct established by external professions. Ethical principles are ways of acting that protect others, including five concerns: autonomy, nonmaleficence, beneficence, fidelity, and justice. Ethical theories are balancing, considering the greatest gain for the greatest number and the least harm for the least number, and universalizability, or generalizing to the deepest and widest universal application.

The Association for Experiential Education has developed seven ethical guidelines related to competence, integrity, responsibility, respect, concern, recognition, and objectivity. Competence refers to not working beyond your capability. Integrity refers to using honesty, fairness, and respect with client interactions and peer relations. Responsibility refers to caring for the clients' well-being

as well as the environment's. Respect refers to the fundamental rights, dignity, and worth of clients and peers. Concern refers to clients' physiological and psychological needs and well-being. Recognition refers to social responsibility toward the community and society's needs. Objectivity refers to not establishing relationships with clients beyond the roles of leader and client. These seven guidelines do not necessarily substitute for ethical decision making; they merely shepherd you through the process of resolving ethical conflicts or dilemmas.

QUESTIONS TO THINK ABOUT

1. Which of the two options (OC and SD) in the attracting corporate customers scenario do you prefer and why?

2. At which step in Kitchener's model had you made up your mind?

3. Using Kitchener's model, determine your ethical decisions for each of the remaining two scenarios at the beginning of this chapter.

4. Outline the process you went through to arrive at your decisions and argue your logic with a partner.

REFERENCES

Association for Experiential Education (AEE). (1992). *Ethical guidelines of the therapeutic adventure professional group (TAPG)*. Boulder, CO: Association for Experiential Education.

Gass, M.A. (1993). *Adventure therapy: Therapeutic applications of adventure programming in mental health settings.* Boulder, CO: Association for Experiential Education.

Gass, M.A., & Wurdinger, S. (1993). Ethical decisions in experience-based training and development programs. *Journal of Experiential Education, 16*(2), 41-47.

Hunt, J. (1990). *Ethics in experiential education.* Boulder, CO: Association for Experiential Education.

Johnson, B.L., & Fredrickson, L.M. (2000). "What's in a good life?" Searching for ethical wisdom in the wilderness. *Journal of Experiential Education, 23*(1), 43-50.

Jordan, A.E., & Meara, N.M. (1990). Ethics and the professional practices of psychologists: The role of virtues and principles. *Professional Psychology: Research and Practice, 21*(2), 107-114.

Kant, I. (1964). *Groundwork of the metaphysic of morals.* New York: Harper & Row.

Kitchener, K.S. (1984). Intuition, critical evaluation, and ethical principles: The foundation for ethical decisions in counseling psychology. *The Counseling Psychologist, 12*(3), 43-55.

McAvoy, L. (1990). Rescue-free wilderness areas. In J.C. Miles & S. Priest (Eds.), *Adventure education* (pp. 329-334). State College, PA: Venture.

Mill, J.S. (1975). *On liberty.* New York: Penguin Classics.

Mitten, D. (1994). Ethical considerations in adventure therapy: A feminist critique. In E. Cole, E. Erdman, & E.D. Rothblum (Eds.), *Wilderness therapy for women: The power of adventure* (pp. 55-84). New York: Harrington Park Press.

Mitten, D. (2002, January). An analysis of outdoor leaders' ethics guiding decisions. *Proceedings from The Coalition for Education in the Outdoors 6th Biennial Research Symposium* (pp. 55-73). Bradford Woods, IN.

Williamson, J., & Gass, M.A. (1993). *Manual of program accreditation standards for adventure programs.* Boulder, CO: Association for Experiential Education.

Zygmond, M.J., & Boorhem, H. (1989). Ethical decision making in family therapy. *Family Process, 28,* 269-280.

Trends and Issues

*A*round the beginning of the 20th century, not one of the futurists predicting our prospective lives mentioned anything remotely connected with the computer.

—*John Sculley, former CEO of Apple Computer*

Predicting the future can be a difficult and dangerous undertaking for any profession. Nevertheless, in this chapter we outline six key trends and issues associated with adventure programming and outdoor leadership: growth, the environment, technology, burnout, professionalism, and research. To better understand these trends and issues, let's first examine some of the factors at work in them as well as some of the resulting growth areas.

FACTORS AT WORK

In their 2004 report, the Outdoor Industry Association reported 16 million additional participants are involved in outdoor pursuits and that participants going into the outdoors tend to be younger, more diverse in terms of culture and race, and more dedicated in their outdoor pursuits with more frequent and dedicated outdoor use. Showing steady growth in numbers over the past six years, this brought the total number of people participating in outdoor experiences to 145.7 million Americans, or two-thirds of the national population (OIA, July 28, 2004). This change is increasingly stressing the natural environment, and it will result in more nonrecoverable damage to the resource base. In short, more people are currently loving the outdoors to death!

At the same time, the world is shrinking due to continually developing communication and transportation. The ability to instantaneously store, retrieve, and deliver a rapidly expanding information base may mean that the dominant global culture will move toward being more empirical, rational, utilitarian, and manipulative. As a result, global markets for goods, services, or ideas will become easier to access, yet heavily competitive for customers and resources. The global economy is currently shifting orientation from industry to service with lower work pay and longer work hours.

Many factors are changing, affecting both the workplace and the home. More dual-income and single-parent families are translating into increasing numbers of latchkey kids spending less time with their families. The status and roles of women in society continue to change. The average age of the population continues to increase. More people will switch careers in their working lifetimes.

What does it all mean? Society may become more consumptive, dominant, and manipulative and less moral, conservative, and compassionate. People are increasing their debt, mortgaging their futures in order to sustain their affluence. Growing intellectual, cultural, and ethical anomie, or unrest, among young people may result in more drug abuse, crime, and teenage suicide. Among all of this, litigious attitudes will prevail, and lawyers will play a more influential role in determining what takes place in adventure programming. Two questions that need to be asked given these societal trends are (1) will adventure programming continue to thrive in such conditions and (2) can the field possibly even change some of these societal trends?

GROWTH

*I*n a summary of his speech presented at the 1996 Outdoor Industry CEO Roundtable Breakfast, Jim Lyons [Under Secretary of the Head of the U.S. Department of Agriculture who oversees the U.S. Forest Service] noted that growing recreation demands are failing to be met by the current [Federal] budget. He noted that in terms of recreation facilities, the Forest Service was underfunded by $818 million. Attendees were informed that outdoor recreation only receives 21 percent of the monies allocated to the total 1996 National Forest Service budget. On the other hand, when analyzing gross domestic products resulting from Forest Service functions, outdoor recreation contributes 74.8 percent with mining and foresting [on U.S. Forest Service lands] being less than 25 percent. . . . Lyons stated, "If we don't provide a high quality natural environment, people won't* *come back to the lands, and you won't sell your products."*

—Mentuck, 1996, p. 3

Since Lyons' presentation, matters have only become worse with these budgets and the days of "free access" to U.S. federal and state lands are becoming a thing of the past. In 2003, the U.S. Congress submitted the H.R. 3283, the Federal Lands Recreation Enhancement Act, to make the once "demonstration program" collecting for participation on public lands a permanent program. This program has been added to the 2005 Fiscal Year Appropriations Act for implementation.

—OIA, December 6, 2004

As a result of the factors Ewert and Miles identified, several trends and growth areas seem probable. Adventure programs and activities will continue to grow in popularity (Friese, Hendee, & Kinzinger, 1998). Some growth will probably be due to the need for greater leisure opportunities, and some may result from the need to use adventure experiences to address societal problems. This trend is already obvious from the increasing numbers of participants in, and revenues from, outdoor recreation. For example, according to the OIA study (July 28, 2004) the bulk of outdoor "participants" and "enthusiasts" in the United States are involved "in the cornerstone activities of bicycling (87 million/20.4 million), hiking (71.8 million/10.5 million), and camping (68.8 million/10.8 million). Known as 'gateway' activities, these pursuits are the primary anchor for attracting new participants and provide an affordable non-intimidating entry point to other outdoor activities. The most significant additions of new participants since 1998 came in trail running (6.4 million new participants a 20.5% increase); kayaking (5.7 million new participants, a 235.7% increase); canoeing (4.3 million new participants, an 18.1% increase); and snowshoeing (3 million new participants, a 203.4% increase)" (pp. 1-2).

Other growth factors include the following predictions:

The size and number of professional organizations will increase. Since the first Association for Experiential Education (AEE) Conference in 1974, for which 130 individuals preregistered (Garvey, 1990), this organization, seen by many individuals as the leading agency concerned with adventure programming, now has over 2,000 members in 20 countries. AEE has professional and special interest groups in experience-based training and development, schools and colleges, therapeutic adventure, and universal programming. While AEE's numbers have maintained their levels over the past six years, numerous member and spin-offs have been created for specialized niches of the adventure programming marketplace. Examples include the International Conference on Outdoor Recreation (ICOR), Association of Challenge Course Technology (ACCT), Coalition for Education Outdoors (CEO), International Conference on Experiential Learning (ICEL), National Association for Therapeutic Schools and Associated Programs (NATSAP), National Society for Experiential Education (NSEE), and Council for Adult and Experiential Learning (CAEL). Other organizations include the Bradford Institute on Americans Outdoors (BIAO), Adventure Travel Trade Association (ATTA), Institute for Earth Education (IEE), Adventuresports Institute (ASI), Wilderness Education Association (WEA), Project Adventure (PA), American Mountain Guides Association (AMGA), National Outdoor Leadership School (NOLS), and Outward Bound International (OBI).

The profession will expand and diversify. For example, the latest version of the AEE's *Directory of Experiential Therapy and Adventure-Based Counseling Programs* (Gerstein, 1992) lists over 257 organizations that utilize adventure experiences for therapy. Within this listing are programs for clients who are at-risk youth, in adult corrections, families, psychiatric inpatients, addicts, terminally ill patients, in juvenile corrections, sexual victims, sexual perpetrators, and developmentally disabled. In the wilderness therapy industry alone, the Chicago Tribune (January 19, 2004) estimated over $200 million a year was spent on wilderness therapy programs for youth-at-risk. We can also expect an increased number of other client types in the adventure profession, particularly in school-based programs.

Adventure will be more often adopted by the schools. Classroom settings will slowly incorporate the concepts and methods of adventure programming into their conventional schooling. For example, "wilderness learning," or the Outward Bound approach, has already met with success in physical education through Project Adventure. Other curricula will likely benefit from including adventure programming, for example, expeditionary learning.

Programs will be brought to the learner, rather than vice versa. With the interaction of shrinking wilderness, accessibility, fiscal restraints, and efforts to make concepts more applicable to clients' real lives, several professionals have called for adventure programs to center efforts more around the learners and the "adventures" in their own environments. One example of this is the growth of urban adventure programming (Proudman, 1990). Urban adventure has several potential advantages over wilderness-based programming, which include greater accessibility to a larger number of clients; clients who can directly benefit from adventure, such as 10- to 15-year-olds from disadvantaged backgrounds; environments with cultural diversity; immediacy of human problems and solutions; availability of differing resources; continuing support systems; greater transferability to clients' futures; and a wide range of learning environments and programming options, such as cultural events and information sources.

Program operations will be more regulated and complex. Less governmental funding and more injuries to humans and damage to the environment all bring increasing regulation from resource managers. Concerned with their liability and visitor safety, these managers set policies and procedures to moderate resource use. Resource-management agencies, such as the National Park and Forest Service, have introduced guidelines governing permit use, program licensing, and access fees. On some public lands, adventure programs must obtain permission via a lottery, be accredited by the AEE (Association for Experiential Education) or AMGA (American Mountain Guides Association), and pay a fee for using those lands. These measures have been implemented, in part, to cover shrinking bureaucratic support and increased use.

Artificial adventure environments will begin to dominate program settings. To some extent this is already the case. Group initiatives and ropes and challenge courses have all but replaced the classic outdoor pursuits with corporate clientele. A proliferation of ropes-course builders has led to the creation of the Association for Challenge Course Technology (ACCT) to standardize construction methods and safety inspections for the thousands of American courses in use today. The sophistication and organization of ACCT continues to grow in North America with similar patterns to follow in other countries (ACCT, 2005). The shrinking of natural outdoor settings coupled with the cost and danger of transporting clients (the most dangerous part of most programs) will necessitate

alternatives. Some alternatives include the already popular climbing walls, ski slopes, kayak roll tanks, and white-water canoe chutes. Others have yet to be invented.

The profession will slowly mature through self-examination. By formulating ways to investigate and theorize about adventure programming, the profession will grow more professional. One important step toward this growth is developing a unique body of knowledge. This has already been accomplished in part by the creation of professional safety guidelines (Priest & Dixon, 1990) and the construction of program accreditation standards (Williamson & Gass, 1993). These publications highlight the profession's ability to identify, document, and refine the expression of practices to practitioners and consumers alike. Moreover, we can see other such evolutionary benchmarks in written works about how adventure programming applies to specific populations. For example, Bandoroff & Newes (2004); Schoel & Maizell (2002); Richards (2002); and West-Smith (2001) have all published books on the therapeutic applications of adventure.

ENVIRONMENT

Rock climbing activity has increased dramatically at Acadia National Park (ANP) over the past 10 to 15 years. The effects of climbing use in ANP are most evident at Otter Cliffs. Significant erosion is occurring around belay trees. Many of them are close to dying and may not be available as anchors within a few years. The proliferation of social trails are largely the result of climbers seeking privacy while "answering the call of nature." Human waste is an aesthetic problem, a possible health hazard, and an ecological concern.

The use of Otter Cliffs by organized groups is contributing to this resource damage. We estimate one-fourth of all climbing use at Otter Cliffs in 1994 was from groups. In addition, the presence of large groups may affect the climbing experience by causing crowding and congestion. It has also caused other climbers to seek new locations to climb in the park.

In order to protect these resources from further damage and to preserve the unique sea cliff climbing experience, ANP will begin to regulate use of Otter Cliffs beginning in 1996. This is the first of several actions which we intend to take at Otter Cliffs and throughout the park to accomplish protection of resources and the visitor experience.

Regulation of group use at Otter Cliffs will likely include a group size limit of twelve, including instructors, and a limit on the number of groups allowed per day at the site. Twelve is the group size we are currently using for commercial operations. Reservations would be required in advance.

We want to remind you that any groups charging a fee for climbing services or for any program must have a commercial use license even if they are a nonprofit group. The fee for commercial use licenses is $50, and special conditions are attached to the permit regarding the time and location of climbing activity, safety equipment, or other conditions as needed.

—Letter from P. Haertel, Superintendent,
Acadia National Park, June 23, 1995

Many recognize that climbing is a very high-impact activity. We are on the "radar screens" of decision makers and their fingers are on the "buttons" of regulations. Make no mistake about it: climbing will be managed and regulated in the future. It is no longer a question of choosing between self-regulation or external regulation. It's too late for that. The Access Fund, American Alpine Club, and other national and local groups are working aggressively to preserve as much freedom as possible for climbers, but we must accommodate the competing values of other outdoor users, impacts on wildlife, soil, and vegetation, and members of our own community, who often climb for very different reasons. In short, we need to promote a new environmental ethic in climbing.

—Lenard, 1995, p. 200

No question about it, the environment is reeling from the actions of many untrained people. Their increasing numbers have degraded wilderness and other natural areas, so much so that resource managers are restricting access. Their carelessness has led to constraints, such as licensing, permits, and fees, on the very freedom they seek to enjoy.

In 1995, the administration agencies for Joshua Tree (southern California) and Red Rocks (Nevada) national parks decided that only those adventure programs accredited by the AMGA or the AEE would be permitted to conduct rock climbing in those parks. At the time of this publication, this policy remains in place. While such requirements only exist in these two areas, it could possibly be expanded to other areas. If such requirements expand throughout North America, they could greatly influence how adventure programs use rock climbing or other outdoor pursuits to conduct their services.

Furthermore, the popularizing of wilderness areas has produced several other changes in adventure experiences, including wilderness areas becoming less remote or wild. People turning to the wilderness for solitude and "opportunities for self-sufficiency" (McAvoy & Dustin, 1981) often encounter crowded conditions that hamper or eliminate many of the reasons they go there. Increasing management by governmental agencies, heavily influenced by advances in wilderness rescue technology and a growing litigious society, has also reduced many of the advantages and attractions of going to the wilderness.

One solution advanced by McAvoy and Dustin (1981, 1983) is rescue-free wilderness areas. "In these zones, the wilderness users would be completely responsible for their own safety. The government agencies managing these rescue-free zones would be absolved, indeed prohibited, from conducting or sponsoring any search and rescue operations for wilderness users in the area. The managing agency would be responsible for informing users of the principle risks in the area and . . . no government rescue services would be available for a recreationist there. . . . [This] is not a proposal championed by insensitive people. Rather, it is an attempt to preserve a few places to experience what wilderness was intended to be, the untrammelled experience full of opportunities for self-reliance, risk, challenge, and growth" (McAvoy, 1990, p. 329, 333).

TECHNOLOGY

Recently, a friend and his partner overtook another party high on the Bastille Crack in Eldorado Canyon, Colorado. Noticing that the belayer hadn't fastened the waist belt on his harness properly—like most buckled harnesses, this one required that the tail end of the webbing be doubled back through the buckle—my friend immediately pointed out the grave potential danger of the situation. Offended, the belayer replied that he had been climbing for almost two years, had always buckled his harness with a single pass, and that how he buckled his harness wasn't anyone else's business in any case. Taken aback, my friend—a product manager for a large outdoor firm—pointed out that his company had tested the same harness, buckled in an identical manner, and found that the webbing started slipping through the buckle under as little as 250 pounds of force. The response was chilling. The belayer turned and very clearly explained, "But I only weigh 170 pounds!"

Nothing came of this incident, but let's get out the crystal ball and take a somewhat pessimistic look at where climbing might be in the year 2000. With liability a major concern, all but a few retailers have stopped selling climbing equipment. Insurance, when it's available, costs far more than any potential profit, and only the largest shops can sell enough gear to justify the expense. Retail prices are astronomical. A carabiner is $50, a harness $300, and a rope $750, as manufacturers pass on the costs of insurance and safety features to the consumer. Every item of climbing gear sold comes with a detailed technical manual and extensive warning label, both mandated by law. So much redundancy is built into climbing equipment that the average carabiner (locking models only are available) weighs 8 ounces and fails at 20,000 pounds; harnesses and ropes are similarly heavy, foolproof, and complex.

Since the federal ban on all forms of individually-placed protection in 1995, initiated by the newly-formed American Climbing Club (ACC) and the Department of the Interior, all of the country's routes have been equipped to an acceptable standard: glued-in 1/2 inch bolts, at least 6 inches long, 10,000-pound test hangers, and triple-bolt anchors with chains and descending rings at all belays. Protection bolts are no more than one body length apart, and pitch lengths on longer routes have been standardized at 60 feet to allow easy top roping and rappels with a single rope. Hexes, stoppers, Rocks, Friends, TCU's, and RP's are museum pieces;

the fine for anyone actually caught using this antiquated gear is $2000 for the first offense, double that for the second.

—Kennedy, 1989, p. 6

Technology is changing more quickly than people can get a handle on it. Note the need to constantly upgrade computer hardware and software as new designs are released as well as the growing inclusion of computers in adventure programming (Carter, 1998; Hester & Hirsch, 1999). Witness the recent advances in climbing protection and belaying devices. Are these driven by a concern for safety, efficiency, litigation, or other forces?

What are the environmental impacts of technology? Battery-powered electric drills have made bolting widespread. Bolting is the practice of drilling holes in the rock face and hammering expansion bolts into the hole to make foolproof or "bombproof" anchor points. A proliferation of bolts is offensive to some climbers and the constant noise of the drills is disturbing to others, not to mention the deteriorating aesthetic values and damage to nature. Consider this illustration:

In early October, bolting was banned in the Boulder Mountain Park system, which includes such popular areas as the Flatirons and Flagstaff Mountain. Park officials are also looking at ways of removing existing bolted routes from formations under its jurisdiction. Park officials have seemingly been loath to compromise either, taking the unilateral position that "bolting, all fixed hardware, and the use of rock drills are strictly prohibited in Mountain Parks." Although they hope to obtain compliance through education and self-regulation by the climbing community, they can (and apparently will) issue summonses to offenders, with fines of up to $300 and/or 90 days in jail. (Kennedy, 1990, p. 10)

As an outdoor leader, you should be aware of changing technology, particularly if it relates to safety. Failure to use readily available technology could lead to a lawsuit. Consider the recent availability of cellular phones and global positioning (satellite) systems (GPS). GPS is a locating device that scans for the location of at least 3 of 24 satellites orbiting around the planet and uses their locations to triangulate its location on the map pinpointed by a six-digit grid reference accurate to within a few meters.

At the time of publication, these devices were available for well under U.S. $100. What would be the result if a group was lost and injured without either cellular phones or GPS? What would be the loss of wilderness atmosphere if both were brought along on a trip? How do you balance these costs and benefits?

Technological improvements and equipment advances may actually undermine adventure programming by hindering clients' abilities to achieve their goals (Browne, 1986; Gass, 1993b). By using gear that is more convenient or comfortable and less difficult or complex, clients learn to rely on technology instead of themselves.

For instance, ultralight and super convenient backpacks allow clients to load their pack "any old way" so that they lose out on valuable dynamics and natural consequences that lead to discussions of more important life issues. Top-of-the-line tents may not require as much sharing, learning, creativity, and problem solving as figuring out as a group how to rig a tarp shelter with a variety of different knots.

While state-of-the-art equipment maximizes safety in high-risk environments and under adverse weather conditions, it is often very expensive. Having the best gear may predispose people to venture into situations they might not normally choose. Furthermore, clients may not always treat expensive gear with the care and respect it demands. For example, they may be better off with inexpensive rubberized rainsuits than with expensive Gore-Tex ones. In short, the best money can buy is of no value if the client has lost, broken, or refused to use it.

Although those operating an adventure program would not want to compromise the safety of clients by using negligent or substandard equipment, you may find unexpected benefits from returning to older designs. Clients can learn to make and fix equipment and to live with the ramifications of their craftsmanship. Rather than simply adding water to dehydrated meals, group members can learn to bake from scratch, thereby gaining important life skills in cooking, teamwork, cooperation, and interdependence all at the same time. Clients who demonstrate care for older equipment may be given the responsibility of caring for newer equipment. Last, damage to equipment can often indicate that clients are having trouble coping with the demands of the adventure experience. "When clients end a course with the equipment neatly organized and accounted for, their spirits and sense of accomplishment and responsibility are high" (Browne, 1986, p. 19).

The availability of GPS can be helpful for travel in outdoor settings, but how does the use of technology change the wilderness experience?

BURNOUT

Often I encounter people who are largely ignorant of the outdoor education field and who conjure up images of scaling peaks, running white water, living out of doors and incredibly, making money to boot! What they don't see is the extent to which I envy them in their stable 9 to 5 lives with predictable parameters when the not-so-romantic aspects of my job press upon me. I have become an outdoor educator by profession and although the rewards of the life make it worthwhile, the romantic sheen of the profession has certainly become tarnished to a more realistic hue. I find myself from time to time weighing the pros and cons, totaling up the balance sheet, and seeking out the issues and conflicts that confront me in this profession.

—Kesselheim, 1981, p. 20

Leading outdoor experiences can be a very enriching experience, but at the same time the profession can be extremely draining. Gass (1993a) identified this paradox by pointing out that the very features that attract individuals to becoming outdoor leaders often lead to professional burnout when not properly addressed. We can define burnout as a "state of physical, emotional, and mental exhaustion [that is] caused by long term involvement [with] demands most often caused by a combination of very high expectations and chronic situational stresses" (Pines, Ayala, & Aronson, 1988, p. 9).

Indicators of burnout are both subjective and objective. Subjective factors may include loss of self-esteem, resulting from feelings of professional incompetence or job dissatisfaction; physical depletion without an identifiable origin; helplessness and hopelessness; disillusionment; exhibition of negative attitudes toward work, coworkers, or life itself; and problems with concentration, irritability, or negativism. Objective factors often involve a significant decrease in work performance as measured by lower quality, decreasing effectiveness, absenteeism, and a general loss of interest in work issues (Schaufeli, Maslach, & Marek, 1993). These subjective and objective factors may vary in intensity, duration, frequency, and consequences as well as vary from one individual to another. Several features that make outdoor leaders particularly susceptible to professional burnout are commitment, independence, lifestyle, experience base, and hopes and dreams (Gass, 1993a).

Most of us are strongly committed to our work, serving in a very altruistic manner that requires us to give certain self-sacrifice and service to others. Such high commitment can produce great energy, empowerment, and positive results for clients, but can also prove expensive to us personally. Long hours, physically exhausting work, and working with clients on emotionally charged issues are laborious. As outdoor leaders, we often pour so much effort into others that we neglect to take care of ourselves. We fall into the trap of expecting coleaders to have the energy to accomplish tasks that we would never ask clients to consider doing.

Compared with other professions, we as leaders are quite independent and self-sufficient. Such independence allows us the flexibility to meet a wide variety of needs for a broad range of populations. But such independence also leads us to overlook the strengths and advantages of being connected with mainstream issues. MacArthur (1987) probably best described this quality with the term *mainstream fringe:*

> We hang around the edge of the mainstream, putting up with the problems of interpreting why we do what we do, hoping that others will see the light. We are not really willing to make the full commitment to mainstream ways. As a survival technique, this probably makes a lot of sense. However, this may also mean that we are not committed enough to change politically. We are too transient in life to commit to one community, too concerned about our own freedom to invest in one place or one group of people for very long. Hence, we cannot sustain the momentum for significant change in our communities. (p. 6-7)

One of the advantages of adventure programming is that it allows you to combine your avocations, which include hobbies or life interests, with your vocation: it is a lifestyle investment for most outdoor leaders. This makes tasks intrinsically rewarding, yet can give the appearance that you are always on vacation. However, blurring the boundaries between work and play can be depleting rather than replenishing. Interpersonal and business relationships, maintaining ethical behavior, and the need to regenerate yourself can become complicated, leading to burnout when your work becomes so closely associated with your life outside of adventure programming.

As you well know, experience-based learning lies at the heart of most adventure programming. While we have identified many advantages and disadvantages of experiential learning, additional concerns contribute to professional burnout. One is that a profession that solely focuses on experience can lead to personal imbalances, particularly if you ignore the wealth of educational theory inside and outside the field. If you live only by your own experiences, then the extent of what exists for you will be only the length of your lifetime.

Most outdoor leaders hope that adventure programs will improve difficult situations. Change processes center on empowering clients in dysfunctional situations to attain healthier goals and lifestyles. Performing such work and living up to such expectations can be draining, especially when you don't reach such goals or expectations. Holding high expectations can lead to programming excellence, but it can also cost you a great deal of energy, resulting in burnout.

To prevent and combat professional burnout, Gass (1993a) proposed a model based on the interconnected qualities of security, success, financial support, and balance. The model stresses that adventure programs need to position themselves so that these qualities are accessible to leaders. Security means that a program places you in positions with the potential to grow, receive constructive feedback, and regenerate your professional efforts. Success allows you to expect and achieve a sense of quality in what you do. This includes establishing appropriate boundaries, often by identifying nonnegotiable values, that is, values you are not willing to forsake to achieve client goals. Financial support addresses the idea that you must be paid in concert with the quality of work you do and the function you perform. As with other professionals, if educating, then be paid as educators; if providing therapy, then be paid as therapists. Balance refers to your receiving the means to acquire and possess the necessary time, resources, support, and perspective to maintain professional quality.

PROFESSIONALISM

In the summer of 1990, two incidents occurred involving deaths of adolescents in private wilderness programs, which spurred regulatory activity in Utah and other western states. On May 9, 1990, fifteen-year-old Michelle Sutton died of dehydration and exposure while hiking in the Summit Quest program. The program was based in Utah, but the death occurred on a program expedition in Arizona. On June 27, 1990, sixteen-year-old Kristin Chase died of heat stroke while hiking in the Challenger program in Utah. Both incidents led to criminal investigations, and the founder of the Challenger program now faces criminal charges. The parents of both adolescents, who placed their children in the programs because of behavior problems, have brought wrongful death actions.

Even before the Challenger and Summit Quest incidents, Utah's child protective agency had removed several children from the Challenger program due to allegations of maltreatment. The deaths, however, prompted the Utah legislature to enact legislation enabling the state's Department of

Human Services to adopt and enforce licensing standards for wilderness programs. The new standards were developed and implemented in the fall of 1990 (Utah Code, 1990). In addition to general standards applicable to all residential facilities, the standards governing staffing, equipment, admission and screening, nutrition, First Aid and general safety, transportation, and environmental precautions were developed. They do not, however, include safety rules for specific outdoor activities. Since that time, Utah's Office of Licensing has granted licenses to 13 wilderness programs, suspended the licenses of two programs, and denied licenses to two new applicants.

—Mathews, 1993

This extract was written about incidents that occurred in 1990, and it regards programs not following many of the standards of that time. Unfortunately, in 1994 a similar tragedy occurred when Aaron Bacon died while participating in the North Star program, also in Utah. While the factors that resulted in these three deaths are rare in genuine adventure therapy programs following professional standards, they call into question the concept of professionalism in adventure programming.

Ewert (1989) and Gass (1993b) have compiled lists of several characteristics that determine the viability of a profession: the establishment and utilization of a unique body of knowledge supported by a theoretical structure; integrity, dictated by an ethical code of conduct, including moral standards; the organization and representation of the field by professional organizations; skills that require extensive training; and the fulfillment of an indispensable social need particularly pertaining to client health and welfare.

We have already addressed each of these components to some degree in this text, summarizing a portion of the broad base of unique knowledge that exists concerning adventure programming. We have described in detail ethical principles addressing competence, integrity, and client and social responsibility as well as respect for the rights, well-being, and dignity of clients. A number of professional organizations, most notably the Association for Experiential Education in North America and the National Association for Outdoor Education in Britain, the Comenius Institute in Europe, and the Australian Outdoor Education

Council, have been organized to enhance these perspectives. Moreover, we have identified the skills and training necessary to conduct effective adventure experiences. The intent and outcomes of adventure programs are clearly directed toward the needs and welfare of the clients. Adventure programming is a profession by definition, yet the question remains, "Is it professional?"

Consider the recent and rapid growth of corporate adventure programs. Many operators work with this clientele for the large amounts of money it generates. While some use these profits to offset the cost of running a youth camp or to subsidize hospital outreach efforts, many more are drawn simply by the opportunity to make a decent living. As a result, a number of programs claiming to be "corporate" are poorly facilitated. The operators simply repeat the programs they might conduct for their regular clients without adjusting the program to suit the corporation's needs or the participants' abilities. The programs become ineffective in the long run. To use a fast-food analogy, these programs fill clients up, but the clients soon become hungry again.

Not only do ineffective programs affect the adventure operator's survival, they also can adversely impact the entire profession's image since customers have difficulty differentiating good providers from bad. Consider a corporation looking for a developmental team-building program that receives a recreational fun and games program instead. The transfer is absent and so the corporation remarks, "All this adventure stuff doesn't work!" The entire industry gets a negative reputation as evidenced by recent columns in the popular press, for example, Lenconi (2003); the *New York Times,* and *Wall Street Journal* suggest adventure training is a waste of money with limited transfer of learning.

How does a consumer differentiate good programs from bad ones—or at least those that profess to conduct valuable experiences from those that are inadequate? Program accreditation can be one indicator that the provider has met certain criteria for safety, ethics, and experientiality. Beyond this, Priest (1991) has suggested a list of 10 hallmarks for corporate programs: safe, confidential, personalized, flexible, fast and efficient, enjoyable, educationally transferable, ethical, effective, and evaluative.

All adventure programs must be clearer about the level of programming they can supply. And consumers must understand the type of programming they need: recreational, educational, developmental, or therapeutic. This requires you

as an outdoor leader to be clear about the level at which you can capably facilitate and the techniques you can effectively use, such as funneling, frontloading, and framing. Until we are all open and honest about our strengths and weaknesses and have sufficient research or evaluation to counter the arguments against adventure programming, the profession will continue to suffer from this credibility crisis.

RESEARCH

In the late 1970s Endeavor Enterprise (not a real name) was generally acknowledged by many professionals as an effective and innovative adventure program. Sponsored by its local government and funded by tax dollars, EE received court-referred young people, who were at risk of imprisonment if they continued their behavior. For two decades, EE changed the lives of countless youth, putting them on the road to becoming productive members of society.

In the early 1990s, financial cutbacks brought an end to this top-rated program. Despite numerous protests from the staff and participants of EE, the powers that be canceled the program and refused to fund any similar programs that provided wilderness "holidays for criminals." While EE claimed to make an important difference and many experts agreed they did, EE could not present evidence of their impact. They could not prove that their recidivism rate was lower than other programs or that their program cost less than prison and other treatment alternatives.

The EE program had not bothered to conduct any program research or evaluation. So like many other programs, it suffered a very real end to its prosperity. Indeed, the lack of research and evaluation often leaves the profession on the fringe, unable to claim its effectiveness when seriously challenged. Thus, more programs are being terminated due to decreases in subsidized (governmental) funding. More research and evaluation would further establish credibility for our field by demonstrating its effectiveness; more evaluation would enhance its current practices and methodologies (Priest, 2001). In other words, research can prove how and why adventure works and evaluation can improve the way programming works.

Specifically, as a profession, we need to do more research and evaluation to provide evidence that adventure programming is more than just fun and games and that it can serve as a powerful impetus for change. Several specific areas of study are necessary, including examining the elements of adventure programming and the means by which these elements bring about change (Nichols, 2000). We also need to examine how these changes transfer to the client's real life and how to sustain such change in the face of an unsupportive environment (for an example of one such study, see Gass, Garvey, & Sugerman, 2003). In other words, we need to ask, "What transfers from the experience, how much of it, for how long, and because of what program elements or barriers?" We must organize studies that examine program duration, that is, one-day versus multiday programs; content, including activity numbers, lengths, types, and debriefings; location, that is, indoor or outdoor; setting, whether urban, rural, or wilderness; follow-up, including transfer strategies, reflection, and integration; clients, including types, ideal numbers, and gender segregation or mixing; and leadership, including facilitation techniques, teaching styles, and gender. Some of the better studies examining these issues have been done by Hattie, Marsh, Neill, & Richards (1997) and Russell (2003), but many more efforts are needed.

With an understanding of the need for and the methods of research and evaluation, you can contribute to its production and consumption. As a producer, you can assist others or conduct your own studies. Learn how to be a researcher or an evaluator by taking a course in research or evaluation. Get help from university faculty and support students doing studies in order to graduate. As a consumer, you can read and critique existing published research and evaluation. When reading a study, check that the flow is logical and organized, that the intent of the study (purpose, questions, or hypothesis) is connected to the outcomes (findings, discussion, or conclusions), and that the study is easily understood (written well, clear tables, or reasonable recommendations). When critiquing a study ask yourself two questions: "Does this make sense? Can I apply its findings to my program?" The first question refers to validity and reliability: Can I explain the outcomes by some other sensible explanation? The second question refers to generalizability: How are the outcomes and their context the same as or different from my adventure program? You don't have to be an expert in research and evaluation in order to examine and comment on such studies; common sense is often sufficient.

Researchers and evaluators are likely to encounter a few routine difficulties when investigating adventure programming (Priest, Attarian, & Schubert, 1993). First, remember that credible adventure programs operate under the ethic of challenge by choice (see chapter 4), which means subjects are voluntary and random sampling can be difficult to implement because the participants are all at least somewhat ready to take risks. Second, small groups of 8 to 12 people, typical of adventure programming, make distributions more likely to be abnormal, requiring nonparametric (distribution-free) tests. Nonparametric statistics are generally less accepted by scholars than parametric procedures. Third, you cannot overcome this sample size concern by combining several groups from the exact same adventure, because effective programs often customize the activities to meet the clients' needs. If the program gets modified to suit the study, then the program suffers; and if the reverse is done, then the study suffers. Fourth, obtaining control groups (those not engaged in a program) is extremely difficult, because the experimental groups (those involved with the adventure) can often "contaminate" the purity of the controls by sharing their experiences outside the study. Since controls may be selected from the same learning situations as the experimentals, you can expect the two groups to interact at home, school, work, or play, influencing the way both groups respond to the study. Fifth, the phenomena studied in adventure programs are mostly human qualities, which are not easily quantifiable. Since few valid and reliable instruments for measuring exist, the use of qualitative methods to measure qualities appears most logical. Sixth, some adventure programs and their clients simply do not want to be studied in case an inquirer discovers that they are ineffective in some way. Furthermore, research and evaluation can interfere with running a smooth program by interrupting processes or preventing people from concentrating.

Good research and evaluation follow some basic tenets of ethical behavior. First, informed consent is expected, except in cases in which deception or concealment is both justified and necessary for the intent of the study (i.e., participant observation). You must obtain the approval of the ethical human subjects committee (or its equivalent) of your organization before conducting this kind of study. Informed consent means that subjects must have the risks and responsibilities of the study explained to them verbally or in writing and that they should provide signed consent. Verbal agreement to participate is acceptable in general public surveys, but not in experiments in which subjects are assigned to treatment or control groups. Second, you must guarantee confidentiality by stating that individual responses will not be named, but instead will be reported in aggregate or averaged forms. Real names will be changed to protect subjects, and the names of organizations (clients or programs) will be withheld for privacy. Third, as a researcher and evaluator, you should resist the temptation to overgeneralize. Lack of random sampling techniques, often due to the predetermined client group, may mean that you cannot generalize results beyond the groups or clients studied. Generalization is frequently limited to a particular program or training treatment. The perfect study is rare, as most research or evaluation is limited and flawed to some extent. People who fail to acknowledge these flaws in their studies are claiming credibility that simply does not exist and may be misrepresenting the authenticity of their work. Fourth, research and evaluation should be given a peer review or refereeing process as is done in scholarly or academic journals. Other researchers and evaluators critique the work, drawing attention to the possible flaws. This can either improve marginal studies or prevent poor studies from being disseminated to consumers. Releasing research or evaluation in prepublished manuscript form to anyone other than fellow researchers and evaluators is unwise.

GROWTH CURVES AND LIFE CYCLES

All these trends and issues don't mean much unless we can use them to see common patterns and predict the emergence of new patterns based on the old ones. Tools to do this include the growth curve and repetitive waves. The growth curve is a standard phenomenon found throughout nature. A familiar school experiment that illustrates the curve collects bacteria and grows them in agar on a petri dish. A time plot of the daily individual bacterium cell or colony counts, as shown in figure 24.1, results in the standard bell-shaped curve with five typical stages that we will call birth, growth, plateau, decline, and death.

In birth, the bacteria have an abundance of food and they multiply without restraint. During growth (which can be separated into early and late periods), the increase in numbers becomes exponential. At the plateau, cell division slows so replication of new cells maintains the amount in stasis. Decline (also split into early and late periods) brings a slow, then rapid drop in numbers. Death eventually results from exhausted food supplies or accumulated waste products. Adding food or removing waste allows new growth, but the effect is only temporary and may bring a greater crash afterward.

In a closed system such as this, most organisms (from mice in a cage to cattle on the range to the human population on earth) follow this pattern, although the curves may be taller and thinner or shorter and fatter. Business uses these same growth curves to describe the life cycles of products: Early adopters buy and try newly introduced products. As marketing and advertising drive sales, more and more people purchase the product until the novelty wears off and a decline in purchases leads to the ultimate death of that product. Eight-track tapes, exercise equipment, and adventure programming all follow this same pattern!

If you reread the history chapter (chapter 3), you can trace the global evolution of adventure programming through a similar life cycle. Birth

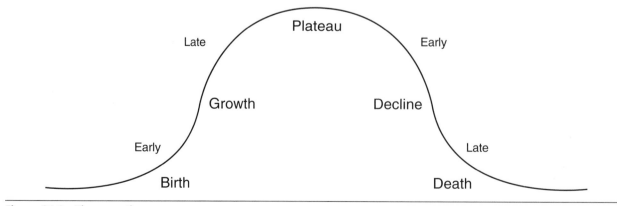

Figure 24.1 The growth curve.

is the inception of Outward Bound. As Outward Bound was cloned in countries around the world, and as these nations spun off their own versions of these programs, adventure programming grew exponentially. Many countries are still in their birth stage, some are deep into growth, while a few are on the plateau. Figure 24.2 suggests some countries' positioning on the growth curve based on 2003 trends and issues as well as on the authors' personal travels to study adventure programming in over 40 countries around the world.

An argument could be made that adventure programming in the United States and United Kingdom is beginning to decline as programs are cut back, closed, and canceled. One reason for decline might be the accumulation of waste products in the form of government regulations, litigation, and financial restrictions that prevent adventure programs from operating. Another explanation might be the lack of research to justify program efficacy or bad press in the public media toward adventure. Alternatively, food could be running out as reality TV shows make adventure programming seem tame by comparison for most of the public.

Countries further back on the growth curve can learn from the mistakes of those nations ahead of them. Table 24.1 examines 10 benchmarks from birth to decline. Perhaps you recognize some of these in your country or in some of the nations you have read about.

Countries like China, India, Indonesia, Brazil, and many more are in the birth stage. They are just beginning to run their first recreational programs from base camps. The public is discovering the outdoors as a place for leisure. Program staff members are sharing ideas within their organization but not with outside competition. They are looking at what and how they do and how they

do it to loosely improve. They view outdoor leadership as hard-skill competence and imagine the road to safety is paved with some sort of certification of leaders. Litigation and facilitation, although unrelated, are not present.

Belgium, Singapore, Netherlands, South Africa, Norway, Japan, Germany, New Zealand, Canada, Australia, and Ireland (to name a few) are in various stages of early to late growth. As they offer more programs, skeptics question the value of their programming. Programs move from being mobile to having a fixed center with climbing walls, challenge courses, and other artificial adventure environs. Programs organize into conferences where staff members share program ideas, where basic methods of facilitation become more widely accepted, and where attempts are made to identify acceptable common practices. Meanwhile, increased public use of the outdoors damages local resources and causes more frequent search and rescues for lost or injured people. This reflects badly on the adventure programs, which in turn have their own accidents and the occasional fatality with resulting lawsuits. Outdoor leadership is seen to be more than hard skills and universities begin to prepare leaders with a semblance of soft skills.

The United States is on the plateau in 2003. Adventure programs are prescribed for specific and diverse populations as there becomes an adventure answer for every problem. This is possible because facilitation techniques have become quite sophisticated. Challenge courses and climbing walls abound as the outdoors is overrun by the public. Government begins to restrict access to the resources and mandates rules and new technology in place of judgment and the old ways. Major centers and gigantic spin-off organizations develop and shine at conferences where journals, textbooks, and other resources share best practices. The emerging profession attempts to standardize the industry. Voluntary program accreditation replaces leadership certification by taking a holistic perspective on safety and by not just concentrating on the competence of program staff. Outdoor leadership is seen as more than soft and hard skills as metaskills become important. However, litigation becomes common and many program decisions of safety and practice are made in fear of lawyers instead of with the clients' best interests in mind.

By 2004, the United Kingdom is in decline. Program numbers are dwindling, major centers are closing or being sold, and well-known organizations

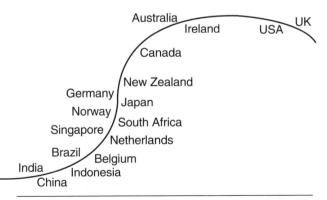

Figure 24.2 Approximate national positions on the life cycle of adventure programming.

Table 24.1   Ten Hallmarks From Birth to Decline

Stage	Program	Centers	Professional	Environment	Safety
Birth	First program met with curiosity and fresh enthusiasm	Very few centers, most programs go from base camps	First meeting of loosely organized staff and leaders	More and more people going to nature for leisure	User participation in the outdoors is on the rise
Growth	Skeptics oppose large number of novelty programs	Proliferation of centers, first use artificial environs	First conferences, formation of professional group/ association	Increased use and more damage of fewer resources	Increased SAR and user accidents are a public concern
Plateau	Programs become more prescribed, specific, and diverse	Overreliance on artificial environs and formal centers	First journals and textbooks, spin-off organizations form	Resource access restrictions are added by government	Technology added to safety, rules replace judgment
Decline	Program numbers begin to dwindle, merge, and combine	Centers begin to close because of fiscal restraints	Research (too late) creativity lost, and failure to prove value	Government legislation begins to choke programming	Well-publicized fatalities tarnish professional image

Stage	Practices	Certification/ Accreditation	Leaders	Litigation	Facilitation
Birth	Self-examination and criticism of program practices	Early attempts to certify leaders fail (one puzzle piece)	Hard skills form basis of leader certification	None to very little depending on national laws	Nonexistent (recreation programming most common)
Growth	Identification of acceptable and common practices	Higher education takes on role of preparing leaders	Soft skills (+ hard) become the new gauge of leaders	Rising number of civil lawsuits due to poor protection	Basic methods (educational programming most common)
Plateau	Standardization of best practices, ethics considered	Voluntary program accreditation and not certification	Metaskills (+ soft) become the true measure of leaders	Litigation begins to drive decision-making process	Intermediate (developmental programming most common)
Decline	Required standard of professional practices with ethics code	Mandatory program accreditation and government licensing	Staff burnout is a common/growing leader concern	First criminal proceedings with more expected	Advanced methods (therapeutic programming most common)

are merging or reorganizing. Although program facilitation has become highly sophisticated, the value of the programs has not been clearly communicated to the public. A lack of research has failed to counter the public press's portrayal of adventure as a dangerous undertaking with well-publicized accidents and fatalities. Government regulations and requirements are staggering as programs lose their flexibility to operate in all but one singly acceptable standard. Creativity is all but lost as staff members are burned out and constrained by licensing agreements against trying new procedures or approaches. Many staff

still work like they did decades earlier. Mandatory licensing looms on the horizon and staff members fear possible criminal proceedings if they make a mistake.

REBIRTH OR DEATH?

In the product life cycle, successful businesses release a new product in the old product's late growth stage, as in figure 24.3, just before the plateau and definitely not during early decline. Akin to adding food or removing waste, this new release

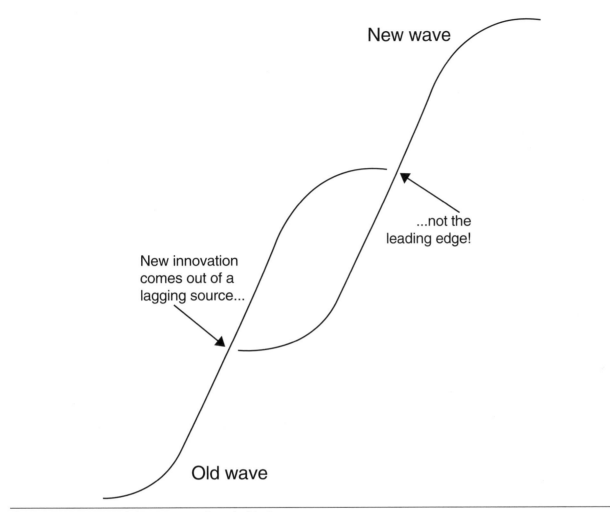

New wave

New innovation
comes out of a
lagging source...

...not the
leading edge!

Old wave

Figure 24.3 Waves of change come from behind.

brings new growth. Take computer hardware and software as examples. The newest computer or operating system comes on the market just as we are getting familiar with our old ones. This successful marketing ploy is designed to keep us wanting the latest version and to keep technology companies in business.

Repetitive waves build on this concept of change. Figure 24.4 shows a sequence of waves we could easily relabel. On the one hand, humans have evolved from hunters and gatherers through agrarian societies to the industrial era on into technology and the information age, with the virtual age coming next. Rest assured that those who were best at one way of living were not the innovators for the new way of living: they were too busy living the old way and dealing with the consequences of the old ways. The new ways came from people somewhere in the middle of the wave who said, "There must be a better way to do this!" and "We're not going to blindly follow the others!"

In adventure programming, we can see the same sequence repeated for facilitation methods. The satisfied experts of the "experience speaks for itself" were not the ones who came up with the idea of "speak for the experience!" Similarly, the successful leaders of debriefing and funneling didn't envision direct frontloading. And the best isomorphic framers couldn't imagine paradox and double binds. These paradigm shifts came from folks in the background who looked for a new solution because they were not stuck in the old one.

As a result, do not look for future innovations to come from the United States or United Kingdom. They will be too mired in lost creativity and choked by government regulations to innovate. Look for the new ideas to come from countries like Australia, Canada, and New Zealand. Being on the leading edge is not all that it is cut out to be. The nations who lag behind the leading edge are in an enviable position. They can learn from the

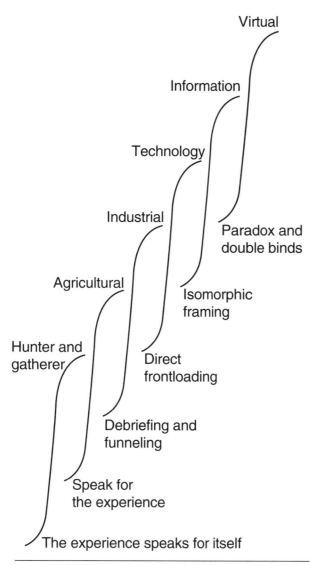

Figure 24.4 Repetitive waves of change.

mistakes of those ahead. They are not necessarily destined to repeat the errors of earlier nations, unless they ignore history.

Unfortunately, these lagging nations are also in a hurry to catch up. They import ideas and methods from America and Britain and devour them with increasing hunger. Rather than consuming what the overseas expert offers without questioning, why not develop their own brand of adventure programming that especially suits their unique culture? Perhaps they can create a version of adventure programming that avoids past mistakes or generates new growth.

Lastly, waves can also split as in figure 24.5. If we look at adventure programming activities, we can see an evolution from wilderness pursuits to two separate and distinct waves: ropes (challenge) courses and group initiatives. Later, we see ropes courses split again into climbing walls and team challenge courses (perhaps in response to the need to focus on teamwork). The group initiatives wave splits again into portable initiatives and prop-free initiatives (perhaps to avoid becoming tied down to constructed facilities).

What will be the next splits? If innovative ideas are coming, what will they be about? At the start of this chapter, we said the key to predicting the future lies in identifying and combining patterns. For example, technology is a new innovation that fits the pattern but has yet to be incorporated into adventure programming. What if technology were applied to any of these waves? Perhaps we would have Internet challenge courses (www. virtualteamworks.com) or GPS-based team building (www.geoteaming.com).

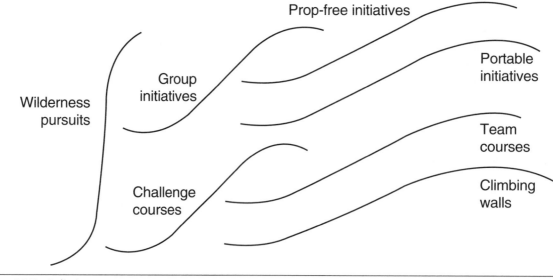

Figure 24.5 Splitting waves.

◄ *EFFECTIVE OUTDOOR LEADERS* ►

- ► Are aware of the trends, issues, contributing factors, and growth areas of adventure programming in order to be ready for the future.
- ► Are careful to use technological improvements and equipment advances to enhance program quality, not undermine it.

- ► Know how burnout arises and how to avoid it.
- ► Understand their roles in maintaining a professional image.
- ► Comprehend how to help the research and evaluation process.

SUMMARY

A number of trends and issues in adventure programming are influenced by global and social factors, including increased population, increased environmental damage, improved communication and transportation, worldwide economic competition, decreased family association, decreased discretionary moneys, decreased work time, and decreased conservation and compassion.

These factors suggest that adventure programs will continue to grow in popularity and that the size and number of professional organizations will increase as the profession expands, diversifies, and matures through self-examination. Adventure programs will find their ways into schools and urban centers as greater use is made of artificial adventure environments and as the natural environments become more regulated or managed. Programs will see greater restrictions on using natural resources through outdoor licenses, use permits, and access fees. Wilderness will become even more popular and controlled, causing some to use rescue-free zones for greater challenge.

Technology will also impact the environment and the feeling of wilderness through such inventions as battery-powered electric drills, cellular phones, and GPS units. Equipment advances may work against program intents, and you will need to be careful that equipment does not undermine the adventure experience.

Burnout will continue to be common among staff members due to a number of subjective and objective factors relating to loss of self-esteem; feelings of incompetence or dissatisfaction; physical depletion without identifiable origin; helplessness or hopelessness; disillusionment; negative attitudes toward work, coworkers, or life itself; problems with concentration, irritability, or negativism; and decreases in work performance, quality, effectiveness, attendance, and interest. You may remain susceptible to burnout due to your commitment, independence, lifestyle, experience base, and hopes and dreams. You can reverse burnout by working for programs which espouse security, success, financial support, and balance.

Recent deaths in programs lacking credible practices yet licensed by Utah have highlighted the need for greater professionalism in adventure programming. A profession has a unique body of knowledge and ethical integrity, is represented by governing organizations, uses skills that require extensive training, and fulfills indispensable social needs. Although adventure programming qualifies as a profession by definition, it does fall short on a few professional behaviors. Most notable is its systemic and occasional inability to deliver the goods. As a result, its professional image has become tarnished by the popular press claiming that adventure programming is a waste of time and money. Program accreditation and 10 benchmarks may help consumers distinguish the effective providers from the ineffective ones. We encourage programs to be clear about their competence, and we caution you not to facilitate for a program purpose that is beyond your abilities.

Research and evaluation establish professional credibility as well as demonstrate effectiveness. While research proves how and why adventure programming works, evaluation improves the way it works. Future research and evaluation ought to answer several questions: What transfers? How much of it? For how long? Which program elements or barriers affect outcomes? Participation in research and evaluation should be voluntary with small groups in customized programs compared to a control group if possible. As a profession, we must use more qualitative, as opposed to quantitative, methods to understand the quality of the experience. Moreover, we must follow certain guidelines for ethical research and evaluation:

using informed consent, maintaining confidentiality, avoiding overgeneralization, and obtaining a peer review or refereed critique of the study.

Combined with these factors is the growth in the participation of adventure experiences. According to a recent OIA study (July 28, 2004) the bulk of outdoor "participants" and "enthusiasts" in the United States are involved in the cornerstone activities of bicycling (87 million/ 20.4 million), hiking (71.8 million/10.5 million), and camping (68.8 million/10.8 million). Known as "gateway" activities, these pursuits are the primary anchor for attracting new participants, and provide an affordable non-intimidating entry point to other outdoor activities. The most significant additions of new participants since 1998 came in trail running (6.4 million new participants, a 20.5% increase); kayaking (5.7 million new participants, a 235.7% increase); canoeing (4.3 million new participants, an 18.1% increase); and snowshoeing (3 million new participants, a 203.4% increase)" (pp. 1-2). Such growth has tremendous influence on all of the trends mentioned in this chapter.

QUESTIONS TO THINK ABOUT

1. Identify the factors and growth areas in this chapter that are global and those that are local. Add any new factors or growth areas you come up with.

2. Which of these factors and growth areas influences each of the six trends and issues mentioned in this chapter?

3. In the role of program coordinator, write a response to the statements of the ANP superintendent found in the first vignette of the "Environment" section in this chapter.

4. A very real threat is posed by increased mountain biking in wilderness environments. After doing a background search on mountain biking in your region, debate this issue with a colleague or class. Be sure to cover the real potential to have trails closed to mountain bikes.

5. Describe your attitudes toward technology. Can you think of a technological improvement that has had a major effect on the outdoor experience, either positive or negative?

6. Describe a time when you felt burned out. What did you do about it?

7. How can you contribute to the adventure programming profession?

8. How can you help research and evaluate adventure programming?

REFERENCES

Association for Challenge Course Technology (ACCT). (2005). ACCT website homepage. Retrieved January 10, 2005 from the World Wide Web: www.acctinfo.org/index.html

Bandoroff, S., & Newes, S. (2004). *Coming of age: The evolving field of adventure therapy.* Boulder, CO: Association for Experiential Education.

Browne, D. (1986). How to use equipment therapeutically. *Journal of Experiential Education, 9*(3), 16-19.

Carter, M.W. (1998). A portable paradox? Laptop computers and outdoor learning. *Journal of Experiential Education, 21*(1), 40-45.

Chicago Tribune. (January 14, 2004). The last resort: Therapeutic education industry booms as parents seek programs for their troubled children. Retrieved May 12, 2005 from http://pqasb.pqarchiver.com/chicagotribune.

Ewert, A. (1989). *Outdoor adventure pursuits.* Columbus, OH: Publishing Horizons.

Friese, G., Hendee, J.C., & Kinziger, M. (1998). The wilderness experience program industry in the United States: Characteristics and dynamics. *Journal of Experiential Education, 21*(1), 40-45.

Garvey, D. (1990). A history of AEE. In J.C. Miles & S. Priest (Eds.), *Adventure education* (pp. 75-82). State College, PA: Venture.

Gass, M.A. (1993a). Enhancing career development in adventure programming. In M.A. Gass (Ed.), *Adventure therapy: Therapeutic application of adventure programming in mental health settings* (pp. 417-426). Dubuque, IA: Kendall/Hunt.

Gass, M.A. (1993b). The future of the profession of adventure therapy. In M.A. Gass (Ed.), *Adventure therapy: Therapeutic application of adventure programming in mental health settings* (pp. 411-416). Dubuque, IA: Kendall/Hunt.

Gass, M.A., Garvey, D.E., & Sugerman, D. (2003). The long-term effects of a first-year student wilderness orientation program. *Journal of Experiential Education, 26*(1), 34-40.

Gerstein, J. (1992). *Directory of experiential therapy and adventure-based counseling programs.* Boulder, CO: Association for Experiential Education.

Hattie, J., Marsh, H.W., Neill, J., & Richards, G.E. (1997). Adventure education and Outward Bound: Out-of-class experiences that make a lasting difference. *Review of Educational Research, 67*(1), 43-87.

Hester, K., & Hirsch, J. (1999). Computers in experiential education: The learners' perspective. *Journal of Experiential Education, 22*(2), 80-84.

Kennedy, M. (1989). Money talks, nobody walks. *Climbing, 114,* 6.

Kennedy, M. (1990). Trouble in paradise. *Climbing, 118,* 10.

Kesselheim, A. (1981). A look at the life of an outdoor educator. *Journal of Experiential Education, 4*(1), 39-41.

Lenard, M. (1995). Toward a new climbing culture. *Climbing, 150,* 200.

Lenconi, P. (2003). *The five dysfunctions of a team.* San Francisco, CA: Jossey Bass.

MacArthur, B. (1987). Habits of the heart. *Journal of Experiential Education, 10*(1), 5-11.

Mathews, M. (1993). Wilderness programs offer promising alternatives for some youth: More regulation likely. In M.A. Gass (Ed.), *Adventure therapy: Therapeutic application of adventure programming in mental health settings* (pp. 441-450). Dubuque, IA: Kendall/Hunt.

McAvoy, L. (1990). Rescue-free wilderness areas. In J.C. Miles & S. Priest (Eds.), *Adventure education* (pp. 335-343). State College, PA: Venture.

McAvoy, L., & Dustin, D. (1981). The right to risk in wilderness. *Journal of Forestry, 79*(3), 150-152.

McAvoy, L., & Dustin, D. (1983). In search of balance: A no-rescue wilderness proposal. *Western Wildlands, 9*(2), 2-5.

Mentuck, A. (1996, August 18). Lyons speaks to industry leaders. *Outdoor Retailer Daily Exposure,* p. 3.

Nichols, G. (2000). A research agenda for adventure education. *Australian Journal of Outdoor Education, 4*(2), 22-31.

Outdoor Industry Association (OIA). American outdoor recreation participation continues six-year ascent (2004, July 28). Retrieved January 7, 2005 from the World Wide Web: www.outdoorindustry.org/press.oia.php?news_id=708&sort_year=2004

Outdoor Industry Association (OIA). OIA analysis of recreation fee program. (2004, December 6th). Retrieved January 10, 2005 from the World Wide Web: www.outdoorindustry.org/gov.press.testimony.php?news_id=912&sort_year=2004

Pines, B., Ayala, L., & Aronson, E. (1988). *Career burnout: Causes and cures.* New York: Free Press.

Priest, S. (1991). Shopping for a corporate adventure training program. *Personnel: Journal of the American Management Association, 68*(7), 15-16.

Priest, S. (2001). A program evaluation primer. *Journal of Experiential Education, 24*(1), 34-40.

Priest, S., Attarian, A., & Schubert, S. (1993). Conducting research in experienced-based training and development programs: Pass keys to locked doors. *Journal of Experiential Education, 16*(2), 11-20.

Priest, S., & Dixon, T. (1990). *Safety practices in adventure programming.* Boulder, CO: Association for Experiential Education.

Proudman, S. (1990). Urban adventure. In J.C. Miles & S. Priest (Eds.), *Adventure education* (pp. 335-343). State College, PA: Venture.

Richards, K. (2002). *Therapy within adventure.* Augsburg, Germany: Ziel.

Russell, K.C. (2003). A nation-wide survey of outdoor behavioral healthcare programs for adolescents with problem behaviors. *Journal of Experiential Education, 25*(3), 322-331.

Schaufeli, W., Maslach, C., & Marek, T. (Eds.). (1993). *Professional burnout: Recent developments in theory and research.* Washington, DC: Taylor and Francis.

Schoel, J., & Maizell, R.S. (2002). *Islands of healing: A guide to adventure-based counseling.* Hamilton, MA: Project Adventure.

West-Smith, L. (2001). Body stories: *Research and intimate narratives on women transforming body image in outdoor adventure.* Boulder, CO: Association for Experiential Education.

Williamson, J., & Gass, M.A. (1993). *Manual of program accreditation standards for adventure programs.* Boulder, CO: Association for Experiential Education.

Author Index

Subject Index

Note: Information contained in tables or figures are indicated by an italicized *t* or *f*.

About the Authors

Simon Priest, PhD, (left) is president and chief executive officer of virtualTEAMWORKS.com, which specializes in experiential learning on the Internet. He is also a retired full professor from Brock University in Canada and the executive director of the Corporate Adventure Training Institute, a research center of excellence. He was an interim director of Canadian Tire's corporate university. A member of the Association for Experiential Education (AEE) since 1983, he chaired their research task force, safety practices task force, and student research grants committee while also contributing on the journal editorial board, scholarship committee, conference steering groups, and journal editorships.

Dr. Priest's contributions to the field of adventure programming have had an international impact. He has been a scholar in residence and has been awarded visiting fellowships in Australia, New Zealand, Canada, the United States, England, and several other European nations. He has studied and taught about outdoor leadership in more than 40 countries around the world.

Dr. Priest has researched and written extensively on the topic of adventure programming.

He has authored or edited several books and book chapters, and his articles have appeared in publications such as the *Journal of Adventure Education and Outdoor Leadership,* the *Journal of Experiential Education, Journal of Leisure Research, Leisure Sciences, Leisure Studies,* and the *Journal of Physical Education, Recreation and Dance.* Dr. Priest received his doctorate in outdoor recreation from the University of Oregon in 1986.

Michael Gass, PhD, (right) is a full professor and chair of the department of kinesiology and member of the award-winning outdoor education program at the University of New Hampshire (UNH). This accredited program is recognized as one of the best undergraduate and graduate training programs in the world, and its students are some of the finest emerging professionals in the field of adventure programming. Dr. Gass has helped to produce numerous pivotal books for the field, including *Book of Metaphors: Volume II, Adventure Therapy: Therapeutic Applications of Adventure Programming,* and *Program Accreditation Standards for Adventure Programs* with Jed Williamson. He has conducted numerous international workshops and trainings, and his writing has appeared in professional journals around the world. He currently directs several evidence-based research projects for the American Youth Foundation and Project Adventure to validate and promote best practices in the field of adventure programming.

Dr. Gass served as president of the Association for Experiential Education (AEE) in 1990 and was the chair of AEE's Therapeutic Adventure Professional Group in 1992-93 and 1995-96. He also was the chair of the American Alliance for Health, Physical Education, Recreation and Dance's Council for Outdoor Education in 1994. Currently he is the editor of the *Journal for Therapeutic Schools and Programs* and serves on the review board for the *Journal of Experiential Education.* He also served for 10 years on AEE's Program Accreditation Council.

Dr. Gass received his PhD in experiential education from the University of Colorado at Boulder and completed postdoctoral studies in marriage and family therapy. When not with his family, he can be found climbing or wilderness running.